The Deutsche Bank and the Nazi Economic War Against the Jews

This book examines the role of the Deutsche Bank, Germany's largest financial institution, in the expropriation of Jewish-owned enterprises during the Nazi dictatorship, both in the existing territories of Germany and in the area seized by the German army during World War II. The author uses new and previously unavailable materials, many from the bank's own archives, to examine policies that led to the eventual genocide of European Jews. How far did the realization of the vicious and destructive Nazi ideology depend on the acquiesence, the complicity, and the cupidity of existing economic institutions to individuals? In response to the traditional argument that business cooperation with the Nazi regime was motivated by profit, this book closely examines the behavior of the bank and its individuals to suggest other motivations. No comparable study exists of a single company's involvement in the economic persecution of the Jews in Nazi Germany.

Harold James is Professor of History at Princeton University and the author of several books on German economy and society. His earlier work on the Deutsche Bank was awarded the Financial Times/Booz–Allen Book Award and the Hamilton Global Business Book of the Year Award in 1996.

The Deutsche Bank and the Nazi Economic War Against the Jews

The Expropriation of Jewish-Owned Property

Harold James
Princeton University

CAMBRIDGE
UNIVERSITY PRESS

PUBLISHED BY THE PRESS SYNDICATE OF THE UNIVERSITY OF CAMBRIDGE
The Pitt Building, Trumpington Street, Cambridge, United Kingdom

CAMBRIDGE UNIVERSITY PRESS
The Edinburgh Building, Cambridge CB2 2RU, UK
40 West 20th Street, New York, NY 10011-4211, USA
10 Stamford Road, Oakleigh, VIC 3166, Australia
Ruiz de Alarcón 13, 28014, Madrid, Spain
Dock House, The Waterfront, Cape Town 8001, South Africa

http://www.cambridge.org

First published 2001

Printed in the United States of America

Typeface Caslon 224 10/13.5 pt   *System* QuarkXPress™   [HT]

A catalog record for this book is available from the British Library.

Library of Congress Cataloging in Publication Data

James, Harold.
    The Deutsche Bank and the Nazi economic war against the Jews/Harold James.
        p. cm.
    Includes bibliographical references and index.
    ISBN 0-521-80329-2
        1. Deutsche Bank (1957–) – Political activity. 2. World War, 1939–1945 –
Economic aspects – Germany. 3. World War, 1939–1945 – Jews – Germany.
    HG3058 D4 J36 2001
    940.53'1—dc21   00-048651

ISBN 0 521 80329 2 hardback

Contents

Preface of the Historical Commission Appointed to Examine the History of the Deutsche Bank in the Period of National Socialism   *page* vii

Author's Preface   ix

Selected Abbreviations Used in the Text   xi

1 Business and Politics: Banks and Companies
   in Nazi Germany   1

2 The Structure, Organization, and Economic
   Environment of Deutsche Bank   11

3 National Socialism and Banks   21

4 The Problem of "Aryanization"   36

5 Deutsche Bank and "Aryanization" in the Pre-1938
   Boundaries of Germany   43

6 Deutsche Bank Abroad: "Aryanization," Territorial
   Expansion, and Economic Reordering   127

7 Jewish-Owned Bank Accounts   196

v

8   The Profits of the Deutsche Bank   204

9   Some Concluding Reflections   211

Notes   219

Bibliography   245

Index   255

Preface of the Historical Commission Appointed to Examine the History of the Deutsche Bank in the Period of National Socialism

The studies of the Historical Commission of the Deutsche Bank, in contrast to the studies of various governmental and some other commissions assigned the task of dealing with the role of business in the National Socialist period and Holocaust assets, are to be viewed as the products of the individual scholarship of its members. The ultimate responsibility for what is said in our studies rests with the author of each work produced under the auspices of the commission. Although it certainly is to be expected that historians sharing the same basic moral and political values and confronted with a certain basic set of facts can and should reach a reasonable level of agreement or consensus about their basic significance and interpretation, it would be unnatural and unreasonable to expect that each of us would tell the same story in exactly the same way and that there would not be differences of nuance and of emphasis in the way we would present our material and findings. The commission has and continues to see as its task the careful reading and detailed discussion of the studies completed by its members to ensure that the works in question meet the highest standards of scholarship and that they reflect a defensible and responsible presentation of evidence and conclusions. In discussing the Gold report and this study, we have vigorously debated the person and role of Hermann Josef Abs, and each of us has and will interpret that complex and important individual in a slightly different way. Similarly, in the case of this study, we have all thought long and hard and have discussed at considerable length what might and might not be said about the level of profits made by the bank from "aryanization" on the basis of the available information. We achieved a consensus that it was impossible to present a convincing total bank profit from "aryanization," and Professor James has refrained from doing so. We were less of accord when it came to coming to conclusions about the probable significance of those profits for the bank on the basis of the available evidence, and each of us reserves the right to come to different conclusions if the evidence seems so to warrant. Indeed, the pace of research and new findings in this field being what it is, we are duty bound to adjust our interpretations if new information so demands. This said in order to clarify and make transparent our procedure, the commission is very pleased to have the previous work by Professor Steinberg and the present work by Professor James appear under its auspices.

Avraham Barkai, Gerald D. Feldman,
Lothar Gall, Harold James, Jonathan Steinberg

Author's Preface

This book has had a long gestation. I began thinking about the theme in the late 1980s, when the Deutsche Bank invited me to write one chapter in a history to be published on its one hundred twenty-fifth anniversary, in 1995. The aim at that time was – from the point of view of the bank – a very courageous one, in that it was prepared to allow an outside team of scholars to write an uncontrolled, uncensored, and unexpurgated history of the bank. In the course of the later 1990s, after the book was published, a great deal of public interest and attention focused on the role and behavior of corporations in the Nazi period in the wake of class actions in U.S. courts. Much new material became available at the same time: in central Europe and Russia, as a consequence of the end of the Cold War; in the United States, as records relevant to the Second World War and its aftermath were declassified; and in Germany, as (at least some) corporations tried to assemble all the documentation relevant to their history.

In 1998, the Deutsche Bank invited five historians (the other four were Avraham Barkai, Lothar Gall, Gerald D. Feldman, and Jonathan Steinberg) to form a commission to examine the history of the bank in the Nazi era and to assess the new documentation that was becoming available. Jonathan Steinberg prepared an initial report, on gold transactions during the Second World War. This is the second study produced in the context of this commission. The other members of the commission offered very helpful comments on the draft manuscript, but – as is usual with academic manuscripts – they are not responsible for the contents.

This report focuses on the role of the Deutsche Bank in the expropriation of Jewish-owned enterprises in Germany and in the areas occupied by the German army, which was termed at the time "aryanization" (the German version of this book, which is published simultaneously by C.H. Beck Verlag, Munich, is entitled *Die Deutsche Bank und die "Arisierung"*). It does not systematically deal with the behavior in regard to the exploitation of forced and slave labor of some of the large enterprises (such as IG Farben or Daimler-Benz) to which Deutsche Bank gave credits.

The Deutsche Bank documents used in this study are all available for consultation by scholars.

The staff of the Deutsche Bank's Historical Institute, under the direction of Professor Manfred Pohl, provided much help, without intervening in any way in the investigation or the writing of the study. Angelika Raab-Rebentisch helped greatly with the overall logistics of the project. Jutta Heibel worked very hard, with enormous integrity and perseverance and with imagination and intelligence, in assembling archival material not only from the bank's own archive but also from many other archives. Dr. Monika Dickhaus, Thorsten Maentel, and Dr. Martin Müller also helped me greatly in the Deutsche Bank archive.

I am grateful to many archivists. Věra Pospíšilová in the Finance Ministry of the Czech Republic was extremely helpful in very difficult circumstances in Prague. In Poland, Senator Władysław Bartoszewski and Professor Daria Nałęcz, the director of the State Archives, greatly helped in obtaining access to a wide range of documentation. Dr. Marzenna Kowalik James and Marion Milo assisted me with interpreting and translations. The research expenses for this book were paid by Deutsche Bank.

Harold James
Princeton, New Jersey
November 2000

Selected Abbreviations Used in the Text

AG   *Aktiengesellschaft* (joint-stock company)
ANN   New archive, Warsaw
BA   Bundesarchiv
BAB   Bundesarchiv Berlin
BAK   Bundesarchiv Koblenz
BDB   Bundesverband Deutscher Banken archive
BDC   Berlin Document Center
BUB   Böhmische Union-Bank (Union Bank of Bohemia)
CFM   Finance Ministry of the Czech Republic, Prague
DAF   Deutsche Arbeitsfront (German Labor Front)
DAIB   Deutsche Agrar- und Industriebank (German Bank of Agriculture and Industry)
GmbH   *Gesellschaft mit beschränkter Haftung* (limited-liability company)
HADB   Historisches Archiv der Deutschen Bank, Frankfurt
HTO   Haupttreuhandstelle Ost, the major administrative agency responsible for the reordering of industry in the East
NA   U.S. National Archives and Record Administration, Washington, D.C.
NBS   Archive of the National Bank of Slovakia, Bratislava
ÖstA   Austrian State Archive, Vienna
RHG   Reichswerke "Hermann Göring"
SAM   Special Archive (Captured German Documents), Moscow
StA   State Archive, Leipzig
UBB   Union Bank Bratislava (Union Bank of Bratislava)

1

Business and Politics: Banks and Companies in Nazi Germany

Recently there has been a remarkable increase in interest in the business history of Germany in the Nazi era, and especially in the economic history of the Holocaust – the analysis of the economics behind discriminatory measures that prepared the way for the mass murder of Jews and other racially or biologically defined groups who lived in Germany or in the areas conquered by German soldiers. For a long time, there was relatively scant academic interest in the story of the expropriation of German Jews and its function in German economic life.

There is certainly an extensive literature on the relationship of big business and National Socialism; consequently, the revival of interest in this theme in the 1990s may appear quite puzzling. Much of the older literature, from the 1930s on, concentrated on the extent to which the support – especially the financial support – of business facilitated Adolf Hitler's rise to power. The analysis that emphasized the antidemocratic consequences of large concentrations of economic power underlay Allied wartime and postwar plans for the restructuring and democratization of Germany. For the United States, the problem lay in cartels, trusts, and big banks, and the occupation authorities consequently embarked on decartellization, detrustification, and a regionalization of banking along U.S. lines (where banks were restricted to one state). This view was reflected in the reports compiled for the Office of the Military Government of the United States (OMGUS). For the Soviet Union, a parallel interpretation involved the transfer of large corporations and agricultural estates to state control.

1

In the 1960s and 1970s, a substantial literature was devoted to an analysis of the origins of "fascism" and tried to suggest that fascism was the final outcome of a general crisis of capitalism, in which business used the most radical and destructive means in its attempt to defeat a challenge from labor and the left. This approach took up many of the themes from the older critical literature of the 1930s.

A great deal of the discussion of business took for granted that the major motive of business was a search – relentless and ruthless – for profit. Robert Brady, for instance, in 1937 explained in *The Spirit and Structure of German Fascism* that the ostensibly hostile Nazi rhetoric about business was merely a camouflage for the real interests of business. "The objective, in short, is profits. If in an organized economy the community must be made to believe that service comes first, it can be argued that profits are no more than the just reward for success in this labor of public love. But for the initiated there can be no confusion; the single, sole, and dominating purpose is necessarily profits."[1] Such discussion largely ignored the ways in which the government of Nazi Germany tried to limit profits (by restrictions on dividend, by tax measures, etc.). It also forgot that managers in a large corporate hierarchy may not have the same interest as shareholders in profit and may find size, power, and prestige more attractive and more compelling incentives for action. Peter Hayes's groundbreaking study of IG Farben rightly pointed out that "the dynamics of capitalism do not entirely explain the Farben case."[2] One of the aims of this study is to attempt to assess the nature of the motivation for actions that appear morally dubious.

The older literature emphasized violence and terror as the hallmarks of a new aggressive imperialism, in which business was fully complicit. It devoted little attention to the victims of National Socialism. To be sure, not all analysts were as naïve as Cambridge economist Claude Guillebaud, who in his book *The Economic Recovery of Germany*, published in 1939, wrote of the new prosperity of the German business elite: "The present writer was told early in 1938 that there had latterly been an enormous increase in the sale of pictures, old furniture, objets d' art etc. in Berlin, and that this was a sure sign of great prosperity in the business community; it might of course also be interpreted as a sign of fear of future inflation (though there was no evidence of this in other directions), or of a desire to escape future taxation."[3] Guillebaud did not think that the sales might be a product of the regime's persecution of Jews.

Only in the 1990s did an approach that put victims at the center of historical writing about National Socialism change the perspective. In large part this change is a consequence of a shift in historical sensitivities, in which power and the powerful are no longer seen as the core of the historical process, but in which empathy for victims is a part of restoring morality and compensating for past injustices. There is also a geopolitical element to this development, in that the many victims of Nazi injustice and persecution who lived behind the Iron Curtain of the Cold War era – by the 1990s, of course, quite elderly people – had never received restitution or compensation for the evils perpetrated against them.

One of the most important impetuses to a new assessment of company history was provided by the class-action lawsuits launched on behalf of victims of persecution and brought before U.S. courts.

In the rewriting in the 1990s of the history of persecution, the experience of victims has been more central. For heavy industry, where attention had previously concentrated on the contributions of industry to the armaments economy and Germany's military push, this meant a concentration above all on the exploitation of slave labor. Older accounts had been more interested in the oppression of the German working class and its experience of suffering. The pioneering work of Ulrich Herbert raised the general issue.[4] Until the end of the 1980s, many business histories simply omitted the question of forced labor. The most egregious example was Hans Pohl's work on Daimler-Benz, but Pohl was not alone.[5] There were also some positive examples, notably Peter Hayes's account of IG Farben, which dealt extensively with the firm's employment of forced foreign workers.[6] Subsequently, business histories, often commissioned now in the hope of presenting a complete and accurate picture of business involvement, devoted considerable space to this issue. Hans Mommsen's history of Volkswagen devotes 215 pages; Wilfried Feldenkirchen's history of Siemens, 10 pages; and Manfred Pohl's account of Philipp Holzmann, 14 pages.[7] Since the mid-1990s, there has been a proliferation of work on this subject.[8]

What was the participation of business in the process of exploitation and destruction? This question arose especially in the case of the large German chemical company IG Farben. Peter Hayes devoted a substantial part of his history to explaining the background of Farben's decision to build a plant at Auschwitz.

These stories had much to do with the barbarization and systematic destruction of human life but less to do with the earlier phases of discrimination, marginalization, and victimization. There had been some work on so-called "aryanization", the takeover of Jewish businesses, but with a few exceptions, this work rarely connected with the general history of persecution and genocide. The first systematic study was that of Helmut Genschel (1966), and there followed in 1987 Avraham Barkai's book on the economic struggle of German Jews. The story of the dispossession of small-scale assets, furniture and household goods, was told in detail for the first time by Frank Bajohr as late as 1997.[9]

Yet this process of despoliation was a crucial link in the cumulative radicalization of a process of discrimination that ultimately led to genocide. Restricting occupational activity and stripping property was a way of stripping dignity and converting citizens into surplus people whose welfare and even existence could be a matter of passive indifference for the population at large. Hans Safrian has made this point very clearly in relation to the brutal expropriation of Austrian Jews (which proceeded much more quickly than the analogous process in Germany). He quoted a 1938 memorandum by "Reichskommissar" Bürckel of Vienna: "We must never forget that, if we wish to aryanize and to deprive the Jew of his livelihood, the Jewish question needs to be solved as a whole."[10] Violation of property rights was a major element in the violation of human rights.

For heavy industry, or automobiles, the issue of "aryanization" played a comparatively small role. There was little Jewish ownership of German heavy industry, with the exception of the substantial holdings of coal fields by the Czech–German industrial dynasty of the Petscheks (see discussion), so that the expansion of industrial activity in Germany did not rest substantially on the takeover or seizure of Jewish businesses. For textiles, printing, tobacco, and the retail sector, the story is very different: Few postwar German companies have reached the size or dominance to make this a major focus of analysis.

Banks, on the other hand, are historically a central part of the German corporate landscape. They figured prominently in postwar American investigations of the corporate origins of National Socialism.

Their power had already been a topic of intense political debate at the end of the nineteenth century.

They did not produce anything. In that sense, the slave labor discussion is an issue that usually concerns banking only indirectly, insofar as particular bank managers or directors sat on the supervisory boards of companies that employed slave labor and in this sense bore an indirect responsibility for the policies of companies. They did, however, employ relatively small numbers of forced laborers in clerical jobs and sometimes also in construction of bank buildings.

On the other hand, banks administered accounts of business and personal customers. In this way, they were inevitably involved in shifts of assets and transfers of property. In the currency-exchange legislation of the 1930s, they took over some public functions: Foreign exchange, gold, and foreign securities were required to be registered with a *Devisenbank,* a bank (which could be a commercial bank) licensed to deal in foreign exchange. Even the way bank officials referred to themselves in Germany gave some indication of their public role: the counter clerk was a *Schalterbeamte,* with *Beamte* carrying a civil-service connotation. Periodically, such officials were reminded in the 1930s that it was their duty to give a positive impression of the legislation brought in by the new state. In addition, banks had traditionally in Germany been heavily involved in the financing of industry and in industrial restructuring.

If we take a narrowly defined view of what banking involved, the "aryanization" of businesses in Germany in the 1930s and the large-scale looting and expropriations undertaken in occupied Europe were merely particular instances of such industrial restructuring.

The focus on the economic side of persecution is quite novel: For instance, when the United States Holocaust Memorial Museum in Washington, D.C. decided in the mid-1990s to microfilm large parts of the captured German documents held in the Moscow Special Archive, it did not think the files of the Reich Economics Ministry or the Four-Year Plan sufficiently central to the analysis of the genocide to be worth including in the copy order. Only a few years later, such themes were central, largely as a consequence of the intense public debate that began in 1996 about the wartime role of Swiss banks, their holdings of the "heirless assets" of the victims of persecution, and their role in gold transactions and other measures that allowed the continuance of the German war economy. In December 1997, an international conference, held in London and organized by the U.S. Department of State and the British Foreign Office, examined the question of "Nazi gold." But at the conference, there was almost no discussion of the German policies and institutions that had caused the whole problem. Instead, the focus was on other countries, often but not always Germany's trade partners: Switzerland, Sweden, Spain, Portugal, Argentina, but also the Vatican.

Inevitably, however, these discussions eventually focused attention back on the behavior of German corporations and on the extent to which they had been accomplices, beneficiaries, or profiteers of state and party measures. The voluminous documentation that was then released, in Russia and the United States as well as Switzerland and Germany, produced some new surprises. In the course of the investigation of German gold transactions with Switzerland, microfilm copies of some of the Reichsbank's gold ledgers were rediscovered in the National Archives and Records Administration in Washington, D.C. They revealed that the two largest German commercial banks, Deutsche and Dresdner, had purchased gold from the Reichsbank. Tracing the destiny of individual gold bars demonstrated in addition that a large share of this gold was derived directly from the victims of persecution. In response to the new revelations, both banks asked commissions of independent historians to produce analyses of these gold transactions. The studies by Jonathan Steinberg on Deutsche Bank and Johannes Bähr on Dresdner Bank were published as books within a few weeks of each other at the beginning of 1999. (The Deutsche Bank report had been available for longer on the World Wide Web.)[11] Deutsche Bank invited a commission of five historians, three of whom had already been involved in the preparation of a comprehensive history of the bank published in 1995, to produce a number of specific studies of its history in the Nazi period. They are Professors Avraham Barkai, Gerald D. Feldman, Lothar Gall, Harold James, and Jonathan Steinberg. The extent of public concern made it crucial to undertake the expensive task of locating and centralizing all historical records, including those previously held by bank branches in more or less forgotten record depositories, back rooms, and cellars. The first such study was Jonathan Steinberg's gold report.

The second study prepared under the auspices of Deutsche Bank's historical commission is unlike the first. The bank's participation in the process of so-called "aryanization" was neither a forgotten secret nor a minor and obscure part of the bank's history. The author of the current report, Harold James, had already tackled this question at some length in the chapter he prepared for the history of the bank published in 1995.[12] There are now more documents available for the study, with the consequence that the present report represents a comprehensive overview of all currently available evidence:

1. The papers of branches of Deutsche Bank were collected, inventoried, and analyzed in Eschborn, on the outskirts of Frankfurt, from 1998. Credit files and general correspondence provide a detailed picture of the activities of the bank's branches, which were largely responsible for handling most of the cases of "aryanization." These branch files give some information about some of the profits derived by Deutsche Bank from "aryanization". They are not, however, uniformly comprehensive. The papers of branches from southwestern Germany are relatively complete, but there is much less from the industrial heartland of Rhineland-Westphalia. Files from former branches of Deutsche Bank in eastern Germany were preserved in the public archives of the German Democratic Republic (GDR). Regional and city archives in Poland, however, appear not to contain Deutsche Bank material. Neither was it possible to locate papers from Sudeten-German branches of the bank in archives in the Czech Republic or Slovakia.

2. In connection with the analysis of the gold transactions, Deutsche Bank Controlling discovered preliminary material for the preparation of annual accounts, material that had previously been unknown to Deutsche Bank's own historical archive.

3. The papers of Hermann Josef Abs were not available to Harold James when he prepared his chapter in the 1995 history. The material in his office subsequently turned out to include some Deutsche Bank files, evacuated from Berlin to Hamburg in 1945, which Abs had used in the early 1970s in preparing his court case against the historian Eberhard Czichon.[13] There is

7

relatively little documentation in these papers from Deutsche Bank files between 1933 and 1945 that was not previously known: most of the files were taken by the Allies and used by the OMGUS in preparing preparatory reports on Deutsche Bank. On the other hand, Abs's personal papers, have been blocked for historical use until 2014. These papers relate overwhelmingly to the postwar period. But the author was able to see the most important pre-1945 source, a substantial number of note cards, detailing appointments and the contents of discussions, in Abs's own rather small and semilegible handwriting. These cards may have been weeded by Abs himself, in that for a number of Abs's most sensitive contacts, there are no note cards in the collection. Thus there are no cards for contacts that we know existed between Abs and oppositional or semioppositional figures or foreigners (Helmuth James Graf Moltke, Hjalmar Schacht, Per Jacobsson) and also not for some crucial bureaucrats (Hans Kehrl, Joachim Riehle), or for one central former Deutsche Banker who headed the Böhmische Union-Bank (hereafter referred to as the BUB) during the war (Walter Pohle).

4. It was also possible to use more files in central Europe and Russia than had been used for the 1995 history. These included most importantly the captured German documents in the Moscow Special Archive and the records of the Česká Banká Union in the Ministry of Finance of the Czech Republic.

One group of records that might reveal significantly more about the controversial issue of the level of profit involved in "aryanization," the documents of tax offices [*Finanzämter*], are blocked under the Federal Republic's archival law for eighty years after their creation.

The conclusions of the 1995 history in respect of "aryanization" require not revision but merely amplification. This is not really a new history. James's verdict then in 1995 – that the worst and most exploitative case of "aryanization" involved the takeover of a Czech bank, the Česká Banká Union, or the BUB – is amply substantiated by the surviving records in Prague of that bank. Those documents show how brutal but also how illegal were the bank's actions in occupied Europe and how intimately connected was the bank in the terroristic world of military authorities, the party, the SS, and the Gestapo. As in the case of Jonathan Steinberg's gold report, some problems relate not only to actions between 1933 and 1945 but also to the post-1945 aftermath.

The reader of the following pages will notice that there existed room for maneuvering for individual bankers and that bankers behaved in different ways, which makes it difficult to generalize about the behavior of the firm as a whole. This does not mean that there is not room for other ways of presenting the same material. In particular, there is a difference between a historical way and a legal way of looking at the same problem. Both depend on a reconstruction of facts, on what actually happened. But lawyers and historians will view responsibility in a different way.

The difference will be clear if the reader reflects on the law of sexual harassment in the United States. Sexual harassment is an action of individuals, and they may be liable for criminal action. But legally, the responsibility rests with the company that permitted the inappropriate activity, and in working out financial settlements it is this responsibility that will be reflected.

A historical account, as offered here, offers an indispensable basis for working out what kind of responsibility existed. The reader will see that reconstructing the dynamics of business decisions at this period shows how rational-bureaucratic structures, such as a firm, began to break down under the weight of a pervasive and pernicious ideology.

This book begins by examining the structure of the bank and the economic environment within which it operated (Chapter 2). It then asks in what ways such an institution could be affected, and permeated with, the evil ideology of National Socialism (Chapter 3). The exclusion of Jews from German economic life is treated in general (Chapter 4), before the book examines in detail the progressive involvement of banks, and of Deutsche Bank, in the purge of Jews from German economic life in the 1930s (Chapter 5). It looks at the general political, legislative, and economic framework, then at the relationship of the bank with Jewish-owned banks, at the personalities involved in some of the very large cases of "aryanization," and at the different responses of the branches of the bank. A further chapter (6) examines the much more radical policies outside the German frontiers of 1937 but also tries to explain why very different courses were followed in the three countries first invaded by Nazi Germany: Austria, Czechoslovakia, and Poland. Chapter 7 looks at how bank accounts were affected by the expropriation of Jews. Finally, there is an attempt (Chapter 8) to explain how far the involvement of the bank brought profits.

2

The Structure, Organization, and Economic Environment of Deutsche Bank

In the 1930s, as now, Deutsche Bank was the largest German bank whose economic power was the subject of debate and controversy. At that time, its full name was Deutsche Bank und Disconto-Gesellschaft.[1]

Deutsche Bank had been founded in 1870, when a new law permitted the establishment of joint stock banks in Prussia. This was a few months before the unification of Germany and the creation of the German Empire. The bank's founders had a national-patriotic purpose in mind, which was indicated by the (rather ambitious) title they chose for their bank. It was supposed to challenge the preeminence of London in the financing of overseas trade.[2]

In the first years of its existence, it very rapidly emerged as an energetically expanding international bank. It participated first in the establishment of the "German Bank of London" in 1871, and in 1873 then created its own London agency. In 1872 and 1873, it bought into New York and Paris banks, and in 1872, founded agencies in Shanghai and Yokohama. In 1874, it participated in a South American bank, and in 1886, created its own institution for South America, the Deutsche Übersee Bank (later Deutsche Überseeische Bank or Banco Alemán Transatlántico). Besides trade finance, it carried out a number of important operations for the German government – including the sale in Asia of much of the Prussian stock of silver, as the empire prepared the transition from a silver- to a gold-based currency.[3]

One of the first managers of the bank was Georg Siemens, who had previously worked for the electrical firm Siemens und Halske, founded by his father's cousin, Werner von Siemens. This enterprise was a

11

major beneficiary of the creation of the new empire and its demands for communications technology. Georg's bank rapidly became involved in industrial finance.

One founder of the new bank was a prominent liberal politician, Ludwig Bamberger. As a young man, he had been a participant in the abortive revolution of 1848 in the Palatinate, had been sentenced to death, and fled to London, where he worked in a bank owned by relatives of his mother. He later moved in the same business to Rotterdam and Paris and learned about the interconnections between economic and national development, or between money and politics. In 1868, he had been elected to the Customs Union [*Zollverein*] parliament, the predecessor of a national parliament, and after unification he became a member of the Reichstag. There, his major achievement was as rapporteur to the committee that created the legislation establishing a new central bank (the Reichsbank).[4]

The early years set a pattern in which the new bank moved in the interstices of international finance, industrial finance, and politics. Before the First World War, it played a major role in the growth and consolidation of German industry, especially the electrotechnical industry. It promoted the formation of syndicates, in which businesses were grouped in cooperative partnerships, as well as a wave of mergers, which left the German electrical industry dominated by just two large firms by the beginning of the twentieth century: Siemens and AEG. Deutsche Bank also played a prominent part in the financing of the great project of the extension of German power into the Balkans by the construction of a Berlin-to-Baghdad railway.[5]

Organization of the Bank

At first the Deutsche Bank had been a Berlin-based bank, with branches only in the two port cities (which were not yet members of the German customs area), Bremen and Hamburg. It was only in 1886 that Deutsche Bank opened a branch in Frankfurt; it opened a branch in Munich in 1892 and one in Dresden and Leipzig in 1901. In the first decade of the twentieth century, it took a substantial number of participations in the industrial basin of the Rhine-Ruhr. These were amalgamated with the bank only after 1913. In 1914, the bank took over one of the largest regional industrial banks, the Bergisch-Märkische Bank. It was only really in the 1920s that the bank became a truly multibranch bank, with tentacles spreading all over Germany. At the time of the merger in 1914, the Deutsche Bank had only 15 branches, whereas the Bergisch-Märkische Bank had 35. By the end of 1926, there were 173 branches.[6] Branches clearly brought the bank into a new sort of business: customer accounts and smaller-scale financing of small and medium-size enterprises. One of the attractions of a larger branch network was that it brought a stable supply of deposits, and the bank tried to develop this business by launching savings accounts. In the 1920s, however, the Deutsche Bank, like the other big joint-stock banks based in Berlin, still dealt mostly with large-scale industrial finance and with international trade and was frequently and bitterly criticized for its neglect of small-business [*Mittelstand*] customers.[7] This criticism, which was in the later years of the Weimar Republic most radically expressed by the National Socialist German Workers' Party (NSDAP), may have been one reason why some of the managers of Deutsche Bank believed that they should become more involved with the financing of small and medium-size business and hence participated in the "aryanization" of such enterprises, which is the major theme of this book. Most *Mittelstand* finance, however, was conducted by other sorts of financial institutions, small private banks, regional banks, or the many savings and cooperative banks spread over Germany.

The biggest of the bank mergers took place in 1929, with the Disconto-Gesellschaft, one of the four so-called D-banks (besides Deutsche, the others were the Dresdner and the Darmstädter- und Nationalbank). The Disconto was more conservatively managed than Deutsche had become, and its high management regarded itself as less tainted by expansion. The complexities of the merger had not been fully digested before the full fury of the world depression hit Germany.

How was such a complex institution as Deutsche Bank managed, and how did it do business? The immediate executive responsibility lay, as with all German companies, with a board of management [*Vorstand*], composed in 1932 of ten members. Each had responsibilities for a particular region and for some particular function of the bank. This was a body of equals, though one member might be delegated as the speaker [*Sprecher*].

A supervisory board [*Aufsichtsrat*] was chaired by convention by a former member of the board of management. Its other members were prominent business figures, usually from major companies with which Deutsche Bank had had a long-standing business relationship. In 1932, this board had 102 members, in addition to two representatives from the works council. This was clearly a very unwieldy institution that met infrequently and could not exercise any real control. Like almost all German supervisory boards, its function was social rather than operational. A committee of this board, however, met more frequently, and this committee's role was strengthened in the course of institutional redesign during the depression. It then became known as the credit committee, and its major function lay in supervising large credits, which had been one of the problematic areas of bank policy before 1931.

In the course of this redesign during the depression, the number of members of the supervisory board was reduced dramatically, to fourteen plus the two members of the works council by the beginning of 1933. But later, as it was important to accommodate politically influential figures in the new regime, such as tobacco magnate Philipp Reemtsma, the number increased again, so that there were twenty-nine members of the supervisory board by 1936.

Another way for the bank to expand its business contacts was through the institution of a large "main committee" [*Hauptausschuss*], which took over from the larger, pre-1932 supervisory board. This was complemented by a nationwide pattern of regional advisory committees [*Beiräte*].

Members of the board of management were members of the supervisory boards of industrial enterprises, and they derived a substantial amount of their income from the remuneration as members of those supervisory boards (these fees were called *Tantiemen*). From this resulted a deep relationship between banks and industry, in which a bank would characteristically first give loans to an enterprise, sometimes secured, sometimes in the form of a current account overdraft [*Kontokorrentkredit*].[8] When there was a favorable moment on the stock market, banks would organize new issues of shares or bonds and would use their customer base as a market for the newly issued securities. Many customers kept their securities with the bank, in custody or *Depot* accounts, and the bank would then use these securities to vote in the general meetings of companies. It was the mixture of different financial products that gave the German "universal" banks their particular power, a power that probably reached its height in the first decade of the century, at the time of the great wave of mergers and the establishment of many large trusts.

Such a board system worked well at a time when most of the business was Berlin based or foreign oriented. It did not really fit well with the organizational structure required by an extensive branching system. There was a central Berlin office that dealt with branches [*Filialbüro*], supervised by one member of the board of management. In addition, each member of the managing board had general responsibility for a particular region. But the large companies might have had a particular relation with another managing director.

The branches behaved in many ways as if they were miniature versions of the bank. Between one and three leading managers were called directors, and they sat on the supervisory boards of companies smaller than those on which the bank's managing directors would sit.

The existence of a quite dense network of branches meant that the bank had a much greater contact with a variety of regional and local subeconomies. This meant, too, that it had substantial business interests in those areas of Germany where there was a considerable amount of Jewish-owned business: in Saxony, where there were many Jewish-owned textiles, leather, and fur firms; in Silesia, where Jewish owners worked in textiles and also in heavy industry; in southwestern Germany with its craft traditions, where there were also extensive Jewish-owned manufacturing enterprises and where by coincidence the Deutsche Bank had acquired a particularly dense network of branches as a result of mergers with other banks.[9]

One other institution should be introduced at this point, although it played a significant role only in the Nazi period. The Weimar Republic had established works councils, to discuss issues connected with conditions of work and employment. In the Nazi dictatorship, they were reconstituted as organs in which Nazi trade union representatives assumed a major part.

At the beginning of the 1930s, then, the Deutsche Bank was not a perfectly centralized institution but had an imperfectly articulated hierarchy: It might even be termed a "polyarchy." It looked in some ways like a mirror of a republican state that the theorist Carl Schmitt described as "polycratic" (a term many historians have used to describe the distribution of power in the post-1933 Nazi state).[10]

Depression and Financial Crisis

The whole structure of German banking was thrown into confusion by the trauma of the great German financial crisis of 1931. The worst affected bank was the Darmstädter und Nationalbank (or Danatbank), led by the charismatic Jakob Goldschmidt, who had appeared to Germans as well as to foreign observers to be the incarnation of the power and attraction of the German mixed-banking model. The report of the British Macmillan Committee, which held Goldschmidt up as a model, was by an odd coincidence published on July 13, 1931, the day when the Danat closed its doors. The basic weakness of the Danat lay in a combination of a massive overextension of loans to a single borrower, the apparently very successful and dynamic Bremen firm of Nordwolle, with large-scale purchases of its own shares to support its price in a weakening market. The firm was then swept away by an international wave of panic that followed the collapse in May of the Viennese Creditanstalt. The Danat was merged in the course of a state rescue operation with the almost equally damaged Dresdner Bank, and the old management of both banks was replaced. The fact that the state de facto owned the new Dresdner Bank, and that the replacement of the board was not complete by January 30, 1933, almost inevitably gave the Nazi Party a substantial influence on the bank.

The Deutsche Bank had not been as badly affected by the crisis, but it also depended on government money and had to deposit 72 million Reichsmarks (RM) of its shares with the Deutsche Golddiskontbank, a subsidiary of the central bank, the Deutsche Reichsbank. The speaker of the board of management, Oscar Wassermann, had been responsible for the problematic loans to a bankrupt large brewery, Schultheiss-Patzenhofer, and had failed to check the creditworthiness of Schultheiss. There was also a bitter controversy – stimulated by the management of the failed banks – as to whether Deutsche Bank had not deliberately worsened the crisis to hurt its competitors. This version, actively propagated by Jakob Goldschmidt, was later repeated by then Chancellor Heinrich Brüning, in his posthumously published memoirs.[11] (Brüning apparently had found it hard to write the section on the banking crisis. Whereas most of the manuscript was complete in the 1930s, Brüning wrote the banking section in the 1950s, while consulting Goldschmidt, who had fled from the Nazis to New York.)

Very late in the development of the bank crisis, on July 8, Goldschmidt had proposed a merger of the Danat with the Deutsche. Wassermann had refused, wisely, because it was impossible to gauge the extent of the Danat's losses (and a similar takeover of a problematic bank, the Bodenkreditanstalt, had been responsible for the losses and then the failure of the greatest Viennese bank, the Creditanstalt). A few days earlier, Wassermann had repeatedly spoken at a meeting of industrialists and bankers about a specific "Danat problem," but in reality all banks were vulnerable because of withdrawals and the unwillingness or inability of the Reichsbank to support the commercial banks by discounting bills. Later, Wassermann told the government that the Danat could not be saved, and on July 10 he had informed Chancellor Brüning that the other banks were not threatened. On July 11, the Deutsche Bank's directors refused to participate in a credit for the Danat, and indeed, Wassermann began to insist that the Dresdner Bank was tottering.[12]

After the banking crisis, in October 1931, Deutsche Bank drew up a lengthy memorandum defending itself against the accusation that its lack of solidarity with the other big banks had brought about a general crisis. The memorandum attributed the responsibility for the banking crisis to the international environment; it also criticized very strongly the Reichsbank's policy of restricting credit (rediscounting) to the commercial banks. Indeed, the Reichsbank's actions did not conform to the classic central banking recommendations of Walter Bagehot (who had believed that the central bank in the face of a panic should lend freely, but at a penalty rate). But the Deutsche Bank's memorandum did not take any account of the way in which the Reichsbank had been forced into this course by other central banks, in particular the Federal Reserve Bank of New York and the Bank of England, who had made such credit restrictions a precondition for any international assistance.[13] Throughout the subsequent months, Deutsche Bank remained quite critical of the Reichsbank and its president, Hans Luther. The issue remained sensitive after the war, as in the 1950s former Deutsche Bankers feared Brüning's imminent memoirs, and the bank's dossier on the 1931 crisis was kept with Hermann Josef Abs's personal papers.

It is easy to see how such an attack could be mounted. Whoever was responsible for the banking crisis had significantly worsened the

German depression. Without that worsening, it is quite conceivable that Brüning might have survived longer and that Hitler and his movement might have "faded into oblivion" (as a former British ambassador to Germany had stated rather prematurely in his memoirs published in 1929).[14] In 1953, Brüning had a long conversation about the banking crisis with the past (and future) star of the Deutsche Bank, Hermann Abs. A note on this talk records that "Abs has the impression that Brüning believes this crisis to be the root of all subsequent ills, and has from somewhere gained the impression that the events were very influenced by competition between the banks, and that the Deutsche Bank's unwillingness to support the Danatbank aggravated the situation."[15]

On the eve of the Nazi dictatorship, the Deutsche Bank was, in consequence, vulnerable – organizationally, financially, and politically. Great though that vulnerability was, it was less than for many other banks. The rival Dresdner Bank, in particular, was even weakened by the banking crisis, by the de facto nationalization of the bank, and by the government-imposed merger with the Danat. Three members of its old managing board had been obliged to resign after the debacle of 1931. The bank had a reputation as being "Jewish."[16] The restructuring of its managing board had not been completed by 1933, when there were only four members left. As a consequence, it was much easier for the new regime to influence that bank than it was in the case of Deutsche Bank.

The Economic Circumstances of Recovery

It is difficult to distinguish clearly in the story of Germany's way out of depression and into the economics of control quite what followed more or less inevitably from the financial and economic catastrophes of the depression, and what originated from the political vision of the new masters of Germany. The capital market, for instance, became smaller and less relevant to economic activity. Bank loans recovered much more slowly than did the rest of the economy from the world depression. But both these phenomena were characteristic not only of Germany and dictatorship but also of the development of the whole European economy. Some economists as a result formulated a law of a long-term decline in the demand for loans.[17] The capital market seemed to have been destroyed by the experience of depression and by the organizational measures, such as increased cartelization in financial markets, that accompanied the market failure of the 1920s and early 1930s. It required no National Socialist government opposed to finance capitalism to marginalize the German capital market. In this sense, a large part of the macroeconomics of Germany's 1930s experience would have happened anyway, whatever the form of the government.

At first, little bank financing of new investment was required because of the availability of unused capacity. Later expansion could be paid out of high profit levels, or through government credits in the case of firms producing on public contracts.

The Deutsche Bank und Disconto-Gesellschaft gave substantially more new credits in 1933 (118,000) than in 1932 (17,000), but the total volume of credit fell steadily until 1937. As a proportion of the bank's balance sheet, it declined from 55.4 percent in 1932 to 35.4 percent in 1937. Though there was a brief recovery of bank lending in 1938, during the war, bank loans continued to decline.

Bank lending contracted in part because firms learned the lesson of the depression as meaning avoidance of indebtedness. But banks also had their own reasons to be cautious in the aftermath of 1931, when they had been obliged to liquidate many loans in a great hurry, and in the process had incurred massive hostility from their clients. Any wise banker would draw lessons from the banking disaster. Time after time, the Deutsche Bank urged restraint on its credit officers. Thus, a circular to branch managers in August 1933 read, in part: "We are interested in as far as possible [...] keeping our liquidity at a satisfactory level in the future."[18] Eduard Mosler, the spokesman of the board of managing directors, told branch managers in October 1936: "As a result we needed a certain caution in our credit policy. We should not aim at an extension of credit." Karl Kimmich, speaking to the board in 1938, said: "There is the danger that we will be called on by industry, and we must alter our attitude. [...] We shall try to convert long- and middle-term credits into short-term loans."[19]

Deposits of all the major German banks also contracted in the initial phases of the recovery period, as major firms started to use their deposits for investment.[20] A process of financial disintermediation set in. Foreign deposits dropped particularly sharply, in the case of the

Deutsche Bank to RM 403 million at the end of 1933 (compared with RM 685 million in 1931). But after the end of 1934, the total of deposits rose steadily. Faced with low demand for loans, banks found they could do little in the later 1930s except to channel these new funds into state paper. From 1933, holdings of securities shown in the bank's balance sheet rose. To a substantial extent, these were government securities. After 1937, as the government became more dependent on short-term borrowing, the number of treasury bills in the bank's portfolio also rose. This process was described in Germany as the "silent financing" of a government whose expenditure and deficits rose as it took on ever more tasks. In practice, the result was the financing through the banking system not simply of the government sector of the economy but instead of a rearmament drive.

As the traditional business of the bank in taking business deposits and extending commercial credit contracted, its position within the German economy was diminished. In addition, traditionally a major strength of the German great banks, and that of the Deutsche Bank in particular, had lain in overseas financing. The dramatic reduction of world trade in the depression, the protectionist environment of the 1930s, and Germany's managed foreign trade regime reduced the scope and significance of foreign economic relations. All these considerations combined to ensure that the Deutsche Bank, along with all the other Berlin great banks, lost its share of German banking business.

Organizational uncertainty and financial and political weakness made the bank as a structure vulnerable. At the same time, these circumstances meant that individuals within the structure of the bank who believed that they were dynamic and in touch with the spirit of the new age looked for new opportunities. Such opportunities might easily be presented after 1933 by the new official endorsement of anti-Semitic fears, prejudices, envies, and hatreds.

3

National Socialism and Banks

The National Socialist Party and government were suspicious of banks and their power and took over many elements of older critiques of German banking. They distinguished between productive and speculative, grasping capitalism ("*schaffendes*" as opposed to "*raffendes Kapital*"). In the discussions about bank reform and restructuring that took place in the aftermath of the depression and the banking crisis, they favored public-sector banks, as a less "capitalistic" way of managing money and investment. There were already state-owned banks, such as the Reichs-Kredit-Gesellschaft, and the Nazi state added more for particular investments in connection with the new military and economic priorities: notably the Bank der deutschen Luftfahrt, which was to finance air rearmament. In retail banking, the Nazis unambiguously favored the savings banks [*Sparkassen*], the banks of the little or average people.

The Nazi attitude toward privately owned joint-stock banks was heavily permeated by anti-Semitism. Banking and speculative financial capitalism were castigated as "Jewish," and in a number of instances commercial banks were subject to party-organized anti-Semitic boycotts in 1933. Later, in 1938, there was a brief time when Deutsche Bank was, under official and legal terminology, a "nonaryan" bank. Explaining the character and origins of Nazi anti-Semitism is clearly an enterprise that goes well beyond the scope of this study. The movement had many facets or strands. In the resentments of the interwar years, there was a mixture of social snobbery, old stereotypes derived from Christian teaching, hostility to people who could be identified as different, racialist notions about purity of

21

ancestry and descent, and eugenic concerns with the categorization of genetic groups. But it is worth pointing out one strand peculiar to this epoch that bears directly on the involvement of banks in the process of "aryanization."

Since the middle of the nineteenth century, with the evolution of a new, dynamic, and unstable sort of market economy, Jews had been identified with finance capitalism. At the beginning, the critique often came from the political left. In France, left-wing revolutionary Alphonse Toussenel wrote in 1845 a book entitled *Les Juifs, rois de l'époque: histoire de la féodalité financière* [*The Jews, Kings of the Age: A History of Financial Feudality*]. In Germany in 1843, young Karl Marx wrote an essay, *"On the Jewish Question,"* in which he posed a series of questions. "Let us not look for the Jew's secret in his religion: rather let us look for the secret of religion in the real Jew. What is the secular basis of Judaism? Practical need, self-interest. What is the secular cult of the Jew? Haggling. What is his secular God? Money."[1] The 1848–49 Saxon revolutionary Richard Wagner wrote in very similar terms in *"Das Judentum in der Musik"* ["Jewry in Music"] (1850), "As things stand in the world of today, the Jew really is already more than emancipated: he is in charge, and he will remain in charge for as long as money is the power before which all our strivings are as naught."[2]

With the First World War, price controls, inflation, and the evolution of a black market, large numbers of people were obliged to take up speculative, illegal, or semilegal activities simply to survive. Such actions conflicted with traditional ideas of what kinds of business conduct were legitimate. One powerful argument as to why anti-Semitism flared up so poisonously during and after the First World War is that Germans widely took up activities previously defined as Jewish, hated themselves for this breach of traditional values, and reacted by transferring their hatred to the members of the ethnic group associated with the stereotype of bad behavior.[3] One example of such a transition, in someone who played a crucial role in the development of the Nazi state's anti-Semitic policy, is Joseph Goebbels, who seems to have learned Jew hating as a bank clerk (with Dresdner Bank) during the great inflation of the early 1920s.[4]

In explaining why individuals who were employed by banks took the actions they did, such anti-Semitism – professionally generated – may have played some role. There are instances of such attitudes that will be found over the following pages. But most of the bankers' activity seems, on the basis of the available (written) evidence, to have been much more motivated by a narrowly conceived professionalism. In some areas, bankers disliked or even resisted anti-Jewish measures because they saw them as directed against major and profitable clients of the bank. Professional banking involved a network of social contacts with bank customers, which the bankers did not want to break – and they did not. It is striking how in many postwar restitution negotiations, in obviously completely changed political circumstances, the victims of persecution worked on friendly terms with the old bankers to reach restitution settlement – against the purchasers of Jewish property and against the German state. Where there were no such professional contacts, in the occupied countries and especially in central and eastern Europe, the bankers behaved on the whole very differently (and there was certainly no assistance in restitution agreements).

The history of Deutsche Bank in the Third Reich is the story of the clash of two fundamentally contrary strategies of adaptation: on the one hand, self-defense against the intrusions of party and state; on the other, accommodation and compromise. The management of Deutsche Bank might well have tried to retreat to purely economic activities, but it lived under a regime that had declared economic actions to be political.

There are four critical questions that arise in forming a judgment about this policy of accommodation:

1. To what extent did the German business elite recognize the implications of the new anti-Semitism?
2. To what extent did the business elite seek to profit from the new political and ideological circumstances?
3. To what extent were companies open to influence from the party and the state?
4. How did the new environment affect the functioning of the organization?

The Business Elite and Anti-Semitism

In the Weimar Republic, anti-Semitism had not in general been a socially acceptable attitude among the business elite, and especially among the banking elite (in sharp contrast to the communities of academics, and more so of students, or the world of small-business owners and small shopkeepers, where anti-Semitism was considered normal and even acceptable). Of course this does not mean that some, or even many, owners and leaders of big businesses might not have shared elements of a set of widely shared prejudices. But they did feel some hesitancy about expressing those prejudices. Many of the most influential bankers of the Weimar Republic were Jewish – to name only a few, Jakob Goldschmidt, the brilliant head of the Darmstädter Bank; Oscar Wassermann of Deutsche Bank; Max Warburg, the great Hamburg banker who had several times been considered as a candidate for the position of foreign minister of the republic. It is striking that when Hitler tried to pitch an appeal to business leaders during the depression, he avoided anti-Semitic rhetoric almost entirely and campaigned against "marxism." By 1933, however, there could be no doubt that the party was massively anti-Semitic, and in late March 1933 the SA (Sturmabteilungen, or Storm Troopers) organized a ferocious campaign of boycotts aimed at Jewish-owned stores. The banks – including Deutsche Bank – were vulnerable to attacks and were accused of being "plutocratic" or "Jewish."

One defense mechanism was to purge Jewish directors. This purge coincided with the aftermath of the great banking crisis of 1931, which had been resolved only with an injection of public funds. Part of the price of state reconstruction was a purging of the bank officials who were thought to have been responsible for the mistakes of the 1920s. The two purges – anti-Semitic and banking – came together.

In the first months of 1933, politics intruded into banking in two very specific ways. No one would deny that the magnitude of the 1931 crisis revealed severe shortcomings in the German banking system and in the behavior of its luminaries. The discussion about bank reorganization in the aftermath of 1931 personally threatened the leading figures involved in that debacle. But by the time of the National Socialist "seizure of power" [Machtergreifung] the personnel issues had been by no means completely resolved, and an additional element now entered the calculation. How far should the banks reflect the beliefs of what was thought to be the new Germany, beliefs expressed by the new political leadership, and in the streets, but also in the press, by many bank customers and not least by some bank employees? Second, the NSDAP used the opportunity of bank restructuring to attack the position of Jews in German economic life. The fact that the structure of business organization had been so severely shaken by the Great Depression made a purge much easier.

In Deutsche Bank, Oscar Wassermann as spokesman of the managing board [*Vorstandssprecher*] had been in charge of the bank's overall policy in the late 1920s and was widely blamed for the 1931 crisis. He was also subject to attack as a Jew and a Zionist. Two non-Jewish managing board directors bore a heavier responsibility than Wassermann for the mismanagement of Deutsche Bank's business. Werner Kehl resigned from the managing board because of the large speculative foreign exchange positions of the Düsseldorf branch in 1931, which fell within his regional domain. Emil Georg von Stauss was held to account for the bank's losses on loans to the fraudulently managed Schultheiss-Patzenhofer brewery, over whose supervisory board [*Aufsichtsrat*] he had presided.

Then in May 1933, a new purge of the managing board began, carried out for very different reasons. Here the new Germany made itself felt. As part of the political concessions made by the bank to National Socialism, Jewish directors Theodor Frank and Oscar Wassermann resigned from the managing board. As spokesman of the managing board, Wassermann had been in a particularly exposed position.[5] In his absence, Reichsbank President Hjalmar Schacht had spoken (on April 6, 1933) with two leading figures in the bank, Georg Solmssen and supervisory-board chairman Franz Urbig, and suggested the removal of some of the Jewish members of the managing board.[6] Wassermann initially agreed to leave by the end of 1933, but on May 20, his colleagues decided to announce the resignation in advance of the bank's annual general meeting scheduled for June 1. The bank's spokesman was thus pushed out prematurely.

The chairman of the supervisory board, Franz Urbig, concluded a memorandum on Wassermann's handling of Deutsche Bank's problems in the crisis years:

> Where was the man who really could not ignore where such isolated cases were leading? Where was the hand that, while such things were still in preparation, ruthlessly intervened to halt the mischief in time? Where was the fist pounding on the table to bring back to their right minds colleagues who had lost all sense of a tenable risk? Where was the

primus inter pares who, less burdened with seats on supervisory boards, had with unfailing continuity to maintain an overall view and influence over the whole and who in this direction inevitably felt some moral responsibility vis-à-vis the bank and its management? Where was Mr. Wassermann? [...] Whether Mr. Wassermann was Jewish or Christian no longer had anything to do with it.[7]

Did Urbig really convince himself of the last point? It is difficult to know, and, in July 1933, when this was written, it clearly mattered a great deal whether Wassermann was Jewish.

The bank clearly found these changes profoundly embarrassing and emphasized the nonracial and nonbusiness grounds for the departures. The press communiqué pointed out that Wassermann was 64 years old and Frank 62, and it stated an intention of electing them to the bank's supervisory board ("to be put forward for election to the supervisory board"), though neither of them did in fact move upstairs. They were replaced on the managing board by Karl Kimmich, who had been a director of the Disconto-controlled A. Schaaffhausen'scher Bankverein until its merger with Deutsche Bank in 1929, and Fritz Wintermantel from Deutsche Bank's main Berlin office. Georg Solmssen, who had been spokesman of the managing board in 1933 and whose father had been born in the Jewish religion, also moved onto the supervisory board. Three additional new members of the managing board in 1933 – Oswald Rösler, Hans Rummel, and Dr. Karl Ernst Sippell (who took responsibility for the bank's personnel department) – made for an almost complete change of leadership. The only figures remaining from the pre-1933 world were Eduard Mosler, who succeeded Solmssen as spokesman, and the bank's foreign specialist and German delegate on the Standstill Committee, Gustaf Schlieper.

There were pragmatic reasons not to be openly anti-Semitic in 1933. Suppose the National Socialist revolution was not permanent? It was by no means clear, at least until the so-called Night of the Long Knives in June 1934, that the dictatorship was stable. The papers of the bank contain some fascinating documentation of the tergiversations of the leading bankers. When Wassermann and Frank were not made members of the supervisory board, Franz Urbig, the chairman, wrote to another board member:

I, and I'm sure this goes for you too, do not like to think that a promise delivered in this form may be forgotten. Different times may one day return, and in the bank's interests we must make absolutely sure that no one can ever accuse the supreme administrative organ of the bank of having, through its representatives, contributed towards making it necessary for non-aryan board members to leave the premises.[8]

However, after June 1934, this sort of pragmatic argument against anti-Semitism faded away, and bankers were faced with a choice of how to adapt to a series of changes that looked increasingly permanent.

There was now an increasingly thorough racially driven purge of the bank. Bank directors in branches were forced to resign, allegedly in response to local circumstances, but in some cases as a preemptive measure. There seems not to have been a uniform strategy across the whole bank. In Breslau and Essen, Jewish branch directors were dismissed. On the other hand, Ludwig Fuld, the influential director of the Mannheim branch, remained until 1935.

The director of the Nuremberg branch, Hermann Oppenheim, who had a particular position as a "severely wounded front-line serviceman" (and who would not have been liable for dismissal under the Law on the Restoration of a Professional Civil Service), was in a specially sensitive region, immediately exposed to the rabid anti-Semitism of *Gauleiter* Julius Streicher and *Der Stürmer.* In April 1934, he was visited by a member of the managing board, Alfred Blinzig, who explained that he could resign under more favorable circumstances if he would take the step voluntarily, before a press or party campaign against him might begin. Oppenheim's memorandum of this conversation records the following argumentation:

> Of itself, the board would apparently never have conceived the idea of getting rid of me, partly because I have always been a valued member of it; he [Blinzig] was also clear in his own mind that my departure represented, at the moment, a loss for the branch. The fact was, I was told, while I was still out of the public eye (*Stürmer, Fränk. Tageszeitung*) and had not yet been targeted, as they say, the board could make any agreement with me that it liked; however, things would be different as soon as the least little newspaper article, for instance, coupled my name with that of the bank. Then, every conceivable agency would take the

matter up immediately; awkward questions would be asked about my compensation, etc.

Oppenheim pointed out that Dresdner Bank had a prominent Jewish employee in Nuremberg, and that Commerzbank even had two. In subsequent correspondence, Eduard Mosler of the Berlin managing board made it clear that Oppenheim could not expect much help from the bank in looking for a position in Berlin rather than in Nuremberg.[9]

Jewish employees were dismissed rather later, in 1937–38, and again often on general grounds ("because of cutbacks"). There is no material in Deutsche Bank archives that allows a detailed reconstruction of the chronology and extent of the personnel purge, such as has recently been undertaken by Dieter Ziegler for Dresdner Bank.[10] Deutsche Bank was subject to state laws and decrees, which in 1937–38 required the expropriation of Jewish businesses. It felt rather vulnerable: Indeed, for two months, between mid-June and mid-July 1938, the bank was legally classified as a Jewish enterprise. Organized anti-Semitic demonstrations were in some cases accompanied by generalized protests from the party and others against banks. Immediately after the pogrom of the so-called Reichskristallnacht, for instance, the Munich branch of Deutsche Bank complained that it was threatened.[11] Local branches of the bank adapted themselves to particular conditions, so that in some cases Deutsche Bank consulted with Dresdner Bank on the simultaneous dismissal of Jewish staff.[12] In some cases employees were transferred to foreign branches.

In addition, bank directors and employees played a role in their capacity as supervisory board members in the exclusion of Jews from many other businesses.

The government's and party's attitudes, and particularly their anti-Semitic policies, had a major effect on the relationship of banks with the rest of German business. A mixture of official pressure and threats from below led to the removal of many Jewish company directors. Bank directors played their part in this development.

This was not because the bank's leading managers were "Nazis." On the contrary: The managing board had no Nazi member until 1936, and then it was someone who had a peculiar function, in dealing with personnel, over which there had been many conflicts with the party.[13] At the beginning of 1936, a new personnel director was appointed –

Karl Ritter von Halt, who had come from the Munich private bank Aufhäuser.[14] Von Halt filled the intended role perfectly: He had been a war hero in the Great War, had been wounded on three separate occasions, and had received a Bavarian knighthood.[15] He also was awarded the Austrian Military Cross, Third Class, and the Bavarian Military Cross, Fourth Class.[16] After the war, he had distinguished himself principally as a horseman and athlete, and above all, he was a member of the NSDAP. He organized in 1936 the Olympic Winter Games in Garmisch, and he made sports a major part of the life of each Deutsche Bank employee. In Berlin, he frequented the Hotel Kaiserhof, located close to the Reich Chancellery, where many of the most powerful Nazi leaders liked to relax.[17]

There was no further appointment of a member of the NSDAP to the board until 1943, when again the addition was the result of the dynamics of party pressure, and in particular of a new anti-Catholic campaign of the party. The political balance of the board had been disturbed in 1938 and 1940 by the addition of two practicing Catholics who came from outside the bank: Hermann Abs from Delbrück Schickler & Co., and Clemens Plassman from the Rudolph Karstadt AG (*Aktiengesellschaft,* or joint-stock company). Because there were already two other Catholic members of the managing board, Oswald Rösler and Erich Bechtolf (the latter, however, was nonpractising), critics in the party began to call the Deutsche Bank the "Catholic bank."[18] In May 1943, an additional party member besides von Halt was taken on after the party and the SS started to attack[19] the presence of two new Catholics, Plassman and Abs. The new man was Robert Frowein, head of the Frankfurt branch since 1938 and a member of the NSDAP since 1936.[20] But Frowein also remained in his Frankfurt position and was rarely in Berlin, moving there only in February 1945.[21] He was hardly an effective National Socialist presence.

An initial suggestion that came from the party was that Landrat Hellmut Boernicke, director-general of the public-sector Girozentrale Brandenburg and a militant party member, should be the new commanding figure in the Deutsche Bank. But this proposal for a more intimate involvement of the party in the affairs of the bank was vetoed by the party chancellery. Hitler and the "Secretary of the Führer" Martin Bormann made it clear that they agreed with the general aim of a "pushing back of bank influence," but for this reason they should not allow the party to take direct responsibility for running the nerve centers of finance capitalism. "He [Hitler] believed that these plans [of the Deutsche Bank] could not be carried out, because there could not be any question of the party taking responsibility for banks." The banks should certainly appoint and promote party comrades, but this should not be interpreted as the state supporting private capitalism. "If the Deutsche Bank had itself suggested Herr Boernicke for the Board of Managing Directors, there would on the other hand have been no objections."[22]

Eventually, the Deutsche Bank chose as the party man on the board Professor Heinrich Hunke, the editor of the journal *Die deutsche Volkswirtschaft* (*The German Economy*), a civil servant (*Ministerialdirektor*) in the Propaganda Ministry of Joseph Goebbels, and in the late 1930s the most influential of National Socialist economic theorists. Hunke had been educated as a primary school teacher and only later entered the university and eventually obtained a doctorate with a dissertation on "the acoustic measurement of intensity." He was in the odd position of completing the university matriculation requirements only in 1929, after finishing his doctorate. In 1935, he was awarded the title of honorary professor at the Berlin Technische Hochschule. From 1927 to 1933, he had worked in the Army Ministry. He had joined the NSDAP in 1928[23] and in 1932 became a Reichstag deputy. In 1933 he became vice president of the Werberat der deutschen Wirtschaft (Advertising Council), an institution created in 1933 as part of the new autarkic stance and intended to use advertising to influence consumer behavior. In 1934, he wrote an article advocating the nationalization of the Great Berlin Banks.[24] In the Propaganda Ministry after 1940, he was responsible for the Foreign Department and propagated schemes for a new European economic order and economic community.[25] Abs and Rösler had initially asked Hunke to join the board of Deutsche Bank in the course of an overnight train journey to Vienna, but at first he declined. He apparently later changed his mind as his relations with the Propaganda Ministry deteriorated.[26]

When discussing Hunke, the Deutsche Bank Working Committee explicitly discussed the dangers of a political appointment and the implications for the functioning of the board of managing directors. "In particular the Board of Managing Directors has always maintained the principle of collegiality, which is the only system possible for a private bank, and in particular our bank, rather than the *Führerprinzip.*"[27]

What about the bank's branch directors? A list prepared toward the end of the war gives details of eighty-four branch directors. Of these, forty-four were party members. None of them had joined before 1933. Most branches at that time had two directors, but there seems to have been no attempt to make a balance. In a few branches, such as Danzig (Gdansk), both were party members; in others, such as Kattowitz (Katowice), neither were.[28] This statistic seems not untypical of German business life in general. It certainly makes it clear that neither party membership nor nonparty membership were prerequisites for a successful career in banking.

To What Extent Did the Bank Seek to Profit from the New Anti-Semitism?

Perhaps the question of how anti-Semitic or how Nazi businesspeople and bankers were is of little relevance in actually making assessments of their behavior. Personal identification with anti-Semitic beliefs is not a prerequisite for a willingness or even a desire to profit from discriminatory measures. The initial response of the bank at the highest level was thus simply denial, but as the new regime became more established, it began to treat the political circumstances as part of a general business context, in which profitable business could be generated. This development is the concern of a great part of the story told in the following pages.

Subsequently, after 1945, bank profits from "aryanization" in the Third Reich began to exercise a fascination in some commentators, with wildly exaggerated estimates of the extent of profitability. Some even see in the illegitimate profits from the spoliation of Jews in Germany and occupied Europe the immoral foundations of the prosperity of the Federal Republic. The reader who is looking for confirmation of this interpretation in the following pages will be disappointed. Many of the transactions undertaken by the bank in regard to Jewish property were not very profitable, and in some cases even produced losses. The case of the Česká Banká Union (Böhmische Union-Bank, or BUB), which is treated in great detail here, was not a source of great revenue for Deutsche Bank. The fact that a bank might have sustained losses in the course of serving the ends of an evil regime should not, it needs to be pointed out, make its actions any better morally.

Because so many different banking transactions were involved in the transfer of Jewish property (not just commissions on sales but also fees from handling mortgages, accounts, foreign transfers etc.), it is difficult to fully gauge all the additional revenue that came to the bank as a consequence of the Nazi plundering of Jews. The method adopted here is to identify what revenues were regarded as profits from "aryanization" at the time and to add additional revenues clearly derived from the spoliation.

To What Extent Was the Bank Open to Influence from Party and State?

The discussions about Jewish property took place in the framework of a radical control of the economy, in which banks were subjected to criticism and attack. The banking crisis of 1931, in which all of Germany's major banks required support from the state to survive, had been the most significant single event in the history of the German depression. It worsened the cyclical downturn substantially. As banks came under strain and called in loans, manufacturers, shops, and farms went bankrupt. The National Socialist new order inherited a network of controls from the depression governments and proceeded to make it ever more extensive. In 1934, a system of managed trade was inaugurated, as well as allocation of raw materials and the restriction of dividend payments, and after 1936 came a far-reaching regulation of prices. Jewish property was subject to what were at first apparently spontaneous attacks from local fanatics, then to official discrimination and, in the end, to expropriation.

With the exception of the racially motivated attack on Jewish possessions, the fundamental principle of private ownership was left untouched. The laws defining what ownership involved, people's "property rights," however, were utterly transformed. Germany remained a private economy, but without the guidance of those signals usually associated with the operation of a market: freely determined (not administered) prices, interest rates, or exchange quotations. It was an economy without a market mechanism, which was supposed to behave as its new masters wished. Prices are essential to the market: Their suppression and distortion leads to a command economy.

Because the banking system had historically been a transmission mechanism for market signals, in the 1930s it faced potential redundancy as the enthusiasts of new forms of economic organization took over. The crisis of 1931 seemed to teach the lesson that a banking system only harmed the rest of the economy. Would it not, they argued, be more efficient if the state directly realized its objectives by administrative fiat?

As the traditional business of the bank in taking business deposits and extending commercial credit contracted, its position within the German economy was diminished. In addition, a major strength of Germany's big banks [*Grossbanken*], and of Deutsche Bank in particular, had traditionally lain in overseas financing. The dramatic reduction of world trade in the depression, the protectionist environment of the 1930s, and Germany's managed foreign-trade regime reduced the scope and significance of foreign economic relations. All these considerations combined to ensure that Deutsche Bank, along with all the other Berlin *Grossbanken*, lost its share of German banking business.

If banks existed more and more to channel private savings into state debt, was there any justification at all for their continued independent activity? In the directed economy, did not banks belong to the apparently discredited world of the individualistic nineteenth-century past? Such was the tenor of the arguments put forward by believers in the new economic doctrines of management and control through party and state. Banking, particularly as it had developed in Germany, is concerned with identifying and assessing risks in a capital market, or (more generally) in evaluating the future. In the 1930s, many politically inspired commentators believed that the state could do all these tasks better – and above all more closely in accordance with the dominant social and political doctrines of the time. And this is where the character of the new regime made a distinct difference.

The new doctrines had been defined unambiguously by Hitler in a series of programmatic writings and speeches. He frequently declared "unalterable" the twenty-five-point NSDAP party program of 1920, which included the demand for the "breaking of the servitude of interest" and (point 13) "the nationalization of all businesses which have been formed into trusts." Again and again he declared that the economy should be subordinated to the good of the people.

Throughout the duration of the National Socialist dictatorship, the party launched periodic attacks on banks and bankers. It associated them with the allegedly defunct economy of "liberal individualism" and found them to be at odds with its notions of state-led economic activity.

How should banks respond to dramatic changes in political and moral values? Bankers recognized quite well that the new principles of Germany in the 1930s aimed fundamentally at the destruction of the economic system in which and for which they functioned. Yet at the same time, their historical role in evaluating and judging future trends meant that they could not but take the new doctrines seriously.

How Did the New Politics Affect the Organization of the Bank?

The removal of Deutsche Bank's Jewish directors was an acutely painful process. Georg Solmssen, spokesman of the managing board in 1933, saw more clearly than anyone else in the bank what was happening. A letter he wrote on April 9, 1933, to the chairman of the supervisory board, Urbig, is both moving and chillingly prophetic. It is worth quoting at length[29]:

> Dear Mr. Urbig,
>
> The expulsion of Jews from the civil service, now enshrined in law, prompts one to ask what further consequences for the private sector will flow from measures that even the educated section of the population has accepted almost as a matter of course. I fear we are only at the beginning of a development that is deliberately aimed, in accordance with a well-thought-out plan, at the economic and moral extermination of all members of the Jewish race living in Germany – quite indiscriminately. The total passivity of those classes not belonging to the National Socialist Party, the manifest lack of any feeling of solidarity on the part of everyone who, in the firms concerned, formerly worked side by side with Jewish colleagues, the ever-clearer readiness to take personal advantage of the fact that jobs are now falling vacant, and the dead silence that greets the ignominy and shame irremediably inflicted on those who, albeit innocent, find the foundations of their honor and livelihood undermined from one day to the next – all this points to a situation so

34

hopeless that it would be wrong not to look matters in the face without applying any makeup, as it were.

Certainly those concerned, seeing themselves apparently abandoned by all their professional associates, are entitled to think of themselves and no longer allow their actions to be dictated by regard for the company to which they had devoted their lives – unless, of course, that company shows towards them the same loyalty as it expected to receive from them. In our circle, too, colleagues discussed the question of collegiate solidarity. My impression was that, possibly as a result of the heterogeneous composition of the board, the idea met with a very lukewarm response and that, were one to decide to implement it oneself, such action would be more in the form of a gesture than for the purpose of out-and-out resistance and would therefore quickly collapse. I accept that in the relevant deliberations distinctions are drawn between the board members figuring on the list of proscribed persons. Nevertheless, I have the feeling that, at the same time as I seem to be regarded as someone whose work is valued as an asset and who is perhaps respected as embodying what is now a 70-year-old tradition, I too would be dropped as soon as the call came from outside in a decisive manner that I should be included in the "cleansing campaign."

I must have it made clear as soon as possible [...]

The new politics also opened a way for much greater pressure from ambitious junior employees, who saw positions opening up. Deutsche Bank had a radical National Socialist works council, which kept up the political pressure on the management. Later, with German military expansion, it was frequently the junior staff and managers who played a radicalizing role in banking policy in the occupied countries.

Was this a peculiarly German response of bank employees? They were certainly as a group spineless, and many enthusiastically sought compromises with the new regime. But there is actually nothing that the author – or, as far as he knows, any other historian – has seen in any German files of quite the rancor of the post-Munich (September 1938) submissions of Czech bank employees' associations, which demanded the closure of Jewish banks and the sacking of Jewish employees.[30] Nevertheless, the internal dynamics of bank bureaucracy helped to permeate National Socialist ideology through the bank.

4

The Problem of "Aryanization"

With the Nazi seizure of power in January 1933 began a government-sponsored drive to exclude Jews from German economic life. As a result of a series of pressures – from local party officials, from public authorities who played a prominent role as customers, from party members in the enterprise and in the reconstituted works councils, from ambitious managers who wanted rapid promotion – Jews were removed from the managing boards and supervisory boards of major corporations.

Deutsche Bank was no exception in this general story. Believed by National Socialist ideologues to be all-powerful, represented on many supervisory boards, often holding the chairmanship, Deutsche Bank was inevitably involved in what amounted in practice to a large-scale purge of German economic life.

This purge is and was sometimes termed "aryanization." This is a loose or elastic concept that encompasses both the economic effects of racial discrimination by customers and suppliers ("ordinary Germans") and restrictive administrative practices (in giving permits to trade, in allocating foreign exchange) and finally concrete legal measures in 1938 that completed the exclusion of Jews from German business life.

Some writers consider that the first kind of "aryanization," which came to be a major feature of the early years of the dictatorship, was in fact already under way well before Adolf Hitler became chancellor of Germany on January 30, 1933. Avraham Barkai wrote: "The anti-Semitic boycott had already begun several years prior to the Nazi seizure of power and was intensified particularly during the

1929–1932 Depression. Both the appeal and the impact of this boycott were enhanced by the fact that Jewish economic activity was concentrated in a small number of especially prominent or crisis-prone branches of the economy."[1] Such areas included banking, which came under regular attack from the party for being intrinsically speculative and "Jewish,"[2] but also department stores (which had the same reputation),[3] the garment and shoe trade, and cattle dealing. Some Jewish business fields were vulnerable on purely economic grounds. Probably the most extreme example of a "pre-Nazi crisis" is the Leipzig fur trade, which collapsed during the world depression (see Chapter 5.)

Most Jewish trading (according to Barkai, eighty-five percent) in fact occurred in medium-size specialty shops. These were the subject of resentment by business competitors and also sometimes by customers. Especially in periods of large price movements – either the increases of the inflation era or the collapse of the depression – many ordinary people felt inclined not to hold abstract macroeconomic forces responsible but rather to place the blame on specific malevolent agents. Owners of small shops and traders were particularly attractive targets. Cattle traders, who were very largely Jewish, appeared responsible for the pressure that produced falling livestock prices. But these were not areas in which the Berlin big banks on the whole had a great deal of contact (with a few exceptions, discussed in Chapter 5: the Saxon fur trade had good bank connections). In the 1930s, these kinds of businesses were victims of what might be termed a "petty or non-state aryanization:" They were harassed by party functionaries and competitors. In the destruction and sale of these businesses, which have been studied in the case of Hamburg in an exemplary way by Frank Bajohr, NSDAP officials frequently tried to press down prices and extract personal advantages from the racial purge.[4] Such operations were rarely conducted through the mediation of banks.

Major firms were initially less affected by the anti-Semitic boycott. Where they were vulnerable to a boycott, and where such party effects threatened the prospects for economic recovery, the Nazi government often intervened in the initial phases of the Third Reich to support the enterprise. The most famous case is the rescue of the Hermann Tietz department store, to which Hitler personally gave his approval. By late 1936, 360 larger firms had been "aryanized," but only in 15 or 20 of these cases was there a takeover by another large firm.[5] The involvement of banks (including Deutsche Bank) in these cases was thus rather limited, although there were important exceptions (for Deutsche Bank, notably the great Jewish-owned publishing house of Ullstein). The larger firms then even more abruptly felt the new intensification of government pressure after 1936–37, when the regime moved to a full-out attack in which legislation was used as an instrument of policy. This was then a "state-driven aryanization." A major motive of state policy was here the extraction of economic advantages for the state: the acquisition of assets in a period in which the funding of the rearmament-driven government debt was becoming increasingly problematic, and, as German war preparations advanced, a desperate search for foreign exchange [Devisen], needed to acquire otherwise unavailable raw materials. Consequently, the state was concerned that individuals should not derive excessive benefits from the process: The Four-Year Plan authorities wished the tax authorities to assess whether "the price was right" and whether there was not a substantial "aryanization profit" [Arisierungsgewinn] that might fall into the hands of the purchaser, the seller, or intermediaries such as banks or lawyers. In such cases, the state imposed a special "aryanization levy" [Arisierungsabgabe].[6] It should be needless to add that such concern on the part of the state was in no way motivated by any trace of concern for the rights of Jewish owners but instead reflected a desire to maximize the resources that might be looted by the state.

The Reich Economics Ministry [Reichswirtschaftsministerium] appeared in particular in very large cases as a major blocking force to Deutsche Bank's attempted involvement in "aryanizations" (see the Chapter 5 discussion of Adler & Oppenheimer AG (A&O), Bankhaus Mendelssohn & Co., and the Austrian Creditanstalt). Such interventions of state agencies came at a time when the state was generally increasing the tax burden on enterprises. The rate of corporation tax was raised from twenty percent in 1935 to forty percent by 1939–40. But there was a particularly intensive campaign to curtail extra profits by corporations. In early 1939, a supplemental tax [Mehreinkommensteuer] of fifteen percent was applied to profits for 1938 that were higher than those for 1937. This tax thus applied at the most intensive moment of state-imposed "aryanizations."[7]

There is yet a different meaning of "aryanization:" namely, an ideological demand requiring not simply the expropriation of Jewish owners but also the removal of names that gave an indication of the contribution of Jews to the course of German economic development. This operation might be termed "nominal aryanization." Again, it took place on the basis initially of informal pressure of the party and its press organs, and finally, in an administrative decree of March 1941, requiring the alteration of the names of "aryanized" enterprises, through compulsion. Deutsche Bank was associated with this development, too: A striking example is the pressure from the party's *Gau,* or administrative-district authorities, in the late 1930s to rename the Dresden bank of Philipp Elimeyer, in which there had been no Jewish capital participation since the 1920s.[8] An analogous case was an Austrian enterprise with a Jewish name, M. B. Neumann's Söhne AG, whose ownership had passed into the hands of a bank in the 1920s but which was still regarded as a Jewish enterprise. Deutsche Bank participated in a change of name and ownership in this case also.

In the literature on the massive transfer of ownership as a result of the threatened or actual use of force, two particularly acrimonious historical debates have been fought out. First, was it correct to argue, as many German individuals and businesses did after the war, that because the whole process had originated with state actions they might be justified in explaining their participation in a morally insalubrious exercise with *force majeure?* The Allied occupation authorities addressed this issue very explicitly in the immediate postwar era. Law No. 52 of the British military government on the restitution of confiscated property explicitly stated (Article I, 2):

> Property which has been the subject of transfer under duress, wrongful acts of confiscation, dispossession or spoliation, whether pursuant to legislation or by procedures purporting to follow forms of law or otherwise, is hereby declared to be equally subject to seizure of possession or title, direction, management, supervision or otherwise being taken into control by Military Government.

U.S. Law No. 59 stated (Article I, 3): "Regulations standing in the way of restitution such as are designed to protect acquirers in good faith are disregarded, except where this law provides otherwise."

The Allied Supreme Command instructed the Reichsbank on the application of this law:

While there is no intent that property acquired for full value, in due course of law, and with the full consent of the former owners be subjected to any restrictions not imposed upon other unblocked business enterprises, the entire so-called aryanization process was predicated upon such total disregard for the rights of former non-aryan owners, that duress, dispossession and wrongful acts of confiscation *must be inferred* in the absence of absolute proof to the contrary. The relatively unsupported statements of present owners as to the proper manner in which their properties were acquired in the aryanization process does not constitute such absolute proof; neither does the stipulation that the process was consummated in full accordance with existing German law suffice, since patently, such laws were entirely discriminatory to the rights of the non-aryan former owners."[9]

The military laws were taken into German law: in the American Zone of Occupation, the military government's Law No. 59 was enacted on November 10, 1947[10]; the French military government enacted its own draft on the same day.[11] In the British Zone of Occupation, an analogous restitution law was promulgated only on May 12, 1949.[12] This extensive conception of restitution was never modified by law or restricted by case judgments in the Federal Republic.

Secondly, a great deal of debate has centered around the question of whether bank participation in these takeovers helped to ensure that they were "helpful," "cooperative," "friendly," or "fair." This sort of language regularly appears in affidavits and declarations of the immediate postwar era, in which bankers tried to justify or explain their role under the dictatorship. Sometimes the previous owners submitted testimony to this effect in support of their successors. But the same words appear in historical writing. Wilhelm Treue, writing in 1972, spoke of a "friendly takeover" of Mendelssohn.[13] Christopher Kopper used the same word [*freundschaftliche*] in 1995, although he put it in quotation marks.[14]

On the other side, much of the interpretative literature written from a standpoint hostile to banks and banking has emphasized the profiteering aspect of bank mediation. The OMGUS report on Deutsche Bank used documentation to demonstrate "how readily Deutsche Bank took advantage at the expense of Jewish property-owners living abroad." Karl Heinz Roth concluded that "in the service of the Nazi war machine Deutsche Bank had devised a program of plunder unique in its brutality." Tom Bower's book *Blind Eye to Murder: Britain, America and the Purging of Nazi Germany – A Pledge Betrayed* claims that forced takeovers, including the "forced purchase of Jewish companies at knockdown rates," were the secret of Deutsche Bank's "sudden and phenomenal growth."[15] This unsubstantiated assertion is based on nothing other than the author's vivid imagination. A recent study of the profits of Deutsche Bank and Dresdner Bank relies on figures that are simply guesses – or, less politely, inventions.[16]

The debate about whether the transactions were "fair" or "profiteering" is rather sterile. For an interpretation of the events of the 1930s and 1940s that is more sensitive, in both a historical and a moral sense, the question of what alternatives, what interests, what time horizons, and what legal consequences were involved in these transactions needs more intense study.

1. What were the *alternatives* for the future, or the further existence of the previously Jewish-owned enterprises, given the policy of the regime? Options included bankruptcy, liquidation, sale to a number of competing German firms, absorption by the state, by quasi-state institutions (such as the "Reichswerke" Hermann Göring [RHG]), or by party or SS organizations. The German Labor Front (Deutsche Arbeitsfront [DAF]) developed some economic activities; during the war, the SS developed an immense economic empire. How did private business interests shape the outcome of such debates? Much of the construction of new forms of industrial and trading organization took place on the basis of Jewish property. One of the peculiarities of the era, which greatly influenced the form of the takeovers, was that the future economic order was the subject of intense debate. Many powerful figures in party and government believed that the future lay in a state-dominated economy. Private businesspeople tried to counter such tendencies and to organize alternatives that might have a chance of appealing to the political leadership and thus of being politically implemented.

2. What *interests* were involved in these transactions? The state wanted to prevent the accretion of excessive profits to private corporations or individuals. Local branches of the Nazi Party

were often massively corrupt and sought advantages for local party bosses and their friends. Businesses wanted to expand their enterprise, but they also needed to calculate what might happen if political conditions changed. Some "aryanizations" were accompanied by tacit agreement – which in the event were not always observed after 1945 – concerning restitution after the end of the Nazi regime.[17]

3. How did *expectations about future developments* influence the transactions? Views of the political future were subject to a considerable change over the twelve years between 1933 and 1945. In the initial months of the regime, many still thought that this was an unstable order that might not last long. After the summer of 1934, the dictatorship consolidated itself. In 1938 and 1939, the likelihood of war threatened new upheavals. After the summer of 1940, a long-term reordering of Europe along German or Nazi lines looked probable. From 1942, it appeared less and less likely. In each of these chronological phases, the balance of interests changed.

4. What was the *legal aftermath* of the property transfers? How were legal claims by the legitimate owners dealt with after 1945, how were valuations undertaken in the 1930s adjusted, what compensation was given, and how was the role of intermediaries (the attorneys and the banks) regarded? In some cases, banks were held liable for shares that they had resold to their investing customers (see the discussion of Salamander AG in Chapter 5).

5

Deutsche Bank and "Aryanization" in the Pre-1938 Boundaries of Germany

This chapter deals with the Deutsche Bank's involvement in the takeover and reorganization of Jewish property in Germany prior to the enlargement of the Reich as a result of diplomatic and military pressure after 1938. Initially, the major push on the part of the state and the party – and also of the bank – was to secure a change of *management,* rather than new *ownership.* According to the priorities of the regime at this early stage, Jews were to be removed from positions of influence in the German economy, in line with the idea of building a new type of state with a new German management. Especially where business had clearly wider social and political influence, as for instance in newspaper publishing, or when there existed large public contracts, official authorities moved quickly to combat Jewish influence.

Some, but not all, of these cases also involved the transfer of property, but discussions of ownership had largely been secondary in the years immediately after 1933. After 1937, however, such issues were the driving forces. A much more radical phase began, in which the regime (and especially Hermann Göring, then at the height of his powers) saw the takeover of Jewish property as the most obvious answer to the fiscal crisis produced by rearmament. Germany's Jews were to be made to pay for Germany's war. Local party activists also saw their own opportunities for enrichment, as did business rivals and would-be entrepreneurs. In this phase, Germany's banks – the big Berlin banks, the regional banks, but also the dense network of publicly owned savings banks [*Sparkassen*] – frequently played an active role in brokering deals and in finding buyers and sellers and often also putting up finance for purchases and acquisitions.

This was a competitive business, and the question arises: Why should the Deutsche Bank have been successful (as it was on its own terms) in managing a very substantial number of "aryanization" transactions? Was it the extent of its political contacts, even though these were not as extensive as those of the rival Dresdner Bank and, on a local level, not nearly as compelling as the savings banks, which could and did present themselves as the institution of the ordinary German? Was it a particular trust that the bank had with customers who might be potential buyers or also sellers of "aryanization" properties? In many transactions, trust indeed played a prominent role. It operated on the basis of contacts between individual managers rather than in an abstract institutional way. This chapter examines a number of cases in which that trust seems to have been – even to the critical eye of the historian – well placed, but also cases in which trust (the basis of orderly business life) was broken as the pernicious and corroding exploitative ideology of National Socialism took over.

Many of the transactions in which the Deutsche Bank was involved were ones that involved cross-national property issues. Here the bank, as an institution with a substantial range of international contacts, had a clear advantage. The question arises here: Did the activity of the bank in the pre-1938 German areas encourage the interest of the bank, and especially of its younger and more ambitious and politically well connected managers, in a wider area of activity?

The Bank and Informal Pressure, 1933–1936

Well before the onset of "state-driven aryanization," Deutsche Bank was involved in economic discrimination against Jews through its extensive business contacts and its representation on the supervisory boards of other corporations. This did not always involve a sale of the enterprise. A characteristic process for firms was to push for the removal of Jewish managers or directors to claim the status of "Aryan enterprise" (even though until 1938 there was no formal or legal definition of what this involved).

Two examples will show how the bank became enmeshed in the policies of the new regime. Lorenz Hutschenreuther AG (Selb), where Deutsche Bank's supervisory-board chairman Franz Urbig held the chair of the supervisory board, was one of Germany's most famous

44

manufacturers of porcelain, with a substantial and important export market. In October 1933, two NSDAP functionaries replaced representatives of the Weimar Republic works council on the supervisory board. They immediately demanded the dismissal of Jewish members of the board, including the manager of the Mannheim branch of Deutsche Bank, Ludwig Fuld. The firm felt sensitive because, as it argued, ninety percent of its domestic sales were made through retailers organized in the NS-Hago, which might impose a boycott of the firm's products.[1] Urbig responded by attempting to secure the voluntary resignation of the members of the supervisory board who had been attacked, but two refused to give way, pointing out the dangers of compliance (yielding on this issue would be a *"Vogel-Strauss-Politik,"* or "head-in-the-sand policy"[2]) and adding the commercial argument that obvious and visible acceptance of the National Socialist racial priorities would damage the company's export order book.

For a year, nothing happened and the Jewish supervisory-board members stayed in place. Then the party renewed its offensive, through the local *Kreisleiter* district leader. He summoned the manager of Hutschenreuther to come to the town's Brown House and explain himself. When the manager explained that he could not remove a member of the supervisory board, the *Kreisleiter* claimed that this should properly be the responsibility of Deutsche Bank.

> Mr. K. [*Kreisleiter* Kellermann] then asked whether Deutsche Bank could not make decisions just like that, by virtue of its own shareholding or authority. [...] Mr. K. thereupon explained that one had to assume that either Deutsche Bank did not wish to intervene – which, however, was scarcely conceivable – or that its capital ratios were such that it was unable to intervene.[3]

The tactic of putting pressure on central office in Berlin to influence local conditions proved eminently successful. As a result of renewed and more insistent pressure from Urbig, the two members of the supervisory board resigned their seats. Fuld, and another Jewish colleague in Mannheim, Dr. Mandel, were later (in October 1935), as a result of direct pressure applied by public-sector bank Rentenbank-Kreditanstalt, removed from three other supervisory boards, the Hefft'sche Kunstmühle AG, Mannheim; the Deutsche Mühlenvereinigung AG, Berlin; and the Osthafenmühlen-AG, Berlin.[4]

The second example concerns Johannes Jeserich AG (Berlin), a major construction firm [Tiefbau] with road contracts all over Germany, especially in the north. Dependency on public-sector orders made a company of this sort especially vulnerable to political pressure. On April 1, 1933, the day of a nationwide anti-Jewish boycott, four representatives of the National Socialist Factory Cell Organization (NSBO) walked into a director's office and demanded the immediate dismissal of the company's Jewish employees. The director, Lothar Fuld, responded at once by terminating the contracts of just two workers. But the action of the Jeserich employees turned out to be only the beginning of a much bigger campaign. The company directors were themselves extremely vulnerable. The *Staatskommissar für das Tiefbauwesen* responsible for Berlin, *Regierungsbaumeister* Fuchs, rejected Jeserich bids for road repair work on the grounds "that the firm concerned is Jewish." The Charlottenburg NSBO then demanded the removal of the Jewish directors – Lothar Fuld and Ernst Stern.[5] The two directors went without making any protest, and at a meeting of the supervisory board on April 13, the bank representatives, who again included Ludwig Fuld from Deutsche Bank Mannheim, as well as Director Ottomar Benz from Berlin, agreed "that, in the interests of the company, which might otherwise obtain no further public contracts, the request made by Mr. Fuld and Dr. Stern must be granted."[6] One of Jeserich's remaining directors, Dr. Eugen Feuchtmann, then said that it had become clear that the supervisory board required restructuring and that the five Jewish directors on the supervisory board should resign. They did. Both supervisory board and managing board were in consequence almost entirely depleted. Feuchtmann tried to fill the vacancies with obviously politicized figures, which were at first rejected by Benz. But in the end, Benz was pressed into accepting appointments to the supervisory board that included the leader of the NSDAP group in the Württemberg parliament [Landtag], Hermann Kurz, and, as the representative of the Jewish banking house of H. Aufhäuser Munich, non-Jewish party member Dr. Karl Ritter von Halt.[7]

A similar case of a building firm with a high degree of dependence on public works, creating a vulnerability to party pressure, was Philipp Holzmann, where Alfred Blinzig from Deutsche Bank helped to push Charles Rosenthal first from the managing board and then from a position as company representative to Latin America. But here it was very clear that the source of the demand for a purge of Jewish directors was external to both the company and the bank.[8]

In the cases of both Hutschenreuther and Jeserich, the initial pressure for the purge came from inside the firm. In the porcelain firm, it originated from the firm's employees as reorganized, after the introduction of a new labor law, into the National Socialist Works Council. With Jeserich, the radical agitation by the workforce ultimately had its source in one of the firm's directors who deliberately used politics to take management into his own hands.

The use of physical violence in intimidation that had characterized 1933 diminished as the National Socialist revolution consolidated itself. By the later months of 1933, the anarchical conditions that had characterized the early months of the year had been succeeded by the imposition of political centralization and the reestablishment of state authority. For the moment, official anti-Semitism seemed to abate. In the case of reconstructed department store Hermann Tietz & Co., where Deutsche Bank was a member of the bank consortium that ran the Hertie-Kaufhaus-Beteiligungs GmbH (*Gesellschaft mit beschränkter Haftung*) many of the Jewish employees were sacked: by August 1933, 500 of a total of 1,000. But the party then made peace and tried to build bridges to the new managers (though these improved relations were to be paid for by the department store). The SA in Karlsruhe, for instance, suggested that "our house there should take over as sponsor of certain impecunious members of the SA."[9]

The result of the pressure of 1933 had been that many Jewish firms were purged or sold. More followed in subsequent years. In 1932, there had been approximately 100,000 Jewish-owned firms in Germany (using a religious definition of Jewishness), whereas in 1935 a contemporary estimate suggested that the number had fallen to 75,000 to 80,000.[10] By the end of 1937, two thirds of small-scale Jewish-owned businesses had already ceased to operate, including five of six retailers, where Jewish proprietors may have been most visible to the public eye.[11] Many of the larger firms survived until 1938, in part because their disappearance would have jeopardized Germany's recovery from unemployment and depression.

Some enterprises in areas which the Nazi authorities felt to be very sensitive were subjected to a much speedier "aryanization." The

47

most dramatic example in which Deutsche Bank was involved is probably the publisher Ullstein. As the owner of a major sector of the German press (including the highbrow and influential *Vossische Zeitung,* the mass-circulation *BZ am Mittag* and *Berliner Morgenblatt,* and the weekly *Berliner Illustrierte*), Ullstein clearly exercised a direct political influence that the new power elite perceived as threatening. In March 1934, Nazi journalist Fritz Geisler submitted to the Reich Chancellery details of the continuing high circulation figures of the Ullstein press, with the comment: "The style and presentation of the Ullstein papers are more appreciated in extensive party circles, too, and certainly among other sections of the population."[12]

The Propaganda Ministry had already demanded the resignation of Ullstein's general director, the former secretary of state at the Finance Ministry, Hans Schäffer, on March 10, 1933. Hitler himself subsequently took a direct role and on July 12, 1933, received the new "political director" of Ullstein, the conservative but not Nazi Eduard Stadler to discuss the "bringing into line" [*Gleichschaltung*] of the publishing house. Reichsbank president Hjalmar Schacht was to produce a plan for a new financial structure. He conducted most of the negotiations with a member of the Ullstein managing board, Ferdinand Bausback, who had previously been the director of the Stuttgart branch of Deutsche Bank. The aim was to distribute the new shares of Ullstein widely, throughout the major German industrial and commercial firms. In this way, Schacht concluded, "the influence and predominance of the aryan shareholder group would be assured." All non-Aryans, with the exception of one member of the Ullstein family, would leave the managing board.[13]

By 1934, the party and government took a much more radical line, demanding the transfer of the publishers to NSDAP Franz Eher Verlag under Max Amann, president of the Reich Press Chamber and NSDAP *Reichsleiter für Presseverwaltung* (press director). Amann told Max Winkler, who became the critical figure in establishing the Nazification of the press: "Goebbels is finishing off the Jewish press."[14] The shares were bought with public money through a trustee firm, Cautio, and left on deposit with Deutsche Bank. Bausback remained as chairman of the supervisory board. The name of the company was later changed to Deutscher Verlag Kommanditgesellschaft. The financial details of this transaction were managed by Deutsche Bank. In June 1934, Eduard Mosler concluded in minutes marked "confidential":

> Secretary of State Funk (Propaganda Ministry) confirmed today in answer to my question that the transfer of all Ullstein Verlag shares to Eher Verlag has been discussed with the Führer as well as with Dr. Goebbels and has been carried out at his instigation in the Ministry of Propaganda. He told me he had wanted Deutsche Bank to broker the transaction, saying that Deutsche Bank would thus be doing the Propaganda Ministry a great service. Everything as presented to us had been discussed at the Ministry, he said. At my request he added that he would see to it and discuss with Herr Amann that on no account should the party press attach any disparaging criticism to the deal; he would take steps to ensure that the *Völkische Beobachter* carried an approving article.[15]

As far as can be judged by this memorandum, the main incentive for Deutsche Bank to add a cloak of respectability to this transfer was not so much financial as the hope that attacks on the bank from the party press (and perhaps also from the foreign exchange control authorities) would cease, or at least be bought off for a time.

Though many Jewish-owned businesses lasted, many individual business people were subject to pressure and terror from the Nazi Party. In 1935, the owner of the Aronwerke Elektrizitäts AG, Berlin-Charlottenburg, for instance, was subject to harassment by the party and was repeatedly arrested and sent to a concentration camp. Under this pressure, he sold his company, a leading manufacturer of radios (under the trade name Nora) as well as of electrical meters, to the Elektrische Licht- und Kraftanlagen AG, Berlin, which took 3,692,000 shares, and to Siemens-Schuckertwerke AG, which took 1,900,000. In addition, Deutsche Bank kept a further 724,000 shares in its deposit for the Siemens concern. The business was immediately renamed as Heliowatt-Elektrizitäts AG. The shares were sold at eighty-three to eighty-five percent of their par value, rather than the thirty percent valuation that Nazis on the supervisory board had been pressing for. Deutsche Bank made a profit on the transaction by selling the shares to Siemens at a price of RM 86.5, yielding a gain of around RM 188,000.[16] Deutsche Bank had had no previous business connection with the Aronwerke, which dealt mostly through Commerzbank. Commerzbank also took a lead in organizing the sale. At the extraordinary general meeting to restructure the firm and its supervisory board, to which Hans Rummel of Deutsche Bank and Joseph Schilling of Commerzbank were elected, Rummel set out the rationale for the changes: "The share transfer had become necessary in order to prevent this oldest of German meter manufacturers from falling into foreign hands." Neither the banks involved nor Siemens had done anything to put additional pressure on the company, and the price corresponded to the stock market valuation.[17]

Irrespective of morality and immorality, there were good "economic" reasons not to "aryanize" too rapidly. The forced sale of Jewish firms noticeably weakened the quality of German entrepreneurship. At the Cologne meetings of the Rhineland-Westphalian Advisory Council of Deutsche Bank, for instance, a cotton spinner, Emil Engels (of Ermen & Engels AG) complained that the "aryanizations" had reduced the liquidity of firms in the textile branch, and their capacity to keep up payments. "Aryanizations have sometimes led to firms falling into weak hands and he was particularly appealing to bank managers to exercise great caution in connection with the reorganization of such firms."[18] It is impossible to judge whether the underlying reasons for opposition to Nazi measures were based on moral principles or pragmatic calculations of interest. But it is clear that the expressed rationalization for such criticism was *always* expressed on pragmatic grounds.

Forcing the Pace, 1937–1938

Virtual full employment after 1936 weakened the force of pragmatic objections to an economically irrational action. In late 1937, Hitler specified Germany's foreign-policy goals at the meeting recorded in the Hossbach protocol, explaining that neither autarky nor integration in the world economy would solve the German economic problem. Only the use of force would create adequate economic space, or *Lebensraum.* At the same time as foreign policy became much more radical, the regime stepped up the pace in implementing its anti-Semitic program.[19] The goal that had been frustrated in 1933 by practical considerations, the removal of those the state defined as Jews from German business life, could now be realized without encountering obstacles or objections.

Nazi anti-Semitism combined many different elements, and the party's leaders each had different visions of the racist dream. Goebbels saw anti-Semitism in cultural terms, whereas Hitler propagated what Saul Friedländer has aptly termed "redemptive anti-Semitism," "a story of perdition caused by the Jew, and redemption by a total victory over the Jew."[20] What drove much of the terrible logic of the late 1930s, however, was a different rationale and rhetoric, associated with a different personality, Hermann Göring. Göring saw in anti-Semitic measures primarily the chance for gigantic profits, and for a reordering of the economy that would enlarge the public sector.

At the end of 1937, Jewish business activity was restricted at Göring's initiative by a discriminatory tightening of raw-material supplies.[21] On January 4, 1938, a decree defined a Jewish enterprise as one owned or dominated by Jews, in the sense that either one member of the executive board or one personally liable manager was Jewish in the sense of the Nuremberg laws, or that one quarter of the supervisory board was Jewish. On June 14, 1938, the Third Ordinance on Reich Citizenship reaffirmed and partly redefined the specific criteria for the assessment of what was a "Jewish" enterprise. On April 26, 1938, the Ordinance on the Registration of Jewish Assets required the registration of Jewish property exceeding RM 5,000 in value; Section 7 allowed the Commissary for the Four-Year Plan to take measures "that are necessary in order to ensure that the notifiable property is deployed in accordance with the interests of the German economy."[22] A few days earlier, the Ordinance Against the Support of Camouflage by Jewish Businesses provided penalties (of not less than one year in prison) for German citizens who "through selfish motives help in this connection deliberately to obscure the Jewish nature of a commercial operation with a view to deceiving the authorities."[23]

During the course of the year attacks increased until they reached an apogee in the pogrom of the so-called Reichskristallnacht, November 9, 1938. This was followed (November 12) by an Ordinance on the Exclusion of Jews from German Economic Life and the imposition of a twenty-five percent tax on assets [*Sühneleistung*, or reparation]. At the same time, Jewish enterprises were threatened with prosecution under existing legislation for actual or alleged "capital flight" – attempting to bring their assets to safety beyond Germany's frontiers. The transfer of Jewish-owned property into "aryan" hands was at first left to private initiative. Reich Economics Minister Schacht had in 1935 defined one of the tasks that "the economy must solve itself" – namely, "how to finance the transfer of Jewish businesses into aryan hands."[24] A follow-up decree of December 30, 1938, required the *"Reichstreuhänder der Arbeit"* to appoint a director [*Betriebsführer*] "who would meet the blood requirements for the acquisition of Reich citizenship" for businesses with Jewish owners.[25]

There were some problems for banks in implementing these decrees, as until the beginning of 1939 they had no means of knowing with certainty who was "Jewish." The Munich branch of Deutsche Bank at the end of 1938 wrote to the legal office in the Berlin headquarters explaining that it had had "some very unpleasant arguments with customers [...] whom we assumed to be non-aryans but who in reality were of aryan extraction."[26] The Gesetz über die Änderung von Familiennamen und Vornamen (Law Concerning Alteration of Surnames and Given Names) required Jews after January 1, 1939, to designate themselves with a specifically "Jewish" name, and to add *Israel* or *Sara* if they had no such name. The Private Banking Business Group (Wirtschaftsgruppe Privates Bankgewerbe) advised its members to alter their account files correspondingly. From then on it was entirely clear who in Germany was a Jew.[27]

On December 6, 1938, at the Air Ministry, Göring gave a dramatic speech to the assembled *Gauleiter* in which he attempted to assert his control of the "aryanization" process, and its profits, and to limit the gains of private businesses (and banks). He said, characteristically calling on the highest authority to support his claim:

> However, the Führer has coined the following dictum: the benefit of all aryanizations shall accrue to the Reich and the Reich alone, i. e. in this instance to the administrator, the Reich Finance Minister, and to no one else, for only then will it be possible to implement the Führer's arms program [...]. It goes entirely without saying that a check [on previous and future aryanizations] can be made at any time. It also goes without saying that in particularly important instances aryanizations or at least the relevant negotiations are from the outset effected

at the top, that here every possible control is put in place to make the benefit really accrue to the Reich. I shall in fact be ordering the reversal of certain aryanizations that have been made hitherto, and they will then be binding.[28]

Throughout 1938, the number of Jewish-owned businesses for sale increased, and banks played a major part in brokering the sales. In dealing with the new attack on Jews in German business life, the banks responded with the twin strategy that characterized much of their response to National Socialism. On the one hand, they looked for business opportunities that would strengthen their individual competitive position; on the other hand, they looked to business solidarity as a way of establishing a united front against those aspects of the new policy that they felt to be threatening or unacceptable to their own interests. Banks had already been involved in some cases of managing the transfer of Jewish-owned property.

In late 1935, the headquarters of Deutsche Bank sent out a series of circulars to their branches warning about the dangers of credits to "non-aryan" firms. Many firms "under Jewish influence," the first memorandum observed, had experienced falling sales. The consequence might be illiquidity, unprofitability, and even bankruptcy. "Our job must therefore be to ensure that we recognize the situation in time, so that we are not forced by the pressure of state institutions to provide further resources to enable wages etc. to be paid and thus increase our credit exposure above the limit that we judge acceptable." The best way to forestall such difficulties was by providing full details of "businesses in acute danger" to the public authorities. Deutsche Bank should ensure that such firms inform the authorities, including the party offices (Gau Economic Advisers and Gauleiter). The circular particularly requested that there should be written evidence of such attempts to make the firms report their difficulties, in order to defend the bank against possible recriminations from the party. A further circular urged particular caution in cases where business owners were abroad, and a third circular demanded a listing of all credits over RM 20,000, and an indication of the total amount of credits under that amount.[29]

In August 1937, Deutsche Bank asked its branches to report cases of Jewish-owned firms with debit positions. It justified the inquiry by the argument that the owners were liable to leave Germany suddenly and without warning.

We are faced over and over again with the unpleasant fact that proprietors of non-aryan firms to which we furnish credit suddenly go abroad, thus ducking their commitments vis-á-vis ourselves as well. In many instances we are then faced with the fact that, despite constant soundings and monitoring on the part of our branches, the financial circumstances of the enterprises concerned have deteriorated so badly that, for us, liquidation of such commitments is possible only at a loss.

We have held a number of discussions with you about how loans to non-aryan customers should be handled and repeatedly requested in the process that, to guard against further surprises, they should be fully secured – in which connection it is only in very exceptional cases that we are willing to forgo the liquid form. A new case now gives us occasion to subject all commitments still current with non-aryan firms to fresh examination in order to ascertain whether in the meantime this viewpoint has been considered and, if not, why you think you are able to deviate from it. To enable us to form a picture of the present level of commitment and to identify any risks that may be associated therewith, please let us have a detailed report by the end of the month, addressing your communication for the attention of our "Branches Office" and enclosing a synopsis.

For the synopsis due on 31 July of this year, you will kindly use the customary form for the list of accounts receivable (Branches Office no. 78). Please list liquid and non-liquid securities separately on the basis of *current* value (i.e. in this instance not nominal value). Any reserves are to be noted separately in addition to securities. In the case of commitments under RM 20,000.–, all that is required for the time being is a summary in a single amount, with the same procedure being applicable with regard to security.

You will kindly advise your sub-agencies from there as appropriate.[30]

But in 1938 these efforts were systematized. A decisive impetus was given by a new state measure of December 15, 1937, reducing the import quotas for Jewish-owned firms and requiring an investigation into "whether the level of foreign-exchange allocations is compatible with the development of economic circumstances." On January 7, 1938, the Reich Chamber of Commerce (*Reichswirtschaftskammer*) sent out a circular in which it emphasized that this ten percent reduction was only a minimum demand.[31]

Deutsche Bank felt the pressure quite directly, as the Berlin Chamber of Industry and Commerce sent an obviously formulaic letter addressed to Eduard Mosler, inquiring whether Deutsche Bank was a "Jewish commercial enterprise": "Having received such a response regarding your firm, we should be obliged if you would undertake an examination of the question in the light of the guidelines and notify us as soon as possible of the outcome of your inquiry." Deutsche Bank promptly replied that it did not meet the government's criteria of a Jewish firm: There were no Jewish members of the managing board, Jews had no decisive capital control, and they did not constitute more than one quarter of the supervisory board. Nor was "Deutsche Bank in fact under the dominant influence of Jews."[32]

In the immediate aftermath of the government decrees of January 4, 1938, and of the Reich Chamber of Commerce document, a letter from the managing board to branch managers, dated January 14 and signed by Hans Rummel and Karl Kimmich, asked for a listing of the "non-aryan clientele" of the bank's branches:

> We have recently had numerous discussions with you about dealing with our non-aryan commitments, and we told you only a few days ago how we see the future development of these firms. We then heard from you that you are in constant contact with such enterprises and have offered your services or intend to offer your services at their request in connection with aryanization.
>
> Since we have so far received only an overview of those non-aryan firms in your branch territory that number among your accounts receivable while on the other hand knowing only a little about your non-aryan accounts payable, please send us another list of your non-aryan accounts receivable and accounts payable, namely those that are candidates for aryanization. What particularly interests us in this connection is how far aryanization of the enterprises concerned has progressed and to what extent you are involved in the process yourselves.
>
> The intended purpose of this list so far as we are concerned is for us to be able to consider here at headquarters whether, in the light of the many enquiries that reach us daily and the overview that these afford, we can support you in your endeavors, although we are of course keen for the immediate negotiations to continue to be conducted by yourselves.
>
> The whole matter needs to be handled carefully and with forethought, and great skill is required lest tactical mistakes should provoke instances

of irritation and ill-will that, as has already been our experience, can lead to consequences for business; that must of course be avoided.

In this connection, we should also be interested in those major non-aryan firms in your branch territory that are not customers of yours but are also potential candidates for aryanization, be they private firms or joint-stock companies – in the case of the latter we are keen to discover in whose hands any major shareholdings lie – so that here too we can be in a position to offer our services in the event of a possible transfer.

We take this opportunity to send you for your kind attention a document that we have received in confidence from the Private Banking Business Group, a circular from the Reich Chamber of Commerce to Reich Groups regarding the definition of a Jewish enterprise for the purposes of allocation of foreign currency and raw materials. Under the terms of clause 3 a) of this ordinance, note that the word "Jewish" means the same as "a Jew" – with the result, for example, that a joint-stock company is deemed to be Jewish if there is *one* Jew on the board.[33]

On June 14, 1938, the definition of a Jewish enterprise was tightened further. Enterprises in which one or more members of the supervisory board were Jews were now to be counted as Jewish. Section 2 stated that "if in the case of a joint-stock company or no member of the managing board or supervisory board on 1 January 1938 was a Jew, the assumption is that Jews are not decisively involved in terms of capital or voting rights. The contrary assumption is made if on the said day one or more members of the managing board or supervisory board were Jews."[34]

For Deutsche Bank, the problem was that at the determining date, January 1, 1938, Georg Solmssen had been a member of the supervisory board. Solmssen, a baptized Christian, was the son of one of the directors of the Disconto-Gesellschaft (a predecessor of Deutsche Bank), Adolph Salomonsohn, and had been spokesman of the bank's managing board in 1933. There were extensive discussions with the Berlin Chamber of Industry and Commerce. Deutsche Bank pointed out that Solmssen had moved abroad in 1937 and had in practice taken no part in the supervisory board, and that it would have been needlessly expensive to hold a special meeting to remove Solmssen. The most peculiar feature of the legislation was clearly its retrospective character. Until June 14, Deutsche Bank had not legally been a Jewish enterprise; just as clearly, after June 14, it was – and there was nothing that could be done about this status. Eventually, on August 15, 1938, the Chamber of Industry and Commerce issued the appropriate certification that Deutsche Bank "is to be regarded as a non-Jewish business in the sense of the third order under the Reich Citizenship Act [Reichsbürgergesetz]."[35] For two months, between mid-June and mid-August, Deutsche Bank had legally been a Jewish enterprise.

As a repository of shares, Deutsche Bank also had to deal with requests from businesses responding to the inquiries of their chambers of commerce for information on the "racial" character of their shareholders. Deutsche Bank complained in an internal note: "Replying to such queries is extremely time-consuming and laborious, and in many cases it is also not possible without ambiguity."[36] Such detailed lists of who owned which parts of German business implied a new danger at a time when the ordering of the economy and of ownership was once more becoming an acute political issue.

The bank also consulted with its major competitor about the best way of dealing with a process that might bring the threat of a new socialization. On July 2, 1938, Deutsche Bank's supervisory-board chairman Eduard Mosler spoke with his counterpart, Carl Goetz of Dresdner Bank. The Reich Economics Ministry was planning the creation of a new "rescue company" [*Auffanggesellschaft*] to administrate Jewish property. Shares in major industries and banks would be consolidated and would give the state an opportunity to influence the business strategies of the companies concerned.

The banks did not directly feel vulnerable to a possibility of using "aryanization" as a way of extending state influence. Dresdner Bank calculated that of its shares about RM 7 million (nominal value) were owned by Jews. But Mosler was worried about the extent of influence elsewhere and proposed meeting the other big banks (Dresdner Bank and Commerzbank) to discuss an alternative:

> [...] that in place of the Reich we should acquire the businesses and firms to be taken over from the Reich and give the Reich part of the value of the Reich loan devoted thereto as a down payment or advance, then, when the enterprises concerned are resold, as they quickly should be, make the payment to the Reich or, if it can be managed, to the previous (Jewish) owner, possibly also, in the event of exorbitant prices being achieved, issue income and adjustment bonds or the like up until completion of the sale or reception of the purchase price.[37]

In a subsequent discussion, Goetz explained that there was an urgent need "to prevent these Jewish enterprises from being placed, as seems to be the intention, in a large holding company and there, to the detriment of the economy at large, being fed into channels that in his view were not the right ones." Kimmich was even more hostile to the proposals and did not want to be involved in the assessment of values and the transfer of property, pointing out

> [...] that in the interests of keeping our foreign credit, which even in this question we have to put first, we should prefer not to make a profit out of this transaction and also to have no part in setting the prices for the Jews; that [he said] is the job of public agencies and it also strikes me as best that, were there to be any kind of positive reaction to what he proposed, then public or semi-public agencies should take matters in hand.

At the same time, he wanted to ensure that shares and property remained in private and not in state ownership:

> In connection with this last part, banks would need to play a substantial role, as indeed they did in the past. I was able to disclose to him that we had already successfully aryanized a large number of enterprises. The whole question, in fact, was not so much one of capital, more one of people. If the progress of matters hitherto had been too slow for the state and he was looking for a complete solution, I could only imagine the matter being dealt with in this way.

Subsequently, Kimmich added a further note: "that in order not to forfeit our foreign credit we should not draw attention to ourselves in this matter and that it is also not our job to deal in real estate." He then made a series of suggestions for "aryanization," which he proposed to discuss with Reichsbank President Hjalmar Schacht. Jewish shares, according to this plan, would be taken over by a consortium managed by the Bank für Industrie-Obligationen. All banks and large industrial firms should participate in the consortium, because, after all, they had an interest in avoiding a sharp decline in share prices. It would be financed by treasury bills, make no profits, and be guaranteed against losses. The banks would not deal in real estate at all but would leave this business to an analogous consortium of mortgage banks and insurance companies. Nonquoted shares would be handled by yet another consortium and make "immediate payment in correspondingly small amounts to the non-aryans, since here, of course, the risk is very much greater, not to say unlimited." Finally, "Jewish enterprises not transferred into aryan hands by a date yet to be fixed will be taken over by a rescue company." This would act as a trustee: Half of the capital required to buy up enterprises would come from the state, and the other half would come from the relevant industrial group or a specially formed group of enterprises, such as the Adefa (Arbeitsgemeinschaft deutsch-arischer Konfektionsfabrikanten, or Working Group of German-Aryan Clothing Manufacturers, which at the end of 1937 had launched a campaign to label clothing as German-made if all stages of production were securely in "non-aryan" hands). The Adefa also played a central part in the political pressure applied to remaining department stores such as Schocken.[38] This would solve the question of entrepreneurship ("the trickiest aspect of the whole aryanization problem, which plays a crucial role particularly in the Jewish-controlled intellectual sectors, namely the question of how the business is to be managed in future").

Banks should continue to look for individual purchasers for companies with which they already had business contacts:

> As now, though, it is up to the banks to find suitable buyers for the businesses in question. For the time being this applies with regard to those firms with which they are already connected. However, it is not impossible for Deutsche Bank, for example, if it has a good prospective purchaser for a connection with Dresdner Bank, to present this and in this way subsequently secure bank transactions with the firm concerned for itself.[39]

But the initiative lay clearly with the state, not with the banks. The Reich Economics Ministry called a meeting on September 1, 1938, to discuss the question of credits, possibly guaranteed by the state, for the purchase of Jewish property. Deutsche Bank expressed its opposition to a "complete solution through government institutions."[40]

On September 6, the bank noted that the Berlin district economic adviser [Gauwirtschaftsberater] had announced his intention to place commissars in all Jewish property that had not been "aryanized" by October 1.[41]

The bank now sent out letters signed by Kimmich to some of its major business customers setting out the problems and opportunities for non-Jewish Germans that arose in the course of the discussion of "aryanization," suggesting that branches of businesses should on their own initiative form consortia to take over Jewish property. "For economic groups this procedure offers the great advantage that they keep control of the aryanization process and in particular intervention by the state [is] avoided that may have disturbing effects with unforeseeable consequences so far as the government itself is concerned." Such a method would avoid "losses as well as market disturbances." The model for this sort of scheme was to be the Adefa.[42]

Almost unanimously, these customers rejected such a scheme as impracticable, as requiring too high a guarantee. Richard Freudenberg, the major leather producer from Weinheim, who had participated at an early stage (1933) in the "aryanization" of the Tack shoe company,[43] explained that there were still too many factories and that his own enterprises were working at only two-thirds capacity. He complained that the Reich Economics Ministry did not allow large firms to take over other factories, and he gave a specific instance of a Mannheim factory (Marcus Blaut) whose sale to Gebr. Fahr, a customer of Deutsche Bank, had been obstructed by Dresdner Bank, which believed that Blaut belonged to its clientele. He gave other instances from the shoe industry, where he believed that firms such as Langermann or Wieringer (Nuremberg) or Diamant (Strausberg) could not really continue without the entrepreneurial activities of their Jewish directors.[44] Heinz (Girmes & Co. AG) drew a similar conclusion for the velvet and plush industry. "Economically, though, it was a mistake [he said], since the value of these businesses had lain precisely in their Jewish managers, who through long tradition, natural ability, and a multiplicity of connections, particularly abroad, had created these highly fashion-dependent businesses." Julius Graf reported a similar conclusion for the cotton industry. Ultimately, Deutsche Bank believed that there was no option: "that there will be no other alternative than to proceed as hitherto, carefully examining, case by case, the possibilities of aryanization in terms of the financial and particularly the personal aspects."[45]

The pogrom of November 9–10, 1938, changed the climate further, and quite decisively. Immediately after the pogrom, Propaganda Minister Joseph Goebbels, who had been largely responsible for unleashing the pogrom, noted in his diary the results of a conversation with Hitler: "The Führer wishes to take very firm measures against the Jews. They must put their businesses in order again by themselves. The insurance companies will not pay them a thing. Then the Führer wants gradually to expropriate Jewish businesses, and to give the owners securities in exchange that we can cancel at any time."[46] Measures that had already been discussed earlier in the year in the German ministries but had been stalled in the interstices of the bureaucratic apparatus were now rapidly promulgated. The radical precedents from the rapid expropriation conducted in Austria after March 1938 also had an effect in stimulating Göring's cupidity. On November 12, Hermann Göring announced a new principle for the takeover of Jewish property: "The Jew will be eliminated from the economy, ceding his economic property to the state. He will be compensated for it. [...] The government trustee will value the business and decide what sum the Jew is paid." On November 12, a decree forbade Jews from engaging in the retail trade and craft manufacturing, and on November 23, a further decree required the liquidation of such businesses.[47]

The government pressed for special companies to carry out "aryanization" to ensure that private individuals should not make illegitimate personal profits as a consequence of the behavior of the party and the state. At a new meeting in the Reich Economics Ministry to discuss the question of the liquidation of Jewish property, the following figures were given. There was still about RM 2 billion worth of real estate in Jewish possession and RM 1.5 billion worth of securities. According to the minutes of the meeting, the banks again expressed their objections to the accelerated sale, on technical financial grounds. "The bank laid great stress on the incalculable difficulties and dangers of restructuring all that wealth not only for the real-estate market but also for the stock market – and in the long term, too." The Reich Economics Ministry official, Kurt Lange, simply stressed that "whatever people think about the immediate expropriation of Jewish property, the necessity needs in any case to be reckoned with as a firm fact." He then invited the banks to discuss the question in the Private Banking Business Group.[48] That meeting occurred the next day, and participants discussed rather higher figures for the value of Jewish property in Germany: RM 2.4 billion in real estate, RM 1.2 billion in businesses [*Geschäftsvermögen*], and RM 4.8 billion in other property (including securities).[49]

Kimmich acted again as Deutsche Bank's representative in this discussion, where the bank representatives suggested:

1. That the Reich should take the Jewish-owned securities at a fixed price
2. That the banks should not immediately attempt to sell these securities on the market ("to protect the capital market")
3. A small bank consortium should give an advance of between RM 300 million and RM 500 million, with interest of 4.5 to 5 percent for a six-month term
4. Banks with securities deposits [*Effektendepots*] should "take the initiative in realizing the securities"

Kimmich noted that in the debate he had argued for the necessity of "centralized, individual treatment of the whole transaction [...], since each case is different [he said], and in this way the banks can best help by providing the unofficial market that the stock exchange can in any case not provide and on which, through the banks, the securities can be sold on to agencies having mobile capital at their disposal." He suggested that the advance should be conducted on the basis of the previously Jewish-owned securities, and not, as proposed by the Reich Economics Ministry, in a nonsecuritized form.[50]

In some areas, a central institution was created to take over Jewish-owned property. The Saar-Pfälzische Vermögens-Verwertungs GmbH (Saar-Palatinate Asset Realization Company) was already set up at a meeting organized by Saarland District Economic Adviser Wilhelm Bösing on November 10: The speed of the meeting demonstrates that the process had already been discussed and prepared in party circles before the November pogrom. A note on the meeting prepared by Deutsche Bank's Saarbrücken director, Max Ludwig Rohde, records:

> By this evening all the Jewish assets in the administrative district [*Gau*] will have been transferred to this company, the usual procedure being that the Jewish proprietor irrevocably authorizes the company to administer his assets and to transfer them to aryan ownership; in individual instances, immediate transfer to the company appears to be planned. [...] The company [*die GmbH*] shall speedily undertake the sale of the assets transferred to it, in which connection banks are expected to offer credit in suitable cases. The takeover by the company

shall be effected at real values, i.e. at the price to be granted to the Jew taking account of all circumstances, notably the compulsory nature of the sale, whereas the sale is to be made at market value. The purpose of this is to prevent unreasonable profits from being made by those acquiring Jewish assets. All Jewish property is to be taken over with the exception of residential real estate, personal effects, and debts by Jews against Jews.

The GmbH would have a seven-person advisory council, on which Deutsche Bank, as well as Dresdner Bank, the Pfälzische Hypothekenbank, and the administrative district [Gau] would be represented.[51] The newspapers carried details of the new company the following day. A notice signed by Bösing stated: "The consequences of the fact are being ruthlessly drawn and can only be that Jewish property is now immediately to be transferred to German ownership [...]. Persons interested in Jewish property will in future only be able to buy it through this newly-founded rescue company."[52]

A similar regional organization was created in East Prussia, the Erich-Koch-Stiftung, whose goal was declared to be "to speed up the transfer of Jewish wealth."[53]

The most decisive and comprehensive piece of legislation came on December 3, 1938: the Decree on the Utilization of Jewish Property [Verordnung über den Einsatz des jüdischen Vermögens].[54] Section 1 provided for specific deadlines for the sale or liquidation of a Jewish firm, and Section 2 allowed the state to impose trustee administration. Göring's aim was to stop "wild aryanizations" siphoning assets away from the state. In addition to the collective fine (Sühneleistung, or "reparation" in the Nazi vocabulary) imposed on December 12 as an initial measure, individual tax offices imposed blocking orders on Jewish-owned accounts, and then the Reich Economics Ministry ordered that the currency legislation should be used to impose such a freeze of bank assets.

The December decree also provided for the sale of Jewish-owned securities. The economic groups [Wirtschaftsgruppen] of the "Reich Group Banks" [Reichsgruppe Banken] were to decide themselves about the sales of Jewish security deposits, which had greatly accelerated as a result of the so-called reparation. But the amounts to be sold were carefully controlled by the banks and the bourse authorities to prevent a sharp dip in the stock market. At first, RM 60,000 to 80,000 in securities a day were sold; by January 1939, the amount was RM 250,000 daily. By the beginning of January 1939, RM 5 million worth of securities had been sold.[55]

Individual branches of the commercial banks conducted their own "aryanizations." Deutsche Bank also compiled a central list of 700 firms, of which 200 were sold by July and 260 by the end of August 1938.[56]

In November 1938, shortly before the anti-Semitic pogrom, Kimmich reported that Deutsche Bank had participated in the "aryanization" of 330 businesses. "The difficulties, notably in personal terms, are not inconsiderable [he said]. Specialists with capital are thin on the ground." At this time, he estimated the total Jewish-owned capital in Germany to amount to RM 6 billion to 8 billion.[57]

A separate tabulation of November 1938, produced by Gerhard Elkmann, deputy director attached to the office of Karl Kimmich, described 569 "major non-aryan firms" as "dealt with"; of these, 363 had been "transferred to aryan ownership or liquidated." Elkmann's brief summary also breaks down the firms concerned by categories (Table 1). The figures show that Deutsche Bank was apparently particularly effective in managing "aryanizations" in branches such as textiles and tobacco, where there was a substantial dependence on foreign imports of raw materials. Elkmann had dealt personally with at least one (eventually unsuccessful) attempt of Deutsche Bank to negotiate an "aryanization," that of the N. Israel department store.[58]

At that time, a draft letter, which survives in the files of Deutsche Bank, referred to government plans for a holding company for Jewish property in terms, which in retrospect have a sinister implication. "In order to create a definitive state of peace for the economy as soon as possible, the supreme authorities in the Reich are currently discussing the idea of a complete solution of the non-aryan problem in the economy."[59] The major purpose of this draft letter, which might never have been sent, was to protest against the likely difficulties of such a total state settlement in the light of the absence of skilled managers who might run the "aryanized" enterprises.

The additional credit business generated as a result of "aryanization" affected the competitive position of Germany's big banks. At a meeting of Bavarian branch managers in June 1938, the increased "generosity" on the part of Dresdner Bank in giving credits to allow firms to engage in "aryanization" was discussed, but Deutsche Bank's

Table 1   Deutsche Bank and the Number of Aryanized Firms, 1938[60]

	Column 1 Dealt With	Column 2 Aryanized	Column 2/1 (%)	Column 2 as Percent of Total	Number of Noncraft Enterprises	Column 2/5 (%)
Textile mills	60	54	90.0	14.9	116,627	0.046
Ready-made clothes factories	59	36	61.0	9.9	146,402	0.025
Leather/Shoes	32	21	65.6	5.8	5,287	0.397
Iron	20	16	80.0	4.4	3,561	0.449
Tobacco	7	7	100.0	1.9		
Paper	11	9	81.8	2.5	17,046	0.053
Retail	223	129	57.8	35.5		
Furniture/Wood	11	5	45.5	1.4		
Wine (wholesale trade)	7	2	28.6	0.6		
Various	139	84	60.4	23.1		
Sum	569	363	63.8	100.0		

managing board urged caution: "Mr. Rummel once again points out with emphasis that we do not wish to allow ourselves to be driven off course in our credit policy. It is the board's intention [he said] that in the foreseeable future, however great the requests for credit addressed to the bank, we should have sufficient capacity to issue good loans."[61] But Deutsche Bank in practice certainly responded to the demand for bank loans, though in some cases, such as Leipzig, it made no explicit "aryanization loans" at all.[62]

On May 12, 1939, a circular to bank branches, signed by Kimmich and Abs, listed as a desired activity of the bank "to promote Jewish emigration."[63] In fact, as an internationally active bank, Deutsche Bank played a significant part in transferring abroad the small sums left to Jewish owners under the terms of increasingly draconian exchange and transfer regulations.[64]

Were all banks treated equally? What price was paid for properties subject to "aryanization"? The Dresdner Bank produced a revealing memorandum in May 1938, after a visit of a bank official to the Economics Ministry, in which the valuation principles were set out. It gives a glimpse of the way different banks were treated differently and supplied with inside price information. The memorandum began:

> It is intended within a not too long time frame to either transfer to aryan ownership or liquidate all non-aryan businesses. The appropriate specialty Economic Group or the local chamber of commerce will have to decide whether an aryanization is desirable. In consequences, in cases when there is an overcrowding of businesses, the liquidation of the non-aryan firm and the transfer of inventories to aryan ownership is preferred. Apart from this the Economic Ministry does not require a forced aryanization.

The ministry rejected the idea of particular payments to party offices:

> In general, local offices cannot make particular financial demands for the authorization of aryanizations. It is certainly not the rule that parts of the aryanization profit have to be transferred to party or other offices. The Economics Ministry only requires payments in cases in which the aryan purchaser buys at an especially favorable rate because of the absence of the non-aryan seller. In these cases, the purchaser is required to make a payment to the [government owned] Golddiskontbank.

For the valuation, there should be no special calculation of a "good will" content; there should be a reserve to cover "the increased risks to the purchaser." The *Gau* economic adviser [*Gauwirtschaftsberater*] generally suggested an "estimation" of twenty percent "of the own capital of the enterprise," "so that aryanizations are authorized on the basis of between two thirds and three quarters of the original wealth. In part, the party believes that the non-aryan seller should receive no higher price than if the enterprise were liquidated." This information, the Reich Economics Ministry official had specified, should not be made generally available "since he did not want to create the impression that a particular bank had been treated favorably."[65]

Banks in Germany

The "aryanization" of banking was a special case, both because of the problematic character of the business – in the National Socialist world view it was "speculative" or "Jewish" – and because of the close business and personal links that already existed among the banking elite. In some cases, therefore, "aryanization" was conducted in close cooperation with the legitimate owners, and with a substantial amount of care for the protection of their interests. This was particularly the case with the involvement of Deutsche Bank in the sale or liquidation of two of the most important private banks in Germany, Mendelssohn of Berlin and Simon Hirschland of Essen.

In the case of smaller banks, Deutsche Bank was cautious and hesitant. At the beginning of 1938, Erich Weinmann of the Prague-based Živnostenska Bank wrote to the manager of the Saarbrücken branch, Eduard Martin, to say that he had just dined with Sigmund Wassermann of the Bamberg bank A. E. Wassermann. Weinmann, who was a close acquaintance of Martin's, talked about Martin, and Wassermann then asked him to inquire whether Martin might not join the Bamberg bank as a partner. Weinmann explained: "You are aware that A.E.W. is one of the best-financed and oldest private banks in southern Germany and is Jewish-owned. This firm is now, at the request of the proprietor, to be aryanized – not in any camouflaged way, either, but genuinely." He suggested that Martin should acquire twenty to twenty-five percent of the capital, either with his own money or with borrowed money, presumably borrowed from Deutsche Bank. Martin immediately informed Arnold Schwerdtfeger, of Deutsche Bank's Berlin secretariat, and suggested that this might be an interesting involvement for Deutsche Bank. "At the moment, then, without knowing the details, only the most basic aspects can be discussed, namely whether it might be interesting for our firm to become involved in the clearly imminent reorganization of Wassermann." Schwerdtfeger then discussed the issue with Deutsche Bank's managing board. He replied to Martin by return post:

> As regards the Wassermann affair, we learned of the plans several months ago in a different connection. As such the projected aryanization is note-worthy from a general standpoint, but here at the bank we are not directly interested. [...] We welcomed the fact that you spoke quite openly in this connection, but since we do not intend to participate finan-cially in the matter in any way whatsoever – you will be aware from your own experience that here at the bank we have tended in recent years more to avoid other private banks than extend our commitment in the sector – in this instance too there is no intention of departing from the line adopted hitherto.

Martin then told Weinmann that he could not accept the proposal to join Wassermann as a partner: "Despite the fact that in a private bank I should enjoy far more independence, I should not like to acquire this at the expense of giving up what has for years been my familiar circle of responsibilities and intimates."[66]

Mendelssohn and Hirschland, however, were special cases because of their size and importance and the close personal nature of their links to Deutsche Bank's management. These two had resisted Nazi pressure for a long time with relative success. Some famous private banks had already sold out at the turn of 1935–36: Gebrüder Arnhold (Berlin and Dresden) and A. Levy & Co. (Cologne). Many smaller banks had simply been liquidated. It was frequently difficult to find qualified purchasers for businesses that produced nothing but relied on personal contacts and business judgments. In the middle of the big wave of "aryanizations" in 1938, the journal *Die Bank* commented that "the development opportunities of a production enterprise are usually rated very much more highly nowadays than those of a bank, whose services are largely subject to pretty strict regulation of pay-ments."[67] The majority of small and medium-size Jewish-owned private banks thus simply disappeared as a consequence of liquidations, some taking place as late as 1938: Bass und Herz, Frankfurt; Boehm & Reitzenstein, Berlin; S. Frenkel, Berlin; Gumpel, Hanover; Hagen & Co., Berlin; Hardy, Munich; A. Kohn, Nuremberg; Marx, Munich; Schwabe & Co., Berlin; or Jacob Stern, Frankfurt.

What were the alternatives to liquidation? The easiest was the transfer of the bank to one or more former employees – this was the path taken in the case of M. M. Warburg. Second, the bank might be sold to another private banker. This is what occurred in the case of the old Berlin house of Jacquier & Securius, which was taken over by Richard Lenz & Co. The "aryanization" of Simon Hirschland, Essen, ran in an analogous way. Thirdly, parts of the business could be transferred to another bank: This is what occurred in the case of Mendelssohn.

Richard Lenz, who had been a member of the NSDAP since 1933, was a well-connected banker who was in charge of the admissions office [*Zulassungsstelle*] of the Berlin stock exchange. In addition, he was regional director [*Landesobmann*] of the Reich Group Banks, the umbrella organization of German banks. His initial contact at Deutsche Bank was Ernst Eisner, the bourse director for Berlin. Lenz apparently played an active role in the protection of Jews and continued to employ some Jews, who were disguised from their coworkers as business customers, until 1943. In 1943, Lenz left the NSDAP under rather unclear circumstances.[68] In March 1938, Deutsche Bank helped in putting up the capital for Lenz's purchase. Initially, it supplied capital of RM 1 million, one third of which was paid back in 1939 and the rest in 1941. At that point, Deutsche Bank realized a profit net of interest of 115,454 RM (or 11.5 percent of its original investment), which was booked as "realized reserves in long-term holdings."[69]

With M. M. Warburg in Hamburg, Mendelssohn and Hirschland represented the pinnacle of German-Jewish private banking, Mendelssohn specializing in government finance and overseas trade finance, and Hirschland in the politically equally sensitive area of industrial finance. The involvement of a major Berlin bank in their "aryanization" attracted critical comment; correspondingly, when the Munich house of Aufhäuser was taken over by an individual without the assistance of a Berlin bank, the financial press commented: "If now, as appears to be the case, it has happened in Munich without the involvement of big banks [*Grossbanken*] as partners, basically this can only be welcomed."[70]

Bankhaus Mendelssohn & Co., Berlin

The struggle preceding the liquidation of Mendelssohn, Germany's most significant private bank, was a war of all against all: the Jewish owners against some of the employees, the party and the Reich Economics Ministry against the bank, and against the commercial banks – notably Deutsche Bank – which intervened in the process. Even the term used to describe the end of the firm played a role in these struggles. By a strict definition, there was no "aryanization," because only some of the assets were transferred to Deutsche Bank and there was no sale. The assets were precisely matched with the liabilities. Wilhelm Treue wrote that Robert von Mendelssohn remained grateful to his partner Rudolf Löb for preventing "aryanization" and securing through a liquidation an "end befitting the status of the institution [*standesgemässen Abschluss*]."[71] Löb later set out his major goal in the negotiations as the avoidance of Nazi or Nazi-sympathizing partners and the prevention of the disappearance of the firm's name. "These two objectives could be achieved only if the Jewish-named firm was taken out of operation for an indeterminate period."[72]

Mendelssohn was one of the oldest names in German banking. The bank had been created in 1795 by Joseph Mendelssohn, the oldest son of the Enlightenment philosopher Moses Mendelssohn. Franz von Mendelssohn played a major part in the business and industrial politics of the Kaiserreich and the Weimar Republic as president of the Deutscher Industrie- und Handelstag and was also a member of the Reichsbank's general council [*Generalrat*]. In the 1920s, for the first time, three nonmembers of the family became partners: Paul Kempner, Rudolf Löb, and Fritz Mannheimer (who, however, conducted most of his business in Amsterdam). But they held only a minority of the shares, and three quarters of the bank's capital remained in the hands of the family.

Mendelssohn remained a successful bank for the first five years of the Nazi regime and continued to be a member of the consortium issuing government debt. But it was riven by internal tension, both within the family and among the employees. In 1935, Franz von Mendelssohn and Paul von Mendelssohn-Bartholdy both died, and the internal agreement regarding the distribution of property within the dynasty was consequently reworked. In November 1937, Franz's widow, Marie von Mendelssohn (née Westphal), was entered in the commercial register as managing partner [persönlich haftende Gesellschafterin], but Paul's widow Elsa was not. Some of the employees began to worry about their future, either fearing that a Jewish-owned bank could not survive or hoping to step into the shoes of the Jewish partners and take over the business.[73]

In confronting the Nazi threat in 1938, Mendelssohn was in a much weaker position than Hirschland in Essen or the Hamburg house of Warburg. Those banks had foreign affiliates (in both cases in Amsterdam) that could be used in negotiations about the transfer of assets. Mendelssohn's Amsterdam branch, however, which like those of the other German private banks had been founded in the turbulent inflationary years that followed the First World War, was run by an independent and brilliant speculator. Fritz Mannheimer had engaged more and more in French politics. (He was a close friend of the French politician Paul Reynaud.) His extravagantly ostentatious expenditure aimed explicitly at recreating the life of a banker of the France of Honoré de Balzac and Alexandre Dumas. He named his country residence at Vaucresson outside Paris "Monte Christo." But by 1938 his bank was in serious trouble, mainly because of its personal loans to Mannheimer. On May 1, 1938, Mannheimer owed the bank HFL 5.8 million and, in addition, it had given a credit of HFL 6 million on the security of Mannheimer's fine art collection. He killed himself in 1939 when its bankruptcy became unavoidable.[74]

In the course of 1938, the pressure to exclude the remaining Jews in the bank increased. The vice president of the Reichsbank, Fritz Dreyse, spoke with Löb and explained that the bank would face increased pressure ("for political reasons, difficulties must increasingly be reckoned with.") The Reich commissar for credit, Friedrich Ernst, also advised Löb to begin immediately with preparations for Aryanization. Dreyse told Löb that the Reichs-Kredit-Gesellschaft (RKG) was willing to buy the bank, and Löb replied, according to Hermann Abs's account, that he would rather deal with Deutsche Bank and Abs. Thus, he went immediately from Dreyse's office in the Reichsbank to see Abs of Deutsche Bank.[75]

At this point, the Mendelssohn partners were Rudolf Löb, Paul Kempner, Fritz Mannheimer (who were Jewish), who owned about one quarter of the bank; Robert von Mendelssohn and Marie von Mendelssohn (who were classified as half-castes under the Nuremberg laws); and two "aryan" widows of the Mendelssohn family, Giulietta von Mendelssohn and Elsa von Mendelssohn-Bartholdy. Of 180 employees, 27 were Jewish.

In June 1938, the Reich Economics Ministry negotiated with the deputy head of the bank's work council [Betriebsobmann], Erich Kluge, a member of the party and chief employment manager [Hauptstellenleiter]. The officials responsible for banking in the ministry, and the Reich commissar for banking, originally supported the option favored by Kluge, an "aryanization" that would leave the bank as an independent entity. Kluge, in a detailed report on the bank prepared for the Reich Economics Ministry, claimed that the bank's Jewish directors and officials preferred a dissolution of the bank. Retaining the bank under "aryan" control would be a means of securing the continued employment of the bank's non-Jewish personnel.

> This will achieve the preservation of one of the few remaining private banks as a necessary institution that both in domestic German business life and in dealings with abroad would provide exceptionally good service in terms of full exploitation of the firm in the interests of the National Socialist economy; it will further achieve, as a result, retention of 150 jobs.

Kluge suggested that the easiest way of accomplishing this was through the exchange of shares with Mendelssohn & Co., Amsterdam, whose main partner was Mannheimer: In this way, "the Berlin house could be cleared of Jews."

He also mentioned a third option, sale to a big bank. The main objection to this in his eyes would be that the jobs of the employees (and their unusually generous salaries) would be at risk. But he added that such a takeover would destroy the valuable institution of the private bank and have the economically undesirable consequence of increasing concentration in banking.

The chief legal problem with the option favored by Kluge and the Reich Economics Ministry lay in the question of the "standstill credits" [Stillhaltekredite]. Mendelssohn had about RM 27 million of foreign credit lines that had been frozen in the banking crisis of 1931 and that were then subject to the annually negotiated German Credit Agreements. Kluge explained to the Reich Economics Ministry:

> In connection with these credits [...] liability also lies with the proprietors personally, in fact, through their private assets, and, under the provisions of the Standstill Agreement, the part amounts concerned when a proprietor withdraws would fall due immediately, payable in foreign currency. [...] As long as the standstill credits remain in place the foreign standstill creditors have right of relief over foreign-currency assets, i.e. when the proprietor withdraws immediate payment can be demanded in foreign currency, as a result of which it follows that Jewish assets located abroad would be jeopardized.

The consent of the foreign creditors would be needed to transfer these credits to another bank or to the German government. The possibility of such claims made emigration very difficult. For this reason, the Jewish partners were pressing for another German bank to take over Mendelssohn.

Kluge's approach to the Reich Economics Ministry was intended to generate official pressure on the bank to purge itself:

> *Only the authorities* [original emphasis] could compel the Jews at least to proceed simultaneously to take all the steps required to transfer the operation to aryan ownership, and previous experience suggests that there is no doubt that such a request, if made by a government agency (Reich Economics Ministry, Reichsbank, or Bank Commissar), would in fact be complied with.[76]

Kempner and Löb, however, stated in the discussions that they were not contemplating any "further structuring" of the bank, because any changes depended on the solution of the standstill credit problem. But they also implied "that without Jews, i.e. under aryan management, [the bank] would not be as successful commercially as hitherto."[77]

In September 1938, the Reich Economics Ministry was still advocating the transfer of the Jewish-owned shares to Robert von Mendelssohn. The solution that was now proposed for the standstill credits was that Deutsche Bank should take over the current business of the bank, along with a $2 million (almost RM 5 million) credit line. The minutes of the negotiations record that: "The American creditors are apparently in agreement with the commitments being taken over by Deutsche Bank. No other solution appears feasible." Bank Commissar Ernst was still trying to find a way to rescue Mendelssohn as an independent firm.[78]

Abs of Deutsche Bank had started to hold discussions with Löb immediately after the initial warnings (March 14, 1938) from Reichsbank Vice President Fritz Dreyse about the unsustainability of the bank's position. The Deutsche Bank managing board first discussed the matter ("Mr. Löb's idea") on July 25, 1938, but decided against it. The young man who reported the managing board's vote to Abs (who was in Amsterdam), Walter Pohle, was rapidly developing into the specialist for business takeovers.[79] If the project came off, it was because of renewed interventions of Abs. Löb later praised Abs's "tact, wisdom, and firmness," as did Robert von Mendelssohn.[80] At the end of August, Paul Kempner told Abs that the Mendelssohn employees agreed to the Deutsche Bank solution;[81] in fact, however, the longer the Reich Economics Ministry hesitated in its decision, the more turbulent and fractious those bank workers became.

Some did not stop at personal denunciations to the authorities. After the pogrom of November 9–10, 1938, one Mendelssohn employee (Walther Beyer) wrote, complaining that Löb had been "the real driving force behind the whole plan with Deutsche Bank," that he had just paid RM 740,000 to the tax authorities, apparently in settlement of the *Reichsfluchtsteuer* (Reich Flight Tax), and that the holder of the power of attorney, Dresel, had also written a check for RM 50,000 and was leaving immediately: "this very evening [he plans] to leave Germany for Amsterdam."[82]

According to the takeover plan, RM 68 million in assets and liabilities were to be transferred to Deutsche Bank, and RM 2 million were not taken over. The customers ("the customer business in its entirety") were all assumed by Deutsche Bank. Deutsche Bank did not pay a particular sum for the new business: The assets and liabilities were simply transferred and the outstanding balance was paid. The remaining firm (Mendelssohn in Liquidation) kept the capital of the bank and foreign assets and some German assets that could not be liquidated. In addition, it retained the real estate. According to the agreement, Deutsche Bank would also take over the non-Jewish employees and, for a period of three years, pay them at the higher rates customary in Mendelssohn. (This had been one of the most contentious points in Abs's negotiations with his bank.) Deutsche Bank also took over the pension obligations of Mendelssohn. At the time, the journal *Die Bank* commented: "Meanwhile it would in no way accord with the facts were one to seek by such historical reminiscences to point in the Mendelssohn case to a desire for expansion on the part of Deutsche Bank. As has already been suggested, the causes of the transfer are different here. All the same, Deutsche Bank will welcome the additional business."[83]

The Jewish employees were to be dismissed, and on December 5, three days after the Reich Economics Ministry agreed to the plan, Löb, Kempner, Mannheimer, and Marie von Mendelssohn all left the bank. Löb went first to Buenos Aires, then to the United States. Kempner went via London to New York. As a result of the Reichsbank's judgment that he had been helpful in the question of negotiating the transfer of foreign credits to Deutsche Bank, he was allowed to take some of his personal furniture with him. Otherwise, he was left with only RM 50,000. Löb was permitted to transfer RM 210,000.

On December 1, 1939, the bank was liquidated. The journal *Bank-Archiv* commented that this liquidation "heralds the final phase of the aryanization of the private-banking industry" but emphasized that the special role of Deutsche Bank made this an "exception."[84]

In January 1939, a further memorandum restated the case against the takeover by Deutsche Bank and urged instead that the bank raise new capital through a bank consortium, especially from the Reichs-Kredit-Gesellschaft, and that it should be managed by Robert von Mendelssohn. The document claimed that this solution was supported by the Berlin District economic adviser, by the Private Banking Business Group, and by the Jewish Affairs Department (Judenreferat) of the Reich Economics Ministry.[85]

In the detailed provisions of this suggestion, one of the bank's key men was to play a particular role. Robert von Mendelssohn should be joined by one or more new partners in the direction of the bank.

> Mr. [Alfred] Kurzmeyer has belonged to the firm for many years and can be described as one of the pillars of the enterprise. He enjoys excellent foreign connections and should fulfill all that is expected of a new partner. Mr. Kurzmeyer has Swiss nationality. That fact, together with his resultant ideological position, could speak against him, or at least make it

seem advisable to bring in a third partner. Mr. Kurzmeyer [...] is also one of the leading personalities in the Mendelssohn Bank who are in favour of the firm continuing and who are unreservedly positive about the possibilities of such a course.

In fact, Kurzmeyer had already appeared on October 25, 1938, at Deutsche Bank to speak with Abs and Kimmich. He said that he had had alternative offers, from Warburg and Aufhäuser, in the event of an "aryanization". Carl Goetz of Dresdner Bank had offered him at least four positions, at the level of the Dresdner Bank managing board. But he then said "that at the age of 58 he naturally attached importance to earning something and that it was not a matter of indifference to him whether he received RM 100,000 or RM 200,000." Deutsche Bank offered him a position as director, directly below the managing board, and promised that he would have a department rather than simply an office job. His initial responsibility would lie in "building on the Mendelssohn business and bringing it back to greater standing within Deutsche Bank by acquiring customers with the aid of incorporation of officials etc." Eventually his responsibilities would be broader: "Mr. Kurzmeyer felt he was particularly suited to customer business, also for giving advice on stocks and shares, but in addition for foreign business, in which connection he was thinking particularly of his contacts in Belgium, France, Switzerland, etc." Kimmich and Abs noted that "Mr. Kurzmeyer also gave an impression of being very agile as well as knowledgeable about business, in fact there appears every justification for believing that the bank is here gaining a businessman."[86] And indeed, Kurzmeyer joined Deutsche Bank on February 10, 1939, and played an important role in the foreign business of the bank over the subsequent six years.

Mendelssohn in Liquidation was renamed in 1943 as von Mendelssohn & Co. i.L. In 1941 Elsa von Mendelssohn-Bartholdy, the widow of Paul von Mendelssohn-Bartholdy (after a remarriage, Countess Kesselstadt), left the partnership, and so at the beginning of 1942 did Giulietta von Mendelssohn, leaving Robert von Mendelssohn as the only partner and, with Ferdinand Kremer, one of the two "liquidators with authority to sign." By 1943, the liquidation had almost been completed, and there remained only some Hungarian investments, real estate, and "compensation claims vis-à-vis the German

Reich" on the asset side, with RM 4 million in liabilities. The bank in liquidation eventually moved to the premises of Deutsche Bank (the Deutsche Bank Kameradschaftshaus at Behrensstrasse 15) after a bombing raid destroyed the previous offices in a Reichsbank building.[87]

When Kremer prepared a report for OMGUS after the war on the takeover by Deutsche Bank (in which he, too, praised the role of Hermann Abs), he mentioned that in the course of negotiations the intention was developed "to revive the firm of Mendelssohn & Co. as soon as the right political and economic conditions obtain." But this aspiration was never realized.[88]

Simon Hirschland, Essen

Simon Hirschland was founded in Essen in 1841. At the end of 1937, it had a capital of RM 84 million and standstill credits worth RM 38 million. There were 160 employees, of whom 36 were Jewish. By October 1937, the Gestapo was attacking the Hirschland bank as the "focal point of Jewish financial dominance in the Ruhr District," complaining about its irregular business activities, but also about the Reichsbank – which, according to the Gestapo, was developing a plan to make Hirschland a "camouflaged Christian" bank.[88]

In the course of 1937, Georg Hirschland began discussions with the Reichsbank and the Reich commissar for banking about a possible transfer of the bank. They both urged that the bank continue as an independent entity. The Hirschland family proposed to continue its banking abroad, through the Amsterdamsche Crediet Maatschappij (ACM) and the Compagnie voor Belegging en Administratie (Coba), in which they already held participations. ACM was founded after the First World War, with the principal goal of financing German enterprises. Between 1924 and 1930, and again in 1934, Simon Hirschland increased its capital participation. ACM had a considerable part in the Dutch standstill credits to Germany. Simon Hirschland owned in addition HFl 282,700 (nominal) shares in Coba, which was intended to buy up problematic engagements of ACM.

A consortium managed by Deutsche Bank was supposed to buy up the Hirschland shares, according to a preliminary agreement drawn up by Hirschland's lawyers.[90] Capital in the firm (a limited partnership, or

Kommanditgesellschaft) would be provided by major Ruhr industrialists, including Fritz Thyssen and Friedrich Flick as well as the Munich bank of Merck, Finck & Co. Deutsche Bank would take over the standstill credits. The managing partners (*persönlich haftende Gesellschafter*) would be Otto Burkhardt and Dr. von Falkenhausen, the director of Deutsche Bank's Essen branch. Gotthard von Falkenhausen had been a close friend of the Hirschland family since 1935, and the bank also had good business contacts with Karl Kimmich.[91] Jewish employees would be dismissed, but all the "aryan" employees of Hirschland would stay in the new firm.

However, this solution was bitterly opposed by the Essen district government (*Gauleitung*) of the NSDAP, and in particular by *Gauleiter* Josef Terboven. District Economic Advisor Paul Hoffmann wrote to Reich Economics Minister Walther Funk that the plan was

> completely out of the question, since the political leadership does not wish this business to survive, because if it did the result would be to usher in a fresh version of the Essen banking industry [...]. This preliminary agreement gives such unilateral preference to Deutsche Bank and further provides for such powerful dependence on the part of Deutsche Bank that there could be no more talk of a "private bank" in the strict meaning of the phrase.

Instead, the bank should be liquidated.[92]

Originally, other banks had been interested in acquiring Hirschland – the National-Bank AG in Essen (which was linked to DAF, the Nazi trade-union organization) and Dresdner Bank. The Reich commissar for banking supported the notion of a continued independent existence (as he had in the case of Mendelssohn). In particular, he was concerned about stopping any increase in the influence of Deutsche Bank.[93] The Reich Economics Ministry's bank department pointed out that the compelling argument for the sale to Deutsche Bank lay in the need to transfer the standstill credits, because the repayment in foreign exchange would be too costly for Germany.[94]

On July 20, 1938, Otto Abshagen (Deutsche Bank) and Hirschland's lawyer Fritz Fenthol visited the Essen district-government offices (*Gauleitung*). Hoffmann began the discussion by saying that he had spoken with Economics Minister Funk, who supported the *Gauleiter*'s position. He then said that *Ministerialdirektor* Kurt Lange had been misinformed about the interests and needs of the Ruhr business community. "Following the takeover, Deutsche Bank would only launch a major publicity campaign aimed at industry, bringing nothing but unrest into the district as a result." He was opposed to the possibility of Deutsche Bank's achieving a unilateral advantage through a profitable "aryanization." The standstill credits were a red herring, because almost all of them carried a guarantee from the Deutsche Golddiskontbank. "After all, if the worst came to the worst a law could be passed to prevent the foreign creditors from making difficulties for the German Reich." Fenthol pointed out that "the foreign creditors would be entitled to assert their claims if the name of Hirschland disappeared and no legal successor was found." Hoffmann then denied this and repeated his arguments.[95]

After this meeting, a district-authority official, Wolfgang Müller-Klemm, told Hirschland's lawyer that "Deutsche Bank had made the big mistake of not contacting the district authorities very much earlier [...]. It was also quite out of the question that Deutsche Bank should come into Hirschland's entire inheritance." The National-Bank AG wanted to acquire specific shares from Hirschland (Kahla Porzellan AG and Hamburger Hypothekenbank). Finally, Müller-Klemm indicated that it would be possible to rescue the Deutsche Bank plan only if "some of the Gauleiter's industrial friends become personal and financial partners in the new firm." In addition, the district authority rejected the entry of von Falkenhausen into the proposed new bank.

Subsequently, Müller-Klemm visited Georg Hirschland, who explained that "he could not in fact give his consent to a liquidation, as requested by the district governor, because on the one hand he was committed vis-à-vis Deutsche Bank." Meanwhile, Fenthol advised Hirschland: "Since the district authority wants liquidation, he should decide this himself, provided that it is possible in terms of foreign indebtedness and does not involve any foreign debts becoming payable." Hirschland accepted this advice.[96]

At the beginning of August, in the offices of the Reich commissar for banking in Berlin, a new discussion took place with Hoffmann and Müller-Klemm. The Reichsbank official responsible for the standstill credits, von Wedel, explained the legal position regarding the credits, and emphasized that, of Simon Hirschland's RM 28 million to 30 million credits, only RM 8 million were guaranteed by the Golddiskontbank.[97]

The new bank, Burkhardt & Co., was thus established in line with Deutsche Bank's plan. Deutsche Bank paid the entirety of von Falkenhausen's capital participation and gave a RM 35,000 advance to Burkhardt.

The foreign credits under the standstill were divided up between Deutsche Bank and Burkhardt. Deutsche Bank assured $3,382,976 U.S. liabilities (RM 8,421,000), £933,011 (RM 11,401,000) for standstill credits from Great-Britain, 1,583,940 Swiss francs (RM 878,000) from Switzerland, and 4,508,403 French francs (RM 328,000) from France, but almost all of these positions were balanced out with "provisional currency claims." Burkardt kept an uncovered U.S. credit position of $311,642 (RM 776,000) and some largely covered English and Swiss credits (£671,291 and CHF 6,375,575, or RM 8,203,000 and RM 3,639,000).[98]

Under the terms of the arrangement with the Reichsbank's Foreign Debts Department of September 30, 1938, Hirschland was left with HFl 1,760,000 worth (RM 2,416,000) of shares in the ACM, HFl 287,700 worth (RM 395,000) of shares in Coba, and $106,300 worth (RM 265,000) of shares in the New York Hanseatic Corporation. In return, the firm surrendered RM 500,000 in foreign currency to the Reichsbank, HFl 400,000 (RM 549,000) to the Golddiskontbank, and RM 8 million to the Golddiskontbank. After the pogrom of November 9 the family members fled abroad, leaving some of these payments still to be made. "Following the events of 8 and 9 November 1938, the applicants refused to pay the amounts still outstanding." Consequently, in April 1939 District Economic Adviser Hoffmann went to a meeting in the Amsterdam German consulate with the representatives of the Hirschland family. These explained that buildings, a children's home, and a synagogue belonging to the bank had been destroyed; paintings by Marées, Menzel, Caspar David Friedrich, Cézanne, and van Gogh had been confiscated; silver and jewelry had been blocked in Germany; and the family had paid for the support of numerous refugees who had fled to Holland. In the end, to legalize their emigration, the family agreed to a payment of £40,000 (RM 488,000) and that their planned payment of HFl 400,000 should be reduced to HFl 200,000 (RM 275,000). The Hirschlands would buy HFl 1,840,000

(RM 2,525,000) of ACM shares from Fried. Krupp AG, in part to be paid in guilders, in part through the cancellation of a foreign-exchange credit of Hirschland to Krupp. Georg Hirschland would sell the paintings ("some of them coming under the Art Protection Act [Kunstschutzgesetz]") to the Essen district authority for RM 350,000. Other silver and jewelry would be allowed to be shipped. Hoffmann promised to secure passports valid for five years.[99]

The connection of the Hirschland family did not end with this forcible expropriation. The model for a postwar settlement was provided by the agreement that Erich Warburg reached with the partners of Brinckmann Wirtz & Co. (the former Bankhaus M. M. Warburg). After restitution negotiations in 1949, the family held thirty percent of the capital of Burkhardt & Co. In addition, the Burkhardt bank was obliged to pay the Hirschland interests the sum of DM 800,000.[100]

This agreement was more amicable than the relations among the former "aryanizers" had been. Gotthard von Falkenhausen and Burkhardt had already quarreled before the outbreak of the war, and only the military call-up of von Falkenhausen in 1939 had prevented an open clash.[101] In addition, after the currency reform of 1948, von Falkenhausen engaged in a bitter controversy with Deutsche Bank as to whether the bank's financing of his takeover of Hirschland had been a loan (which would have been reduced in the ratio 10:1 by the currency reform) or a trusteeship, in which case Deutsche Bank would have a much larger claim to a share of the capital of Burkhardt. In the course of this altercation, von Falkenhausen accused Deutsche Bank of having made a large profit on the sale of securities previously held by Hirschland, a charge that Deutsche Bank attempted to refute.[102] After the 1950 settlement, Burkhardt worked closely with the newly founded New York Hirschland bank.

Deutsche Bank did not take over any major banks in Germany in the 1930s (by contrast with the experience of the 1920s, when it had been massively acquisitive).[103] This was not because of self-restraint, moral scruples or doubts about the process of "aryanization," or an unwillingness to expand. Rather, the absence of takeovers was a consequence of government policy and of the unwillingness of the Reich Economics Ministry and the bank commissar (in charge of banking supervision) to see an extension of the economic power of Deutsche Bank. The same sorts of calculation, augmented by personal and institutional greed, drove local party authorities to try to conduct bank "aryanizations" through public-sector banks. Of the two large banks with which Deutsche Bank dealt, Mendelssohn and Hirschland, Mendelssohn was liquidated and its current business transferred. The Reich Economics Ministry was eventually satisfied with this outcome, because of the need to secure the cooperation of the bank's foreign creditors. Hirschland went, with the assistance of Deutsche Bank, to manage a former Deutsche Bank branch. In both cases, the involvement of Deutsche Bank provided a significant service, subsequently recognized in the postwar period, to the Jewish owners and partners of the banks under threat.

Industrial Enterprises in Germany

In the case of industrial enterprises, Deutsche Bank did not aim to be a buyer of Jewish businesses but was frequently an intermediary, either in complete sales or in holding shares on its own account for some period of time. When it managed a straightforward sale, it usually received a commission of between one and three percent. In cases in which it held shares, it might profit from the rise in share values during the period that the bank owned an equity participation. One case dealt with in this section, Adler & Oppenheimer, represents the largest single "aryanization" profit made by the bank. It arose because of the delays in carrying out the transaction, which meant that the surge in asset prices during the inflationary circumstances of war affected the shares held by the bank.

The brokering of "aryanizations" was a competitive business between German banks. Other banks, especially regional banks and savings banks (*Sparkassen*) were looking to expand their own businesses and capture long-term customers as a result of managing an "aryanization." The actual profit from commissions on the transaction probably mattered less than the hope of establishing longer-term business relationships with the new owners. In this competition, the major advantage of Deutsche Bank lay in its activity as an international bank. This allowed it to deal with the complexities of trade financing in a world of exchange control, with the consequence that firms with substantial foreign-trade links were more likely to use the services of Deutsche Bank. The international contacts of Deutsche Bank meant that it could also play a part in transfer of Jewish assets abroad, after sales had made these assets liquid.

The sales of most Jewish businesses, even of quite substantial corporations, were handled by the branch office responsible rather than by Deutsche Bank's central office. In some cases, however, the sales involved high-level negotiations with other banks, frequently with the state-owned Reichs-Kredit-Gesellschaft, which could be carried out via only the Berlin offices.

A characteristic "aryanization" – so to say the basic type – looked like the following case: The Mafrasa Textilwerke AG (originally Marschal, Frank, Sachs Aktiengesellschaft) was a major Saxon textile producer, based in Chemnitz but with additional factories in Zschopau, Willichthal, and Magdeburg. It produced mostly underwear. In 1934, it had a share capital of RM 4 million and was owned by Frank, Sachs, and Bernstein. By 1937, there was mounting pressure to sell. Originally, the sale was to have been managed by the Reichs-Kredit-Gesellschaft, with whom one of the Mafrasa partners, Kurt Bernstein, had good business relations. Then the sale was handled by Deutsche Bank, which managed the transaction through a consortium with the Reichs-Kredit-Gesellschaft and the Sächsische Staatsbank, Dresden. The Reichs-Kredit-Gesellschaft and Deutsche Bank each placed about forty percent of the shares with their customers; the Saxon State Bank retained a holding of twenty percent. The shares were sold at nominal value, but their bourse price soon fell because of the need to undertake substantial write-offs, and in the period 1939–41, no dividend was paid. During the war, about half of the shares were bought by Awag AG, Berlin (also an "aryanized" business: previously it had been the Wertheim department store), which was controlled by a non-Jewish member of the Wertheim family, Ursula Lindgens.[104]

What was the responsibility of banks in such sales of shares? The Stuttgart branch of Deutsche Bank bought shares of Laupheimer Werkzeugfabrik at a price of seventy-five percent and then resold them at seventy-eight percent. In a postwar restitution case, Deutsche Bank argued unsuccessfully that this was not an "aryanization," because the owners had left Germany before the sale, and thus the company legally was owned not by "Jews" but by foreigners.[105]

A similar but much more complicated case was that of the largest German shoe producer, Salamander of Stuttgart-Kornwestheim.

Salamander (Kornwestheim) was the largest and most modern shoe producer in Germany in the 1920s. A family-owned enterprise, it was founded in 1891 by Jakob Sigle and Max Levi, as Jakob Sigle & Co. In 1905, the company joined Berlin shoe retailer Rudolf Moos and established the Salamander Schuh GmbH. The calculation underlying the firm's strategy was a bet on a developing mass market. Sigle explained a quite radical new philosophy: "We make our shoes not for the count and the countess but for their servants, since there are a lot more of them."[106] By the 1920s, Salamander was by far the largest German shoe producer and the only enterprise that could compete in scale and efficiency with the Czech Bata works. Salamander drew from Bata the lesson that it needed to expand its own retail network even further. At the end of the 1920s, the firm had a nominal capitalization of RM 14 million equally divided between two families, the Sigles and the Levis, but estimates of its worth ran to about two and a half times the nominal capitalization. In September 1929, Sigle wanted to sell some RM 2.5 million worth of stock to foreign owners and made contact with Deutsche Bank's Stuttgart branch, even though the firm's regular bank connection was with Commerzbank.[107] This transaction came to nothing, because of the stock-exchange crash of the following month. But the firm took over the Salamander-Vertriebsgesellschaft, and the capital was raised, through the issue of new shares, to a nominal RM 32 million.

Bata had been a major object of attacks by small and medium-size producers, and Salamander was also very vulnerable, simply because of the threat it posed to conventional shoemakers and retailers. Anti-Semitism, too, played a major part in the controversy about the role of Salamander. The Levis, but not the Sigle family, were Jewish. In 1933, Salamander supplied 2,000 sole distributors in Germany, of which around a quarter were owned by Jews.[108] The Nazi press refused to take advertisements by Salamander, and retail branches were boycotted in March 1933 and some closed by the SA. On March 30, the firms put an advertisement in major newspapers, declaring that the company "is under German management, uses only German materials, and provides German workers with wages and food."[109] On April 20, the firm gave RM 10,000 as part of the "Adolf Hitler Donation." But the firm's management rapidly came to the conclusion that such cosmetic adjustments to the new Germany would not be sufficient.

By 1934, a fifth of the Jewish distributors had been "aryanized."[110] But what about the company itself? In 1933, as part of a so-called bringing into line of the enterprise, the firm discussed a proposal to sell ten percent of the capital from the Levi portion. Originally, Dresdner Bank proposed to manage this transaction, at a commission of 0.5 percent of the entire capitalization of the firm. Deutsche Bank Stuttgart quickly suggested an alternative strategy and a potential purchaser, the Henkel concern. Deutsche Bank Stuttgart pointed out "that another means of foiling the attempts by competitors and other groups to deny the aryan character of the company was the fact that a major aryan prospective buyer with a resounding name was found and joined the supervisory board." The representative of the Levi interests allegedly supported this strategy suggested by Deutsche Bank.[111] Deutsche Bank Stuttgart now proposed a consortium for the issuing of Salamander shares, in which Deutsche Bank and Dresdner Bank would each take a forty percent share, and Commerzbank, twenty percent. The Berlin headquarters supported the branch's strategy with the following argument: "Like you we take the view that, given the relations we have with the enterprise, we cannot simply leave the field to Dresdner Bank." Berlin suggested either that Deutsche Bank should be the lead manager or that it should share the leadership with Dresdner.[112] Dresdner Bank was very upset by the appearance that Deutsche Bank was invading a deal that was already almost complete and its Stuttgart manager complained of a "hostile attitude towards my bank."[113] In the course of the negotiations, Deutsche Bank, and especially the manager of its Stuttgart branch, Hermann Köhler, repeatedly insisted that Deutsche Bank saw its function in the negotiations as the defense of the interests of the Levi family, who wanted to sell as little as possible of its stake in the enterprise.[114] The transaction eventually collapsed, not because of the bitter rivalry between the two banks but because the Reich Economics Ministry refused to give consent for the share offering.

In 1933, the owners opted for a much more limited transaction in the hope that this would establish the "aryan" character of their business. One million RM shares had been transferred, but between the two family groups, so that the Sigles now had RM 17 million, and the

Levis, RM 15 million (nominal) in shares in Salamander. The Sigles bought their shares from Bertha Rothschild, the widow of Isidor Rothschild, Max Levi's brother-in-law, who had joined the firm at the turn of the century. In 1935, immediately after the death of the now aged founder, Jakob Sigle, Köhler proposed a new strategy: to sell the Levis' shares without a general stock-exchange issue, or simply to transfer them to an "aryan asset-management company." Köhler thought that this might find official approval because "it would also suit the existing aversion to making business enterprises anonymous." He claimed that Hjalmar Schacht, who was now economics minister, supported this course. "Surely it would be possible surreptitiously (i.e. without attracting the attention of Commerzbank and Dresdner Bank) to trace the agency responsible there [at the Reich Economics Ministry] and explain our plan?"[115]

The necessary political consent must have occurred at the highest political level, because at the beginning of 1936, the Stuttgart branch reported on the sale of RM 5.4 million worth of stock and the transfer of voting rights of ten percent to the Sigles, so that the Levis controlled only twenty percent of the votes. "We are keen to advise you that, the rest of the sale having gone through, the Reich Chancellery [...] regards the condition formerly imposed as having been met even without introduction of the share capital."[116] The Levis continued to sell shares, as family members emigrated. By April 1937, a total of RM 7,192,000 had been sold, of which RM 3,609,000 had been sold through Deutsche Bank, RM 1,415,000 through Dresdner Bank, RM 700,000 through Commerzbank, and RM 1,208,000 by the Sigle family. The remaining RM 260,000 had been sold through a Stuttgart private banker, Joseph Frisch.[117] At that stage, therefore, the Levis controlled less than twenty percent of the firm, and Deutsche Bank Stuttgart assumed that few of the shares had stayed with the banks but that the ownership was broadly spread among the "serious investment clientele." One of the last major Levi owners, Paula Levi, then sold her shares through Delbrück Schickler & Co., with the mediation of Delbrück's rising young star, Hermann Abs. Delbrück bought RM 2,471,000 (nominal) in shares (mostly from Paula Levi), and Mendelssohn & Co. bought RM 450,000 (from Mathilde Weil). These transactions are difficult to reconstruct accurately. In the course of postwar restitution negotiations, however, it became clear that the banks had not simply acted as intermediaries but had instead initially bought Salamander shares on their own account.[118]

In these dealings, the interests of the various banks and of the owners of the Salamander shares repeatedly came into conflict with each other. Paula Levi's case is indicative in this regard. She had been told to approach Delbrück Schickler & Co. by Julius Oppenheimer and Ernst Ullmann of the big leather factory Adler & Oppenheimer (in whose history Hermann Abs later played quite a decisive part). Abs had already acquired considerable expertise in handling retail stores as a result of his involvement in the reconstruction of Karstadt. In November 1935, Abs approached Waldemar Strenger of the Neuerburg GmbH in Cologne and produced details on Salamander based on publicly available information. On November 29, Paula Levi told Abs that she had been unable to get more information about the firm, and Abs immediately wrote to Salamander's board president, Alex Haffner, telling him that the potential buyer was interested in buying a larger number of shares than merely those owned by Frau Levi. When Haffner replied, he expressed some surprise and declared that he had not encountered any difficulties in selling Salamander shares.[119] In fact, these shares were sold only in 1937, after Paula Levi had reached a decision to emigrate, and in handling this transaction, Delbrück Schickler outbid Deutsche Bank's Stuttgart branch.[120] In later restitution negotiations, Frau Levi claimed to have been urged to sell her shares "at the instigation of Salamander AG,"[121] which seems – at least for the 1935 negotiations – not to have been the case. At the time of the initial negotiations, Abs and Paula Levi were pressing, whereas the management of Salamander was hesitant.

In June 1938, after Schacht's departure from the Reich Economics Ministry, the ministry at last consented to a public issue of Salamander shares. Deutsche Bank at first claimed a "moral right" to lead the consortium, because it had handled the preponderant share of free (*freihändig*) sales in 1936 and 1937 that arose "in the wake of the 'bringing into line.'"[122] Most of these sales had been to leather and shoe firms in southwest Germany. In fact, the public share issue was managed by Dresdner Bank.

The restitution negotiations were especially complicated because of the number of banks involved in sales that took place at different times. The documentation of share transactions by Deutsche Bank Stuttgart was destroyed in wartime bombing.

The mixing of interests is also problematic in restitution negotiations. Initially, the firm representing the interests of Paula and Rolf Levi asked Abs to help them prepare their case:

> Recent press coverage and the friendly and obliging readiness of Dr. Schniewind to be the bearer of our letter enables us to ask for your friendly support in the following matter. Mrs. Paula and Mr. Rolf Levi of New York have instructed our company to assert their claims for restitution and reparation. We owe this mandate to Mr. Ernst Ullmann, formerly a member of the board of Adler & Oppenheimer A. G., Berlin. The claims of Mr. and Mrs. Levi relate among other things to an RM 2,380,000.– block of shares in Salamander A. G. As Mr. Ullmann informed us, these shares must have been sold at the instigation of Salamander A. G. The sale was conducted through the Delbrück Schickler & Co. Bank. The relevant negotiations were handled for that institution by yourself. From the particularly fair and understanding manner in which the negotiations were handled at that time, Mr. Ullmann feels able to infer that even today you will be prepared to assist with your information in realizing Mr. and Mrs. Levi's claims vis-à-vis Salamander A. G. May we stress that our company sees it as its responsibility, in the interests of both parties involved in the restitution proceedings, to do what it can to avoid contentious proceedings and achieve relative agreement among the parties in advance? We should like if possible to combine lodging the claim that Mr. and Mrs. Levi have instructed us to make in Bad Nauheim with submitting a corresponding settlement proposal. However, as a basis for such negotiations with Salamander A. G. we require information going into greater detail than Mr. Ullmann was able to provide us with. We should therefore be particularly obliged to you for an account of what happened at the time, as you recall it.[123]

Abs was also, from 1949, the deputy chairman of Salamander AG's supervisory board and, from 1956, its chairman. From 1952, he was spokesman of the managing board of the Süddeutsche Bank AG (SDB), one of the successors to Deutsche Bank.

In a postwar restitution settlement of the Stuttgart District Court (*Landgericht*; *Wiedergutmachungskammer* 1), owners of Salamander shares were obliged to hand over fifty percent of their shares to the Levi family. Shareholders and their interest representatives tried to claim that the shares had been bought in good faith and that it was impossible to tell which shares had been Jewish and which not.[124] What was the responsibility of the banks? The banks had usually bought shares in their own right and resold them ("as self-appointed commission agent"), although in some cases the banks may simply have sold them as a trustee for the Jewish owners. In 1953, the parties in the restitution case reached a settlement. Where Deutsche Bank had sold to the current owner, the SDB in consequence assumed an obligation to make a payment of twenty-five percent of the share value, so that the losses involved in restitution payments were shared equally between the new owners and the bank.

In the aftermath of this proposed settlement, which SDB urged its clients to accept, there developed substantial disputes about which institution had sold which shares to particular owners. Some owners tried to resist the settlement. The banks also tried to evade their commitments. In particular, in the case of the Henkel group, which had acquired a substantial number of Salamander shares (nominal value, RM 1,250,000), it was unclear whether the shares had been dealt by Deutsche Bank or by Mendelssohn. Deutsche Bank's former Swiss director Alfred Kurzmeyer, engaged in an ultimately futile attempt to demonstrate that it was Mendelssohn (for whom he had worked until 1938) rather than Deutsche Bank which was legally liable to Henkel for the Salamander restitution. In any event, Deutsche Bank agreed to make the twenty-five percent payment, but Mendelssohn & Co. (in liquidation) paid Henkel DM 100,000 as a contribution toward the Henkel restitution.

On October 6, 1954, a decision of the Nuremberg Court of Restitution Appeals set a precedent that confirmed the claims of the former Salamander owners, and a second settlement offered less favorable terms to those current owners who had not accepted the first settlement. In all, the former Stuttgart branch of Deutsche Bank paid DM 1,963,000 in restitution payments.[125] Initially, the director of the Stuttgart branch had believed that SDB would have to accept responsibility for around eighty percent of the bank's financing of the settlement, but he started his discussions with the other banks at a figure of sixty percent and allowed himself to be talked up to sixty-five percent. Claims to shares, including some that had been transferred to the

Soviet zone in eastern Germany, were sold by the beneficiaries to a trustee firm owned by the banks for DM 1,200,000.

The negotiations were finally concluded only in September 1957. The bank's contribution, however, cost the bank nothing in that it was repaid with public funds. When Deutsche Bank's Stuttgart manager informed Abs by telephone, Abs noted: "Bravo!"[126] Only with the conclusion of this settlement were Salamander shares once more tradable on the stock exchange. The postwar restitution process quite clearly recognized the responsibility of banks for their part in the prewar transfer of Jewish property.

Adler & Oppenheimer (Norddeutsche Lederwerke Aktiengesellschaft Berlin)

The largest and most complicated industrial "aryanization" conducted directly by Deutsche Bank, and managed directly from Berlin with the involvement of managing-board members over years, was Norddeutsche Lederwerke AG (Berlin), which was originally called Adler & Oppenheimer (A&O) As with Mendelssohn and Hirschland, the legal expropriation of the owners required the participation of a bank with a wide range of foreign contacts and experience. As with the transfer of the Jewish-owned banks, Deutsche Bank was in a strange semicompetitive but also semicooperative relationship with a state-owned bank: in this case, as with Mendelssohn, the Reichs-Kredit-Gesellschaft.

When East German historian Eberhard Czichon used this case to attack Hermann Abs,[127] Abs claimed that he had helped the original owners and delayed the "aryanization." His argument was anecdotally supported by a member of the Adler family: Dr. Hans Adler recalled in 1971 that Abs had told a member of the NSDAP during the "aryanization" negotiations: "Adler (Eagle) is a proud old bird and Oppenheimer is what we call a 'good wine,' so what do you want to 'aryanize' about the firm?"[128] In fact, Abs was trying hard to find suitable purchasers, but the case was complicated by the number of interests and competing government and party agencies trying to shape the outcome.

A&O was founded in Strasbourg in 1872, became a joint stock company in 1900, and moved from Alsace to Berlin in 1920. By the 1920s, it had become one of Germany's largest leather producers. It had a nominal capital in 1937 of RM 18 million and had factories in Neustadt (Mecklenburg) and Neumünster (Holstein). Its business benefited from the recovery of the 1930s, but after 1936 its foreign sales, which had been an important element in the firm's traditional repertoire, fell off very sharply.

Most of the shares were held by the original Adler and Oppenheimer families via a Dutch intermediary, N. V. Amsterdamsche Leder Maatschappij (often called Almy), Amsterdam, that was founded in 1919, with a modest capitalization of HFl 50,000, to facilitate the import of raw materials.

Abs became chairman of the supervisory board in August 1938. A few weeks before, he had been approached by a newly appointed managing-board member of A&O, Ernst Steinbeck, who stated that he would ask the Dutch shareholders of his company "whether and on what conditions sale and repatriation (not to say aryanization) are possible."[129] Steinbeck had been placed in the company as a result of German pressure to ensure its Germanization, which of course also meant "aryanization." Deutsche Bank, as the lead manager of a syndicate which also included the Reichs-Kredit-Gesellschaft, Delbrück Schickler & Co., and Pferdmenges & Co.,[130] started to buy up shares in A&O at a price of 106 percent of the nominal value from Jewish customers, including many who had emigrated. Between September 1938 and May 1939, a total of RM 617,000 was bought in this way. It is quite surprising that these transactions continued even after the outbreak of war in September 1939 across enemy lines in the "phony war."[131] In 1940, Deutsche Bank bought another RM 9,528,000 in shares belonging to the Adler and Oppenheimer families.

There was a great deal of interest in the future of A&O. The party and especially its representatives in the Reich Economics Ministry who saw their mission as protecting the interests of small and medium-size business (*Mittelstand*) were hostile to the idea that a major business might form the basis for an even larger concentration of economic power, especially in what had been a classically *Mittelstand* branch of industry. Some suggested that the concern should be taken over by the DAF. A&O was a major military supplier, and this status allowed the firm to import the leather required for its business. In the struggle that Deutsche Bank conducted against party influence, the military played the part of a helpful ally, as the command was interested above all in securing a continued reliable supply of leather.[132]

Initially, a major part of Abs's negotiations on the transfer of A&O into non-Jewish hands was conducted abroad, during repeated business trips. Erwin Schuller wrote from London to Abs that the Werhahn family[131] was interested in acquiring A&O.[134]

But there were also many large German businesses interested in acquiring the firm. The big south-German leather and shoe producer Richard Freudenberg was blocked by the Reich Economics Ministry, which wanted to prevent oligopolization in the leather industry. Baron Cornelius Freiherr Heyl zu Herrnstein of Cornelius Heyl AG Worms (a large leather producer with a capitalization of RM 12 million) wanted to acquire a minority participation to stop the DAF from acquiring the business.[135] The Reich Economics Ministry blocked Heyl.[136] In 1940, a plan by the Margarine-Union to undertake the acquisition fell through.

At first, the most promising customer was a large Dutch multinational. At the beginning of 1939, Unilever proposed to take between twenty-five and forty percent of the capital of A&O, on condition that Deutsche Bank would also participate and thus hold a majority of the shares together with Unilever.[137] At some time in the future, presumably when political conditions in Germany changed, Unilever would be able easily to acquire a clear controlling majority. In these negotiations, Unilever was represented by one of the Reichsbank directors, Karl Blessing (the future Bundesbank president), who had just been dismissed by Hitler and who had taken a position on the managing board of the German branch of Unilever. By July 1939, Abs had reached an agreement with Hendriks and Rykens, the Dutch representatives of Unilever, which envisaged a twelve percent participation by Deutsche Bank and an overall commission of three percent for the bank.[138] He proposed to use blocked marks from the German chemical and pharmaceutical company Schering in order to be able to make the payment in foreign exchange. This part of the purchase became increasingly complicated and problematic. But when Abs set out his plan, and the alternatives for German ownership, in a discussion at the Reich Economics Ministry, government officials straightforwardly rejected the plan and explained that they would not undertake "definitive recognition of the enterprise as a German and aryan operation."[139] Abs complained that it was almost impossible to find alternatives: he "described it as very hard to find potential buyers as long as the shares remained in Dutch hands and acquisition of them uncertain."[140] From the official standpoint, however, it was crucial to have such a major firm in exclusively German control, but at the same time not in the hands of another major corporation. The Reich Economics Ministry thus suggested that Deutsche Bank should form a consortium to take over the shares and then gradually place them on the market.

Obviously the outbreak of war put a final end to any of the foreign discussions about a sale. But through 1940, there remained a continuous flow of visitors and suggestions to Abs and Deutsche Bank with proposals about the future of A&O. One leather specialist wanted to pull in the Quandt family to finance the transaction.[141] The Stuttgart branch of Deutsche Bank reported that the big shoe producer Salamander AG wanted to buy the company.[142]

In May 1940, the Reich Economics Ministry instructed Abs to drop the name A&O and manage the company as "Norddeutsche Lederwerke."[143] The German invasion of the Netherlands and the integration of the country in the German New Order solved the problem of acquiring foreign exchange to buy out the Dutch interests. On May 3, Deutsche Bank manager Gerhard Elkmann visited the Reich Economics Ministry to speak with the official responsible in the Jewish Affairs Department, Assessor Möhrke. He wrote in his minutes: "The Jewish Affairs Department is also in agreement that we should effect the aryanization in Holland. However, no prior written authorization from the Jewish Affairs Department is necessary for this. All that is required is for us to have been given oral consent." Elkmann explained that the bank was in a hurry to finish the business and had become exasperated with the bureaucratic complexities of the transfer ("we are very keen to speed things up"). The Reich Economics Ministry then explained that it would help if another part of the German bureaucracy became involved and if the bank were to liaise with the NSDAP's "Foreign Organization." Möhrke promised a post facto written permission to acquire RM 9,528,000 in shares "in line with the Jewish Ordinance." For the bank, this permission was crucial, because "the decision itself also contains the observation that we made no aryanization profits."[144] Meanwhile, Abs continued to buy up any blocks of A&O shares that he could find.[145]

But transferring the shares proved to be much more difficult than the German bankers had initially thought. In October 1940, a meeting at the Reich Economics Ministry took place to negotiate the "aryanization" of the foreign shares of the Adler and Oppenheimer families. Some shares had been used as a security for a bank loan from the Amsterdamsche Bank and had been deposited in the United States (these were worth about HFl 1.5 million – almost RM 2 million). Of those shares held by family members, nine percent belonged to people who were by then resident in Great Britain, and these shares could be regarded under German law as "enemy property." But thirty percent belonged to family members in France, where obviously no similar argument could be made after the armistice. The Dutch representatives of Almy proposed a plan to transfer the family shares to Almy, which would then pay the purchase price from the profits of the company. Abs proposed an alternative solution: that assets and inventories in the United States could be used to make the payments, even though they had been blocked by both U.S. Treasury orders and instructions of the Netherlands government in exile in London.

When the Reich Economics Ministry meeting continued, it was joined not only by a representative of the Dutch Affairs Department (Holland-Referat) but also by Assessor Möhrke of the Jewish Affairs Department.[146] The owners were in fact in quite a strong position, because neither the German occupation authorities nor Deutsche Bank had access to the shares of Almy.

Clemens Oppenheimer, negotiating for the family from a base in Ascona (Switzerland), stated as conditions for a transfer of the shares:

1. That $960,000 of Almy assets in the United States should be released
2. That a further $1,000,000 should be transferred to the United States
3. That the family members living in Europe should be given permission to travel to Portugal
4. That HFl 100,000 should be placed in a trustee account in Amsterdam for Almy employees who might be dismissed.[147]

Oppenheimer believed that the Reich Economics Ministry had originally proposed a sum of $900,000.[148] His suggestion thus represented a slight increase. But it was unclear how a German buyer could find the dollars required in this transaction.

At this point, the occupation authorities tried to put further pressure on the Adler and Oppenheimer families through one of the most familiar tricks of the 1930s: claims for vast tax arrears. In early 1941, the firm faced RM 4.3 million in tax payments as a result of the calculation of the profit that they had taken on the devaluation of the Dutch guilder in 1937. Abs noted: "Impossible to effect placement now."[149] In consequence, the amount of foreign exchange that Deutsche Bank was willing to transfer decreased.

Deutsche Bank offered to raise the dollar amount, in return for the transfer of about RM 6 million of assets (the nominal RM 4 million in Nordleder shares), but suggested that it would transfer only $600,000 rather than the $1,000,000 requested. This amount was then transferred into dollars via Switzerland, using a convoluted path to mask the nature of the transaction. Almy had debts to the Schweizerischer Bankverein, which would be paid from a RM 10 million credit that Almy had given to Schering. So that Schering could make the payment, Abs suggested that Schering acquire Swiss commercial papers.[150] But a more obvious way to disguise the transfer was as a transfer of goods from Schering to Ciba, Basel. An alternative would be to deliver leather from the Nuremberg stocks of the Swiss company Bally.[151] The Reich Economics Ministry issued Schering with a declaration intended to mislead the Swiss authorities about the nature of the transaction. The text gives an indication of the complications of masking financial transactions as commercial transactions. The deal was supposed to look simply like a payment for deliveries of a chemical (Oestron):

> For the purposes of presentation to the Swiss clearing house, I confirm with reference to my communications of 8 August, 19 September, and 16 November 1939 and 24 January 1940 and to the permits granted by the Berlin Revenue Chairman (Foreign-Exchange Department) on 29 August, 12 September, 28 September, and 29 November 1939 and 9 February 1940 that I agree to the terms of the loan as they arise from your agreement of 5 December 1939 with Amsterdamsche Leder Mij. and from your

letter of 5 December 1939 to the Chemische Industrie company in Basel
re. purchase of oestron."[152]

The transaction was then further held up because Ciba demanded
freely convertible francs, not *Verrechnungsfranken* (francs in the
German-Swiss clearing), and this required an additional German
export to Switzerland.[153] Eventually, CHF 1,250,000 was paid to the
family (the equivalent of $218,625).

The German authorities demanded proof that three quarters of the
shares were in Aryan ownership, to ensure that the firm was an Aryan
firm under the definitions of 1938. A third share package, worth
RM 3,239,000, was consequently sold to Deutsche Bank with the permission of the Reich Economics Ministry in the fall of 1940.[154] By the
end of 1940, Deutsche Bank had thus acquired three quarters of the
total capital of the company RM 18 million).[155]

As a result of these transactions, Norddeutsche Lederwerke (the
German company) acquired RM 11.9 million in assets, including the
RM 4 million (nominal) in shares of Nordleder (now valued at RM 6
million) and a leather factory in Oisterwijk. The transaction
involved a substantial amount of patience and ingenuity at Deutsche
Bank. The bank was rewarded with a commission. In drawing up and
managing the transaction, it originally claimed a 1.5 percent commission, but in the document this figure has been crossed out and
(with a date of July 3, 1943) the amount RM 120,000 substituted.[156]

But there was also a more substantial gain for the bank derived from
the issuing of Nordleder shares. The Reich Economics Ministry now
stipulated that the shares should be distributed widely, to mop up liquidity and offer the investing public something other than war loans and
treasury bills. Most importantly, it was in line with the principle of preventing the establishment of new trusts or concerns. No more than
RM 100,000 (nominal) in shares should be sold to any individual purchaser, and anyone who wished to buy more than RM 50,000 worth
needed the consent of the Reich Economics Ministry.

Some of those who had originally lined up to buy A&O were con-
soled with other purchases, including those in occupied eastern
Europe. Thus, Deutsche Bank suggested to August Neuerburg buying
shares, worth RM 5 million to 6 million, of the formerly Jewish-owned
firm I. K. Poznanski (a majority of whose shares had been owned since

1930 by the Banca Commerciale Italiana) in Łódź, now renamed Litzmannstadt.[157]

Deutsche Bank disliked the Reich Economics Ministry's concept for distributing shares as widely as possible. It saw it as a blocking effort by the Reichs-Kredit-Gesellschaft, and Hermann Abs was prepared to make concessions such as offering an "aryanization quota" and putting a Reichs-Kredit-Gesellschaft banker on the supervisory board of Nordleder.[158] It instructed its branches not to engage in a wide sales effort and not to leave prospectuses for the issue on its counters. The bank also contacted major corporate as well as individual clients (Thyssen, the Neuerburgs, and Henkel & Cie.) The file note indicates that they should be approached by Deutsche Bank's peripatetic and influential Swiss director, Alfred Kurzmeyer, "to prevent Reichs-Kredit from beating us to it."[159] The public subscription was managed by an issuing syndicate in which Deutsche Bank had a controlling 62 percent, with a smaller participation of the Reichs-Kredit-Gesellschaft (25 percent), Pferdmenges (8 percent), and Delbrück Schickler & Co. (5 percent). The subscription opened on July 18, 1941, when 170 customers of the bank bid for a total of RM 1,288,00 in shares at an issue price of 140 percent. (Abs had originally suggested 130 in January 1941.)[160] But the bank was allowed to allocate only RM 322,000 so that the bids needed to be scaled down to 23 percent, much to the irritation of the bank's customers.[161]

Thus the second element of profit from the Nordleder transaction was the difference in price between the purchase of shares (106 in Germany) and the issue price of 140. In addition, there was another commission arising from the bank's management of the issuing consortium.

After the sale had been managed, Deutsche Bank then set about reducing the capital of the firm as the firm's sales (which lay between RM 25 million and RM 30 million annually in the first four years of the war) looked disappointingly small in relation to the capitalization at RM 18 million.[162]

This was a large transaction that had initially, in 1938, looked relatively simple. The first major difficulty, which postponed the sale, lay in getting government consent, because the Reich Economic Ministry resolutely blocked the involvement of either foreign or large German corporations. Second because the owners held their shares through a Dutch corporation, they were in a powerful bargaining position, quite distinct from the overwhelming majority of "aryaniza-tion" sales.

The occupation of the Netherlands gave the bank a new opportunity to press ahead with the transaction. To do this, it needed to negotiate with more layers of German bureaucracy: with the occupation regime of the Netherlands, with the NSDAP "Foreign Organization," and also presumably (at least indirectly) with the SS over emigration permits. On May 10, 1940, most of the members of the family were already in the United States, South America, Great Britain, or Switzerland, but Franz Ferdinand Oppenheimer was still in the Netherlands, in Scheveningen, and Alfred Adler and Anna Luise Adler were in Graulhet, France.[163] In essence, the bank was taking part in what was also a ransom operation, in which lives were to be exchanged for the consent to a financial transaction.

The general conditions for such a transaction were the result of gov-ernment legislation and policy. But at specific moments, the bank forced the pace to wrap up a complex and convoluted transaction – one which was, however, in the end quite profitable for Deutsche Bank.

The ownership of Nordleder was restituted under the postwar Allied laws. On October 14, 1947, the major German newspapers carried an advertisement of the N. V. Amsterdamsche Leder Maatschappij, asking shareholders of Adler & Oppenheimer AG (i.e., Norddeutsche Lederwerke AG) to report their shares to the Allied authorities because they fell under the terms of U. S. Law No. 59. The immediate reaction by Franz Heinrich Ulrich (who had been Abs's assistant in the wartime management of the transaction), and indeed of Deutsche Bank's postwar central management (*Führungsstab*), was to contest this claim, because – they said – the agreement for the sale in 1942 had been con-cluded with a trustee for the Dutch firm who had been installed by the German military occupation authority. Ulrich pointed out that "it may be a question of the shares of a foreign enterprise that (if the company's head office was the deciding factor) could never be demanded back." In a memorandum of December 1948, Deutsche Bank argued:

> The negotiations were invariably friendly. Deutsche Bank paid an appro-priate price. Moreover, it helped to make it possible for a particularly favorable percentage of the proceeds for the large shareholdings of RM 9,528,000 (nominal) to be transferred. After completion of the sales, the former shareholder families acknowledged verbally and in writing the fair implementation and assistance provided by Deutsche Bank [...].[164]

One Deutsche Bank board member, however, followed a different line of reasoning. Erich Bechtolf[165] pleaded vigorously for an out-of-court settlement and suggested that "a capital reduction followed by an increase does not require any calling-in of shares."[166]

This provided the basis of an eventual settlement with Relda Trading Co. Inc. of New York, representing the Adler and Oppenheimer families. Prior to the agreement, the capital of Nordleder was reduced by 10:3. The capital was then raised by 2,001,200 ordinary shares and 1,000,600 nonvoting preference shares. Relda acquired 1,424,200 voting shares and 103,000 preference shares. Deutsche Bank transferred RM 986,000 (DM 295,800) in Norddeutsche Leder shares to the Dutch company Almy. In addition, Norddeutsche Leder paid Almy DM 550,000 and paid DM 1,200,00 to Relda.[167] The result of these arrangements was to give the families a controlling stake in Nordleder. By this agreement, Deutsche Bank avoided a court case over restitution.[168]

In financial terms, A&O was the "aryanization" transaction that brought the greatest return to Deutsche Bank. It was also by far the most complicated, as a transaction that took an exceptionally long time because of the intervention of state and party authorities in attempting to stop large (and especially large foreign) corporations acquiring a controlling interest. On the other hand, because the shares were foreign-domiciled, there were clear limits on the extent to which the company was vulnerable to German official bullying before the occupation of the Netherlands. As a result of these complications, the transaction had not been completed before the outbreak of the European war in September 1939. The Germanization of A&O then became part of the brutal German occupation policy in the Netherlands. Deutsche Bank had become involved because of the complex international entanglements of the case. But this was also a very personal affair, in which the range of Hermann Abs's contacts could play a vital part.

Personal Contacts of Deutsche Bank's Managing Board: Hermann Josef Abs

In some of the most important and problematic cases of "aryanization," the involvement of Deutsche Bank occurred on a very personal basis, with blurred lines between personal and business relations, and depending on trust or confidence in particular executives. Two of the most interesting examples again involve Hermann Josef Abs. The first is Deutsche Bank's involvement with the German portion of the Petschek concern, a vast empire of coal (primarily lignite) fields controlled (since the death of the founder, Ignaz Petschek, in 1934) by four German-Czech brothers, Ernst, Wilhelm, Karl and Frank Petschek. The Petscheks' most important property in Germany lay in Upper Silesia and was administered by a trust company, the Deutsche Kohlenhandel GmbH. The family resisted attempts to "aryanize" its assets with the utmost vigor, possible only because of Czech nationality. At the beginning of 1939, Karl Petschek apparently told German officials in a meeting at the Reich Economics Ministry: "If it's war you want, gentlemen, I am ready." Hermann Göring appointed a senior official, Helmuth Wohlthat, as a special commissary (*Sonderbeauftragter*) with the task of "aryanizing" the works. The major weapon of the German authorities was the use of allegations of non-payment of German taxes.[169] The Petschek assets attracted Germany's biggest and most powerful mining firms: Wintershall, Salzdetfurth, Mitteldeutsche Stahlwerke, Bubiag (Braunkohlen- und Brikett-Industrie AG), Henckel von Donnersmarck-Beuthen, Gräflich Schaffgott' sche Werke, Deutsche Erdöl-AG, IG Farben, and above all the Flick group all approached the trustee. A Flick manager, Otto Steinbrinck, explained in late 1937 that "expansion of its coal base was a question of survival, which is why it wanted at all costs to participate in the liquidation of the Petschek holdings."[170] The lignite fields were eventually sold mostly to Flick as part of an exchange of property in which Flick would sell hard coal resources to the Reichswerke "Hermann Göring" (RHG).[171]

But there was also a much smaller Petschek field in western Germany. In this case, there appears to have been no rush of interested companies. Of the ordinary shares of the Petschek-owned Hubertus AG, 73.6 percent were owned by Helimont AG Glarus and Deutsche Industrie AG, which formed part of an extensive industrial empire of the Czech part of the Petschek dynasty. Minority participations included 16.2 percent held by the Abs family of Bonn: Justizrat Josef Abs, and his sons Clemens Abs and Hermann J. Abs (who in 1938 had joined the managing board of Deutsche Bank: he had been on the supervisory board of Hubertus since 1925). Abs senior had been associated with the company since its founding in 1905.

At the beginning of 1938, Ernst Petschek talked with Hermann Abs about "aryanization trends." Abs noted simply: "D.B. position."[172] In June 1938, Ernst and Wilhelm Petschek resigned from the supervisory board of the Hubertus AG, and Josef Abs became chairman. The "aryanization" started with an accusation from the tax authorities (Oberfinanzpräsident Hanover) that Hubertus AG had organized a flight of RM 70 million. In October 1938, the firm was obliged to present a complete list of accounts, liabilities, and assets held abroad.[173] A decree of the Reich Economics Ministry in January 1939, based on the Law on Investment of Jewish Property of December 3, 1938,[174] then installed a trustee, Karl Leising of Preussische Bergwerks- und Hütten-AG, and obliged the Petschek group to sell Hubertus by the end of February. Leising, who was placed in charge of all the Petschek coal property in Germany, initially pushed aggressively for a "voluntary aryanization" and threatened to take over the properties himself.[175] The ministry explained that "it does not want an aryanization but a transfer of the commercial operation to aryan ownership. Plans aimed at an aryanization of the company are therefore out of the question, should the Reich Economics Ministry alter its position." When nothing happened, Leising was dismissed and replaced by a Berlin lawyer, Wolfgang Zarnack.

Hermann Abs had originally proposed that the best solution would be to turn the productive facilities of the firm into a new joint-stock company owned by the "aryan shareholders." He considered that a price of RM 4 million would be appropriate: The tax returns valued the business at RM 4.7 million, but this included shares of the Union Rheinische Braunkohlen Kraftstoff AG at par value, and these shares would yield a dividend only in some years' time.[176] Where would the money come from? The Abs family could not pay this kind of price and consequently devised a scheme whereby the price would be covered through share purchases on behalf of the "old" Hubertus AG, which would then be subject to liquidation as a Jewish firm.

This transaction was managed by Deutsche Bank, which sold Hubertus AG in December 1939 to the newly founded Erft-Bergbau AG (with a capitalization of RM 3 million) for the not unreasonable sum of RM 5,750,000. Half the Erft shares were held by the Abs fam-

101

ily. The other half were bought by a company established by the owners of the neighboring mines, Roddergrube, Gewerkschaft Beiselgrube, Rheinische Aktiengesellschaft für Braunkohlenbergbau, and Brikettfabrikation, as well as the banks H. Daelen & Co. and Bankhaus Delbrück von der Heydt. The overall price represented a valuation of Hubertus shares at 205 based on the current stock-market quotation (the average bourse notation for the period July 1938 to March 1939 had been 203.30). For a company whose net profit in 1937 had been RM 327,000, the stock-exchange valuation seems appropriate.[177] This transaction was legally problematic, because the share titles of the Hubertus AG (RM 2,750,000 in ordinary shares and RM 300,000 in preference shares) were held outside Germany – at first in Switzerland – by the Petscheks. How much did the Petschek family know about the Abs family plans? Hermann Abs went to Switzerland shortly after the outbreak of the war and on September 19, 1939, spoke with Ernst Petschek, the oldest of the brothers, in Zürich. But there is no reliable account of what was said. In any case, the Petscheks saw no reason why they should send their share titles to Germany.

In 1950, a West German court established that this sum undervalued Hubertus by some RM 840,000. There is no doubt that throughout the sale, and especially in the restitution process, the Petscheks had confidence in the character and trustworthiness of Abs, their former junior partner, and that Abs assisted after 1945 in the restoration of their position. The postwar story was not a matter simply of goodwill: Abs was legally obliged to cooperate in the process of restitution. He also saw a series of opportunities in restitution.

After the war, Ernst Petschek began a correspondence with the wartime manager of the Erft AG, Hans Kersting. In his initial letter, he explained:

> My brother and I also remain in good health and have meanwhile become American citizens. As you are probably aware, at the time the liquidation of Hubertus was undertaken against the wishes of the majority shares represented by Dr. Hänggi [Paul Hänggi was a client of Schweizerische Creditanstalt and held shares of Hubertus with a nominal value of RM 2.4 million[178]] and myself. Those shares remain safely in our possession. Neither against the company nor against individual members of manage-

ment do I harbor any feelings of hostility, particularly since I have no idea what actually happened. Rather, I cherish the hope that, given goodwill, a way will be found of settling the outstanding questions in the interests of Hubertus and all interested parties in a sensible fashion.[179]

Hermann Abs, who obtained Petschek's address from Kersting, wrote a rather vague account of the wartime transactions:

I greatly regret that my father [who had died in May 1943] could no longer conduct in person the negotiations with yourself that he had always had in mind. The liquidation of Hubertus was pushed through by the then government against the will of the management and all the partners. The setting-up of the rescue company to run actual trading operations was done in the interests of the firm [...] and of the partners. However, in the nature of things it was not possible to take your interests into account directly; instead, they were protected by the loyalty of the partners [...]. The fact that, in consequence, the partners in the rescue company had to take a huge gamble, acting as they did on their own account and at their own risk, yet had to leave open the question of their interests being considered and taken into account for some future settlement – that was unavoidable.[180]

The relationship between Abs and the Petscheks soon became warm and trusting, and Ernst Petschek sent Abs CARE packages as a goodwill gesture; Abs replied with a copy of an article on restitution law. In December 1948, Abs and his brother Clemens Abs resuscitated the Hubertus AG, and in February 1949 three Petschek brothers, Ernst, Charles, and Wilhelm signed, in Westchester County, New York, a power of attorney to Abs in regard to the management of their Hubertus shares. It might be thought that Abs's position was somewhat peculiar, in that he now represented the Petscheks, as well as his own interests. But the financial settlement, by which the Abs family bought the restitution claims of the Petscheks (and thus secured legal possession of the Hubertus AG shares), was laid down by a court. In 1955, the Abs family sold its shares in the Erft AG to the lignite consortium Verges.

Abs continued to work closely with the Petscheks. He had helped them obtain a restitution settlement against the state holding company Viag in 1953 and 1954, and in 1956 he received a general power of attorney in restitution negotiations, now chiefly against the West

German state in regard to the much more extensive Petschek properties that had been taken into the Reichswerke "Hermann Göring" (now renamed as Salzgitter). In May 1963, the Berlin Restitution Chamber concluded a settlement of the claims of the Petschek heirs against Salzgitter. In 1970, the same court awarded the Petscheks DM 9,500,000 in settlement of their RM 105,965,000 in Reich treasury certificates. The story does not necessarily end with this agreement, which concerned only the Petschek property on the then territory of the Federal Republic. After the negotiations between Salzgitter and Abs, Salzgitter noted: "The purchase price does not make up for the opportunities based on the now lost property in the East." Abs reported to Charles Petschek that he had spoken with Dr. Weimar of Salzgitter about the need for additional security: "What is to happen if with the reunification of the Federal and Democratic Republics the brown-coal companies are to be compensated in respect of confiscated assets? (Considering Bonn's policy towards the East [*Ostpolitik*], the chances do not look entirely positive, but Dr. Weimar is asking for an agreement about the 'emperor's beard.')"[181] In short, a new Germany – or the end of the Cold War – would bring a new set of legal problems and issues in relation to indemnification for the German past.

In return, William Petschek also helped Abs in the Stuttgart case against GDR historian Eberhard Czichon by providing a sworn statement that the Hubertus manager, Ewald Droop, who in 1939 had tried to block the Abs family plans, was not representing the interests of the Petscheks. There was thus no evidence that Abs had in any way neglected the Petscheks' interest in 1939 or subsequently, even though he had barely consulted the family in devising his reorganization of Hubertus.[182]

Postwar restitution history does not provide any evidence that the Petschek family mistrusted Abs. On the contrary, Abs helped them to obtain large settlements in the cases that were more important, and more difficult, than that of the Hubertus company. (It is striking that restitution claims against the German state were much harder to negotiate than claims against German companies or individuals.) But that history does show the peculiar, multifaceted character of Abs's activities, in which he continued to play several – not always coinciding – positions.

S. Fischer and Peter Suhrkamp

Samuel Fischer founded S. Fischer Verlag in 1886. As the publisher of Gerhart Hauptmann, Hugo von Hofmannsthal, Alfred Döblin, and Thomas Mann, he played a crucial role in the development of modern German literature. After his death in October 1934, several interested parties immediately tried to buy the house. Would-be purchasers included the Nazi art publisher from Munich, Hugo Bruckmann, whose wife had been an influential patron of Hitler in the 1920s, and book-seller Koehler-Volkmann from Leipzig. The Propaganda Ministry started to press for a sale of the firm. In the end, Fischer's daughter and son-in-law, Gottfried Bermann Fischer, decided to hand the business over to Peter Suhrkamp, a veteran of the First World War and since 1932 the editor of a Fischer journal, *Neue Rundschau,* and a man with a cast-iron reputation for integrity.[183] Suhrkamp required the financial assistance of Hermann Abs, then a young banker at Delbrück Schickler & Co. who came to the attention of the Fischer family through its attorney Fritz Oppenheimer. In December 1936, Abs put together a consortium of tobacco producer Philipp Reemtsma, Christoph Ratjen, and his own brother Clemens Abs, with participations of RM 100,000, RM 75,000, and RM 100,000, respectively. The new partners would buy the publishing house from Fischer's widow for a sum of RM 200,000, and operate as S. Fischer Verlag KG. At the same time, Fischer's son-in-law, Gottfried Bermann Fischer, prepared for émigré publishing by transferring the rights of his authors to a Swiss holding company. (Switzerland eventually denied him a residence permit, without which the new company could not operate on grounds of the danger of "foreign infiltration" [*Überfremdung*].)[184]

The Propaganda Ministry of Joseph Goebbels distrusted Suhrkamp and saw him as a "Kohlhaas" personality. (Michael Kohlhaas was Heinrich Kleist's intransigently rebellious fighter for justice.) But Suhrkamp was far from being intransigent. He had a wide range of contacts – some anti-Nazi such as Kiel banker Wilhelm Ahlmann (who killed himself in December 1944 to escape the Gestapo); but some decidedly Nazi, such as dramatist Hans Rehberg, novelist Felix Lützkendorf, and sculptor Arno Breker. He was arrested in April 1944 after being denounced by a Gestapo spy. On May 2, Wilhelm Ahlmann called Abs and asked to speak about "a matter concerning the

Suhrkamp publishing house." Ahlmann visited Abs on June 1 and explained the circumstances of Suhrkamp's arrest:

> Matter obscure to him too, seems to have had a visitor from Switzerland [the Gestapo spy] and listened to non-communicable conversation. Nothing to do with the publishing house, apparently. There correspondence between S. and Swiss authors, e.g. Hermann Hesse and others, has been seized. S. has every possible privilege [he worked in the prison library] so no serious case, presumably.[185]

Suhrkamp later attributed his rescue to the intervention of Breker.

The firm was renamed at the beginning of 1942, under pressure from the Propaganda Ministry, as Suhrkamp-Verlag, vorm. S. Fischer (the suffix later had to be abandoned).

Suhrkamp later testified to Abs's assistance: "On his initiative this limited partnership [*Kommanditgesellschaft*] quite clearly became an enterprise for the independence of the old-established publishing house. Mr. Abs proved that repeatedly in his attitude from 1937 to 1945 and all along the line."[186] This sort of independence was one, however, bought by a compromise that quite precisely mirrored Abs's own ambivalent relationship with the regime.

Abs's note cards demonstrate the intensity of his involvement in the Suhrkamp story. When the business receded sharply as a consequence of the outbreak of the war, Abs advised Suhrkamp to take an additional RM 50,000 in bank credits. By 1941, the business was doing well: Turnover doubled compared with the previous year. In April 1942, Abs noted the demand of the "Reich Literary Chamber" for a change of name for the firm by the end of April. He also recorded how Suhrkamp secured a paper allocation for the complete edition of Hauptmann's works (as well as reprints of Novalis, August Wilhelm von Schlegel, and Theodor Fontane) by agreeing to print twenty-five volumes for the Wehrmacht in an edition of 5,000 to 10,000 each. At the same time as Suhrkamp was printing – and negotiating with Dutch firms for the supply of paper – 900 "publishing houses have received notification that they will be allocated no further paper." In March 1943, Abs received confidential information that the firm was to be closed "under wartime legislation." He noted on his cards: "Lützkendorf N. S. author helping." The firm was not closed.

Felix Lützkendorf (born in 1906) was a playwright, the son of an officer killed in the First World War. At the end of the Weimar Republic, he had been a member of a socialist youth organization. His first experiment with novel writing, an epistolary account of the love of an inexperienced young officer for a skeptical and slightly older woman, had been published by Fischer in 1938 (*Märzwind: Die Aufzeichnungen des Leutnants Manfred Kampen und ein Nachbericht* [March Wind: The Diaries of Lieutenant Manfred Kampen, with an Afterword]). It is a sentimental work, but it illuminates quite sensitively the concepts of a softer "New Man" – envious of, but lacking the experience of, the trenches – and an assertive and self-confident "New Woman." It is apolitical, says nothing about *Volk* or race, and is in all quite far removed from being Nazi propaganda. But in 1940 Lützkendorf published, also with Fischer, an account of his experiences in occupied Poland, where he had gone to observe the resettlement of Volga and Volhynia Germans. This book is permeated with Nazi racist philosophy and includes accounts of the newly created ghettoes that exude a terrifying inhumanity. Some of the account is pseudoscientific: about Łódź, for instance, he wrote: "In addition the extensive ghetto, which is nevertheless overcrowded, most of the Jews here are proletarianized." In Warsaw, the tone was more hostile: "Presumptuous glances, overdressed women, fat Oriental 'mammas,' their chubby fingers laden with gold rings, swollen-lipped men with black, fur-lined greatcoats and hard hats, very stylish they are too. And on top of everything that screeching Yiddish in which they call out to and greet one another and in which one is repeatedly dismayed to discover sadly ill-treated German words." In Lublin, he blamed the Polish state for the "disaster," using the favored Nazi term *Seuchenherd* (meaning "hotbed of an epidemic") and hinting at miscegenation. "The Polish government has never bothered about them. Hotbed of an epidemic that flares up repeatedly. The innumerable children nevertheless seem to be doing quite well. Surprising how many blond children there are amongst them." Lützkendorf concluded that Poland had no right to exist:

That history, this present – really, Poland could be termed a feminine country. Feminine entirely in the Slav sense. Everything is outward show. Whims, no actual deeds, mendacity in place of alliances, fantasy instead of political reality, gossip rather than honest toil, and this constant urge to be kept by someone. The whole country one enormous whorehouse. And, with it, cruel to the weak, heartless towards the poor, but pious in their myriad churches. That's Poland – and always will be.[187]

This was only a beginning for Lützkendorf's wartime career as propagandist. Later he accompanied the Waffen-SS in France (*Söhne des Krieges* [*Sons of War*], 1942) and drew ideological lessons. "Because truly, the miracle of their victories is not based on their superior weapons alone. It is the spirit of their leader [*Führer*] and commanding officer that makes them invincible; it is this profound faith in the divine mission of the Reich to organize the peoples in its space [*Raum*]."[188] On September 1, 1942, Hitler rewarded him, along with another Suhrkamp author, Hans J. Rehberg, with the Military Service Cross, Second Class.[189]

By the end of the war, he was turning back to drama and in a play on medieval Emperor Friedrich II, presented Schillerian style, dramatized contrasts of philosophy and values. In a scene recreating the great confrontations of Friedrich von Schiller's Mary Stuart with Elizabeth, or Philip II with the Inquisitor, Frederick tells Pope Gregory: "In the state God becomes power, order, law." But destruction and disorder are the outcome of the clash, and by the end, the dying emperor holds up a mirror to contemporary Germany. "Like fire I race through the land, consuming fire with fire – peace is among the things we have lost in the flames – the world I tried to grasp anew crumbles through my fingers like earth – a cloud of blood rises redly into the sky." And as he exhales, he exclaims: "We need continually to reconquer the Reich."[190]

Lützkendorf was only the most political of the Suhrkamp authors. Ernst Penzoldt prepared *Korporal Mombour, Eine Soldatenromanze* [*Corporal Mombour, a Military Romance*], telling a story of Napoleonic love and intrigue (1941). In 1942, Ursula Lange published a series of sonnets about the death of a beloved soldier:

> *unendlich süsse Erde – deine*
> *trunkene Fülle wahrt der Söhne Tod –*
> *ach, vergib mir, dass ich dennoch weine.*
> [*Earth infinitely sweet – your*
> *intoxicated fullness holds the deaths of sons –*
> *ah, forgive me if I weep nonetheless.*]

Viennese author Alexander Lernet-Holenia's 1939 novel *Ein Traum in Rot* [*A Dream in Red*], with its strident anti-bolshevism, was reissued by Suhrkamp in a soldiers' edition in 1943. Its major character explains: "Everywhere, like sheaves of vipers, Bolshevism reared its heads. [...] Horrors that in Europe only the lowest riffraff could have devised are perpetrated by the majority. Wherever a soviet, a revolutionary committee, or a cheka formed, blood flowed copiously, men were tortured and maimed, and total destruction ensued."[191]

With the help of this kind of compromise, the publisher managed to keep the firm running until the last months of the war. In August and September 1944, the temporary manager, Heinrich Gruber, again reported efforts of the party to close down the house. Grubler himself was to be conscripted – first to the Wehrmacht, then to the Waffen-SS. Gruber was then replaced by Herman Kasack. Kasack himself was threatened with conscription in the Volkssturm (militia) in January 1945. He then wrote to the district chamber of commerce, requesting an exemption on the grounds that

> The firm, listed as a military essential at the District Chamber of Commerce, is kept open on the orders of the Reich Ministry for Public Education and Propaganda in order to perform special services for the Ministry, filling export orders and exercising troop-care functions, including for example production of a work that Grand Admiral Dönitz urgently requested in a letter of 10 January 1945.[192]

The report to the partners on the firm's business in 1943, prepared in October 1944, reported the details of Suhrkamp's arrest and imprisonment in the Berlin jail Moabit and spelled out the likelihood that even if Suhrkamp were released from prison, he might remain "in the hands of the Secret State Police [the Gestapo] for further examination of the matter." But the report also referred to the efforts to secure Wehrmacht contracts (there had been eight such new contracts) and explained why the publisher had not been closed down. "The renewed attempt by the old adversaries of the publishing house to include the enterprise in the general shut-down of belletristic publishing has been unsuccessful. Following a fresh decision by Reichsminister Dr. Goebbels, Suhrkamp Publishers remains open within the framework of total wartime measures. Even the theatrical department is to remain open on the Chamber's express instructions." On the other hand, the *Neue Rundschau* was to cease publication in October.[193]

On May 10, 1945, after the occupation of Berlin, the Fischer building in Berlin was burned, with all business papers, the archive, and the stock of unsold books. Most of the documentation of the story of Suhrkamp's compromise was thus destroyed. Some survived in the papers of Suhrkamp's bankers.

The management of Suhrkamp represents more of a personal concern of Hermann Abs than a corporate interest of Deutsche Bank. The stories of Hubertus and of Suhrkamp show in general how difficult it is to distinguish clearly between Deutsche Bank's actions and the individual initiatives of particular bankers. Such a decentralized style of management had been characteristic of the bank before 1933. (Indeed, the initiatives of individuals, uncontrolled by the managing board or the supervisory board, had been responsible for some of the credit disasters of the Weimar Republic boom.) But such decentralization and personalization was fostered and sustained by the search for reliable and trustworthy business partners in a radically uncertain world. The Petschek brothers, Gottfried Bermann Fischer, and Peter Suhrkamp – or, for that matter, Robert von Mendelssohn and Georg Hirschland – placed their faith in individuals, rather than in a corporation, and wanted to work with those people in whom they believed their confidence might repose.

The Branches of Deutsche Bank and "Aryanization"

The number of 330 "aryanizations" quoted by Kimmich in the discussions of November 1938 does not include all the cases in which Deutsche Bank had some involvement in the process, even if only as a provider of credit or as a banker to the new owner. In response to Allied Military Laws Nos. 52 and 59, banks were obliged to report the cases of "aryanization" with which they were familiar. The Mannheim branch alone reported 83 "aryanized" firms.[194] In November 1949, the Hamburg successor bank of Deutsche Bank produced lists of 129 "aryanized" firms and added another 18 names in January 1950.[195] In many of these cases, the only link was that the firm held a current account with Deutsche Bank.

In some branches, as in Kassel, bank directors took some measure of initiative in the very early phases of "petty or non-state aryaniza- tion." When in mid-1933 the "Kampfbund des gewerblichen Mittelstandes" circulated a booklet in which "non-aryan" firms were listed (the list included all the major banks), the branch director asked the Berlin bank to protest to the Reich Economics Ministry against this illegitimate intervention (the Kampfbund "ventures to describe these as Jewish enterprises, contrary to the decisions of Berlin agen- cies regarding the big banks [*Grossbanken*]"). But he also stated that he had asked Hessische und Herkules Bierbrauerei AG to remove three Jewish members of its supervisory board ("at my instigation"), so that the brewery would not be listed as Jewish. He noted in his cor- respondence with Berlin that not more than fifteen percent of the cap- ital belonged to Jews.[196]

Some branches apparently reached the conclusion that they were prohibited from dealing with Jews – or at least they used this argument to justify commissions on transactions that they shared with other firms. The Hanover branch of Deutsche Bank wrote to a mortgage company at the beginning of 1938:

> We advised a certain Mr. Adolf Samulon over the telephone today [...] to apply to yourselves about realizing a very fine first mortgage, you having private capital available. Since on the occasion of the final examination for the professional certificate we were told by the Labor Front two years ago not to work with "non-aryans," could we please ask you, in the event of a completion, to include a one per cent commission for ourselves?[197]

Frequently, party and state authorities intervened and sought to dic- tate the character of the "aryanization," as in Hanover, where the Labor Front (DAF) demanded that Fritz Reuter of Hanover be allowed to take over the rubber factory of Fritz Weingartner.[198]

Occasionally, even late in the 1930s, individual managers made clear their hostility to a policy that they saw as coming from the cen- ter. On the question of the dismissal of a Jewish employee, Erich André, for instance, the Aachen branch protested to Berlin:

> However, I should like to point out that I fail to understand why the removal of our non-aryan employees is questioned by Dresdner Bank. Dresdner Bank took on its own non-aryan officials (one of whom, an

111

authorized signatory [*Prokurist*], left again over 2 years ago) 5 years back and did so with the clear intention of using them to make inroads into our non-aryan clientele. We had evidence of such endeavors at the time, all along the line. Our non-aryan employee served a successful apprenticeship with us from 1 July 1921 to 30 September 1923 and has been on our payroll ever since, i.e. for almost 16 years altogether. Neither his work nor his conduct have given any cause for complaint during that period. In accordance with your directive, we shall dismiss Mr. A. on 30 September of this year, paying his salary until the end of this year and notifying you in due course.

Berlin replied that "certain agreements have indeed occasionally been concluded between the head offices of bank branches to prevent one big bank from being played off against another, as has been observed in a number of places to the detriment of business."[199] At this stage, the banks were still worried that their Jewish customers might react to the dismissal of Jewish staff by transferring their accounts elsewhere. Erich André was dismissed, and he later died in a concentration camp.

In many cases, branches tried but eventually failed to find purchasers; especially with smaller businesses, Deutsche Bank's competitors were often quicker in establishing contacts between sellers and purchasers. Deutsche Bank had, however, a major advantage in cases in which the business was heavily dependent on foreign trade and on imports: in other words, where its foreign connections could be brought into play. As a consequence, the bank played a much greater role in "aryanizations" in industries such as tobacco and leather than in textiles or in retail trade. The bank also took a significant part in transferring Jewish-owned funds abroad: again, a function in which a larger, more international firm would appear more attractive to Jewish business owners.

This section begins with what might be regarded – from the perspective of the bank – as "failed aryanizations," and then details some examples in which bank branches, acting either alone or in agreement with other branches, played a significant part in the transfer of property.

The Frankfurt branch of Deutsche Bank reported on November 8, 1938, that J & S Nussbaum, a wholesale shoe dealer with a shop at Zeil No. 43, had been sold to a Stuttgart businessman, Frey. The price for the inventories was estimated by a state-appointed expert and then reduced by around twenty percent. Frey had business contacts with Dresdner Bank, which managed the "aryanization." But Deutsche Bank managed the payment of RM 24,000 in securities as the tax assessment of one of the Nussbaum partners.[200]

At the beginning of 1938, the Freiburg branch of Deutsche Bank sent details of the Central-Kaufhaus GmbH, Freiburg, to the Berlin Zentrale-Filialbüro as well as to other branches of the bank with the aim of finding a purchaser. This occurred without prior discussions with the owner ("We would, however, point out in this connection that we have ourselves put out no feelers to our customers as yet, with the result that we also have no idea what purchase price might conceivably be considered. But we feel it is not right to approach the firm here until we are in a position to introduce it to a purchaser.")[201] The store had a capitalization of RM 100,000 and was owned by six partners, all based in Munich. Just over a week later, when Deutsche Bank's branch manager spoke with the manager of the *Kaufhaus* (department store), he was told that "a very substantial number of potential purchasers have already expressed an interest in the company, some directly, some indirectly." But the Munich partners felt that the business was running so well that they did not want to sell.[202] In any case, the Berlin bank was slow in circulating details about the Freiburg store. Over a month after the initial inquiry from Freiburg, the Berlin central office wrote back:

> Before we grant your request, however, please let us know whether you have a direct banking interest in the sale or whether it is simply as a favor to your customers that you wish to become involved in the sale as a broker. In the latter event, we have in fact to refrain from publication, since we make our information bulletin available only for the sale of objects in the realization of which we have a direct interest, e.g. using the proceeds to cover or reduce debit balances held with us.[203]

The Freiburg branch replied that "it is very much in our own interests to retain this important and lucrative account in the future, too, if there is a change of ownership, which we feel we shall achieve partly by doing our best to become involved in the sale negotiations."[204] The Berlin office promptly replied: "We should prefer to refrain from publication in our information bulletin because the number of non-aryan firms up for sale is currently very large. However, we shall include the item in our confidential list of firms to be aryanized."[205]

The information bulletin carried notices proposing businesses that were for sale but without naming either the firm or the town, but merely the region: for example: "a well-established (it has existed for many years) non-aryan butchery requisites and sausage-skin whole-saler in a city in western Germany is for sale."[206]

At the end of April, one of the Munich partners told the Munich branch of Deutsche Bank that no negotiations were taking place as to a sale, "though as things stand there is apparently someone prepared to purchase the Freiburg firm. [...] However, he has promised us that if the sale does in fact go through he will of course do what he can to ensure that your [Deutsche Bank Freiburg] connection with the Freiburg establishment continues."[207] When the Freiburg branch came up with a buyer, the Munich owner demanded to know his name; the Munich branch then said that it was not usual for the would-be purchaser to release his name first in these transactions; the owner replied that further negotiations were useless. He insisted "that he already had more than enough serious applicants."[208] The Freiburg Deutsche Bank branch noted that the Munich owners were upset because it had tried to obtain precise sales figures from the employees of the Freiburg store.[209]

Eventually, in August 1938 the transaction was managed by Badische Bank, and the Central-Kaufhaus wrote (already under a new letterhead, with the names of the new partners, Alois Gerber and Oefelein) that that bank had been so helpful "that we can quite understand their request that all our banking business should be conducted with the said institution."[210] The case aptly illustrates Peter Hayes's comment about "business-hungry regional banks" tak-ing a "particularly aggressive stance" in this business.[211] Thus ended the relationship of Deutsche Bank with the Central-Kaufhaus, but only for a few years. In 1943, Gerber approached Deutsche Bank, successfully, to obtain a credit to take over (in partnership with a Hans Feit, a close associate of Robert Ley of the DAF and of *Gauleiter* Adolf Wagner of Munich) a Jewish-owned store (Kaufhaus Merkur) in Mulhouse in Alsace, which had been reannexed to Germany. Gerber wanted to transfer his credit line from Badische Bank to Deutsche Bank (RM 200,000 was secured on the Freiburg store, and another RM 165,000 worth of credit was given on the basis of a mortgage in Freiburg and on the security of goods in store).[212] There is some irony in the story of the Deutsche Bank central office in 1938 being reluctant to push forward with a search for buyers because the old store did not have bank debts and then being so enthusiastic in 1943 about the assumption of a credit line from Badische Bank because the store was then taking on substantial debts in its pursuit of further targets for "aryanization".

An analogous case, in which Deutsche Bank actively sought purchasers for an old credit customer, is the textile firm of A. Gutmann & Co., Göppingen. In 1934 and 1935, Hermann Köhler, the director of Deutsche Bank's Stuttgart branch, approached other local textile firms; one year later, Sigmund Gutmann told the bank "that Dresdner Bank is also trying constantly to find a potential buyer and recently asked for the firm's last three balance sheets. However, the firm did not comply with this request from Dresdner Bank."[213] The sale was indeed managed by Dresdner Bank in 1938, and the new firm retained only a small account with Deutsche Bank. But the Deutsche Bank files contain warm personal letters between Gutmann and Karl Walz of Südwestbank, the successor institution of Deutsche Bank in Nordbaden and Württemberg, and Walz appeared as a witness in the successful Gutmann restitution case in 1950.[214]

There are examples in the files of Deutsche Bank in which it is clear that the failure of the bank to work through a transaction resulted in a financial loss for the Jewish owner. Gebr. Thalheimer, Hanover, a maker of wooden products, was threatened by a case concerning violations of exchange regulations – a common way in which the state began a drive to "aryanize" a particular enterprise. Its owners, already resident abroad, asked Deutsche Bank's Bielefeld branch to manage a sale. The bank noted: "It is also worth pointing out that the gentlemen attach great value to transferring the works into good ownership and are concerned, moreover, to do what they can to look after the firm's long-serving staff, most of whom are in fact non-aryans." The Bielefeld and Hanover branches of the bank identified a suitable purchaser and began negotiations. But then the government imposed a trustee administrator, and the bank reported (in March 1938) that "the aryanization negotiations [...] are thus presumably now settled." It is not clear that the Thalheimer family ever received any money from a sale. Certainly the moment for a transfer of funds had been lost by the government's imposition of a trustee.[215]

When the bank found a willing (and financially and socially competent) purchaser, active or enthusiastic bank managers followed with more offers. When the aristocratic Günther Graf von der Schulenburg-Wolfsburg asked in Hanover about buying municipal property, the bank promptly approached him with a different sort of offer: "We are particularly at your service, with our contacts and our commercial experience, as regards investments of all types, and in this connection we should like to point out that we are currently in a position, in the context of "aryanization," to broker a number of sound and very promising participations in businesses and enterprises."[216]

Max Egon Fürst zu Fürstenberg seemed an ideal purchaser: In 1938, Deutsche Bank managed the sale of RM 1.5 million in shares of a Jewish-owned cellulose and paper factory in southwestern Germany, the Holzzellstoff- und Papierfabrik Neustadt (or Hupag). Fürstenberg did not actively seek to buy Hupag. He was approached by Deutsche Bank's Freiburg branch (while it was the Mannheim branch of the bank that consistently negotiated with the sellers). One week after the invasion of Czechoslovakia, Deutsche Bank asked him whether he might like to buy forests or factories in Bohemia.[217]

Hupag had been founded in 1897. It looked a promising case, because the Four-Year Plan of 1936 gave high priority to industries that promoted autarky, and cellulose began to play an increasingly important role in textile manufacture. In the negotiations over the sale, the government of Baden suggested that Hupag required an additional investment of between RM 500,000 and 750,000 to develop processes for producing artificial silk, and – as a by-product – animal feed. Although Badische Bank, which played a vital part in the discussions of a state-level "aryanization commission," comanaged the sale, Deutsche Bank played a critical role. Again, Deutsche Bank's importance in the transaction stemmed not least from the foreign connections of the case. The Hupag shares had apparently been deposited by their owner, Joseph Blumenstein of Berlin, as security for a loan in the Netherlands and in Switzerland to the Handels-Aktiengesellschaft Grunewald, and as a means of attempting to transfer assets out of Germany. (Later, in the restitution negotiations, the representative of Blumenstein's heirs denied that the shares had been used in this way and explained that it was a bargaining device to obtain a better price in Germany.) The case is a common one. The combination of persecution and exchange-control laws induced a vicious spiral of resentment and persecution. German Jews who moved or attempted to move their assets inevitably fell foul of the control laws and appeared to be "criminals" or at least "speculators" – observations that of course belong to the well-rehearsed arsenal of anti-Semitic stereotypes.

As was often the case, for Hupag the immediate pressure to sell came from official investigations. In Berlin a customs inquiry investigated the currency transactions. Prior to the sale, Deutsche Bank needed to engage in discussions with the Reichsbank and the German Standstill Committee, but also with a police commissar.[218] At the same time as the Berlin authorities were investigating currency movements, the local authority (*Bezirksamt*) in Neustadt took a sudden interest in the inadequate drainage facilities of Hupag. In the course of the discussions about drainage, it became clear that the local authority believed that because Hupag's supervisory board was Jewish, the enterprise should be treated with special severity. In June 1937, a member of the managing board of Badische Bank announced that there were interested purchasers for the company. Then the Baden authorities took a more direct path to intimidate the factory. At the beginning of 1938, the DAF announced that no one would any longer sell wood to Hupag. In March 1938, the factory had almost exhausted its supply of wood, and the question of Aryanization thus became urgent. One member of the Baden government's "aryanization committee," on which Badische Bank was represented, announced that the company's difficulties would not cease "unless the sale is conducted by Badische Bank." On April 4, Blumenstein asked Deutsche Bank Mannheim for a price of 170 percent of the nominal value; three days later, Deutsche Bank, together with Badische Bank, offered a deal at 140 percent. But only after the wood situation had become completely desperate, on June 11, did Blumenstein reach an agreement with Deutsche Bank for the sale.[219]

Joseph Blumenstein, who had emigrated to a residence near Amsterdam in 1933, had been interned, and he died in Bergen-Belsen on February 26, 1945. In an initial restitution settlement case, Freiburg District Court (*Landgericht*) ruled that the Fürstenberg estate owed no restitution to the Blumenstein heirs, because the case had been conducted on behalf of Handels- AG Grunewald. The Fürstenberg attorneys successfully argued that this was not a corporation entitled to restitution under the Allied Military Laws and that it had been obliged to sell shares as a consequence of fines for a nonpolitical offense, of infringements against the currency-control laws of the 1930s.[220] However, on appeal this decision was reversed, in 1953, by Karlsruhe Higher District Court (*Oberlandesgericht*); which now ordered the new Prince Fürstenberg to pay DM 3 million to the heirs of Blumenstein. Fürstenberg paid this amount with the help of loans from Südwestbank and Badische Bank. The settlement of the case was accompanied by a considerable discussion of the character of Blumenstein's business, a discussion not free from anti-Semitic overtones. The main issue was the extent to which Deutsche Bank officials in Freiburg still felt, in the early 1950s, that Blumenstein's currency deals had been an illegitimate manipulation. One official wrote in a business letter:

> My colleague Badenhauser, formerly of Deutsche Bank Berlin, the person responsible in connection with the Blumenstein bankruptcy, once wrote to me that assets were so cleverly moved to Holland and taken out of the creditors' reach that, even after the collapse, the Blumensteins were able to go on living not just well but extremely well and for example undertake spa excursions to Marienbad with a large retinue of servants, companions, etc. It is really interesting that, when he met you again this summer, Alfred Blumenstein shed tears of emotion. But they were a couple of rogues nonetheless.[221]

Even the manner in which the DM 3 million were immediately transferred to Switzerland in 1953, in contravention of German exchange-control regulations, unleashed a substantial press discussion, because the transaction was blamed for a sudden fall in the external value of the mark.[222] The heirs were accused of moving their money so rapidly because they wished to avoid liabilities of the Blumenstein business stemming from the depression. The press termed the whole affair "trafficking in foreign currency." *Badische Zeitung,* for instance, noted that "Wolff, son-in-law of the entrepreneur Blumenstein, is said to have already received 850,000 marks from restitution proceedings back in Backnang and illegally taken them to Switzerland."[223] The ethnic stereotyping and the peculiar consequences of exchange-control legislation did not stop in 1945.

In some cases, Deutsche Bank branches managed the sale of retail stores. But even here, there was a substantial reluctance in many cases because of the unknown character of many of the purchasers. The Heidelberg branch of Deutsche Bank was looking for a purchaser for L. Mayer, a women's fashion store whose owner was discussing emigration and how to pay the *Reichsfluchtsteuer* (Reich Flight Tax) in the summer of 1937. The Kassel branch then established the contact with Wilhelm Degele, who operated a very similar store in Kassel, who was looking for a business for his thirty-year-old son, who was about to be married. The initial proposal was to continue the firm under the old name, to keep the goodwill associated with the name Mayer. When Degele visited Heidelberg, he immediately asked which party officials to contact and was recommended by the bank to pay a call on the district economic advisor (Ernst Kobe, of Portland Cementwerk). The initial price suggested was RM 50,000; in the end, Degele managed to reduce the price to 30,000 reichsmarks. He proposed to finance the purchase in part with a credit from Deutsche Bank Kassel; and Deutsche Bank Heidelberg emphasized that it could give no uncovered credit to finance the purchase to a newcomer.[224]

In the case of another department store, Schmoller in Mannheim, the local Deutsche Bank branch intervened actively with government authorities to press for an "aryanization" rather than a liquidation. The bank had also found a purchaser, through its Dresden branch. On the other hand, the party and the local chamber of commerce were opposed to a takeover, arguing that there were already too many department stores in Mannheim and that most of the existing customers were Jews who would no longer shop at the "aryanized" store. If the new owners tried to create new business, they would only damage the small retail community. The opponents appealed directly to the Baden Finance Ministry to stop the deal, whereas Deutsche Bank's managers went to the ministry to insist that as a major creditor, the bank had a pressing concern with rapid completion of a sale. The finance ministry eventually authorized the transaction but insisted on a reduction in the rent paid by the purchasers as part of the transaction.[225]

It was with larger, trade-dependent enterprises that the bank was more in its element. The tobacco manufacturing industry had a large Jewish presence. It was also highly bank-dependent, in that firms needed substantial credits to finance the importing of raw tobacco. In addition, the process of granting import permits gave plenty of room for foreign-exchange controls to apply pressure on Jewish firms, by reducing the quotas or by insisting on substantial or very speedy payment of customs liabilities.

Roth-Händle AG, Lahr, produced the most popular working-class cigarette in Germany. Of its nominal share capital of RM 1,988,600, thirty-eight percent belonged to "foreign-currency aliens" (*Devisen-Ausländern*). The Adler and Oppenheimer families alone controlled one third of the capital.

In this case, there is some evidence that the increased pressure to sell in 1938 came from the bank rather than from the tax authorities or from the partners, who believed that they were in part protected by the complicated ownership structure and the substantial foreign ownership. But this bank pressure was applied not from the branch in Lahr or the regional branch office in Freiburg but from the central Berlin office. The credit files contain a Berlin branch-office department assessment of the firm's value dating from the beginning of 1938. The Berlin office urged caution in accepting the accounts prepared by the firm as a preliminary to the sale ("for instance, probably substantial reductions have to be made from the assets side"). Inventories had been valued at cost: the relevant sum could be realized only in the course of production. Three subsidiary companies (Ermeler, Jedicke, and Gräff) had been overvalued (at RM 202,000). The claims on the members of the managing board could not be realized. The liquidity of the company was poor. And so on. With such a balance sheet, the requested credit of RM 700,000 to 800,000 was not feasible. Berlin asked the Lahr branch of Deutsche Bank whether the existing credits should not be made against some security.[226]

At the same time, Reemtsma in Hamburg, one of Deutsche Bank's major debit customers, was trying to end its association with Roth-Händle.

The Lahr branch of Deutsche Bank was supportive of the firm and repeated the management's concern to keep Roth-Händle alive, noting that various official agencies are already interested in what happens to the firm, because what is almost the only cigarette factory of its kind, whose brand is very popular in working-class circles, simply cannot be allowed to fold. The local district head of the German Labor Front has [...] repeatedly expressed himself to this effect, saying also that an increase of around 700 in the Lahr unemployment statistics was intolerable and he would therefore do everything in his power to ensure that, in any event, this workplace survived.[227]

The Freiburg branch noted that Deutsche Bank would receive a three percent commission on the sale.[228] And the bank did indeed find a purchaser, cigar maker Johann Neusch of Herbolzheim, who would take eighty percent of the capital. The Lahr branch was rewarded with a commission of RM 20,000 for its part in the transaction.[229]

Deutsche Bank later helped Roth-Händle's new management acquire the previously Jewish-owned Elsässische Tabakmanufaktur in Strasbourg.[230]

How did the bank find out about potential targets for "aryanization?" In many cases, interested purchasers approached the bank. When, for instance, the manager of Tricotindustrie C. M. Koblenzer, Hechingen, was summoned to the Reich Economics Ministry in Berlin, along with the owner of this knitting factory, to discuss "aryanization," the Deutsche Bank branch in Tübingen asked head office "to introduce Mr. Thieliant to your aryanization experts, should the occasion arise."[231] But there were also less direct paths.

The Hamburg branch of Deutsche Bank heard from an information agency (*Auskunftei*) that in October 1938 the manager and the partners of the Norddeutsche Überseegesellschaft in Hamburg m. b. H. had been arrested for violations of the exchange control laws. Deutsche Bank immediately blocked the firm's account. The *Prokuristen* (holders of powers of attorney) then visited the bank to prevent a cancellation of credits and a financial collapse. The district economic advisor, a Dr. Wolf, then made a telephone call and arranged a meeting with Deutsche Bank, at which he argued that the firm should continue in existence and promised to "protect" the firm from the "authorities" (the currency-control offices) and accept the appointment of a trustee nominated by Deutsche Bank. Representatives of the British Chartered Bank, a major creditor of the firm, were furious with Deutsche Bank for tipping a good firm into insolvency, and Deutsche

Bank eventually gave in and agreed to unblock the accounts if the firm agreed to the appointment of a trustee.[232]

The government also insisted that banks act as its agent in collecting information on Jewish-owned assets. Deutsche Bank at the same time used the data compiled for this purpose to attempt to buy its own shares from Jewish clients and resell them to other bank customers.[233] By the beginning of 1939, most of the branches of Deutsche Bank had compiled the lists demanded by the state, although very few of their Jewish customers had actually given the formal notification to their bankers required under Paragraph 11 of the Law on Investment of Jewish Property. Some branches refused to give out names and invoked the principle of bank secrecy, but the violence of November 1938 helped to break down this attention to legal norms.[234] Even after the pogrom, when the Celle branch asked the Hanover branch how to respond to an inquiry by the tax office into Jewish accounts, the Hanover branch replied: "Since you cannot know which persons among your customers are to be regarded as Jews under the law, you cannot provide the information in the form requested. Please therefore make an agreement with the tax office to the effect that they present you with a list and you give them particulars, using that list, as to whether those individuals maintain accounts and deposits."[235]

Some estimate of the scale of this business is provided by figures from the Frankfurt branch, which indicate that in 1938, RM 35 million of deposits and RM 15 million of accounts payable were "non-aryan." In all, 16.5 percent of the overall business of the branch was regarded as "non-aryan."[236] This branch undoubtedly saw "aryanization" as a threat to its business and not in any sense as an opportunity. It weakened the bank, and it brought politics further into the world of finance. For the Stuttgart branch's Gymnasiumstrasse office, the result was similar. Because of the repayments of loans by Jewish businessmen, the total credit volume fell within two years by over seventy percent.[237] Losses on this business were not compensated by commissions on the additional share transactions generated by the process of "aryanization."

The Leipzig branch likewise complained explicitly at the beginning of 1939 that it had lost deposits ("there were also not inconsiderable credit-balance withdrawals by non-aryan account-holders") and that it was facing a liquidation of its credits to Jewish firms. This branch's

"Jewish commitment" amounted to an estimated RM 500,000 to 600,000. The branch noted: "Discontinuance thereof, together with the loss of the ancillary business associated with the credits (turnovers, bill discounting, guarantees, etc.), will also result in a certain diminution of returns."[238] For such branches, "aryanization" did not look like good business in any sense of the term. Credits of Deutsche Bank generally fell more rapidly than did Jewish deposits, as business sales resulted in cash deposits increasing.

For the bank as a whole, we have only data regarding credits. Credits to "non-aryans" fell rapidly: In October 1935 they had amounted to 13.6 percent of the bank's overall exposure ("incorporated total accounts receivable"), but by July 1937 the sum had fallen to 7.3 percent, indicating the extent to which Jewish business activity in Germany had declined. By the end of November 1938, that ratio had fallen even further, to 3.1 percent (or RM 69.8 million).[239]

The level of interest in possible purchases varied according to the branch of industry concerned. In an internal note of July 25, 1938, the bank noted a growing shortage of suitable firms in metals and chemicals (i.e., in those branches that benefited most from the rearmament boom) and complained: "It is not always possible to steer these potential purchasers towards other branches."[240]

The Leipzig branch reported in response to the Kimmich circular of January 14, 1938:

> Your circular S.5/38 gave us occasion once again to review our non-aryan clientele from the standpoint of possible aryanization. Making such a review, we were again able to establish that the number of firms in our district that are in any way potential candidates for aryanization is not very great, which mainly has to do with the fact that there are no sizeable non-aryan industrial enterprises in our business area.

The majority of debit accounts related to furs, skins, and brush factories, most of which would be liquidated only if they were punished through the reduction of exchange allocations. Only one firm, W. & C. Seckbach, was a suitable candidate for a takeover by two non-Jewish *Prokuristen*. At the same time, the branch reported the successful cases of "aryanization" "involving ourselves," which included Kossack & Böhme, Leipzig. But the other cases listed (Offenburger Rosshaarspinnerei, and three woolen firms in Kassel) were not in the Leipzig area.[241]

Leipzig had had a large Jewish community. Many Jews of Russian or Polish origin had built up a substantial fur trade, but most of the fur firms had run into difficulties early in the 1930s. They were hit first by the economic crisis, and then by currency controls, which from the beginning in 1931 discriminated against luxury goods. In 1930, Deutsche Bank refused unsecured credits to Gebr. Assuschkewitz AG; there were mortgage loans in 1934, but in 1935 credit was again denied. D. Biedermann ("far and away the wealthiest man in the district") had a business that was liquidated on his death in 1931. Chaim Eitingon AG was also liquidated after the death of the owner in 1932. In the case of Allalemjian, Mirham, Deutsche Bank canceled acceptance lines as early as the spring of 1934. One of the most substantial firms, J. Ariowitsch, which had been in business contact with Deutsche Bank since 1900, let its German business dwindle quickly after 1933 and moved its activities instead to associated London and New York firms, Ariowitsch & Jacob Fur Co. Ltd., J. Ariowitsch & Company, Anglo-American Fur Merchants Corporation. Ariowitsch was weakened by a denunciation by a former employee, one Haimson, who was aggrieved when the firm's owners would not agree to send him to represent the firm in the United States. Herr Haimson accused his former employer of tax avoidance and infringement of the currency-control regulations.[242] The denunciation had the consequence that both Haimson and Max Ariowitsch left Germany, but the business continued in operation until 1938. None of these Jewish-owned fur firms was "aryanized," and Deutsche Bank had run down its credit lines from an early stage in the depression.[243] The crisis was not a peculiarity of the Jewish fur merchants: The few non-Jewish firms in the trade, such as Theodor Thorer, suffered similar difficulties.[242] Deutsche Bank's business contacts with the Leipzig fur trade were only sparse in the future.

In November 1938, Babel of Josef and Moritz Kassner, Leipzig, told Deutsche Bank that the two Kassner brothers were unlikely to return to Germany and that "the aim of this management is therefore not the dissolution of the firm but its transfer to aryan ownership." He reported on two alternative purchasers, the first another firm, Mautner & Ahlswede, which would require permission from the foreign-exchange control, whereas the second was the long-time *Prokurist* of the firm, Herr Kuhne.[245]

The Leipzig branch of Deutsche Bank gave credits as part of a bank consortium to a storage and auction house, Deutsche Rauchwaren Gesellschaft, founded in December 1940 with the goal of procuring furs: "It is thus meant to help attain the end-objective of reinstating Germany and Leipzig at the center of the European and overseas fur trade." The company's objects included the following: "to participate in fur-trading companies where as a result of an official directive, request, or recommendation these have been set the task of procuring furs in specified areas." The memorandum justifying the new company – which was initially opposed by the "Reichsgruppe Handel" as a dangerous step toward monopolization – explained that there were few companies left in Leipzig with wide-ranging international connections. "Building up such personal contacts after the war would cost the individual entrepreneur long years of hard work, in which connection it must remain an open question whether the old importers that have now disappeared will be replaced by sufficient new elements suited to the task who are not as today at the same time manipulators – and intend to remain so."[246]

It is of course difficult to make completely sharp generalizations about the behavior of bank branches in Germany. Some actions, especially in 1938, were the results of pressure from the outside, of new legislative initiatives and of inquiries from the Berlin central office of the bank (the January 14, 1938 memorandum), but before this, and even during 1938, much depended on individual circumstances and even on the character of particular managers. A bank is a complex social and economic organization, and it would be quite misleading to think of its actions as being all centrally directed. Some features stand out, however: In cities in which there were large Jewish business communities, such as Leipzig or Frankfurt am Main, the bank's managers saw anti-Jewish measures as a threat to the local economy, and thus to their own business, and hardly welcomed the developments of 1937 and 1938. Bankers were in these cases in the middle of a social and economic environment that they hesitated to tear: in the informal phase up to 1937, but even in 1938, when the legal circumstances changed. On the other hand, where there was a smaller Jewish presence, participation in "aryanization" looked more attractive. In short, anti-Semitism of this economically driven type was easiest where there were fewest Jews. This distinction is evident in the negotiating strategy of some Jewish owners. It is striking, for instance, that the Blumenstein family wished to negotiate the sale of Hupag through the Mannheim branch – but not the Freiburg branch – of Deutsche Bank.

Some bank managers were additionally active in adding anti-Semitic invective to their business correspondence. The director of the Hildesheim branch informed his colleague in Hanover in relation to the sale of Metall- und Farbwerke AG, Oker, that "the content of the same is well-suited to establishing how Jewish infamy has contrived in recent years to exploit this enterprise for itself alone. [...] I am glad, at any rate, to be able to prove that from the start of my managerial activity I have been unrelenting in my efforts to lance this boil."[247] There are at least a few instances where the bank's branch clearly swindled Jewish businesspeople. In Rheydt, when L. Stern & Co., a large shoe factory with 2,309 employees, was sold in November 1938 at a cheap price to its managers, the owner repaid to Deutsche Bank the credit secured on his property. But because the new owners could offer no adequate security for their credit, the bank simply retained Stern's mortgage liability.[248]

In every case, Deutsche Bank was competing with other banks. In general, it was most successful in "winning" "aryanization" cases in which the bank as a whole had particular advantages: This meant mostly in cases in which businesses had foreign branches, foreign owners, or a high degree of dependence on either imports or exports. It was the range of Deutsche Bank's international contacts that gave it a particular profile in carrying through "aryanizations."

6

Deutsche Bank Abroad: "Aryanization," Territorial Expansion, and Economic Reordering

T he business considerations that frequently worked to limit the extent of involvement in "aryanization" – were there moral constraints as well? it is hard to tell – in the pre-March 1938 borders of Germany largely fell away when it came to the expansion of Germany that followed after the Austrian Anschluss. There was no longer any fear of tearing apart an existing business community. Quite the contrary, such a "reordering" gave new entrants into the banking scene substantial advantages. The behavior of occupation authorities, of industrial and financial companies in occupied Europe, also influenced the actions of the same figures when they dealt with German problems after 1938. It is often noted that the Anschluss marked a new phase in the radicalization of economic anti-Semitism. The rapidity and brutality with which the Jews who fell under German power in March 1938 were expropriated created a model for Germany itself to follow later in the year, and which was then applied in the countries of occupied Europe.[1] Most clearly, perhaps, in the Netherlands, where the leading plunderers of 1938 in Austria, Arthur Seyss-Inquart and Hans Fischböck, played a leading role in running the German occupation.

One of the remarkable features of the great German trade expansion to southeastern Europe in the 1930s had been that it was accompanied by almost no investment flows. Alan Milward has commented that "history indeed records no greater disproportion between foreign trade and investment than that shown in the economic relationship between Nazi Germany and south-eastern Europe in the 1930s. It might be just as logical to ask the question, Why, when the proportion of foreign trade with Germany was so very high for these countries, was the level of German investment there so low?"[2] After the Munich agreement of 1938, German policy makers changed course and began to devise a strategy that would include dominance through control of capital.

However, the experience of Germany's big banks varied substantially between different countries in occupied central and eastern Europe. In the course of the war, Deutsche Bank built up a "concern," based on its ownership of Austrian, Czech, and Slovak banks.

In Austria after the occupation, there was a powerful political lobby, based within the Nazi Party, to keep Deutsche Bank out of Austrian banking. (There was more sympathy with Dresdner Bank, which had been allowed to take over the Mercurbank.) On the other hand, within the Reich Economics Ministry in Berlin, arguments about the importance of trade finance gradually became more important, with the consequence that by 1942 Deutsche Bank was permitted to acquire a majority stake in the largest Austrian bank, the Creditanstalt.

The Czech case is very different, in that here – from the beginning of the expansion, with the seizure of the Sudetenland, and as plans were made for a more extensive intervention in Czech affairs – the German government wanted the two largest German commercial banks, Deutsche Bank and Dresdner Bank, to involve themselves in taking over Czech banks, in particular those banks with a large German-speaking clientele. The banks appeared as heralds of the German New Order, with a Dresdner Bank manager discussing the reordering of Sudeten-German banks in the summer of 1938, before Hitler had finally stepped up the pressure on the Czech state. A Deutsche Bank official went to Prague to negotiate about the future of Czech banking in March 1939, just two days before the German invasion. What did the banks offer to the German state that apparently made them so indispensable in economic imperialism directed against Czechoslovakia? What could they do that a state-owned bank, such as, for instance, the Reichs-Kredit-Gesellschaft, could not? First, their foreign contacts were essential in financing the transactions: Deutsche Bank's acquisition of the Deutsche Industrie- und Agrarbank, for instance, was financed through transactions conducted via Switzerland in blocked marks (*Sperrmark*). Second, they could handle the extensive "aryanizations" involved in such a way as to win the confidence and cooperation of greedy and hungry

German and Czech industrialists, who might in this way be firmly bound into the military economy of the "Protectorate of Bohemia-Moravia."

Finally, there was some banking activity in occupied Poland, but because the industrial economy here mattered much less for the German war economy than in the Czech case, the pressure from the German authorities to involve the German big banks was not as great. In territories seized from the Soviet Union, industrial management (and hence a banking presence) was even less of an issue. Banks, including Deutsche Bank, established branches in Poland (but not in the Soviet territories.) They were of relatively little commercial importance, but they were deeply implicated in the horrors of the occupation regime.

In Austria, the Nazi Party – and to some extent the German government – tried to keep Deutsche Bank out, but it wanted to be involved in a major and profitable area of business. In the Czech lands, the government saw Deutsche Bank and Dresdner Bank as vital accessories in the process of economic domination. In Poland, banking was of less interest – either to the German authorities or to Deutsche Bank.

The Österreichische Creditanstalt-Wiener Bankverein

The Creditanstalt was the most famous Austrian investment bank and held many important long-term industrial assets. It had been founded in 1855 and had a major capital participation of the Rothschild family, so that it was often held to be a "Rothschild bank." Its international fame became even greater after May 1931, when its failure precipitated a general banking and financial crisis in Austria that then spread to the whole of central Europe and eventually brought down German banks as well. It was rescued by an expensive intervention of the Austrian state, and in 1934 it was merged with another crisis-torn Austrian bank, the Wiener Bankverein. By 1938, the resulting institution had a capitalization of 101 million schillings and a balance sheet worth a total of around 700 million schillings. The estimates for the total cost to the Austrian state of the rescue operation were around 1 billion schillings.[3]

The Creditanstalt combined two sets of banking business. It was a gigantic industrial holding company whose assets had collapsed in value

129

during the depression and had brought the bank to ruin. This part of the bank would be vital in any plan for the rearrangement of Austrian business. Second, the Creditanstalt had wide-ranging contacts in the former Habsburg territories and beyond, in southeast and Balkan Europe, and played an important part in international trade finance.[4]

Its pre-1938 management was regarded with suspicion by the German and Austrian Nazis, because of the extent of the bank's linkage with the Austrian political system. Two members of the managing board were Jewish: one, Franz Rottenberg, left the bank almost immediately after the Anschluss; a second, Oscar Pollack, stayed for a few months. Board president Josef Joham also resigned, leaving only one board member, who was an engineer rather than a banker. The chairman of the supervisory board resigned, whereas the deputy chairman, Franz Hasslacher, "is an enthusiastic supporter of the new Greater Germany [*Gross-Deutschland*]."[5] The new Nazi authorities complained that the predecessors had failed to proceed with sufficient vigor against the allegedly criminal actions that had led to the failure of the bank in 1931.[6]

In German dealings with Austria, political arguments consistently overrode any economic logic. In late February 1938, in anticipation of the Anschluss, the Reichsbank had rapidly produced a plan for the currency union of Germany and Austria on the basis of an exchange rate of 2 schillings to 1 Reichsmark, which corresponded to the Berlin market quotation. The Reichsbank's economists recognized that this rate did not reflect the higher purchasing power of the schilling but saw in their suggestion a way of stimulating the Austrian economy.[7] Their view was supported by the Reich Economics Ministry but eventually rejected on the grounds that it would be unpopular with Austrians, who thus eventually received their marks at the more favorable rate of 1.50 schillings. This rate created a substantial overvaluation relative to productivity of the Austrian currency, similar to that experienced by East Germany after the monetary union of 1990, with a similar consequence of a massive shock to the Austrian economy and many bankruptcies and subsequent demands for special measures to protect the Austrian (*alpenländische*) areas. How could Austrians be reconciled with the newly composed *Vaterland?* Hermann Göring envisaged an immediate, massive work-creation program to absorb Austria's 600,000 unemployed.

As an additional response to the Austrian difficulties, Göring arranged a bank consortium to give credit to Austrian business (including agriculture) with the intention of "rehabilitating Austrian enterprise and performing functions that will serve the Foreign and Four-Year Plan in the land of Austria."[8] The syndicate was to be led jointly by the Creditanstalt and the Mercurbank, which absorbed the Austrian subsidiary of the Parisian Banque des Pays de l'Europe Centrale, known in Austria as the Länderbank, to become the second major Austrian bank. The Mercurbank was owned by Dresdner Bank. Deutsche Bank and Dresdner Bank were eventually also brought into the syndicate and took an equal share to those of the two leading banks. In the first year, a total credit volume of RM 25 million was envisaged; this was extended by 1940 to RM 65 million.

Immediately after the Anschluss (March 12, 1938), Eduard Mosler, the spokesman of Deutsche Bank's managing board, tried to see Bank Commissar Friedrich Ernst, to tell him "that we are currently considering establishing branches in Austria on the basis of annexation by Germany but that a decision in this regard is still dependent on discussions with the Austrian Creditanstalt-Wiener Bankverein concerning a different type of close collaboration with a bank with which we have been close friends for a very long time."[9] A few days later, Deutsche Bank sent Hermann Abs, together with Hellmut Pollems and Walter Pohle from the Berlin secretariat, the latter a young man who quickly emerged as a major figure in dealing with the banking consequences of the military reordering of central Europe. The attractions of the Creditanstalt did not lie principally in its Austrian business alone. For Deutsche Bank, the acquisition of the Creditanstalt would be the beginning of a drive to build contacts in an area of Europe that was increasingly subject to German political and economic pressure.

The Creditanstalt began the discussions by saying that

> in the light of the friendship that already exists and the many years during which Deutsche Bank has been represented on the C.A. board of directors, it would welcome the support of Deutsche Bank in order to be able, as a result, to continue in future to meet the requirements of the Austrian economy as an independent institution operating in accordance with economic standpoints.

That would be "the best solution economically." A participation of Deutsche Bank in the Creditanstalt ran into opposition from the new Nazi government of Austria. Economics Minister Hans Fischböck announced his reservations. (Fischböck, a member of the NSDAP and a former manager of the ill-fated Bodenkreditanstalt and of the Creditanstalt in Austria, had been the economic adviser of the Austrian Nazi leader Arthur Seyss-Inquart; in March 1938 he was appointed trade minister and in May became minister of finance.)[10] This impression was confirmed when the dismissed president of Austria's Nationalbank, Viktor Kienböck, told Abs of his interview with Wilhelm Keppler, Hitler's economic adviser and *Reichsbeauftragter für Österreich,* on April 12: "very nasty atmosphere against Deutsche Bank", he noted. Keppler had said to him, "D.B., with robbery in mind, has arrived in Vienna with twenty men to take over the C.A." Kienböck had apparently then told Keppler that "Abs was very new and unburdened by matters with which Keppler might have reproached D.B. in the past. Keppler said: Abs was still the best of them all."[11]

Deutsche Bank representatives were certainly quick off the mark in establishing the appearance of control. The general meeting of the Creditanstalt on March 25, 1938, was chaired, in the absence of Hasslacher, by Abs.

One day later, on March 26, a contract was drawn up regulating relations between the two banks, according to which, "given a corresponding material relationship between Deutsche Bank and the C.A., Deutsche Bank is prepared to conduct its southeast Europe business as far as possible through Vienna. The C.A. was told in this connection that the pre-condition was a minimum 75 per cent holding, because then Deutsche Bank must also be able to amend the articles of association without having to rely on the agreement of the other shareholders."[12] Branches of Deutsche Bank in the "Altreich" (pre-1938 Germany) immediately began to advertise their close connection with the Creditanstalt. ("We are able to say that we have at our disposal exact knowledge of all relevant circumstances within Austria.")[13]

Keppler blocked this agreement: "Following consultation with all Reich agencies, i.e. Economics Ministry, Finance Ministry, and Reichsbank, [it has been] decided [...] to leave the majority of shares in the possession of the Austrian government. All the same, consideration should be given as to whether minority holdings could be sold to the Reichsbank – D.B., Reichskredit, and/or Viag." In fact, the state-owned German bank Reichs-Kredit-Gesellschaft and the state-owned industrial holding company, Vereinigte Industrieunternehmen AG (Viag), which owned the Reichs-Kredit-Gesellschaft, appeared to have much better chances in the race to control the Creditanstalt. Their primary interest lay in the industrial assets of the Austrian bank. Fischböck claimed that Hjalmar Schacht had told Abs that Deutsche Bank could not take the Creditanstalt – Abs noted in response that he had had no meeting with Schacht at all in 1938. Instead, the Creditanstalt started to discuss the sale of a stake to the state-owned Viag. Deutsche Bank was "disappointed" at the decision made by the Economics Ministry. Abs noted that "the southeast European business that I have so often stressed met with no appreciation whatsoever."[14] The thirty-five percent stake in the Creditanstalt owned directly by the Austrian state was sold to the Reichs-Kredit-Gesellschaft, and another thirty-nine percent, owned by the Österreichische Industriekredit AG and the Österreichische Nationalbank, was sold directly to Viag, which thus controlled seventy-four percent of the Creditanstalt stock.[15]

Fischböck put considerable pressure on the Creditanstalt, which now had to send denials of its contacts with Deutsche Bank to the ministry. In June, the Creditanstalt stated:

> It is not true that we handed over to Deutsche Bank or to any other institution a list of our industrial holdings with a view to having purchasers for such industries directed to us from the Old Reich. We have absolutely no cause to look for purchasers for our industrial holdings since, so far as the majority of our industrial holdings is concerned, purchasers present themselves without our doing anything about it.

In any case, as Deutsche Bank later pointed out, the accusation was absurd in that the lists of industrial holdings were actually published in the Creditanstalt's annual reports.[16]

A Deutsche Bank executive, Helmut Pollems, contacted Rudolf Brinkmann of the Reichsbank and the Reich Economics Ministry and obtained some support for the idea that Deutsche Bank was best placed to develop business with southeast Europe.[17] But this was just before Brinkmann had a catastrophic nervous breakdown, which led him to distribute bank notes to the amazed public in the streets of Berlin before he was removed to a sanatorium. The economic office (*Wirtschaftsstab*) of *Gauleiter* Josef Bürckel also seemed to have some sympathy for the arguments of Abs and Pollems. Deutsche Bank's argument was that it was unfair to let Dresdner Bank take the Mercurbank and not to give Deutsche Bank some equivalent business.[18] In May 1938, Deutsche Bank produced a lengthy memorandum in which it emphasized the long-standing nature of the contacts with the Creditanstalt (going back to 1873, when the three-year-old Deutsche Bank had held two seats on the board of directors of the four-year-old Wiener Bankverein). It complained that the Viag sale had led to "elimination of its [Deutsche Bank's] activities in Austria" and again suggested a merging of foreign activities of the Berlin and the Vienna banks. "Above all, however, bringing together the foreign business of the Creditanstalt and Deutsche Bank would make it possible to process the main provision and marketing areas of the southeast in a very special way." In addition, establishing a link between the Creditanstalt and a Berlin big bank would facilitate the flow of credit and capital to Austria.[19] In September 1938, in a letter to the *"Reichskommissar für das Kreditwesen,"* Deutsche Bank repeated its proposal to take a majority holding in the Creditanstalt, and, failing this, a twenty-five percent stake on condition that at least another twenty-five percent was held by the Golddiskontbank.[20]

By the autumn of 1938, the Reich Economics Ministry supported the idea of a close cooperation between the Reichs-Kredit-Gesellschaft and Deutsche Bank in the Creditanstalt, with a roughly equal capital participation.

> However, for the purposes of cultivating foreign commerce Deutsche Bank should be granted some influence in Vienna. It is in line with the interests of the export trade that it [Deutsche Bank] should conduct its Balkan business through the Credit-Anstalt. Deutsche Bank is apparently already represented in Romania and Bulgaria. The Credit-Anstalt (we are told) has bank branches or participations in banks in Hungary and Yugoslavia.[21]

It was therefore clear, as the Reich Economics Ministry noted, "that the foreign interests of Deutsche Bank and the Credit-Anstalt complement each other in an exceptionally favorable manner and consequently, if both take effect together in the close tie between Deutsche Bank and the Credit-Anstalt, will pack a bigger punch."

The conclusion of these reflections was that Viag should sell its share in the Creditanstalt to Deutsche Bank, but if that were not practicable, because of the opposition of Viag, Deutsche Bank should conclude a friendship treaty with the Creditanstalt "that secures the co-operation of both banks' systems."[22] In return, Deutsche Bank would not set up its own branches in the Austrian territories.

In fact, the leading managers of Viag were quite prepared to cooperate closely with Deutsche Bank to be able to use the latter's considerable expertise in commercial banking and trade finance. In September 1938, Alfred Olscher of Viag told Abs that when the Austrian Finance Ministry was dissolved in the spring of the following year, German banks would be permitted to operate in Austria. He also discussed a proposal to acquire Creditanstalt shares and then sell a minority stake to Deutsche Bank,

> ...the idea being that, in addition to its new holding of 39 per cent of the capital Viag might acquire the federal government's 36 per cent, so that it would then own 75 per cent. Of that holding, possibly $1/3 = 25$ per cent could be ceded to Deutsche Bank. At the same time there could perhaps be an agreement between Deutsche Bank and Viag providing for joint consultation between both partners on all questions, with Deutsche Bank being seen as the specialist in banking matters.[23]

Fischböck continued attempting to restrict the Deutsche Bank share to ten to fifteen percent. He was a genuine socialist in his vision of banking, arguing that "the major credit banks should be state banks. If no such state institutions exist, in his view they should first be created."[24] But this was not quite the view of the Reichsbank – or of the German Reich Economics Ministry, which looked more favorably at Deutsche Bank plans. In "Austrian business circles and on the part of the government and the party, such a participation by Deutsche Bank would be very warmly welcomed."[25] Abs argued that Deutsche Bank could not accept a share of less than twenty-five percent. The Reichs-Kredit-Gesellschaft then proposed to Abs a division of southeast Europe into spheres of influence: Hungary and Yugoslavia would be managed by the Creditanstalt, through the branch in Budapest and a majority in the Allgemeiner Jugoslawischer Bankverein; Bulgaria and

Turkey by Deutsche Bank, through the Kreditbank Sofia and the Deutsche Bank branch in Istanbul; whereas Dresdner Bank would be left with Greece "in order to develop a certain equality in terms of settlement."[26] By this stage, Deutsche Bank's plans were also supported by State Commissar Josef Bürckel, who noted that "both banks' representations in the south east complement each other exceptionally well." The Creditanstalt should sell its industrial holdings and concentrate on trade finance.[27]

Fischböck became chairman of the Creditanstalt managing board but in practice played little role in banking business. His major official function lay in dealing with the bank's personnel. In any case, his attention was rapidly engaged by the business of "aryanizing" the Netherlands, on the model that he had developed in Austria.

Most of the Creditanstalt's major industrial holdings were stripped out in 1938 and sold to the Reichswerke "Hermann Göring," which took over controlling shares in the Steierische Gusstahlwerke AG, the Kärntnerische Eisen- und Stahlwerksgesellschaft, Feinstahlwerke Traisen AG vorm. Fischer, Steyr-Daimler-Puch AG, Maschinen- und Waggonfabrikations AG in Simmering vorm. H. D. Schmid, and the Erste Donau-Dampfschiffahrtsgesellschaft. But in the course of the very rapid "aryanization" of the Austrian economy in 1938, it acquired a substantial number of new shareholdings, including companies in paper, stone, bridge building, and foreign trade.

A report of Heinz Osterwind of Deutsche Bank in May 1938 describes the quick brutality of "aryanization" in Austria. Osterwind explained that the preference of the authorities – in particular Walther Rafelsberger as the state commissar responsible for appointing temporary administrators and temporary "supervisory personnel" – lay in a takeover by Austrians. "It emerged, however, in connection with the aryanization of larger enterprises, that both the financial and the technical prerequisites for this are not always present, with the result that it will not always be possible to do without some assistance from Old Reich circles." Osterwind explained how the sale prices of Jewish-owned enterprises were being forced down: "In the case of larger enterprises, the ownership is passed to a trustee, and the sale price is only determined after a valuation by an auditor. The valuation of the auditor is decisive in ascertaining the price. The basis is a general assumption of 'bad will.' The future profitability of the enterprise shall be valued on the basis that a non-aryan enterprise would not take part in the nation's economic recovery."[28] In consequence, some German officials, such as Rudolf Brinkmann from the Reich Economics Ministry, argued that although it was undesirable that "a surfeit of Jews should then be replaced by a surfeit of Germans from the Old Reich," in an emergency there should be a greater participation from the *Altreich*.[29]

The "aryanization" of Austrian business life occurred in a different manner to that of the Old Reich. Smaller cases were settled through an asset-management company, whereas larger cases were managed by a "control bank" (*Kontrollbank*), under the supervision of the Finance Ministry. Fischböck saw the institution of the control bank as the best way of carrying through "aryanization" as quickly as possible. A special "aryanization tax" was levied, and Jewish owners received barely any compensation.[30] The control bank, its task accomplished, was wound up at the end of 1940. Far more businesses were shut down than were taken over. In all, of 13,046 Jewish craft-trade firms in Austria, of which 12,550 had been in Vienna, 11,357 were closed down and 1,689 "aryanized." Of the trading firms, numbering 10,992 (7,900 in Vienna), 9,112 were closed and 1,870 "aryanized."[31]

Most private banks were simply liquidated. Of 105 Austrian private banks, only 10 were classed as "aryan," and only 2 of these were of any significant size.[32] The two largest and most important Jewish-owned banks, Rothschild and Gutmann, were taken over by the Munich private bank Merck, Finck & Co. The Reich Economics Ministry noted:

Merck & Finck Bank is an old-established Munich bank operating as an exchange bank. Mr. von Finck is regarded as a highly experienced businessman who is also up to tackling difficult jobs. He is also, to my knowledge, a long-standing member of the party with excellent party connections. I should imagine he is capable of satisfactorily organizing all aspects of the affairs due for consideration according to the letter from the SS commander [*Reichsführer SS*].[33]

The Creditanstalt played a significant role in the process of Austrian "aryanization" even though that development was driven – much more clearly than had been the case in Germany – by the state. It registered all the Jewish assets in its deposit accounts. It asked to buy Jewish assets paid into the Prussian State Bank (the Seehandlung) in

Germany as part of the "Jewish property levy" of November 1938. It attempted to buy Jewish firms, such as Bunzl and Biach AG[34] but was defeated by a rival syndicate organized by Dresdner Bank and had to be content with a smaller stake in the enterprises.[35] There were also Creditanstalt loans to "aryanized" companies, such as the leather case and purse manufacturer Brüder Eisert AG. This enterprise required Creditanstalt credit lines, even though their owners had "made their shares available," as the report prepared by the Deutsche Revisions- und Treuhandgesellschaft for the Austrian credit syndicate euphemistically put it, "partly for nothing, partly against payment of a small sum (max. RM 10 per share)."[36] The records of the agency that administered the barely semilegal theft of Jewish property indicate that in at least three cases Deutsche Bank directly intervened in the transfer of Jewish-owned shares. The fiche cards record the name of one of the victims, Emil Feichtmann, at Wipplingergasse 15.[37]

All businesses in Austria, not just Jewish-owned businesses, were negatively affected by the choice of an inappropriate exchange rate in the Austro-German monetary union. There was thus a demand for new capital from Germany, which became increasingly urgent in the course of 1938 and 1939. These circumstances made the political authorities suddenly more sympathetic to Deutsche Bank plans that they had previously rejected.

Deutsche Bank and Viag decided in a "consortium agreement" of December 30, 1938, to sell twenty-five percent of the Creditanstalt's share capital, 48,500 ordinary and 35,000 preferred shares, to Deutsche Bank. Viag would have three representatives and Deutsche Bank two on the supervisory board of the Creditanstalt; each would supply one vice president for the supervisory board, which would be under the presidency of Franz Hasslacher.

Deutsche Bank sent bankers to supervise the restructuring of the business, and it recommended that the Creditanstalt send its managers to study the banking practice of branches of Deutsche Bank. Otherwise, it would be impossible for the Creditanstalt to break out of its unprof- itable existence: "According to the discussion held with you recently, it seems likely that your bank can hardly expect, during the current year, given the altered business and economic situation, to meet in full the requirements of sound viability."[38] The reorganization included "de- judification of the staff" (*Entjudung der Angestelltenschaft*), as reported on October 22, 1940, to a meeting of the working committee (*Arbeitsausschuss*).[39] In November 1940 (i.e., after the German occupation of Belgium), Deutsche Bank bought Creditanstalt shares of a nominal value of RM 525,000 from the Société Générale de Belgique, and of RM 262,500 from the Compagnie Belge de l'Etranger, so that its holdings now increased to thirty-six percent. The Société Générale welcomed the opportunity to dispose of southeastern European assets, which had been in fact very costly since the depression. At the end of 1941, preliminary discussions began about the purchase of some or all of Viag's fifty-one percent stake in the Creditanstalt. The critical argument that Deutsche Bank made in discussions with German officials rested on the proposals for a coordinated economic development of southeast Europe: "If things develop as Deutsche Bank wishes and has described, then Deutsche Bank welcomes the strengthening of the Creditanstalt's south-eastern business, even at the cost of Deutsche Bank." As part of the conditions for Deutsche Bank's ownership, the sale of further industrial participations was discussed. In particular, the holdings of the following companies seemed marketable, and were used to pay Viag for the transaction: Universale Hoch- und Tiefbau AG, Vienna; Ostmark-Keramik AG; Eisenwarenfabriken Lapp-Finze AG, Graz; Hutter & Schranz AG, Vienna; Kassen-Aufzugs- u. Maschinenbau AG; F. Wertheim & Co, Vienna; Wiener Brückenbau- u. Eisenkonstruktions-AG; and Semperit Gummiwerke AG, Vienna.[40]

Already in 1940, the Creditanstalt had started to develop as a major player in the financial reorganization of Austria's neighbors. Without consulting the German banking authorities, and to their astonishment and irritation, it bought the Slovak branches of the Czech Böhmisch-Mährische Bank (Legiobank), which had been attacked by the Slovak government.[41] At the same time, at the initiative of Fischböck, the Creditanstalt took over the Cracow branch of Deutsche Bank.

In May 1942, an agreement was reached under which Deutsche Bank would acquire a majority holding, by buying RM 17,675,000 worth of Creditanstalt shares and then selling the rest of the Viag holding (amounting to about ten percent of the total capital) to small shareholders. "Of the RM 17,675,000 (nominal) Creditanstalt-Bankverein shares = 25 per cent of the share capital of the Creditanstalt left to us we shall retain RM 10,605,000 (nominal) = 15 per cent of the Creditanstalt capital, which we need for the majority, in our own possession. The remaining RM 7,070,000 (nominal) Creditanstalt shares = 10 per cent of the capital will be deposited by ourselves with the Creditanstalt-Bankverein, together with instructions to place those shares in small amounts – max. RM 100,000 (nominal) in any individual case – to Austrian residents, distributing them as widely as possible."[42]

Viag was paid with the industrial holding from the Creditanstalt. At the same time, the Creditanstalt was restructured as a vehicle of financial control in central Europe. It was to take thirty percent of the shares of Banca Comerciala Romana, Bucharest; thirty percent of the Deutsch-Bulgarische Kreditbank, Sofia; and a third of the shares of the Böhmische Union-Bank (BUB), a major Deutsche Bank subsidiary in the Czech lands. The BUB deal was authorized by the Reich Supervisory Office for Banking in October 1942.

Hermann Abs explained the philosophy of control in a meeting of the working committee of the Creditanstalt in August 1941, when he argued that a branch of the Creditanstalt in Budapest could never be effective on its own.

> Since [he said] the business could not for the most basic reasons be run with its own funds alone, consideration must be given to borrowing funds, which a bank that looked externally like a Hungarian institution might be able to do. As regards the partner, Mr. Abs is of the opinion (and all the members of the working committee agree with him) that only the highest-ranking institution could be considered for this, which would be the Pest Commercial Bank of Hungary.[43]

These banks were in addition to be linked through interlocking directorships. The Creditanstalt would send a delegate to each of the boards of directors of the Bucharest and Sofia banks and two to BUB. In addition, a BUB banker would be on the supervisory board of the Creditanstalt. A great controversy developed about the choice of this person: Deutsche Bank initially proposed Walter Pohle, and the Creditanstalt, his older BUB colleague Max Ludwig Rohde. Abs suggested Walter Tron, a director of the Leipzig branch of Deutsche Bank and a party member since 1937, as a member of the managing board of Creditanstalt. He joined the board on July 1, 1942. Pohle blocked the appointment of Rohde and was himself nominated but initially declined the appointment. He eventually joined the Creditanstalt's supervisory board in April 1943. The completion of the 1942 deal marked the completion of a major Deutsche Bank–led banking group in central Europe, which was already earlier frequently referred to by German officials as a *Konzern,* or group.[44]

The Böhmische Union-Bank and Czech Banking

The dismembering of Czechoslovakia[45] in 1938–39, through the September 1938 Munich Agreement and then the invasion of March 1939, was a crucial part of German economic expansion. Czechoslovakia had an industrial base that represented a substantial addition to Germany's armaments economy.[46] To use this new potential, German policy makers aimed at a restructuring of ownership. The Czech lands were also home to a number of banks with German-Jewish histories and with substantial industrial holdings. These banks, and indeed the whole Czech banking system, had been weakened by the depression, and there were many complaints that the country was overbanked. During the depression, many banks had acquired substantial industrial holdings as their customers found themselves in difficulties.[47] In the eyes of the German economic planners, the Czech banks might lend themselves to the goal of a reorientation of the Czech economy and its integration in German economic mobilization for war. A strong German position was built up in the months following the first stage of the dismemberment of the Czech state at Munich. This provided a base for further economic imperialism after March 1939. After Munich, the German government sent lists of Jewish firms in the Sudetenland to the banks together with a demand that the banks should manage the process of "aryanization."[48] In addition, Deutsche Bank prepared a detailed guide on the industrial structure and the character of the major companies of the Sudetenland, as well as of the rest of "Bohemia and Moravia."[49]

The economic guide to the Sudetenland was published very quickly in October 1938 and must already have been prepared before the Munich agreement. Dresdner Bank had been even more provocatively explicit in its preparations for economic imperialism. On July 25, 1938, the director of its Dresden branch, Reinhold Freiherr von Lüdinghausen, had organized a meeting of Sudeten-German businesspeople, including many board members of the two most important German-language Czech banks, the BUB and the Böhmische Escompte Gesellschaft, in the home of a glass manufacturer, Walter Riedel, in Polubny (Unter-Polaun). At this meeting, the businesspeople discussed the potential for "aryanizing" the Czech banking system.[50]

Expansion did not halt there. Just three weeks after the German invasion of the Sudetenland, on October 21, 1938, Hitler ordered preparations by the army that would enable Germany "to conquer 'rump-Tschechei' at any time, if it were to pursue, say, a policy hostile to Germany."[51]

After the German occupation of March 15, 1939, "aryanization" became such a transparent device for the establishment of German preponderance and the Germanification (*Eindeutschung*) of Czech business that for that reason – more than from any deep-seated moral objection – Czech industrialists and the Czech government of Emil Hácha voiced increasing hostility to the German policy and demanded measures for the confiscation of Jewish assets "where disturbances of public order might occur."[52] The resulting clashes between German and Czech concepts produced a further brutalization in the Jewish policy in the Czech territories.

There can be no doubt that the German political authorities provided the ultimate driving force in this process of establishing German control. The major German banks, and especially Dresdner Bank and Deutsche Bank, played an important part as accessories. Their motivation was complex. In part, they were driven by competitive calculations: If they neglected expansion in the new territories, they would lose out to their German rivals. Deutsche Bank noted and complained about each instance when it felt that the military regime or the party was favoring Dresdner Bank unfairly. In some part, the banks were also driven by tax concessions and other subsidies from the German government. Third, the process of expansion developed a dynamic of its own. As the German banks established their hold over Czech business, the young, ideologically driven managers who were now placed on the frontier of German imperialism saw a chance to make a name and reputation, and they developed their own initiatives. Such spontaneous ideas, emanating from the middle levels of the banking hierarchy rather than from the Berlin executives, eventually fitted in perfectly with the turn to radicalization in occupation policy in

September and October 1941, after Reinhard Heydrich came to Prague.

Why did the German banks take over the commercially less important and financially vulnerable Czech banks, the Escompte Bank (Dresdner) and the Union Bank (Deutsche) rather than the much more powerful and attractive Živnostenska Bank? This reflects the logic of politics rather than the preferred business strategies of the German banks. The German political authorities recognized the need to cooperate with Czech businesses if they were to succeed in their goal of making Bohemia-Moravia central in the new militarized greater German economy. German interests could be adequately secured by letting the Berlin banks take over the previously largely Jewish-owned Prague banks. Thus the Živnostenska remained untouched, even though both Dresdner and the Commerzbank tried to buy the Jewish-owned shares of that bank, and the six percent holding that was in the hands of the Böhmische Escompte Bank. The *Reichsprotector*'s office simply blocked such suggestions.[53]

The Transfer of Banks and Capital Restructuring

After the Munich Agreement of September 30, 1938, and the annexation of the Sudetenland by the German Reich, Deutsche Bank took over sixteen branches of a Czech bank with a large German-speaking customer base, the Česká Banká Union, or Böhmische Union-Bank (BUB), as part of a reordering of Sudeten banking under the direction of the Reich Economics Ministry. It had originally been interested in acquiring the Sudeten-German branches of a larger and more successful Czech-German bank, the Böhmische Escompte Bank (Bebca), but in early October 1938, German Bank Commissar Friedrich Ernst agreed to allocate the branches of the Escompte Bank to Dresdner Bank.[54] The commissar was responsible for granting permission to take over branches and also for decisions on the closure of individual branches.[55] In discussions within the German political authorities imposed on the Sudetenland, BUB was regarded with the least sympathy. A discussion in November 1938 about which banks could be used to extend German influence concluded that BUB "is ruled out as a point of concentration, being a purely Jewish bank."[56] Alternative schemes existed for solving the Sudeten banking problem. Wolfgang

Richter, for instance, whose title was "Economic Advisor to the Reich Commissar for the Sudeten-German Areas," favored reorganizing banking in new regional banks. The joint-stock banks, he declared, were "all more or less part of an international Jewish network." Commerzbank also expressed its interest in taking over BUB.[57]

In a telephone discussion with Hermann Abs on October 8, 1938, Friedrich Ernst asked about the contacts of Deutsche Bank with BUB, and Abs said, "The only information I had received from Amsterdam, not at our own initiative, was that possibly at the beginning of the week a meeting could be arranged with members of the managing board of BUB." Abs continued to insist that Bebca suited the structure and interests of Deutsche Bank more closely and that Deutsche Bank had no interest in BUB "because in our view BUB has a large Jewish clientele and is more biased towards the textile industry and the textile trade, whereas Bebca has a broader range of industrial-finance business."[58] Immediately after this conversation, Abs was called by a Dutch intermediary who explained that Leopold Stein, a managing director of BUB, had been approached by the Saxon regional bank ADCA but rather wished to work with Deutsche Bank. He was also assured that BUB had good relations with the Czech porcelain and ceramics industries.[59] Abs quickly ascertained that BUB did indeed have a substantial portfolio of industrial participations: Bitumia Bergbau und Chemische Industrie AG, Karlsbad (Karlovy Vary); Bohemia Keramische Werke; Karlsbader Kristallglasfabriken AG; Zettlitzer Kaolinwerke AG; Mühlig-Glas; Plüsch-Loewi; Petzold-Kaolin; Neudeker Wollkämmerei; Eisenwerk Rohau-Neudek, Kupferwerk Böhmen, Böhmische Metallwerke, Mannesmann Komotau (Chomutov); Reichenberger Brauerei; Weikersdorfer Textilwerke Samt- und Druckgewerbe; Hermannsthaler Papierfabrik; Troppauer Zuckerfabrik.[60]

But Deutsche Bank had already been in contact with a Czech bank. Bankers sometimes have finely tuned political antennas: The first contacts occurred before the Munich meetings. Oswald Rösler and Abs of Deutsche Bank started negotiations with Victor Ulbrich of the Deutsche Agrar- und Industriebank AG (DAIB), Prague. At the start, the German bankers do not appear to have been very enthusiastic about the new business prospects. Abs noted on the cards he kept detailing his business contacts: "our intentions, in which connection we need to make it perfectly clear to him that a full takeover of the branches, let alone of the whole business, is out of the question."[61]

On October 14, 1938, the bank commissar agreed that Deutsche Bank might begin negotiations with BUB as well as with the DAIB "for the purpose of taking over the Sudeten-German business of those banks." The suggestion was that Deutsche Bank should take over the whole business but might make reductions in the number of branches.[62]

The Deutsche Agrar- und Industriebank

The Agrarbank was founded in 1912 as the Deutsche Agrarbank für Österreich (Sitz Prag). It had lost heavily as a result of its large holdings of Austrian state paper during the First World War. A financial reconstruction in 1925 had been largely unsuccessful. The bank's capital had been further reduced in the depression (in 1930), to CKr 48 million. By 1938, it had some CKr 82 million of state deposits, securities, and guarantees in its assets that had originated in a depression bailout by the Czech government.[63] In an initial note, Deutsche Bank observed that the board of directors and the supervisory board as well as the entire staff ("except for two lesser members of staff") were "aryan". "In the clientele, only a small amount of business is done with Jewish customers."[64] Rösler of Deutsche Bank recorded that this was the only joint-stock bank "that has always emphasized its German character and maintains good relations with the Sudeten-German party." Ulbrich's brother-in-law was a member of the NSDAP "Auslands-Organisation." In the pre-Munich discussions, Ulbrich told Deutsche Bank that "plans already exist within the party regarding a reordering of Sudeten-German banking in the event of cession, plans in which Dresdner Bank, which is said to be interested in Bebca, also plays a certain role." Rösler believed that Ulbrich was chiefly worried about "his own future" and promised "that, if we open up a new operational area in Sudeten Germany – whether through a regional bank or through a branch system – and he contributed to this by bringing in his own organization or the business of other Czech banks, he could expect us to give him a or indeed the major position in Sudeten-German business."[65]

The largest block of shares (75,144 out of a total of 150,000 shares) was owned by a Swiss-domiciled but German-controlled institution,

Agraria Vermögensverwaltungs AG Schaffhausen, which held them as a trustee for the Zierhut-Spina group (Spina and Zierhut were Sudeten-German parliamentary deputies in Prague).[66] Agraria had developed in the 1930s as a channel for clandestine support to Germans outside the boundaries of the Reich, in particular in Poland and in the Sudetenland. It had been founded in 1930, with a capital of CHF 520,999 and in 1935 had taken over the restructuring (*Sanierung*) of the Kreditanstalt der Deutschen in Prague. Another part of its business lay in buying up low-priced foreign-domiciled German bonds and then reselling them with an arbitrage profit in Germany.[67]

There was also a small participation of the Wehrli Bank, Zürich. To buy out the Agraria, Deutsche Bank proposed to use £80,000 to obtain "blocked marks" (*Sperrmark*) as an injection of new capital. (Originally, these were marks derived from German financial payments on the credits of the 1920s, interest, amortization, or repayment, which had been blocked under the provisions of the German currency control after the banking crisis of 1931, but there was also a category of "emigrant blocked marks" (*Auswanderersperrmark*), because the assets of emigrants were blocked at the moment of their departure.) Blocked marks could be used only for long-term capital investment in Germany, the payment of insurance premiums, travel expenses, or for some sorts of export that were categorized as "additional." The deposit of the Czech state that had originated in attempts at rescue during the depression would be paid off by the cession of a mortgage (Grab, Prague) worth nominally just over the state deposit of CKr 30 million. The "Swiss" owners would be compensated with fifty percent of the nominal value of the shares.[68] In return, the DAIB would hand over its Sudeten branches to Deutsche Bank (Aussig [Ústí nad Labem], Benisch [Benesov], Bilin [Bílina], Bischofteinitz [Horsovský Týn], Bodenbach [Podmokly], Freiwaldau [Jeseník], Freudenthal [Bruntál], Gablonz [Jablonec], Komotau [Chomutov], Krummau a.d.M. [Ceský Krumlov], Landskrona [Lanskroun], Mährisch-Schönberg [Sumperk], Mährisch-Neustadt [Uničov], Mährisch-Trübau [Moravské Trebová], Marienbad [Márianské Lázne], Mies [Stribro], Neutitschein [Nový Jicín], Oberleutensdorf [Horni Litvinov], Postelberg [Postoloprty], Reichenberg [Liberec], Römerstadt [Rýmarov], Rumburg [Rumburk], Saaz [Zatec],

Schluckenau [Slukov], Teplitz-Schönau [Teplice], Teschen a.d.E. [Tecin], Troppau [Opava], Zwittau [Svitavy][69]; and the Czech branches would be sold to a Czech bank but would continue an independent existence as a bank with an exclusively German customer base. (Subsequently, Deutsche Bank was obliged to close half of the twenty-eight DAIB Sudeten branches. The annual report for 1938 lists only the following branches as newly acquired: Aussig, Bodenbach, Freudenthal, Gablonz, Komotau, Mährisch-Schönberg, Marienbad, Neutitschein, Reichenberg, Rumburg, Saaz, Schluckenau, Teplitz-Schönau, Troppau, Zwittau.) Deutsche Bank explained:

> Restricting the investors to German circles will protect the institution against sudden withdrawals in the event of political difficulties and thus reduces the risk of foreign currency having to be transferred to Prague on liquidity grounds. [...] It seems to us particularly important that there should be a bank in Prague under Reich-German control that is capable of looking after the interests of Germany and to which all domestic elements can turn for advice and information.[70]

There would be a government guarantee of RM 470,000 as security against the assets represented by Jewish debtors of the Sudeten branches. The final negotiations for the transfer occurred in Prague on March 7 and 8, 1939.

The original plan for the blocked marks envisaged that the Czech National Bank should raise the £80,000 from the Bank of England, which the Deutsche Golddiskontbank, a subsidiary of the Reichsbank, would exchange for blocked marks, which could be then used to cover the DAIB's bad debts. This did not prove realistic, because after the German invasion on March 15, 1939, the Bank of England blocked the Czech accounts. Deutsche Bank subsequently engaged in a complicated plan, initiated by the Reich Economics Ministry "by agreement with the Golddiskontbank [...] since the Golddiskontbank does not at the moment have the appropriate amounts of emigrant blocked marks available in cash."[71] The plan involved the purchase of foreign securities from German-Jewish emigrants at a very slight premium to the rate offered by the Golddiskontbank (6.1 or 6.2 percent rather than 6 percent; the Golddiskontbank originally proposed that Deutsche Bank could conduct the operation at the rate of 6.5).[72] In appealing to the Reich Economics Ministry to continue this device for the takeover of foreign banks, Deutsche Bank complained that Dresdner Bank,

> which to our knowledge was allowed to restructure the Czech banks it had taken over totally through blocked marks, was able to complete the takeover of the banks some time ago without loss to itself, whereas we are still, through no fault of our own, in fact to our regret and to the disadvantage of the Prague banks that the Reich arranged for us to take over, a long way from completing those takeovers, have in any case to pay for those takeovers at considerable loss to ourselves, and on top of that were again, in connection with providing transfer possibilities to strengthen the Prague banks' liquidity, obliged to accept substantial discrimination vis-à-vis Dresdner Bank.[73]

Deutsche Bank then circulated a request among its branches:

> Which of your larger Jewish deposit customers are possible candidates for such blocked-mark transactions? [...] How are those customers' deposits composed? Their form is of supreme importance because there is a possibility that some kind of time commitment could be imposed on us in respect of the securities to be taken over. We should also be interested to learn whether any emigration applications on the part of those customers have already come to your attention and what you think of the prospect of prompting those customers to emigrate by means of the offer we have outlined.[74]

The larger branches of Deutsche Bank then prepared lists of customers who had security accounts of RM 100,000 or more which might be sold in this way.

Deutsche Bank's chief economist, E. W. Schmidt, proposed another tactic, namely approaching the largest realtors in Berlin, Frankfurt, Breslau and Mannheim (i.e., cities with very large Jewish communities) and asking about Jewish real-estate sales (which required permission under the decree of December 3, 1938).[75] One firm in Berlin, Betzen (formerly Israel Schmidt), had for instance around RM 20 million worth of real estate.[76] These sums might then be used to make the transfer into Czechoslovakia. The political situation changed with the invasion of March 1939, but the question of the currency transfer remained until the currency union of Germany and the "Protectorate of Bohemia-Moravia" was declared in October 1940.

In June 1939, a new circular to Deutsche Bank branches announced that the bank would prefer to take over Reich loans and that the conversion rate would be only 6.1 percent. For cash, a slightly higher rate of 6.2 percent could be paid.[77]

By October 1939, eighty-nine Jewish "emigration accounts" (amounting to a total of RM 3,549,770) and seventy-six share portfolios of Jewish emigrants (RM 8,371,331.95) had been transferred into pounds in this way.[78] Of the £80,000, £62,000 had been used, but the operation continued, and British pounds continued to be paid out to emigrants. The £80,000 were used to acquire RM 15,782,000, of which RM 11,639,439.23 went to the DAIB and RM 4,142,477.04 to BUB.[79]

As early as November 1938, in discussions with *Reichskommissar* Friedrich Ernst, Deutsche Bank's representatives announced their interest in taking over not just the Sudeten branches but also the Prague office and the rest of the Czech business of the DAIB.[80] The story of the DAIB ended on June 20, 1940, with a new capital reduction, from CKr 32 million to CKr 16 million, and then a merger with BUB, backdated to January 1, 1939.

When Deutsche Bank examined the business of the DAIB, it noted that it was almost entirely in "aryan" hands.[81] Nevertheless, the property of Jewish emigrants was used to manage the financing of the acquisition of this bank. In turn, this institution would then be used to take over the Sudeten branches of BUB and/or Bebca.

The Böhmische Union-Bank

The BUB had been founded in 1872, with a capital of 10 million Austrian florins. It was substantially weakened by the depression but was in a far better position than the much more exposed Agrarbank. Because of the German character of the BUB and the Bebca, and of other Sudeten banks, and because they were believed to have substantial assets in Germany, these German banks were subject to depositor losses of confidence and bank runs after the banking crisis of July 1931.[82] Both BUB and Bebca had a substantial number of Jewish customers and employees and managers. The takeover of the Sudeten branches of BUB proceeded according to a document dated January 4, 1939, but was to take effect retrospectively from November 1, 1938.

But even earlier, individual Sudeten BUB branches put out signs saying "Deposits for Deutsche Bank accepted here" – to the irritation of the German authorities.[83] Eventually, Deutsche Bank took 23 branches in all, in Asch [Cheb], Aussig [Ústi nad Labem], Bodenbach [Podmokly], Braunau [Broumov], Brüx [Most], Freiwaldau [Jeseník], Gablonz [Jablonec], Graslitz [Kraslice], Hohenelbe [Vrchlabí], Jägerndorf [Krnov], Karlsbad [Karlovy Vary], Leitmeritz [Litomerice], Marienbad [Márianské Lázne], Mährisch-Schönberg [Sumperk], Neutitschein [Nový Jicín], Reichenberg [Liberec], Rumburg [Rumburk], Saaz [Zatec], Teplitz-Schönau [Teplice], Trautenau [Trutnov], Troppau [Opava], Warnsdorf [Varnsdorfi] and Zwittau [Svitary]. It subsequently closed the branches in Braunau, Freiwaldau, Graslitz, Leitmeritz, Trautenau, and Warnsdorf. The assets and liabilities of these branches were transferred to Deutsche Bank, and BUB kept only a few named customers.

Separating the branches from the Prague bank was a complex financial operation. It had major implications for the profitability of the remaining rump of BUB, which had lost branches in the most dynamic industrial areas, with substantial loans to the textile and glass industries. A memorandum of December 1938 presented to the Czech Finance Ministry listed fifty-three firms in which BUB had previously held sizable stakes. Of these, thirty-two had been lost in the Sudetenland. Of the Sudeten firms, the financial position of sixteen was said to be "good," eleven "had prospects," and five were "bad." Of the nineteen firms that remained in the Czech state, however, only one was classed as "good," nine "had prospects," six were "weak," and three were "bad." The bank had lost its best enterprises and was in a "catastrophic state."[84]

Another problem was that claims of the bank branches frequently extended across the new frontier, which was subject to exchange control. Many Jewish customers fled from Germany, across the frontier. BUB guaranteed claims of Deutsche Bank against Jewish debtors to a total of CKr 40 million. The takeover of property, assets, and claims required the consent of the foreign-exchange department in the office of the chief finance officer Berlin, in the form of a permit that required a new application every three months.[85] The conversion of assets and liabilities took place on a split basis: one rate (12 pfennig per CKr) was given for all depositors and borrowers "provided that they do not con-

cern Czech foreign-exchange dealers or other foreigners." Other obligations, including foreign bonds, were converted at 8.6 pfennig. By flee-
ing from the Sudetenland, Jews made themselves into "foreigners" to
whom the German authorities applied this second, less favorable, rate.

A decree of December 2, 1938, required the registration of Jewish
property in the Sudetenland. It brought Sudeten-German Jews into
the process of extraction of Jewish wealth by the German state that
followed the pogrom of November 9.[86] Many Jews living in the
Sudetenland then tried to transfer assets into Czechoslovakia (in
January 1939, such transactions were apparently allowed).

After the outbreak of the European war, the controls tightened. BUB
explained that it was still transferring amounts of up to CKr 30,000
without checking with the finance offices, although the bank assured
the Reich Finance Ministry that it would report the assets of Jews to
the authorities.[87] The chief finance officer in Karlsbad then arranged a
new and much tighter procedure:

> The following agreement has been reached with the manager of Deutsche
> Bank's Karlsbad branch. Deutsche Bank with its Sudeten-German
> branches will immediately inform the tax office responsible for the for-
> mer place of residence of account-holders currently residing in the
> Protectorate of all names, together with former places of residence.
> Immediately on receiving such lists, the tax offices will examine whether
> the account-holders concerned owe any residual taxes or Jewish prop-
> erty tax. If so, the competent tax office will execute the enforcement
> order on the assets or investments held by the bank; otherwise it will
> notify the bank that there are no outstanding tax liabilities or residual
> Jewish property tax. Where no enforcement order or tax-office ruling has
> been received within one week, the bank can effect the transfer in accor-
> dance with Reich Economics Ministry authorization unaccompanied by
> any forms.[88]

But on January 13, 1940, the Reich Finance Ministry agreed that
movements in accounts of less than CKr 30,000 did not require reporting to tax offices but that "accounts of Protectorate creditors" should
be registered.[89]

After the invasion of March 15, 1939, Bohemia-Moravia remained
legally separate from Germany, although it was clearly intended to be
part of a German economic imperium in which the German people
should "secure for itself the sources [...] of the raw materials so impor-

tant for its well-being."[90] By October 1940, Bohemia-Moravia was linked to the Reich by a customs union. But long before that, the banking system had been used to tie the Protectorate's economy to Germany through ownership.

The German authorities generally assumed, after the experience with the Sudetenland, that Deutsche Bank would continue to work with BUB. But one official in a meeting in the Banking Commissariat immediately objected that "Union Bank [of Bohemia, i.e. BUB] being a strongly Jewish-infiltrated enterprise, it therefore seems intolerable that Deutsche Bank should allocate orders to it on a preferential basis."[91] Together with Dresdner Bank, Deutsche Bank sent to the Reich Economics Ministry on March 14, 1939, one day before the invasion, a new plan for the reordering of Czech banks. Whereas the Reich Economics Ministry had tentatively given Deutsche Bank permission to buy the Tatra Bank's holding of the Escompte- und Volkswirtschaftliche Bank, Bratislava, the banks now proposed that Dresdner Bank and its affiliate the Vienna Länderbank should carry out this transaction, as well as a purchase of Bebca's share in the Bratislava Handels- und Kreditbank AG. Half of the Handels- und Kreditbank shares acquired in this way would then be transferred to Deutsche Bank or the Vienna Creditanstalt.[92]

After the actual invasion, Deutsche Bank sent (under the signatures of Hans Rummel and Oswald Rösler) a letter to the Reich Economics Ministry about the Czech banking situation. It would suit the goal of integration in the German economic sphere if

> in future one or more regional banks of a Czech character remain in existence for the time being. However, this is possible only on condition that those banks adapt themselves to the general German interest [*gesamtdeutsche Interesse*], in which connection it may turn out to be necessary that sooner or later German banks themselves participate in such institutions. [...] Another thing to be borne in mind here is that, of the partially transferred Czech banking industry, various institutions will need to disappear for racial reasons or because they are currently insolvent. In connection with the restructuring and liquidation of such institutions it would be necessary, where enterprises of significant size are concerned, to think of involving German big banks, since a regional bank would scarcely be in a position to cope with the problems that will arise in this connection.[93]

Rösler originally wanted to continue to work on a 50:50 basis with Dresdner Bank in taking over Bebca. The Reich Economics Ministry pushed Deutsche Bank to take over BUB instead, to which Rösler replied "that our separation [from Bebca] and our going over to BUB can be achieved only if through a blocked-marks transaction or something similar the opportunity is created of covering BUB's losses and if possible also having a little something left over for the BUB shareholders." Joachim Riehle, the Reich Economics Ministry's bank expert, took a tough line and refused to give a public guarantee for BUB. "Hereupon he spoke of the possibility of exercising coercion over us and received the reply that we could not anyhow be expected to bear the loss of some RM 20 million at BUB."[94]

Deutsche Bank thus continued to work with BUB in Bohemia and Moravia. It took twenty-three more branches (of a total of thirty-four), the twenty-eight branches of the DAIB, and five of the Mährische Bank (BUB's Slovakian branches were incorporated into the Union-Bank Pressburg, which was jointly owned by BUB and the Wiener Creditanstalt-Bankverein).

There exists an account of the events of the German invasion of the Sudetenland in September 1938 and then of Czechoslovakia in March 1939 and the takeover of BUB prepared by the bank's *Prokurist*, Dr. F. Kavan, who remained in this position through the whole of the occupation. Walter Pohle appeared in BUB in Prague on March 13, 1939, two days *before* the German invasion, declared himself to be a senior official and "confidential agent" of Deutsche Bank, and started negotiations about the financial claims of Deutsche Bank following the transfer of BUB's Sudeten-German branches. Clearly, the political atmosphere was already growing more tense. On March 10, the federal Czech government in Prague tried to launch a preemptive strike against Slovak separatism and to dissolve the Slovak government. By March 11–12, there was street fighting in Bratislava, and German minorities flew swastika flags and staged riots in Jihlava (Iglau) and Brno (Brünn). On March 13, Hitler summoned his ally, Slovak separatist leader Father Jozef Tiso, to Berlin. On March 14 and 15, bank panics broke out and the BUB was forced to close.

At least to Kavan, in retrospect it was clear that Pohle knew about the impending invasion; and immediately after the invasion, German military officials demanded a greater German influence over BUB. On

March 16 or 17, Pohle put in another "forceful appearance, saying that BUB was a Jewish enterprise and must therefore, both in its own interest and in that of Deutsche Bank as major creditor arising out of the transaction of the cession of the Sudeten branches, be pronounced an aryanized enterprise as quickly as possible." Pohle's rival at Dresdner Bank, Reinhold von Lüdinghausen, behaved in a similar way, arriving in military uniform in the Bebca offices shortly after the German invasion. A verse circulated about Dresdner Bank board member Karl Rasche:

Who's this, marching behind the first tank?
That's Dr. Rasche of Dresdner Bank![95]

Pohle, according to Kavan, was protected by the Gestapo, and immediately dismissed the Jewish directors and appointed the previous director of the auditing division, Joseph Krebs, who had German nationality, as the new director. The supervisory board meeting of March 16, 1939, began with a declaration by Otto Freund "that his service contract is not being renewed and that he will remain at the bank's disposal as long at it wishes." Such an action was certainly not legal under the bank's existing articles of association. Who had the legal authority not to renew the contract? Freund also stated that Leopold Stein and Schubert "have resigned, which information was registered with regret." At the next meeting of the supervisory board, the existing eighteen members resigned en bloc; only four members returned in the reconstituted supervisory board.[96] Freund, the previous principal director, was arrested fourteen days later by the German police, and soon died in prison, allegedly by his own hand. They were replaced by Deutsche Bank officials, or by people who were acceptable to the occupation regime. The *Tantiemen* (payments to directors by virtue of their membership of other supervisory boards) of the former Jewish directors were then to be paid directly into the bank. In June 1939, Pohle announced the dismissal of the "non-aryan" members of the auditing department. But in January 1940, he still reported that of the 917 employees, 38 were Jewish.[97]

To foreign bankers, however, Deutsche Bank carefully camouflaged the events of March 1939. When Sterling Bunnell of the National City Bank of New York visited Deutsche Bank in May 1939, he was told that in the reordering of Czech banking, "the removal of the Jewish members of the board of directors was effected without coercion by mutual agreement. To our knowledge [he said], the persons concerned had resigned their offices voluntarily in the light of the altered political circumstances."[98]

In April 1939, the Reich Economics Ministry in Berlin demanded "final clarification of the question [...] whether Union Bank of Bohemia [BUB] is to be seen as an aryan or as a Jewish enterprise." Some of the companies in Bohemia and Moravia in which BUB held participations found themselves in difficulties because they were treated by the German authorities as "non-aryan" by reason of BUB's engagement. Deutsche Bank was required to prepare "at the earliest opportunity a memo concerning the current circumstances, both financial (with regard to capital) and personal, [...] which is then to be forwarded to Prague for checking."[99]

Accordingly, Deutsche Bank sent a paper to the Reich Economics Ministry in which it attributed the necessity for a "restructuring" of BUB to the actions of the German government.

> Immediately following the establishment of the Reich Protectorate of Bohemia-Moravia, it was suggested to our bank by Reich Economics Ministry through its representative in Prague that it would be in the general economic interests of Germany that it [our bank] should take BUB under its wing and we were asked to look into the possibilities of restructuring as well as a definitive takeover of the bank by ourselves. It was also encumbent upon us to finish off the restructuring of the German Bank of Agriculture and Industry [DAIB], which had been making no progress for months, while on the other hand further implementation of the Bebca project, hitherto run jointly with Dresdner Bank, should be the sole preserve of the said institution.

The memorandum also explained that the presence of Deutsche Bank bankers in Prague had not necessarily meant a commitment to take over the bank:

> In the light of the fact that BUB had become leaderless following the disappearance of the entire Jewish management, we further agreed that our director Walter Pohle (formerly of the Berlin office) should be appointed to the board and to the executive committee of Union Bank of Bohemia. This also occurred only in order to obviate the most extreme risks and only with the reservation (which was also conceded to us) that no sort of conclusion should be inferred therefrom regarding our intention of finally

taking over BUB which was acknowledged at the time by the Reich Economics Ministry.[100]

On this basis BUB was granted a "certificate of aryanness" (*Bescheingung über den arischen Charakter*) on July 5, 1939.

In his 1950 affidavit, Kavan claimed that Deutsche Bank deliberately made BUB appear to have large losses. "In the circumstances, Deutsche Bank representatives decided to make the BUB balance sheet look so bad that it in fact showed a loss and could be utilized for their further plans." In March and April 1939, Deutsche Bank submitted to the Reich Economics Ministry estimates of the losses on the basis of an audit by the Czech firm Revisni Jednota Bank and of its own – more generous – estimates. The Jednota concluded that the bank had lost all its reserves, as well as CKr 40 million of its capital. Deutsche Bank initially estimated the losses as at least CKr 200 million. It argued that the Jednota had not taken into account the likelihood of losses in Slovakia and Carpatho Ukraine, "losses to be expected on non-aryan accounts receivable," and "reordering costs/dealing with non-aryans."[101]

The main German aim was to reduce the capital by a ratio of 1:10 to make it possible for Deutsche Bank to acquire a majority of the shares. The Czech bankers had originally preferred a smaller capital reduction of 1:4 (Kavan mistakenly claimed 1:5), but the larger-scale German plan prevailed.[102] In March 1939, the capital of BUB had amounted to CKr 150 million (nominal), in 750,000 shares of CKr 200. Of these shares, 100,000 belonged to the British Overseas Bank, London (which also held an option on another 25,000); 70,292 to the Société Générale de Belgique, Brussels; 130,000 to the bank itself; and 80,000 to an enterprise controlled by the bank, the Petschek sugar refinery.[103] Of the other shares, 264,000 were domiciled in the protectorate and 106,000 in the Sudetenland and Austria. Kavan noted that "in fact a substantial number of those shares were owned by non-aryans." In addition there were, as an internal memorandum of Deutsche Bank noted, further "quite substantial amounts [...] in the possession of Sudeten-German industrialists."[104] In May 1939, it was reported that about three percent of the shares were in "non-aryan hands."[105]

The Sudeten-German owners were bought out at a price of twenty-five percent of the nominal value of their shares. In the politically turbulent months of August and September 1939, Deutsche Bank also tried unsuccessfully to buy shares from the London and Brussels banks at a price of ten percent of their nominal value.[106] The Société Générale refused to go along with this plan. Having failed in its move to establish complete legal control, Deutsche Bank instead bought the 210,000 shares of the bank that BUB controlled (at a low price of CKr 20, although the shares were valued in the books at CKr 77.27). This purchase was ratified by the Reich Economics Ministry only on March 16, 1940.

An extraordinary general meeting was held on December 12, 1939, to agree the capital reduction to one tenth of the previous value. Deutsche Bank had 216,000 shares, and in addition had bought another 6,100; 85,448 were in trustee accounts. It asked the Belgian Société Générale to vote for its proposals, but the Belgian bank cabled back with the instruction that its votes should be used to abstain. Walter Pohle expressed his extreme irritation about the Belgian decision. (Two months later, the governor of the Société Générale, Alexandre Galopin, told Hermann Abs that his bank was "not under any circumstances prepared to lend retrospective support to events in Czechoslovakia by taking part in supervisory board meetings or general meetings of BUB.")[107] Only 1,449 shares were represented by individuals, whom Kavan believed to be members of a shareholders' protection association. Again, Kavan's affidavit is quite damning. When Kavan warned Pohle that many of these individuals had detailed inside knowledge of the finances of BUB, Pohle replied: "These people should think long and hard about their demonstration plans, because steps will be taken to ensure that, at the general meeting of 12 December 1939, people from the Gestapo or persons very close to the Gestapo will also be present." At this extraordinary general meeting, Deutsche Bank was sold the shares held by BUB "at the price, laid down by the German foreign-exchange authorities, of CKr 100. – = RM 10. –."[108]

Pohle explained the capital reduction as the quid pro quo for bringing in Deutsche Bank and its support. He also told the general meeting: "We believe that, in our area of responsibility, we can build a bridge from the Protectorate to the Greater German Reich and even farther afield."[109] The latter objective involved Pohle in increasingly ambitious plans for economic and financial reordering, some of which brought him eventually into conflict with the German authorities, as well as with Deutsche Bank's Berlin headquarters.

Deutsche Bank then wanted to turn BUB into a commercial bank and to sell off its industrial holdings. Kavan later cited a BUB letter to Oswald Rösler of May 23, 1939:

> Once Deutsche Bank had achieved complete influence over BUB, a series of valuable assets, notably group enterprises, were indeed sold to Nazi officials at well below their true value. The confidential agents of Deutsche Bank delegated to BUB misused BUB funds on the one hand to finance the German war effort, on the other hand for economic penetration not only within the territory of the so-called Protectorate but also beyond, in the rest of the so-called south east by financing aryanizations and otherwise transferring enterprises and property into Nazi ownership.

Indeed, Pohle had explicitly acknowledged this objective in his explanation of the new philosophy of the bank in December 1939:

> In line with the tradition of our now particularly close associate, Deutsche Bank, we intend to win new customers and keep those already won by satisfying them in every way by what we do, not by binding them to us in terms of capital. On the contrary, we are taking steps to loosen capital ties – carefully, of course, and having regard to our business interests.[110]

Deutsche Bank's argument rested on the observation that BUB had not originally been constructed as an industrial holding company but had acquired its substantial shareholdings largely as a result of depression-era difficulties.

Some of the shares of BUB were sold directly to Deutsche Bank after the seizure of the Sudetenland: the Mühlig-Union Glasindustrie AG; the Petzold-Döll-Werke AG; Bituma, Karlsbad; Reichenberg-Maffersdorfer und Gablonzer Brauereien AG; and Eisenwerke AG Kriebich. Other significant holdings were put on sale, including the ceramics works Bohemia, Karlsbad (Karlovy Vary); Karlsbader Kristallglasfabriken AG; Ludwig Moser & Söhne; Erste Böhmische Glasindustrie AG; Bleistadt; G. A. Fröhlich's Sohn, Weberei; Samt- und Druckfabriks AG, Warnsdorf (Varnsdorf); Troppauer Zuckerraffinerie AG; and Lederer und Wolf.[111]

Deutsche Bank also seemed to the Prague bankers to be striving for greater direct control of Czech affairs. In his postwar memorandum,

Kavan claimed that Deutsche Bank applied the *"Führerprinzip"* (leadership principle) and centralized all decisions in Berlin, so that BUB "was an independent institution in name alone; in reality it was a subsidiary of Deutsche Bank."[112]

BUB in 1939 was in a sorry state. Its commercial position had been eroded by the depression. It was illiquid. Its management had been in large part German-Jewish, and the departure of its senior managers left the bank effectively leaderless. It remained vulnerable to anti-Semitic purges. Its most valuable industrial holdings had been in the Sudetenland. At lower levels, in November 1939 the firm was still employing a large number of Jews.[113] Many of the banks' depositors were Jewish, and many of the credits and industrial assets related to Czech-Jewish firms. In August 1939, a candid letter to a member of Deutsche Bank's supervisory board stated:

> In addition to the partitioning-off of Sudeten-German business, the formation of the Protectorate of Bohemia-Moravia was in the nature of things a further heavy blow for what was left of BUB, for its continued existence as a German-Jewish bank became impossible. On top of the general difficulties of economic reordering in the Protectorate, BUB was particularly effected by the fact that it was almost exclusively Jewish-run and that even today much of its clientele also consists of Jewish firms, whose future is in doubt.[114]

And finally, it had lost CKr 2,461,000 through "speculation at bank risk."[115] It survived by borrowing large sums from its own pension fund (the CKr 20.5 million were repaid in 1942).[116]

After the outbreak of the European war, a further source of weakness emerged. Some of the bank's safe-custody accounts were held abroad, where they were vulnerable to legal action. In November 1940, Pohle reported "on the seizure that has occurred of safe-custody accounts in New York because of actions brought by Jews who have emigrated to the United States for release of their stockholdings and on the only partly completed transfer of such accounts with Dutch banks to Swiss banks; he points out the possibility that in certain circumstances the bank might successfully be sued by customers for damages."[117]

The reordering of BUB had involved a 10:1 capital reduction, so that CKr 150 million worth of capital was reduced to CKr 15 million. The capital was then increased to CKr 100 million through the issue of 212,500 new shares at a nominal value of CKr 400. This required the consent of the Reich Finance Ministry, which was requested in January 1940 and granted on January 18.[118] The capital reduction was followed by an offer from Deutsche Bank to buy out existing shareholders at a price of twenty-five percent of par value. Jewish shareholders were explicitly excluded from this option; CKr 60 million were to be issued to Czech shareholders, and Deutsche Bank led CKr 25 million. With the assistance of the private bank Delbrück Schickler & Co., Deutsche Bank eventually acquired CKr 76,740,000 worth of shares and thus owned seventy-five percent of BUB.[119] (In a subsequent capital increase of CKr 50 million in 1942, the Vienna Creditanstalt took a significant minority participation. As a result, in 1943 Deutsche Bank held fifty-eight percent of the shares, the Creditanstalt thirty-three percent, the British Overseas Bank and the Société Générale two percent, and "other banks" seven percent of the capital.)[120]

Deutsche Bank received permission to buy up Jewish shares at the much lower rate of eleven percent of their value.[121]

The new management of the bank came from Deutsche Bank in Germany. The main figure, Walter Pohle from the Berlin office, was an energetic young man, thirty-one years old, who had briefly been employed by the Reich Economics Ministry before joining Deutsche Bank. He had already worked with Hermann Abs in the attempt to take Adler & Oppenheimer (A&O) into "aryan" hands. Pohle asked Deutsche Bank to keep open the possibility of his return to his old bank at the end of his adventure in Prague. In January 1940, Deutsche Bank gave a written commitment to find Pohle a place "in the co-management of a major branch" or at the head office "if we have no occasion to revise our assessment of you in personal and business terms."[122] The other former Deutsche Bank representative on the board of management, Max Ludwig Rohde, was older, and came from the Saarbrücken branch.[123]

Taking over the management of BUB and installing new directors[124] involved substantial costs for Deutsche Bank. Because the operation had been conducted at the insistence of the German government, Deutsche Bank demanded a public subsidy. Its initial strategy was to try to extend the blocked-marks procedure that had been used to acquire the DAIB.[125]

Eventually, in December 1939, the Reich Economics Ministry agreed to the provision of a subsidy on the grounds that "BUB had [...] always been a German institution. Its collapse would therefore represent a political setback for German-ness [*das Deutschtum*]."[126] As a result, the German state agreed to meet fifty-five percent of Deutsche Bank's losses arising out of Sudeten debtors of BUB through the extension of a Reich guarantee up to a total loss of RM 16.9 million. The guarantee and loss account, it was agreed, would be credited by any gains to Deutsche Bank arising out of a revaluation of the Czech assets of BUB.

From the standpoint of Deutsche Bank, few aspects of this transaction could hold any attraction. In November 1939, the bank explained to the German government that it would not have been interested in the business "if we had been completely free in our decision-making."[127] Internally, it justified the takeover on two grounds: first, that the initiative had lain not with the bank but rather with the Reich Economics Ministry; second, that without any response from Deutsche Bank to the new situation, the expansion of Germany would in reality mean enhanced business for the politically better-connected Dresdner Bank.[128]

From the beginning of 1941, as BUB's profitability revived dramatically, Deutsche Bank tried to obtain a cancellation of the Reich guarantee of BUB claims. The bank explained: "[It does not suit] Deutsche Bank to have within its group a Reich guarantee for its commitments and even less to receive payments in consequence of that guarantee that might be seen as subsidies. The reputation of BUB will also suffer if it is deemed to be in some way underwritten by the Reich."[129] Deutsche Bank now proposed to take the risk of BUB losses, provided the full amount of the loss could be written off against taxes: "[that] no tax disadvantages accrue to it as a result, i.e. if in its profit-and-loss account it can write off against tax, just like any other accounts-receivable loss, the loss it will now incur in its entirety rather than merely at 45 per cent, and if for example waiving its right vis-à-vis BUB to draw on reserves is not put down against it as taxable income."[130]

In the end, the Reich guarantee was canceled only in February 1942, with retrospective effect from the end of 1941. Deutsche Bank at the same time bought the Reich's income and adjustment bonds

(*Besserungsscheine*) of Leibig & Co., Reichenberg, and J. Ginzkey, Maffersdorf.[131]

The extent of the losses tells us a considerable amount about BUB's position. The initial subsidy from the Reich included a provision for CKr 40 million (RM 4 million) claims against "non-aryans." In November 1939, Deutsche Bank estimated its total likely losses as RM 20.6 million of which RM 4.2 million were covered through the transfer to Deutsche Bank of assets from DAIB. In April 1941, a foreign-exchange audit report came to the conclusion that the losses on debtor accounts amounted to CKr 141,138,000.[132] The eventual losses indeed were considerably lower than this estimate – RM 5.9 million, of which the Reich guarantee had covered RM 3.23 million.[133] This was because, after 1941, a quite dramatic turnaround in the bank's fortunes, scope of business activity, and profitability occurred. The overall balance sheet of the bank grew from CKr 5,426.1 million at the end of 1942 to CKr 7,074.5 million at the end of 1943.[134]

In November 1941, the Prague subsidiary (Revisions- und Organisations-Gesellschaft m.b.H.) of the Deutsche Revisions- und Treuhand AG prepared a comprehensive audit of BUB for the Reich Economics Ministry in which it adjusted some of the rather conservative valuations of BUB.

What was the source of the new profitability that allowed the government guarantee to be paid off? By the beginning of 1943, Rohde stated "that on the other hand it is possible to speak of a positive growth in business in the past year."[135] The main source of income was the participation of the bank in a dramatic reordering of Czech and more generally central-European business life.

The "Aryanization" of Czech Companies

The uncertainty about the extent of BUB losses arose in large measure because of the threat that the party and Sudeten-German nationalists would use compulsory "aryanizations" as a way of stripping BUB's assets, which had largely been acquired as a result of nonperforming loans. Thus, the Reich Ministry of Food proposed in April 1939 to seize the Troppauer Zuckerfabrik, on the grounds that BUB, which held a majority of the shares, had remained a Jewish bank.

"The interests of the farmer are so urgent that any bank interests have to take second place." In 1940, the Four-Year Plan authorities took over the operation of the Kupferwerke Böhmen, in which BUB had a substantial holding.[136]

The Kupferwerke Böhmen was a producer of copper, nickel, bronze, but especially of aluminum. It had a capital of CKr 43.75 million, thirty-five percent of which was held by BUB. On October 9, 1940, an option to buy these shares at a price of 175 was sold to Dr. Ing. Emil Hammerschmid.[137] By the end of 1941, Hammerschmid had additionally bought CKr 6 million (nominal) in shares at a price of about 70 from other Jewish owners. Although profits had fallen sharply between 1938 and 1940, the prospects for the firm were good, on the basis of the expectation of greater production for military purposes.

It was textile firms that had been in the greatest difficulties in the depression, and BUB had come to hold a controlling interest in a number of companies. Usually "aryanization," therefore, involved a writing-off of part of the loans. Thus, Hans Kreibich[138] took over Ernst Naundorff Nachf. Holzstoff- und Pappenfabrik, Merkelsgrün, with a reduction of BUB's loan by RM 8,000. On a larger scale, when the Idealspaten und Schaufelwalzwerke vormals Eckhardt & Co. K. G. Herdecke took over the Teplitzer Eisenwerke Schaufel- und Zeugwaren AG, a claim of BUB of RM 317,000 was reduced to RM 110,000.[139]

The 1941 audit listed Hermann Pollack's Söhne as "not yet aryanized." This was a very substantial spinning and weaving firm based in Trübau, but with branches in Braunau (Sudetenland), Neurode (Silesia), Vienna, and Schaffhausen (Switzerland). The Trübau and Neurode plant made small profits, but there were major losses in Braunau and Vienna. Before the war, it had also operated branches in Croatia and Hungary but had ceded these to Swiss banks, which held a claim of RM 6.84 million against the company. The firm had been jointly financed by BUB and Bebca. The total credit of BUB had been CKr 21.8 million in 1938 and had risen to CKr 50.3 million by September 1941. Forty percent of the stock was owned by holding companies, the Polysamplex G.m.b.H. and the Participa AG, which belonged to the banks. The other sixty percent belonged to "the last Jewish owner," Grödl, but as the result of an agreement of early 1939 "that a partner should forfeit his capital share on moving his place of residence abroad," he had, according to BUB and its auditors, lost his share in the firm. The auditors concluded: "With that aryanization is virtually complete, but in the opinion of the Reich Protector some of the agreements still lack the approval of the authorities, who are asking for a dejudification levy [*Entjudungsabgabe*]. The two banks have initially offered the sum of CKr 5 million, but no final agreement has yet been reached."

Uncertainty about valuations, and the extent of depression era losses, also gave substantial scope to the unscrupulous profiteers who descended on many smaller and medium-size Jewish firms. The hat factory Reiniger & Co., Komotau (Chomutov), for instance, had been managed immediately after the invasion by a commissar, Walter Apitzsch, who owned the Dresden firm that eventually acquired Reiniger. In advance of the sale, he reduced the value of the firm by a sale of inventories at undervalued prices, with the consent of the party authorities and the governor of the Sudeten district (*Gau*).[140]

BUB also held almost the entire capital of M. B. Neumann's Söhne Union-Textilindustrie- und Druckfabriks AG in Königinhof (Dvur Králové), a company that had found itself in difficulties in the early 1920s and had in 1924 passed into the ownership of BUB. The company paid no dividend between 1924 and 1938 and had in 1936 reduced its capital by half. The bank had also given a substantial credit to the firm: CKr 26.2 million in 1938, reduced to CKr 10 million by 1941.

A separate firm in the same complex, M. B. Neumann's Söhne, ostmärkische Weberei und Druckerei AG, was also almost completely owned by BUB and also depended on credit from the bank. It had its major production site in Hohenems in the Vorarlberg but maintained the head office in Vienna. The textile works in Hohenems had been started in 1800 by "supplier to the emperor" (*K. K. Hoffaktor*) Wolf Josef Levi. In 1841, after a bankruptcy, it had been bought by Philipp and Josef Rosenthal, and in 1916 the firm passed into the possession of the Bohemian firm M. B. Neumann's Söhne. Since November 1938, the two Neumann firms were run as separate operations. The Austrian firm's capitalization amounted to RM 800,000. Its sales fell sharply between 1939 and 1940, but it started to produce cotton drill, bedsheets, and sacks for the Wehrmacht.

BUB tried to find purchasers, and advertised in the textile trade press in Berlin. In the summer of 1941, the firm feared that it was about to be closed down, and a rapid sale to someone with good political contacts represented the only hope of a rescue.[141] In August 1941 the name was changed to Hohenemser Weberei und Druckerei AG, and in December Joseph Otten bought the firm for RM 728,832 and assumed the RM 1,172,293 debt to the bank. Of that, RM 521,530 were to be paid immediately, and the rest would be spread over four years. Part of the purchase price involved the payment of interest arrears and was accompanied by a commitment of BUB to pay back up to RM 100,000, "provided that you or rather Deutsche Bank receive profits from the new business opportunities introduced by Dr. Otten or Mr. Bührer [from the firm of Esders and Dyckhoff, and an old family acquaintance of the Ottens]."[142] Because BUB had marked its valuation of the Hohenems factory down to RM 175,000, the sale represented a substantial realization of profit. As part of the sale proceedings, Otten paid a RM 11,400 commission to a Herr Hess.[143]

Just a few shares were not in the hands of BUB. As part of the sales negotiations, BUB recorded: "Regarding the two Jewish shares, which we have applied to the Vienna property-transfer authorities to buy, we agreed after discussion that we will buy those shares as soon as we have acquired possession of our 98 per cent."[144]

Otten came from a textile family and was an official of the Reich Economics Ministry and the director of the "Textile Group." According to BUB, which forwarded a credit assessment from Deutsche Bank, he had been very successful in his management of an "aryanized" factory in Mönchengladbach, the mech. Weberei L. Jörissen & Co. In 1939 he had been appointed deputy Reich commissar for silk, artificial silk, and cellulose.[145]

The peculiarity of this case was that although the transaction was not in a conventional sense an "aryanization," because the company had belonged to BUB since 1924, many of the participants assumed that it was: because in 1938 it was not clear whether BUB had been "aryanized," but perhaps also because of the century-long Jewish history of the Hohenems spinning factory. In August 1938, Josef Krebs, the director of BUB, wrote to the director of Hohenems, Alexander Lauterbach: "We have aryanized staff, management, and administration, the qualification in this regard being the as yet unanswered question, which one hopes will find a positive resolution but which in any case requires a further, indeterminate period before it is decided."[146] In December 1938, the firm was still complaining about its uncertain status: "When we approach the various agencies regarding quota amounts or other matters to do with procurement, the question is repeatedly raised as to whether we are an aryan firm. If the question cannot be answered with a simple 'yes,' one finds oneself at something of a disadvantage. In other words, in connection with such important occasions discrimination is possible and to be expected."[147]

In August 1941, in preparation for the sale, the firm was inspected by the Alpine Economic Chamber, whose report stated: "From as early as 1923 the enterprise could no longer be described as Jewish, because there is no proof that a majority of the shares were in Jewish hands."[148] But the district economic advisor immediately expressed his dissatisfaction (he was *verstimmt* [put out], he said) that the bank was conducting sale negotiations without consulting the party authorities.[149]

The firm's name was changed again in June 1942 to Hohenemser Weberei und Druckerei Josef Otten. In February 1943, Dr. Johannes Christian of Deutsche Bank visited Hohenems to recalculate the purchase price, and in October 1944, the credit was transferred from BUB to Deutsche Bank's Friedrichshafen branch.

The wartime sale of Hohenems had some peculiar postwar legal consequences. Otten, who was suspected of having taken illegitimate advantage of his political position in the Third Reich and was distrusted by his competitors in Hohenems as a German and an outsider, was arrested and interned (without trial) between 1945 and 1947. In March 1947, the Austrian minister for property protection and economic planning wrote that Hohenems "passed out of the ownership of M. B. Neumann's Söhne into that of BUB as a result of a share sale and was taken from it by Josef Otten under the duress of the National Socialist seizure of power."[150] In October 1952, Otten concluded an agreement with BUB in liquidation, under which he paid an additional 2 million shillings. "BUB, a state-owned enterprise in liquidation, and Dr. Josef Berkovits as administrator acknowledge that Dr. Josef Otten, in acquiring the said shares, otherwise observed the rules of honest dealing and has therefore become the honest owner and may do what he wishes with the profits withdrawn from the [...] enterprise." But the payments were made not to Prague but to BUB's "representative," Friedrich Freiherr von Kubinsky, with an address in Switzerland. In fact, von Kubinsky was a former shareholder who had no contact with the Prague bank and no authority to represent BUB but who had managed to establish his claims in Austria. In the 1960s, Deutsche Bank tried to reclaim the credit given originally from BUB and then transferred to the Friedrichshafen branch. The case illustrates not only how more sales were regarded as "aryanizations" than actually fit any realistic definition of such a process, both in the Nazi period and in subsequent restitution proceedings, but also how intimately connected BUB and Deutsche Bank were.

The Petschek sugar works, in which BUB had a large participation and which also held some of BUB's own capital, was sold in part to a cooperative organization of rural raw-sugar factories, the Verband der bäuerlichen Rohzuckerfabriken. The money received (some CKr 20 million) was then used to purchase more factories.[151]

BUB repeatedly acted as an intermediary, first buying property on its own account and then reselling the business. For instance, in March 1940, "Director [Viktor] Ulbrich pointed out with reference to the Hatschein sugar works that the bank risked having to grant a large discount in connection with an aryanization by others and that the bank was therefore looking into the question of declaring itself as a prospective purchaser."[152]

In addition, the bank regularly gave credits for "aryanization" sales. Thus, for instance, in the meeting of the bank's credit committee in March 1941, the minutes record: "Grodetsky and Pollak: current account for CKr 2.5 m. for aryanization of the firm by Simm & Söhne, Gablonz-Prague."[153]

Sales of Jewish property in the Sudetenland, which included major companies such as the Teplitzer Eisenwerke, were handled through Deutsche Bank's branch in Reichenberg, which also managed transactions such as the takeover of two Jewish-owned hotels in Karlsbad for use as a branch office of Deutsche Bank.[154]

Almost all of the capital required for the purchase of Jewish property in the Protectorate came from Germany. Deutsche Bank circulated lists to its German branches detailing Czech businesses for sale. By mid-October, a total of 134 enterprises had been advertised in this way. In its circular advising how to approach German companies, Deutsche Bank stated:

> Customers need not make a decision until they have all the details; they should simply express an interest in one of the items on offer in principle. The advantage is twofold: firstly, being in the front rank; secondly, with the aid of the negotiating licence, very rapidly obtaining an entry permit to visit the Protectorate for the purpose of viewing the enterprise concerned.[155]

The purchase price could then be converted into foreign currency, but only at the six percent rate offered by the Golddiskontbank.[156]

BUB sent lists of possible companies that might be taken over to Deutsche Bank, for distribution by Deutsche Bank branches.[157] It also targeted specific enterprises directly. Thus, in June 1939, Deutsche Bank Mannheim was asked to inquire whether the shoe manufacturer Cornelius Heyl was interested in buying the Jewish-owned Edmund Traub leather factory in Podbaba, one of the most famous makers of fine box-calf leather. BUB urged that very prompt action was needed, as there was a great deal of interest in the firm, whose Czech *Prokurist* was planning to hand the firm over to his business contacts.[158]

In some cases, the private purchasers expressed a marginal preference for non-Jewish property. Industry magnate Günther Quandt, for instance, used BUB between 1939 and 1941 to purchase property, preferably but not necessarily non-Jewish property, at favorable prices. Or another example: In June 1941, the largely non-Jewish-owned Metallwalzwerke AG was sold by BUB to Mannesmann.[159] Mannesmann also bought some Jewish-owned enterprises (for instance, Graber & Sohn, Bratislava) through BUB: But in none of the correspondence is there any indication of the question of Jewish ownership being a problematic or controversial issue.[160]

One "aryanized" factory, the Bohemia ceramics works in Neurohlau (Nová Role) near Karlsbad, which had been owned by the Prague investment and banking house of Petschek and which held substantial assets in Germany, was sold by BUB to the SS in 1940. It had paid no dividend since 1922 and had large inventories that were difficult to sell. Deutsche Bank noted that "a purchase-price demand based solely on balance-sheet figures would need to be at what for third parties would be an unacceptably high level."[161] Negotiations for the sale had begun as early as August 1939. Like many struggling Czech firms, Bohemia had substantial debts to its bank, and the sale involved a reduction of the outstanding credit from RM 601,195 to just over half that figure. The loss was shared equally between Deutsche Bank and the German state.[162] These terms were firmly opposed by the only one of BUB's directors who had been part of the pre-1939 management, Joseph Krebs; in the end, the sales contracts were signed by the new men from Deutsche Bank while Krebs was absent on leave. Its chief attraction for the SS lay in its capacity to provide high-grade china artifacts designed in the form of SS kitsch. An SS report listing the SS economic enterprises described the firm as "in qualitative terms the most important porcelain in the whole of Czechoslovakia, for both crockery and figurative porcelain, notably such specialties as underglaze blue (indistinguishable from Chinese and Japanese ware) and what is called 'ice glaze.'" Five percent of its production was reserved, at Himmler's command, "to provide gifts for SS newlyweds, bomb-damage victims, and other needy persons." In 1942, the factory provided spare capacity for use in the armaments economy.[163] The SS management ran the works in Germany as the Porzellan-Manufaktur Allach-München, with a labor force composed in part of prisoners from the concentration camp at Dachau. Allach was one of the first parts of what by the end of the war became a gigantic economic empire under the control of the SS.[164]

Jewish Accounts, Assets, and Safe Deposits

BUB had already had some experience of "aryanization" before September 1938, because it owned a majority stake in the Vienna Bankhaus Rosenfeld & Co., which had been rapidly "aryanized" after the Anschluss of March 1938. In the summer of 1939, Walter Pohle suggested that Deutsche Bank should use Rosenfeld to take over Jewish shares as part of the blocked-marks campaign to finance the takeover of the DAIB: "out of consideration for the campaign planned by Deutsche Bank, whereby Jewish stocks and shares may be acquired in sizeable amounts."[165] But Deutsche Bank had already carried out the maximum amount of blocked-mark conversions by this time.

Already in the national emergency of September 1938, the Czech government had tried to mobilize foreign assets and had ordered a partial opening of bank safes to convince citizens to comply with their patriotic duty in surrendering foreign assets. On March 25 and 31, 1939, under the occupation, the Finance Ministry ordered that the safes of Jews should be opened and inventoried. Czech currency was to be transferred to a "tied – non-aryan – account," and objects of value and precious metals were to be left in the safe but sealed.

The administration of Jewish accounts produced a voluminous and incriminating correspondence with the Gestapo, especially after the change in the occupation regime and the beginning of Jewish deportations in the autumn of 1941. On September 27, 1941, SS-Obergruppenführer Reinhard Heydrich took over the functions of "Reich protector in Bohemia-Moravia" from Konstantin von Neurath, who was placed on sick leave. Heydrich's major mission lay in the Germanification of the new territories and the erosion of the power of the Czech government under Emil Hácha. On November 24, 1941, the occupation authorities conducted the first deportation of Czech Jews to the ghetto in Theresienstadt (Teresín). Theresienstadt occupied a unique position in the world of the Nazi camps: In part designed as a model or display institution, it was intended to lull the Jewish victims of Nazi persecution into a false sense of security. In fact, on January 9, 1942, deportations from Theresienstadt to the killing camps of the occupied east began.

Deportations had obvious financial implications. Banks, including BUB, were presented with numbered lists prepared by the "Central Office for Settlement of the Jewish Question in Bohemia and Moravia." In these lists, Czech Jews were given registration numbers. The banks then had instructions not to take action regarding the account until a second number was placed behind the name: the deportation number. Once Jewish names appeared with these two numbers, the corresponding accounts would be compulsorily transferred.[166] Under the terms of a decree of October 12, 1941, the "Emigration Fund for Bohemia-Moravia" would administer the accounts of Jews listed for deportation. The main emigration fund account was held at the Böhmische Escompte Bank, and other banks were ordered to make the transfer of assets to this account.[167] But BUB also held two very substantial accounts for the fund. These accounts also held some of the proceeds paid as part of "aryanization" transactions, especially arising out of small and medium-size firms.[168]

Valuables, including jewelry, works of art, and precious metals, which had been left by deported Jews in safe-deposit boxes, were sold to German trading company Hadega. Up to July 1942, BUB administered an estimated CKr 364.5 million worth of Jewish property.[169]

The Gestapo ordered the bank to report the assets of Jews "who died in the concentration camp" and to block the accounts in favor of the Gestapo. Some of the funds resulting in this way were transferred to other party institutions. Thus, one account of a Czech Jew was transferred by order of the Gestapo for the use of Lebensborn e. V., Munich.[170]

In November 1943, the list of the bank's "unstable creditors" (sight accounts) amounted to CKr 943,584,000 (or RM 94 million), which included "emigration monies" and "resettlement accounts" (of expelled and "resettled" [i.e., murdered] Jews) worth CKr 271,527,000 and an account of CKr 284,109,000 in the name of the "Jewish Autonomous Administration" of Theresienstadt concentration camp.[171] In addition, there were two term accounts of CKr 312,172,000 each for the Jewish Autonomous Administration of Theresienstadt. Thus, a total of CKr 908,000,000 was on deposit for the victims of Theresienstadt. It demonstrated clearly how BUB's major business lay in the administration of the property of the victims of National Socialism for the benefit of the German state. Again, most of the true owners of this property were the murdered victims of the National Socialist genocide. There was some movement in these accounts, and they were discussed by the bank's credit committee. In November 1944, Director Ulbrich gave a report on the general state of the bank. "He pointed out the big reductions in the investments of financial institutions and the Emigration Fund as well as the resultant diminution of the balance-sheet total and investments in stocks and shares."[172] A final statement (survey of debtors and creditors) produced for February 28, 1945, showed assets consisting mostly of government papers, and liabilities still shown as CKr 287,693,000 in short-term deposits and CKr 617,432,000 in term deposits held by Theresienstadt.[173]

The Industrial Reordering of Central Europe

Initially the economic future of occupied eastern Europe seemed to lie less with the SS than with the gigantic state-run but privately financed holding company, Reichswerke "Hermann Göring." The initial expansion of Reichswerke "Hermann Göring" outside Germany's 1937 frontiers began with large-scale "aryanizations" in Austria; it continued in Bohemia with the takeover of the Petschek lignite mines.[174]

Reichswerke "Hermann Göring's" banking connections had from its beginnings been concentrated with Dresdner Bank. Deutsche Bank had complained frequently and quite insistently about its relative handicap in what promised to be a very rewarding business, and about the apparent favoritism on the part of the state concern.[175] The Reichswerke's manager, Paul Pleiger, told Deutsche Bank's Karl Kimmich, with some irritation, "that the disagreements between the two banks could not possibly continue indefinitely."[176] Pleiger in 1937 had asked Kimmich to do the investment-banking work connected with the launching of the new firm, to prepare a list of companies that would be prepared to work with the Reichswerke, and to prepare a financial plan for the Reichswerke conglomerate. Kimmich arranged a meeting between Pleiger and Germany's major steel industrialists, Friedrich Flick and Peter Klöckner. But Deutsche Bank was subsequently ignored, and Pleiger instead promised the leadership of the issuing consortium to Dr. Karl Rasche of Dresdner Bank.

History repeated itself with a surge of investment-banking activity in Bohemia-Moravia, and Kimmich again complained bitterly to Pleiger that the big transactions of the Sudetenland and the protectorate had eluded Deutsche Bank. The sale of the major industrial concerns – Witkowitz Bergbau- und Eisenhüttengesellschaft (three quarters owned by the Rothschilds of Vienna and London), Skoda (where French firms held a significant equity stake), and Brünner Waffenwerke – to Reichswerke "Hermann Göring" via the Reich Economics Ministry had initially been entrusted to Dresdner Bank.[177] However, BUB congratulated itself when in 1940 it succeeded at least in establishing a business relationship – if only a deposit account, on a credit basis – with Witkowitz.)[178] At the beginning of 1940, BUB secured for itself a twenty percent share in credits to the Reichswerke "Hermann Göring" for the takeover of the Erste Brünner Maschinenfabriks-Gesellschaft (the share amounted to CKr 4,575,758) and the Brünn-Königsfelder Maschinen- und Waggonfabriks AG (CKr 1,952,194).[179]

The transfer of property by sale was central to the Reichswerke "Hermann Göring's" strategy for the wartime reordering of occupied Europe in preparation for a postwar New Order. A sale would have made the transfer much more permanent than the alternative of a German military imposition of trustees to manage foreign or alien property, but it posed major legal difficulties that took years to resolve. The eventual transfer of Witkowitz to the Reichswerke took place only in 1942, and then under a ten-year renewable contract.[180]

Retrospectively, these operations appear hard to comprehend, a bizarre mixture of astonishingly punctilious legalism and insistence on the following of correct procedures with, underlying these, a simultaneous profound immorality and criminality. It is, for instance, a constant surprise for the historian to discover the amount of time and care devoted to finding and transporting often torn and damaged share certificates in occupied Europe and registering the transfer of ownership, with payments made through the reparations and occupation accounts. From the invasions of 1940 until well after the fighting in France began in the wake of the Normandy landings, bank couriers shuttled from Paris to Berlin with sealed suitcases, engaged in the paperwork of creating legality for the New Order. This mixture of correctness, honesty, and order (what Jonathan Steinberg has termed the "secondary virtues") with an ignorance and neglect of the human and moral issues involved was a characteristic of the conduct of institutions and businesses in the National Socialist dictatorship.[181]

In spring 1940, when Göring's prestige in the National Socialist hierarchy temporarily declined, Kimmich believed that there might be a new set of transactions forthcoming as part of a breaking up of the gigantic Reichswerke "Hermann Göring."[182] But as long as the Reichswerke existed, Deutsche Bank believed that it was necessary somehow to establish a relationship with it. In April 1939, Deutsche Bank had sold to the Reichswerke its holding of Bayerischer Lloyd to facilitate the integration of transport on the Danube with the strategic and political priorities of the Reich. BUB appeared to be the ideal instrument in managing such a connection of the bank with the monopoly enterprise in eastern Europe, and in the summer of 1939, for this reason, Deutsche Bank pressed BUB to investigate the possibility of taking charge of the sale of the Witkowitzer Eisenwerke and the Brünner Waffenwerke.[183]

In fact, far from breaking up the Reichswerke in 1940, Hermann Göring launched a new phase in its expansion. On June 22, Göring ordered Reich Economics Minister Walther Funk to prepare the "integration of the areas incorporated in the Reich and the occupied areas into the Greater-German economy" to begin a "reconstruction of the German-led continental economy." Funk promised that the New Order would bring the "beginning of an unsuspected economic flowering." As part of the reorganization, the structure of industrial ownership in Europe would be rationalized.[184] In the wake of the spring invasion of the Netherlands, Belgium, and France, in September 1940 Göring instructed German banks to negotiate the transfer to German control of the major foreign assets of the defeated states. In the National Socialist "new Europe," Germany's "big banks" were to be given back their old function as industrial brokers who built and remodeled vast industrial empires. The difference was that these enterprises were now to be overwhelmingly controlled by the German state.

By 1941 in the Netherlands alone, foreign participations worth over RM 65 million had been acquired "in the wake of *private-enterprise* negotiations" [original emphasis].[185] These purchases occurred at such a rate that they began to interfere with government-directed purchases. In April 1941 the Reich Economics Ministry official in charge of banking supervision ordered the banks to slow down the rush of their private customers to seize Dutch assets. "It was therefore the duty of banks, in the way they advised the public, to recommend unconditional restraint in buying Dutch shares and annuities."[186] The private acquisition of shares in western Europe was to be slowed down, and in the meantime, the state-managed program to reorganize the structure of Europe concentrated on east European assets held by residents of western states.

BUB, which had by now established reasonably cordial relations with the Reichswerke "Hermann Göring" in eastern Europe, as well as with the SS, was an ideal agent for this operation. It bought shares of Czech and also Polish works from west European stockholders: Witkowitz Bergbau und Eisenhüttengesellschaft, Janina, and the Huta Bankowa, which in turn held shares in the Sosnowitzer Bergwerks AG, Sosnowitzer Röhren AG, Radomsko Metallurgia, and Kuxe Renaud.[187] These commercial transactions followed quite logically from the extension of German military rule. As BUB's Walter Pohle wrote in 1940, at the height of German successes, concerning the purchase of shares in the Berghütte from Schneider-Creusot: "If it was possible to buy Schneider-Creusot shares – cheaply, too – this was ultimately a triumph of German arms."[188] In all, Pohle organized the purchase of 110,454 Berghütte shares in France, at a price of RM 137.10 per share, and in addition another 19,170 shares from "Jewish owners resident in the protectorate, which we are to purchase at the demand of the Reich Economics Minister and the Protector." On this transaction, the BUB earned a commission of two percent.[189] Pohle repeatedly emphasized in reporting on the French transactions that they were "by agreement with the Reich Economics Ministry" and that there was no risk to the bank: "the bank [he said] will be indemnified by the HTO [Haupttreuhandstelle Ost; see below: "Deutsche Bank and the Creditanstalt in Poland"] in every respect and the funds presented will enjoy full cover."[190] When Pohle reported the purchase for FF 333 million (RM 16,759,309.31) of shares in the Huta Bankowa and the Französisch-Italienische AG der Dombrowaer Kohlengruben, he added: "this is not a personal transaction but a confidential commission for the government."[191] Such transactions were conducted principally for the Reichswerke "Hermann Göring," but BUB also carried out similar sales on behalf of private German corporations. Pohle spoke about "the purchase of shares of steel rolling-mills in which Mannesmann is interested."[192]

The shares of central and east European enterprises bought by the government or by public-sector institutions in occupied western Europe were sometimes paid through the reparations account, but some were also bought out of the proceeds of sales of French and Belgian domestic securities that had fallen into the hands of the German authorities. The latter included substantial quantities of securities seized from Jews in occupied Europe, most importantly in the Netherlands, where a formerly Jewish bank (Lippmann Rosenthal) took charge of collecting shares turned in to the occupying power on the basis of Decree 141 of 1941 issued by the Reich commissar for the occupied Dutch territories. This operation was conducted in extreme secrecy and, like the rest of such operations, channeled through BUB rather than Deutsche Bank.[193] (Deutsche Bank was not directly a part of this arrangement, although its management knew of the operations.

In 1943 a memorandum noted "that the agreements with BUB had been possible only as a result of the fact that Deutsche Bank had for *general* purposes made a substantial contribution by making securities available, though without wishing to be identified with the Prague business."[194]) The transactions continued until 1944, when in March Pohle told BUB's credit committee: "[...] all French commitments have been wound up, though the individual write-offs have yet to be made. After a projected trip to Paris, it will be possible to close the accounts."[195]

It was BUB rather than Deutsche Bank that had the closest links with Reichswerke "Hermann Göring." At the height of his influence, BUB's director Walter Pohle was chairman of the supervisory board of Berghütte and ran the key firms in the Berghütte complex (Berg- und Hüttenwerksgesellschaft Karwin-Trzynietz, Berg- und Hüttenwerksgesellschaft Teschen (Tecin), and Berg- und Hüttenwerksgesellschaft Wegierska Gorka) and in addition sat on the board of directors of the Böhmisch-Mährische Stickstoffwerke explosives factory, Coburg-Werke, Bandeisen + Blechwalzwerke AG Karlshütte, Friedeck bei Mährisch-Ostrau (Ostrava).[196] Politics here as elsewhere brought dangers to management, and BUB was quite exposed to periodic political interventions.

The first object of Nazi Party and Gestapo hostility was Joseph Krebs, who was accused of political unreliability, membership in a masonic lodge, and contact with Jews. Already in July 1940, the bank had had to write to the security service (*Sicherheitsdienst*) in Prague in defense of its director: "His frequent dealings with Jews are probably an inevitable outcome of his having occupied a high position in an almost exclusively Jewish-run bank with a large Jewish clientele. We ourselves have come to know Mr. Krebs as a man of whose German cast of mind we are not in any doubt." The letter concluded by stating that he was indispensable to the bank's business.[197]

In 1941, he was refused a visa to undertake foreign travel, and a large part of his business transactions then became impossible, so that his duties were redefined as lying exclusively in the Protectorate Bohemia – Moravia.[198] Deutsche Bank's Berlin directors consistently tried to defend Krebs against the political and police attacks. In April 1941, Oswald Rösler wrote to Max Rohde that the bank should protect Krebs:

We need a reasoned, conclusive explanation as to what charges are being brought, and why we must particularly request this is because the board of directors is to pass a resolution that must ultimately bring with it the most serious consequences for the person concerned. If such unjustified demands are too readily given in to, it is easy to see when the next member of the board of directors will have to go the same way, because that member is a nuisance as regards looking after the business interests of some authority or other.

Rösler then consulted with the director of Deutsche Bank responsible for personnel matters, party member Karl Ritter von Halt, and urged Krebs not to proceed with a conflict with the Gestapo but instead reconcile himself to a reduced sphere of activity:

Should Mr. Krebs be unwilling to submit to the demands of the security service, we are prepared to grant him leave to give him an opportunity to organize his defense. That attempt would inevitably (Mr. von Halt also confirms this) prove hopeless and would result in the removal of Mr. Krebs from BUB, since the bank cannot bear the consequences of a dispute between him and the party.[199]

Rösler was right in that the attack on Krebs was only the preliminary to an attack on the rest of the bank's management, and especially on Walter Pohle.

In 1942, as part of the restructuring of Germany's economy to meet the demands of total war, Pohle was pushed out of his influential positions by Major-General Hermann von Hanneken (head of the Reich Economics Ministry's Department II: Mining, Iron and Steel, and Energy Economy). Pohle had consulted the Reich Economics Ministry after he had been asked to buy the IG Kattowitz and Berghütte for a new Göring monopoly organization designed to encompass formerly Soviet as well as Polish metallurgy works.[200] The ministry rejected the indirect control of Reichswerke "Hermann Göring" shares by Berghütte: "The Reich Economic Ministry wants [...] 'Berghütte' to remain tied to the Reich in terms of capital as well, so that the influence of the Protectorate will be that much less."[201] This one false step of attempting to extend BUB's industrial interests at the expense of Reichswerke "Hermann Göring" cost Pohle his functions in the Berghütte industrial enterprise.

The Reich Economics Ministry managed the situation by approaching Rösler and explaining that Deutsche Bank "could do itself a favor by persuading Mr. Pohle to *resign his seat.*" Hans Kehrl of the Four-Year Plan was much more explicit:

> Mr. Pohle, on the other hand, felt he could handle the "Berghütte" question as he thought best, and he constantly placed himself in conflict with the Economics Ministry by holding talks with political authorities in Prague or Upper Silesia without the ministry's knowledge or getting involved in discussions that had caused the ministry endless problems. The ministry had therefore increasingly been forced to accept that Mr. Pohle's conduct had been shady and dishonest.

Rösler then spoke with Pohle and persuaded him to give up the supervisory-board positions. He also wanted Pohle to apologize to Kehrl (he made the point very emphatically in a letter), and he noted of BUB's leading manager:

> He undoubtedly possesses a great deal of vigor, appetite for work, and eagerness to assume responsibility, but in addition an unbridled ambition from which his management style suffers. We were able in the "Creditanstalt" case to gain some idea of the stupidities into which his ambition leads him astray and of how, even in a hopeless situation, he cannot muster the insight to admit his mistake. He is temporarily lacking in the self-discipline required for the development of personal maturity, being very much inclined to see things only from the standpoint of commercial success, never mind how that success has been achieved.[202]

After this conflict, Pohle was replaced on Berghütte's supervisory board by Ambassador Hans Adolf von Moltke, a man of great reputation and decency who was trying to leave the foreign office but who died within a year as a result of an unsuccessful appendix operation.[203] His successor was someone whose sympathies lay close to Deutsche Bank – Karl Blessing, director of the strategically important Kontinentale Öl, which had been set up in 1941 as a model for a future "planned economy using private capital," the intention of which was to "create the situation that, as a great power, Germany needs and deserves."[204] Until 1939, Blessing had been a director of the Reichsbank; he was dismissed after signing the Reichsbank memorandum of January 7, 1939, condemning government policy.

Private capital might have competed with the state concern to acquire east European assets, but the competition was complicated by the fact that both the Reichswerke "Hermann Göring" and its private competitors were producing the same goods, namely armaments, designed for the same monopolistic consumer, the German military Moloch. In the early phases of the war, even private concerns had to negotiate with Reichswerke "Hermann Göring" in attempting to build up industrial assets. In 1940, the Graf von Ballestrem'sche Güterdirektion Gleiwitz established a powerful position in Upper Silesia, using Deutsche Bank and Delbrück Schickler & Co. to repurchase shares in formerly German enterprises that had passed into the hands of the Polish state after 1918: the coalfield operated by Rudaer Steinkohlegewerkschaft, Friedenshütten (which had been ceded under the Versailles Treaty to Poland, with Ballestrem retaining a minority of shares), and machine-tool and boiler-making plants in Sosnowice, Dombrowa and Kattowitz/Katowice.[205] The price paid was RM 12 million, but of this only RM 4 million were paid immediately, and the rest was to be paid out of future profits; the initial down payment could be made out of the profits made in Upper Silesian works since September 30, 1939.

After 1941, as Göring's political role came under attack and his importance in the National Socialist hierarchy waned for good, German private capital could attempt to assert itself further. The Reichswerke "Hermann Göring" conglomerate began to break up. Metallurgia Radomsko, which bought its raw materials from Berghütte Dombrowa, part of the Berg- und Hüttenwerksgesellschaft Teschen (Tecin), was now leased to Oberhütte, despite opposition from the Cracow Armaments Inspectorate.[206] The end of Reichswerke "Hermann Göring" as an industrial conglomerate came only later, as a result of military developments. It needed to use its complex holdings system to minimize the extent of its financial liabilities, and by the autumn of 1944, the Reichswerke refused to give any guarantee for the debts of companies affiliated in the concern and now being overrun by Soviet armies.[207]

BUB's share-purchasing activities were not confined to central European assets with west European owners. It bought up Jewish shares in Hungary. In Yugoslavia, it built up a participation in the Bankverein AG Zagreb and the Bankverein für Serbien AG. Its position within Deutsche Bank's southeast European banking system was confirmed through an exchange of shares and seats on the supervisory board with the Creditanstalt-Bankverein Vienna.[208]

Much of BUB's investment-banking business took place on behalf of state or SS purchasers looking for an apparently respectable financial intermediary to regulate transfers of property. But the war economy, though state dominated, was not entirely socialized, and some private concerns used the same methods.

As the course of the war changed and a German defeat appeared ever more probable, and as the intense involvement of BUB in the economics of imperialism in the east became ever clearer, the Bohemian bank appeared as more and more of an embarrassment to the Berlin managers of Deutsche Bank. The Berlin bank had been dragged in on the crest of the wave of expansionist euphoria in 1938–39 and could now see no way out. In July 1943, Oswald Rösler of Deutsche Bank, the chairman of the supervisory board of BUB, wrote an extensive memorandum about the poor quality of BUB's business, which he attributed to the disruptive consequences of "aryanization" and the impossibility of finding adequate management.[209] But just at this moment, the bank started to become profitable.

Union-Bank Bratislava

At the beginning of 1939, Deutsche Bank had suggested to the Reich Economics Ministry that even before the final dismemberment of Czechoslovakia, it should be allowed to buy a branch in Bratislava: It wanted the Escompte- und Volkswirtschaftliche Bank, whereas Dresdner Bank would take, in a parallel operation, the Allgemeine Handels- und Creditbank. The purchase of ninety percent of the stock of the Escompte Bank was to be a joint operation with the Creditanstalt.[210] The Slovak authorities resented and feared Czech influences. Minister President Vojtech Tuka was still complaining in the middle of the war that the personnel of the former Czech banks were responsible for "constant agitation." In December 1939, the Slovak government correspondingly resolved to turn BUB's Bratislava branch into a "German-type institution."[211]

So it was that in October 1940 the Bratislava branch of BUB began a separate existence as the Union-Bank Bratislava (UBB) and established its own network of branches by taking over other bank branches. The Sillein (Žilina) branch, for instance, was bought from the Böhmisch-Mährische Bank or Legiobank. The capitalization amounted to CKr 60 million: CKr 50 million in capital stock and CKr 10 million of capital reserve.[212] At an initial general meeting, executive-committee (*Verwaltungsrat*) chairman Ludwig Fritscher (from the Creditanstalt, Vienna) gave a speech in which he emphasized the bank's German character:

> UBB works with German equity. It operates here in Slovakia, where borrowed funds will flow into it in the form of investments of all kinds. Those facts place the bank under an obligation vis-à-vis the Reich and Slovakia, yet these are not two conflicting obligations; they both flow together into one: to serve the Slovak-German economic relations that shall bring like blessings upon both peoples, already such close mutual friends. The new bank is not being founded on a private-capital basis; it has not come to Slovakia to exploit the country but in order to assume the necessary role of intermediary in Slovako-German economic intercourse.[213]

Its business looked similar to that of the Prague bank, its most profitable transactions involving the sale of Slovak companies to German firms. Philipp Reemtsma acquired the Vereinigte Holz und Industrie AG, Bratislava, and left UBB as a trustee. The Coburg mining complex was integrated into the gigantic Reichswerke "Hermann Göring" company Berg- und Hüttenwerke. The Antinom Berg und Hüttenwerke AG, Neusohl (Banská Bystrica) was integrated into the Berghütte as well.

"Aryanization" in Slovakia ran on different lines than in the Czech lands. A banker, Nowotny, who had formerly worked for the Prague Bebca, was appointed as trustee for Jewish property, with responsibility for selling at a fixed proportion (thirty-nine percent) of the ascertained value.[214] Mannesmann acquired a Jewish-owned business in Bratislava, M. Graber & Sohn AG, while the bank was still part of BUB. There were some other "aryanizations" of firms associated with UBB: "Sigma" Buchdruck M. Lesay (formerly S. Hauser), but the firm's credit file shows that UBB did not give any loans to facilitate "aryanization" in this case.[215]

As with Prague, and for similar reasons, Jewish credits looked uncertain. The bank's executive committee, on which German bankers sat – Ludwig Fritscher (Austrian, Creditanstalt-Bankverein), Hermann Kaiser, Max Ludwig Rohde (both Deutsche Bank), August Rohdewald (Reichs-Kredit-Gesellschaft) – noted among others cases of credits where the securities for credits involved liabilities of Jewish businessmen (as in the firm of M. Rippers Söhne, in Sillein/Žilina).[216] But the extent of weak loans was infinitely less than for BUB, and there was no collapse of profitability followed by an "aryanization"-driven resurgence. Jewish-owned accounts were also handled in a different way in Father Jozef Tiso's puppet state. Many Jewish deposits were simply transferred to the state-run postal savings bank system, where the state rather than private banks – or the German police – could reap the financial rewards of racial persecution.[217]

The Liquidation of Böhmische Union-Bank

Toward the end of the war, when it was clear that Prague would soon be liberated, BUB sent almost all its assets, and the securities in deposit accounts, to Germany. On March 13, 1945, RM 15 million in German treasury bills from BUB's own account were sent to the Deutsche Bank branch in Hildesheim. The sum corresponded precisely to the nominal capital of the Czech bank. In addition, RM 35 million in treasury bills were sent from the collective deposit account of clients (*Sammeldepot*). Furthermore, other assets were sent to Düsseldorf: RM 1,246,323.63 and a small sum in British bills, £248.5.

The treasury bills lost their value in 1948, as the currency reform canceled without compensation all Reich, Reichsbahn, Reichspost, and Reichsbank debt in the hands of the banks. But surprisingly, in 1956 the Economics Ministry of the state of North-Rhine-Westphalia recognized the transfer of the RM 15 million that had been "left behind" to a Reichsmark account held by BUB.[218]

In 1958, after the recreation of Deutsche Bank, Deutsche Bank Berlin (the "Alt-Bank"), the legal successor to the pre-1945 Deutsche Bank, drew up for the new Deutsche Bank's legal department a complete list of BUB's securities ("assets transferred to the Berlin Disconto Bank AG": this was the successor to Deutsche Bank in West Berlin created in 1949). This documentation included in separate lists those that could be identified as belonging to particular clients, many of whom were Jewish. (But BUB clients also included the German government.) There was a further list of valueless securities (tsarist bonds and the like) and of "securities not amenable to clarification," which included such items as RM 23,000 in shares of the Bohemia Keramik Werke, the factory that had been sold to the SS.[219]

The assets of BUB were used – after court cases had been brought in the Federal Republic – to pay the pensions of former BUB employees in the west, but not to make payments to former BUB depositors.

The chief architect of BUB's wartime strategy, Walter Pohle, died of starvation in a Czech prison. A pathological overeater suffering from "dumping syndrome" as a result of a stomach operation that had removed a large part of his intestine, he could not survive on the meager prison food.

The Czech government quickly nationalized the bank without compensation, by a decree of October 24, 1945, which took almost immediate effect (October 27). This was – as the bank's remaining Czech staff pointed out – a foolish and ideologically motivated move, because the Germans had stripped the bank's assets back in March, moving them to Germany. The result was that nationalization simply meant a default on liabilities, but it made it practically impossible to recover the assets that might have been used to pay such claims. In a memorandum prepared in 1945, the Czech bank in liquidation listed claims of BUB in the Netherlands (HFl 1,827.20), the United States ($88,895.91), Great Britain (£29,862.19, and gold to the value of £185,903.71), Switzerland (CHF 196,047.20) and France (FF 5,439,306.40), as well as smaller amounts from Belgium, Canada, Norway, Sweden, and Yugoslavia.[220] In addition, there were the CKr 160 million (corresponding to the RM 15 million transferred to Hildesheim) and a further estimated CKr 100 million for restitution of individual accounts. These were the claims that the Czech bankers argued that they were losing through the process of nationalization. As a consequence, those who suffered from the Czech government's postwar banking policies included the Jewish victims of Nazi persecution and the Czech population that had been financially exploited during the German occupation.

It might be added that the Czech Republic of the 1990s has not been very interested in the banking aspects of the German occupation. At the time of writing (July 2000), the Czech government-appointed historical commission had still not been given access to the files in the

Finance Ministry that the author of this study had used for the analysis of BUB. (It is true that these files are in terrible condition and have been extensively damaged by damp and mold.)

The takeover of BUB was the most direct contact that Deutsche Bank established with the machinery of wartime exploitation. Its presence had been a major asset for the German government, which had pushed for an involvement of German banks in the ownership of Czech banks. Banks were needed to manage the orderly transition of the Czech economy into the war economy of the Third Reich.

Deutsche Bank and the Creditanstalt in Poland

With the exception of Silesia, which was part of the area brought into the German Reich, industry formed a much less crucial part of German military planning. The military machinery did not need banks in the way they had been required in the Czech case.

There had been a German banking presence in interwar Poland. Both Deutsche Bank and Dresdner Bank had kept branches in Polish East Upper Silesia, in Katowice, under the terms of the 1922 Geneva agreement,[221] which expired on July 14, 1937. Dresdner Bank then closed its branch, and the German authorities suggested that Deutsche Bank should act similarly. Reichsbank President Hjalmar Schacht stated that "the German banks that still maintain branches in Katowice would do well to consider selling those institutions." Eduard Mosler of Deutsche Bank then proposed to sell his branch as part settlement of Polish claims against Germany from transit traffic in the "Polish corridor." But the Polish authorities wanted the German banks to stay, because of their importance in the financing of Silesian heavy industry, and Deutsche Bank remained as the largest branch in Katowice.[222]

Immediately after the German attack on Poland on September 1, 1939, and the German occupation of the western parts of the country, Deutsche Bank looked enthusiastically at the economic opportunities offered by military expansion. It wrote to the German supervisory authorities: "Presumably, then, the Polish banks will have to go into liquidation, particularly since (simply in the light of their many Jewish and Polish accounts receivable) most of them will be unable to avoid forced bankruptcy or at least insolvency proceedings."[223] At this time, the Katowice branch of Deutsche Bank had a staff of ninety, of whom at least eighty were *"Reichsdeutsche"* or *"Volksdeutsche."* Even before the flight of the Polish government (on September 17) or the capitulation of Warsaw (September 27), Deutsche Bank had started to open new branches. It rapidly inaugurated sub-branches in Bielitz (Bielsko-Biała, September 11), Teschen (Tecin, September 11), and Oderberg (Nový Bohumin, September 14).

What did these new sub-branches do? Why was it so important to establish them so quickly, even during the military conflict? The main concern of the German authorities was to seize financial assets – gold, silver, share certificates, foreign exchange, and Polish and Czech currency – which might otherwise be taken from the area under their control. On September 7, 1939, officials of the Foreign-Exchange Tracing and Search Department (*Devisenfahndungsamt*) visited the major towns in the Upper Silesian industrial area. They later noted: "Findings made here showed that banks were almost without exception closed and their owners or managers had fled into the interior of Poland, taking the ledgers and all movable assets with them. The same findings were made regarding wealthy Jews formerly resident in these towns." On the following day, September 8, Regierungsoberinspektor Fischer of the Foreign-Exchange Tracing and Search Department noted: "The Reichsbank representative with the Head of Civil Administration, Councillor Behrbohm, today instructed Deutsche Bank Berlin to buy up the said assets in the Ol'sa District. Deutsche Bank will immediately set up purchasing offices in the largest towns in the district to enable the order to be carried out." But he also saw that the Germans had come too late: "According to the findings made hitherto, the wealthy Jews formerly resident in the Ol'sa District have fled to Cracow with their assets. Because of the rapid occupation of Cracow, they were probably no longer able to move their property farther into the Polish interior." Behrbohm would consequently also establish a Devisenbank in Cracow. The subsequent detailed report of the Foreign-Exchange Tracing and Search Department noted that "after Deutsche Bank had at the instigation of Councillor Behrbohm established branches in Teschen, Oderberg, and Bielitz and been authorized to purchase assets required to be handed over, the order was put into effect in the Ol'sa District on 9 September 1939." There were further plans for the expansion of the bank in eastern areas: "The intention is to set up branches of Deutsche Bank in those towns (Tarnów, Rzeszów) that will then take over the purchasing of assets."[224] But these further plans were never realized.

The conquered territories were divided up by a decree of Hitler's of October 8. Four areas were designated as "occupied eastern areas" and integrated into Germany: the "government district" (*Regierungsbezirk*) of Zichenau, in the north (including the Polish district of Suwalki); the *Reichsgau* of Danzig and West Prussia; the industrial areas in Silesia, which were simply added to German Silesia; and *Reichsgau* Posen (later renamed as Reichsgau Wartheland), which included the industrial city of Łódź. The remaining territories were run under an occupation regime designated as the Generalgouvernement.

At that time, several German banks raced to establish a banking presence in the newly acquired territories.

Deutsche Bank also contemplated a branch in Warsaw, but its directors and managers expressed some hesitation. Johannes Kiehl of Deutsche Bank's managing board noted the progress of the German armies in a letter written on September 19, 1939. "Before long, almost certainly, Warsaw too will be occupied. Then matters will move very quickly towards the founding of a similar institution to the small-loan company [*Darlehenskasse*] set up during the last war and managed by yourself. We must of course try to gain decisive control here [...]. As a bank, however, we must be careful not to be suspected of acting in any selfish interest." But his correspondent, Dr. Felix Theusner (director of Deutsche Bank's Breslau branch), was rather cautious and replied in a noncommittal way: "Should Deutsche Bank feel it must set up a branch in Warsaw (a question that in my view needs a lot of thought and that I should certainly not want to answer in the affirmative in advance), I shall of course be happy to make myself available at any time for the groundwork and discussions in Warsaw."[225]

The banks complained about one other's "aggressive" business methods, and the Reich Economics Ministry tried to preserve Polish banks that the German authorities might then influence and control directly. For instance, Deutsche Bank, Commerzbank, and the Deutsche Genossenschaftsbank complained about the behavior of Dresdner Bank in Łódź (renamed by the Germans as Litzmannstadt).

The Reichsbank office reported that Dresdner Bank was managing the payments of the Zentral-Textil-Gesellschaft, which was then influencing its clients to establish accounts with the bank. In addition, Dresdner Bank had organized a "beer evening with food" in the rooms of the Grand Hotel, "to which we are told more or less all the industrialists of Litzmannstadt and the surrounding area, including ones that do not have accounts with Dresdner Bank, have been invited."[226]

The Reich Economic Ministry also expressed its dissatisfaction with the plans of Deutsche Bank. Deutsche Bank had tried to establish a grip on the officials of the major administrative agency responsible for the reordering of industry in the east, the Haupttreuhandstelle Ost (HTO; Central Trustee Office for the East). Thus in January 1940, HTO officials told the War Economy Research Establishment (*Forschungsstelle für Wehrwirtschaft*) that the best source of information on Polish conditions was a banker named Weiss-Ulog, who had been hired away from the General Bank Corporation or Allgemeine Bankverein (Powszechny Bank Związkowy w Polsce S.A.) in Warsaw by Deutsche Bank.[227] A few months later, Reich Economics Ministry officials noted that another Deutsche Bank representative, Neugebauer, "failed to observe the requisite competitive restraint vis-à-vis the Polish banking industry in an article he wrote and made comments about his situation with the clearly unmistakable intention of denigrating that industry in the public arena."[228] By 1941, Deutsche Bank's successful takeover of HTO was such that at the bank section of HTO's Katowice "Treuhandstelle," all seven or eight administrators had come from Deutsche Bank.[229]

Official agencies were clearly worried about the extent of bank influence on HTO. But sometimes the fact that an official had previously worked in a bank did not guarantee any particular affection for the previous employer. One of the department directors at HTO, for instance, was Franz Hertel, who had previously been the fanatically ideological Nazi factory cell representative on the works council of Deutsche Bank. He was a constant irritant to the bank's management, and the bank had tried, in the end successfully, to make him resign. Hertel, then a *Hauptsturmführer* in the SS, went on to a grand-scale career as an "aryanizer." He took over for himself a large department store in Prague (the Haus der Geschenke) and then bought Czech Jewish real estate. After the war, he tried (unsuccessfully) to petition for compensation for the loss of his Czech property.[230]

HTO administered a large number of sequestered companies and sold some of them, often to the administrators who were provisionally charged with running the firms. Because most of these administrators lacked their own resources, they often required bank credit for the purchase. The Katowice branch of Deutsche Bank dealt with a substantial number of such cases. Wilhelm Rodrian bought the Ölfabrik Siegmund Arzt in Bielitz, and then another similar firm, the Margarinefabrik Paul Hofmann & Co., and took a RM 600,000 credit from the bank.[231] It gave a RM 130,000 credit for Wilhelm Pischner's acquisition of the Elektrische Walzenmühle Dalezman & Co., which worked for IG Farben Auschwitz and also for the SS.[232] The "Kommissarische Verwalter" of Wassermühle Skotschau, Heinrich Rech, bought the mill with a RM 15,000 credit.[233] Similarly, Karl Schubert bought a food producer, Arpol, Bielitz, with bank credit.[234] The list of potential purchasers included not only administrators but also military personnel: The army was to be paid in part in loot. Some quite senior men were listed as interested in the acquisition of Silesian property, including for instance General Joachim von Stülpnagel.[235]

At the same time, the new bank branches in the east had little room for maneuver. They were obliged to give credits when the state had decided to offer a guarantee for a particular project, and, given the wartime conditions, there existed few other businesses or loan prospects in the region. Deutsche Bank angrily rejected Reich Economics Ministry complaints that it had unpatriotically refused such credits. In the late summer of 1940, the bank noted:

This enables us to ascertain that the charges leveled do not, so far as Deutsche Bank is concerned, hold any water whatsoever. None of our branches has refused a loan for which a Reich guarantee was available; they have all acted dutifully in implementing the conditions laid down by the government on issue of the guarantee. [...] That we have furthermore not shrunk from making considerable sacrifices, particularly in the Katowice district especially mentioned, is proved beyond doubt by the past history of our Katowice branch, which is also well-known and generally acknowledged.[236]

Deutsche Bank established, as well as its new branches in Upper Silesia, in Bielitz-Biala, Teschen, Oderberg, a major branch office in Łódź in Reichsgau Posen (Poznań), and in Cracow, in the Generalgouvernement. The head of the Katowice branch of Deutsche Bank in addition requested the establishment of a branch in Sosnowice.[237] In April 1940, the Cracow branch was transferred to the Creditanstalt, after an initiative from Hans Fischböck: "that the Credit-Anstalt should set up branches in Cracow, Tarnów, Rzeszów, and Przemysl and Deutsche Bank cede to the Credit-Anstalt the branches it has established in Bielitz and Cracow. Mr. Abs reserves his position after discussion within the Deutsche Bank board."[238] After the German military offensive against Russia in 1941 brought all of prewar Poland under German control, the Creditanstalt also established a branch in Lvov (Lemberg). The German supervisory authority (*Reichsaufsichtsamt*) disliked the push of the big German banks into the Generalgouvernement. As early as October 1940, it declared its opinion that "from a purely organizational point of view, probably the sensible thing to do would be to limit branches of 'Altreich' banks to Krakau."[239]

By the end of 1940, both the Creditanstalt and Deutsche Bank were discussing the idea of establishing branches in Warsaw. At first one proposal had been to take a Polish regional bank in joint ownership.[240] The Creditanstalt had discussed the possibility of an "expansion of our Polish business," perhaps by taking over the Allgemeiner Bank-Verein.[241] Deutsche Bank wrote to the Creditanstalt rather brusquely: "We once ceded the Cracow location to you after we had established a promising branch there. It is our conviction that, so far as Warsaw is concerned, for the above-mentioned reasons our interests must be regarded as paramount."[242]

In April 1942, Johannes Kiehl of the Deutsche Bank board was proposing to take over the Bank Handlowy, the most significant Polish bank. Bank Handlowy had a capital of 25 million zlotys (RM 12.5 million) and had a substantial foreign ownership. Foreign owners included the British Overseas Bank, London (5.5 percent); Hambros, London (3.1 percent); the Banca Comerciale Italiana (4.8 percent); and the Banque de Bruxelles (3.2 percent).[243] It continued to do a significant amount of business with foreign enterprises in wartime Poland. There were, for instance, substantial movements in the accounts of International Business Machines Corp., New York, and of Watson Business Machines.[244] At the outbreak of war, about half of its deposits came from Polish Jews. Kiehl reported to Consul-General Hugo Winkelmann in Danzig (Gdansk):

> Mr. Bechtolf and I intend to travel to Warsaw on 30 April and possibly also stay there on 1 May. The object of our journey, apart from generally informing ourselves about circumstances there, is particularly to make further preparations in connection with our endeavors to establish a branch of our bank in the Generalgouvernement or, in line with previous tendencies of the competent government agencies, to take over a Polish bank and run it as a regional subsidiary of our bank. This is a matter we have often discussed before. The first potential candidate for such a takeover is the Warsaw Bank of Commerce [Bank Handlowy] as being by far the largest institution.[245]

In 1945 the president of the bank council of Bank Handlowy, Stanisław Wachowiak, wrote an account of the negotiations with Deutsche Bank. He described 1942 as the beginning of "a war on the fundamentals of Polish banking." The Bank control commissar in Cracow, Reichsbankdirektor Fritz Paersch, who was also the director of the Polish Emissions bank (the wartime replacement for the National Bank), told Wachowiak that Economics Minister Walther Funk had issued an ultimatum to merge the Polish banks with German banks. Wachowiak thought that he and his council would resign. Then, on May 1 came the visit of Bechtolf, who was accompanied at first by a secretary and then later spoke alone with Wachowiak:

> When we were left alone, to my amazement, he told me that Deutsche Bank with a one hundred year tradition does not, for the duration of the war, agree with the stand of the Economics Minister of the Reich. Deutsche Bank would not agree to the merger, and, in order to gain time, would send a so-called observer. Asking me to maintain discretion, he assured me that Bank Handlowy would in no way be threatened by the observer. Indeed, with a delay of half a year, the observer arrived, stayed in the Hotel Bristol [then, as now, the best hotel in Warsaw] and visited us twice.[246]

Later in the year, Wachowiak visited the bank supervisor in Cracow, Paersch, and naturally gave a rather different version of the visit of the German bankers. Paersch made a note about this visit:

He gathered from this [he said] that the question of German banks operating in Warsaw would soon become current. He voiced his fear that this could lead to the complete exclusion of the credit institutions active in Warsaw hitherto. [...] I explained to Mr. Wachowiak that the German banks would of course be admitted to Warsaw. [...] I could not at the moment say how and when, but the prerequisites for the reordering of relations in connection with Polish banks were largely in place as a result of the order concerning Bank Polski and the conclusion of the agreements with HTO.[247]

Just before this visit, from October 8 to 10, 1942, negotiations between HTO, the Trustee Administration (Treuhandverwaltung) of the Generalgouvernement, and the Reich Finance Ministry had taken place in Cracow concerning capital participations from the Reich to the Generalgouvernement. A press report noted that "in detailed discussions [...] it was possible to clarify completely the principal questions regarding capital integration of the German Reich and the Generalgouvernement. Those discussions culminated in the conclusion of a series of standard agreements coming into effect immediately."[248] Wachowiak believed that in 1943, four further decrees liquidating Polish banks were prepared but were never published, because of the changing fortunes of war.

If his account is correct, and there is no reason to think that it is not, Bechtolf's trip to Warsaw demonstrates not only the extent of his disillusionment with German policy but also substantial personal courage. Deutsche Bank was not of course operating in a vacuum, and the rival Dresdner Bank consistently expressed its own interest in acquiring the Bank Handlowy. In August 1943, Arthur Glathe of Dresdner Bank visited the bank supervisor in Cracow and asked whether his institution could not take over Bank Handlowy. He "enquired whether we should be prepared to alter the standpoint communicated to Dresdner Bank in writing if, for example, the Polish Bank of Commerce were to continue to operate in Warsaw under its old name and the influence of Dresdner Bank remained invisible."[249] In these circumstances, the continued declarations of interest by Deutsche Bank combined with practical inaction amounted to a protection for the Bank Handlowy.

The Reichsbank and the Polish Issuing Bank (Emissionsbank) were reluctant to see both the Creditanstalt and Deutsche Bank with branches in the same city: "Mr. Paersch is said to have stated in this connection [...] that he could not license Deutsche Bank and the Creditanstalt in the Gouvernement alongside each other but that in that case Warsaw would need to be combined with Cracow and Lvov under one institution."[250]

The Creditanstalt in Cracow was meanwhile engaged in a quite lucrative business. The extent of its credits reduced its liquidity so much that the bank supervisor in the Generalgouvernement several times expressed his unease. What were the credits used for? To a considerable extent, credits were taken to buy firms under trustee administration. Under a decree of September 24, 1940, the property of the Polish state was subject to trustee administration. In addition, private property might be confiscated, or, if declared to be without an owner (herrenlos), taken over (eingezogen). By 1942, 3,296 enterprises were administered by trustees: 1,659 were industrial firms and 1,036 were trading or artisanal units. These enterprises were in part prepared for sale. A 1942 report in the Krakauer Zeitung noted that:

> The sale of the trust businesses can proceed only slowly in view of the state of prewar indebtedness and the poor performance ascertained particularly in connection with formerly Jewish businesses. Where at all possible, the sale will take account of the interests of German soldiers at the front. This presupposes, however, that the businesses are developed in such a way that they are able, after the war is over, to stand comparison with corresponding enterprises in the Reich.[251]

In 1942, in particular, the bank supervisor noted after a visit from Huber of the Cracow Creditanstalt:

> Mr. Huber also announced that enquiries about the grant of loans to purchase enterprises from the trustee administration are on the increase. He had been able, on the basis of previous experience with such loans, to ascertain that the purchase prices set by the trustee administration could be amortized from the proceeds from those enterprises within a disproportionately short space of time (two years).[252]

The Cracow Creditanstalt carried out transfers of money from relatives of concentration-camp inmates. It is clear from the scant surviving documentation that the Cracow bank knew about the massive mortality in these camps.[253] In addition, the same bank administered some of the accounts of the trustee administration, which dealt with confiscated Jewish-owned property.

Half of the profits of the Creditanstalt from its branches in Cracow and Lvov could be transferred, according to the currency-control regulations,[254] to the "Altreich." The Polish profits of the Creditanstalt are shown in Table 2.[255]

But the risks of lending were increasing. In July 1943, Walter Tron, a director of the Creditanstalt, spoke about the risks posed by the bad loans:

> The special review of accounts receivable now introduced has shown that certain commitments need to be terminated or re-arranged – with no certainty yet as to whether and in what amounts losses are to be expected. On the basis of this information, the working committee reiterates the opinion expressed earlier that, in the light of these risks, converting the branches into an autonomous bank would be desirable.[256]

In October 1942, Tron spoke of negotiations with Deutsche Bank about joint ownership of a Polish subsidiary.[257] In August 1943, Tron told the supervisory authority that he would prefer to turn the branches of the Creditanstalt into a separate bank: "It is difficult to handle and supervise business from Vienna." He added that he had already spoken with Deutsche Bank, "which may possibly take a holding in the new regional bank." Such a bank might take over Polish institutions later. ("Director Tron remarked that starting up a regional bank in no way anticipated the subsequent takeover of a Polish bank.")[258]

Table 2   Polish Profits of the Creditanstalt (in Million Zlotys)

Year	Cracow	Lvov	Total
1940	409		409
1941	786	–53	734
1942	1,646	274	1,920
1943	858	324	1,182
TOTAL	3,699	546	4,245

Discussions about the creation of a Polish regional bank were completed only in March 1944, by which time, of course, the German armies were in full retreat. In April 1944, Tron reported that in Cracow and Lemberg "the process of making branches independent [...] is already under way."[259] The "Creditanstalt AG, Krakau" was established in May 1944, with Walter Tron from the Creditanstalt as chairman of the supervisory board and another Deutsche Bank banker, Hermann Kaiser, as a member. It never took over a Warsaw bank.

In June 1944, it seemed that deposits in the Generalgouvernement were still increasing.[260] But some significant accounts were now being closed. On July 27, 1944, the SS "Wirtschaftsamt" transferred its deposit on the account of the "Reichsführer SS" (8 million zlotys, or RM 4 million) to the Kommerzialbank, the Cracow subsidiary of Dresdner Bank, where the Reichsführer had a larger account (79 million zlotys), which the SS also tried to withdraw. The man responsible for these withdrawals was SS-Standartenführer Erich Schellin. Was it more than an arithmetic coincidence that the total in the bank accounts, 87 million zlotys, was close to the 101 million zlotys that Schellin acquired in "spoils" (*Beutemittel*) from the genocide of "Aktion Reinhard"?[261] After protests from the bank supervisor, the SS took only 30 million zlotys from the Kommerzialbank.[262] By September, the business from the Cracow Creditanstalt had moved to Breslau (Wrocław), whereas the Kommerzialbank moved to Leipzig. These moves ensured that – at least in the case of the Cracow Creditanstalt – the overwhelming majority of its files cannot be located. Consequently, the documentation of its activity and an important part of the story of the economic aspects of the persecution and expropriation of the Polish population, including the genocide of Polish and European Jews, is still missing.

Bechtolf's failed negotiations in Warsaw were obviously in part a product of his personal conviction, in 1942, that Deutsche Bank had no business taking over a major Polish bank. But the fact that the Generalgouvernement banking authorities were prepared to tolerate his deliberately dilatory approach indicates a comparative indifference to the issue of German bank involvement. For Deutsche Bank and the Creditanstalt, there was no massive financial control of the key elements of the Polish economy, analogous to the system that Walter Pohle had established in the Protectorate of Bohemia-Moravia. Instead there was an engagement in some relatively small-scale but nevertheless lucrative side business generated by the occupation regime, at the expense of the Poles (including the Polish Jews).

7

Jewish-Owned Bank Accounts

The reason for the discriminatory treatment of Jewish-owned accounts by the German state and by German banks, and then the expropriation through official measures, was the intensified drive, which started at the end of 1937 to exclude Jews from the German economy. One motive lay in using as much of their wealth as could be extracted for the purposes of the Nazi state. Until 1938–39, there was actually no legal way for banks to know which of their customers were Jewish or "non-aryan" in the sense of the definitions of the 1935 Nuremberg racial law. Working on the basis of "Jewish-sounding" names alone was an unsatisfactory procedure and, in a number of cases, led to difficulties and complaints by customers.

Banks anticipated as well as simply responded to state policy. Soon after the passage of the Nuremberg laws, the Deutsche Bank's head office sent a circular letter to its branches, asking for lists of credits of over RM 20,000 to "non-aryan" businesses, and some bank branches went further and compiled lists of credit as well as debit customers.[1] These lists, sketchy at first, became more comprehensive in the course of the subsequent three years. They were not compiled in every branch of the bank, and indeed there was no legal obligation or even any general official request for the banks to carry out such an anticipatory registration.

Before 1938, there existed some restrictions on some Jewish-owned accounts. The accounts of emigrants were blocked and could be converted into foreign exchange only at a rate substantially below the official rate. (The accounts were treated analogously to the foreign credits frozen in Germany in the course of the economic crisis of 1931.) Such blocked accounts (*Auswanderersperrkonten*) could be acquired cheaply for particular specified purposes by foreigners who wished to invest in German securities or make touristic expenditures in Germany.[2] These provisions, however, applied only to those who were emigrating or had already left. The most general way of controlling the disposition of Jewish property was the use of a "security order" (*Sicherungsanordnung*). Before late 1938, these had been relatively infrequently used, most characteristically in cases in which the authorities believed that there existed an immediate plan to emigrate that might make a partial seizure of assets more difficult.

A decree of April 26, 1938, required German Jews to register their domestic and foreign assets (foreign Jews were obliged to register only German assets) and imposed large penalties for failure to comply.[3] This registration made it easier to impose more general security orders. After the pogrom of November 9–10, 1938, the subsequent imposition on November 12 of a fine (*Sühneleistung*) on the Jewish population, and a surge of emigrants who were liable to pay confiscatory rates of tax under the *Reichsfluchtsteuer,* security orders became quite widely applied.[4] A currency decree of December 12, 1938, required (under #59) those subject to a "security order" to create, within five days, a single account at one bank licensed to deal in foreign exchange (*Devisenbank*) a blocked account: *"beschränkt verfügbares Sicherungskonto."* Out of this account, a certain amount could be withdrawn monthly for regular payments. Additional releases of funds were permitted for taxes, payments to the Jewish religious community (*Kultusgemeinde*), and other permitted religious and social institutions, for legal and medical fees, for consular fees and for the purchase of goods in preparation for emigration, and for the repayment of old debts.

More and more of these payments were made to an institution created in 1939, the Reichsvereinigung der Juden in Deutschland, which looked to many Jewish victims of persecution like a valuable self-defense mechanism, in a world in which most Jews were prohibited from following occupations and hence slipped into destitution. (By 1940–41, only one quarter to one third of Jews in Germany were living on their own assets.)[5] In fact the Reichsvereinigung was controlled by the Gestapo and amounted to a channel through which Jews were to pay for their own persecution and its bureaucratic implementation.

Soon after the imposition of the fine, and the new legislation of November 12, 1938 (the *Verordnung zur Ausschaltung der Juden aus dem deutschen Wirtschaftsleben*), the Deutsche Bank's Berlin office called branch offices to explain "that in general Jewish customers could not be allowed to dispose over their accounts in the light of the circumstances created by the new decrees."[6] Some branches reported a police intervention. In Meissen, the political police imposed a general prohibition on payments, but then the same office on Monday stated that "free accounts may be disposed over."[7]

A further decree of December 1938 also provided for the sale of Jewish-owned securities, paid to meet the fine and the emigration tax. The Economic Groups (*Wirtschaftsgruppen*) of the Reich Group Banks (*Reichsgruppe Banken*) were to decide themselves about the sales of Jewish security deposits, which had greatly accelerated as a result of the fine. But the amounts to be sold were carefully controlled by the banks and the bourse authorities to prevent a sharp dip in the stock market.[8]

One example will show how currency control and pressure to sell Jewish enterprises interacted to produce substantial movements in the accounts of Jewish customers – without, however, producing large or disproportionate commissions or profits for the bank (at least in any of the cases that the author has seen). In the first half of 1938, the machine and apparatus manufacturer M. Eichtersheimer of Mannheim came under increasing pressure to "aryanize". Part of the enterprise was sold in July 1938 to the Vereinigte Sauerstoffwerke GmbH, for RM 196,750, which the owner of the firm immediately used to buy securities: mostly German treasury bonds, but also mortgage bonds and IG Farben bonds and shares. The owner seems to have decided to emigrate in November, after the pogrom, and his private house was sold to the Reichsfiskus (Army Administration Mannheim [Heeresstandortverwaltung Mannheim]) on November 22 (for RM 61,500). The main enterprise was only sold, to an Auslandsdeutscher (German abroad) who was returning from Argentina, in the spring of 1939, when the owner was already abroad. A purchase price of RM 424,900 was agreed on, but the purchaser paid only RM 45,360 in free (convertible at the official rate) foreign exchange to the seller's account with the Deutsche Bank. To secure possession, Oberfinanzpräsident (tax administrator) Karlsruhe

insisted that the purchaser pay a further RM 100,000 "without compensation" to the Golddiskontbank and the equivalent of RM 29,640
in foreign exchange, as well as a further sum if the profits of the firm
exceeded a certain amount.[9] In June 1939, the assets in Deutsche
Bank were subject to seizure to pay taxes: RM 70,600 in IG Farben
shares, assessed as worth RM 105,489. A total of RM 290,658 was
claimed in this way, and the taxes specified included RM 73,766 for
the *Judenvermögensabgabe* and RM 106,500 for the *Reichsfluchtsteuer.* In August 1940, the Gestapo seized gold coins, watches,
and other valuables from the safe deposit box of the owner's wife,
which were sold in the course of 1941 and RM 944 credited to the
account. (The actual goods had been auctioned for more: there was a
"surplus" of RM 586.) Almost all of the securities bought by the owner
were sold in July 1939, although a small holding (RM 500 of preferred
shares in the Reichswerke "Hermann Göring") were sold only at the
beginning of 1942. In the course of 1940 and 1941, the Deutsche
Golddiskontbank transferred assets into a blocked account for emigrants or *Auswanderersperrkonto.* (A total of RM 190,605 was paid
in.) Of this, RM 190,184 were promptly paid out again, for further tax
payments, old debts of the company, but also a substantial sum
(RM 15,000) to the purchaser of the machinery factory, and an
equally substantial sum to the Heidelberg law firm that had handled
the owner's German affairs. If there was any excessive charging in
this case, it was by the lawyer acting on the emigrant's behalf. In this
way, the account (as well as the securities depot account) disappeared during the war.

In the course of 1940 and 1941, ad hoc expropriations of Jews
occurred on the basis of very dubious legality – even in the peculiar
legal circumstances of the Nazi dictatorship. There were the payments
of Jews to the Gestapo and SS security services dressed up as contributions to Jewish-run organizations. On August 21, 1941, all Jewish
communities were instructed by the Reichsvereinigung to undertake a
complete inventory of homes and property.[10] There were also direct
local actions. On April 4, 1941, the Reichsführer SS announced the
confiscation of all property of Jews deported from Baden under the
order of October 22, 1940. Similar confiscations took place in
Pomerania and the Saar-Palatinate. These were justified simply by reference to the Decree for the Protection of People and State (the emer-

gency decree following the Reichstag fire).[11] On May 29, 1941, Hitler then decided that seized assets should go to the central state (Reich).[12]

The complete and systematized expropriation of Germany's Jewish population came through the 11th Decree on the Citizenship Law (November 25, 1941: 11. *Verordnung zum Reichsbürgergesetz*). All Jews living abroad lost their citizenship, as did those who were subsequently to leave Germany. Because under previous legislation from 1933 the loss of German nationality meant an expropriation, deportation outside Germany would now entail a complete transfer of assets to the state. German shares were to be administered through the Prussian State Bank (Seehandlung). Other securities (i.e., bonds and foreign shares) were to be processed by the Reichsbank's securities department (*Wertpapierabteilung*).

But implementing this decree proved to be very complicated for the banks. How were they to know of the movement or deportation of their customers? What happened in the case of Jews who were deported but still remained within the boundaries of the German Reich (Auschwitz, for instance, lay in East Upper Silesia, which had been annexed to Germany).[13] There were numerous cases in which bank officials demanded some kind of official information or notification on the fate of their Jewish customers. The Commerzbank's Bielefeld branch, for instance, wrote: "Since we do not know to where the Jew was deported, we cannot ascertain whether it is really a case of a Jew subject to the Decree of 25 November 1941. We inform you that the transfer cannot be effected until we have the appropriate proof in the form of a decision of the Chief of Security Police."[14]

The Wirtschaftsgruppe Privates Bankgewerbe again acted as an intermediary and as a center for the exchange of information and experience between its banking members on the implementation of the decree. It explained the 11th decree in a circular, in which it advised its member banks that it was not necessary to inform its customers of their expropriation. The circular added that the general decree about "cession of wealth" meant that "the reluctance of individual banks to transfer confiscated accounts not yet declared as forfeit to an official payments office or other institution, because of fear of foreign legal cases, is no longer justified."[15]

There were indeed such cases of foreign lawsuits. In March 1942, the Deutsche Bank was still complaining that "we have already been threatened by a case based on the argument that the customer did not fall under the terms of the Eleventh Decree."[16] Not all banks dealt with the application of the decree, and the risk of foreign legal action, in a uniform way. In April 1942, the Wirtschaftsgruppe Privates Bankgewerbe noted: "from repeated discussions of dubious cases relating to the Eleventh Decree, it is clear that the banks do not proceed uniformly in the question of notifying emigrated Jewish account-holders that a cession to the Reich has taken place. The Dresdner Bank and Commerzbank give a short notice in cases where emigrated account-holders issue instructions or ask for statements, while the Deutsche Bank, because in two cases its conduct was questioned by the Oberfinanzpräsident of Berlin, does not issue such notices."[17]

Generally, however, the major banks were involved in lengthy discussions about the execution of the 11th Decree, managed by the Wirtschaftsgruppe Privates Bankgewerbe. They evolved a common procedure "that they only make the transfer to the Oberfinanzpräsident after a prior ascertaining of the cession of account through the Chief of Security police, and make the notification subject to such instruction."[18] For example, the Deutsche Bank provided a letter from the Oberfinanzpräsident Münster, in which the state agency had added to its request for the transfer of funds: "The Jew was deported abroad on January 27, 1942."[19]

The general practice was for the regional Oberfinanzpräsident to send lists of "evacuated" Jews and demand the transfer of the assets that were "ceded to the Reich." Inevitably, there were mistakes in which the tax offices demanded the transfer of Jews who had not been deported.[20]

The confusions and complexity arose precisely because this decree appeared to make legal the completely and abhorrently illegal, and in doing this, produced endless contradictions. Simple expropriation of every piece of property created a state of absolute rightlessness, a denial in law of the existence of a person (because the person is defined by rights.) The complexities were so immense that a further decree on Jewish property was necessary, which made absolutely clear what lay in the future of those Jews in German power. Because it was clear that not all cases were actually covered by the 11th Decree, the

13th Decree stated: "After the death of a Jew his property is ceded to the Reich."

Could there have been in these circumstances, in which the state tried to grasp Jewish funds as completely as possible, "heirless" assets or accounts, analogous to those that in the 1990s created such a justified furor in the case of Swiss banks? The short answer is yes, but not in any substantial volume. The process specified under the 11th Decree was quite complicated, and not all accounts were actually transferred.

Let us again consider one case: Emma K. of Böchingen in the Palatinate, who held an account at the Deutsche Bank Mannheim, had been obliged to sell her land to the Bavarian Farmers' Settlement Agency (apparently without the intermediation of Deutsche Bank). She received RM 4,000, of which RM 1,600 was used to pay the *Judenvermögensabgabe*. Now without a home, she moved repeatedly, first to friends in Mannheim, then to Frankfurt, and then to a Jewish old people's home in Frankfurt (in the Rechneigrabenstrasse). At the beginning of 1942, she paid over what remained of her account, RM 1,800, to the Jüdische Kultusvereinigung Frankfurt. Out of this, the monthly charges of the home (RM 120) would be deducted. On October 6, 1942, the Deutsche Bank Mannheim wrote to the Jüdische Kultusvereinigung to report that on September 26, the Oberfinanzpräsident, Devisentelle Frankfurt, had stated that the "assets of the account holder have been confiscated." But a few weeks later, on October 26, the bank wrote another letter, this one to say that the Finance Office letter of September 26, was "to be regarded as void," and asking the Jüdische Kultusvereinigung to obtain the necessary permission of the Gestapo for the transfer of the account to Theresienstadt (to where Fräulein K. had been deported). There is no reply in the files, and on January 9, 1943, the bank sent a reminder. What had happened between September 26 and October 26, 1942? On October 9, the Wirtschaftsgruppe had sent a new circular with information about the treatment of Theresienstadt: "Deportations of Jews within the area of the Reich usually take place to Theresienstadt (Bohemia-Moravia)." Accounts of such individuals were not to be treated according to the 11th decree. Instead, the accounts were to be marked *"Wohnsitzverlegung nach Theresienstadt."*[21] By the end of 1943, on Fräulein K.'s account there still remained RM 797 in the account (RM 790 at the end of 1945), and the account was labeled with an addressograph print as *"Fräulein Emma K. Frankfurt/M, jetzt*

Theresienstadt z. Hd. Sekretariat im Hause" ("currently Theresienstadt c/o Secretariat of Bank"). The account was converted into Deutschemarks after the 1948 currency reform. The conversion was carried out by the bank without a petition by the owner (as was required from German residents), on the grounds that her last recorded residence was abroad. Initially the law provided for a 10:1 reduction, with half the account blocked; the eventual conversion rate was reduced to 100:6.5. As a result, the account now had DM 50.70, and in 1949 the Südwestbank Mannheim, the successor of Deutsche Bank, deducted 70 pfennigs in fees. On July 19, 1950, a note records, "we request the transfer of the account to the collective account: Owners Not to be Located." The sum of DM 50 was then duly paid one week later into a collective account.[22]

Legally, the postwar situation is clear. The Allied Restitution Law (Military Law 59) required the reporting of assets of victims of National Socialism, and the claims were then transferred to the Jewish Restitution Successor Organization. This organization, to make immediate payments, reached a "global settlement" with the German *Länder,* under the terms of which the *Länder* paid the restitution and took in return the claims on assets. A later decision of the Federal Court (Bundesgerichtshof) in 1955 held that the banks that had managed deposit and security (depot) accounts were still obliged to pay out those accounts to the owners or their heirs without the need for a restitution proceeding. The Deutsche Bank had a number of accounts (not all from victims of National Socialism) that had not been converted at the 1948 reform. The larger accounts (over DM 100) were paid over to the state: A total of 323 accounts worth DM 150,000 were paid in this way. Smaller accounts, under DM 100, were simply booked to the general profit-and-loss account. Thus by the 1970s, no heirless accounts existed. But some such accounts, for small but not trivial amounts (like that of Emma K.) had been canceled well before the general cancellation of the 1970s.

The Nazi state had certainly tried to seize every Jewish asset it could identify, but some assets fell through its bureaucratic web and remained a problem after 1945. Such accounts, small as they may be in comparison with Swiss circumstances, are nevertheless rather more than an accounting problem.

8

The Profits of Deutsche Bank

The published overall profit-and-loss accounts do not show the extent of the profit from "aryanization," although there is a notable (if small) spike in 1938, which reflects the additional business of that year and the income from additional commissions (see Figure 1). The state was concerned to limit private profiteering from "aryanization," at least where nonparty members were concerned, and banks, which on ideological grounds were distrusted, were subject to especially close attention. There was no standard bank commission on "aryanization" transactions: Deutsche Bank generally obtained a figure of between one and three percent.[1]

Nevertheless, the big commercial banks did produce some data on their profits derived from "aryanization." In the case of Deutsche Bank, these figures were found in the balance-sheet material prepared for 1938 and subsequent years, but there is no equivalent data for the period before 1938. This material was found not in the Historical Archive of Deutsche Bank but in its Control Department, which unearthed it and revealed its existence to Professor Pohl and the Historical Institute in the wake of the controversy over "Nazi gold": These documents were also the basis for the report on gold transactions written by Jonathan Steinberg.

Before analyzing these data, it is worth reflecting why they were produced. The special listing of "aryanization" profits clearly reflects a perception by someone that "aryanization" constituted a peculiar and unique revenue, quite distinct from the normal course of business activity. Because the data were prepared at the same time as the bank's tax balance sheet (which differs substantially from the pub-

204

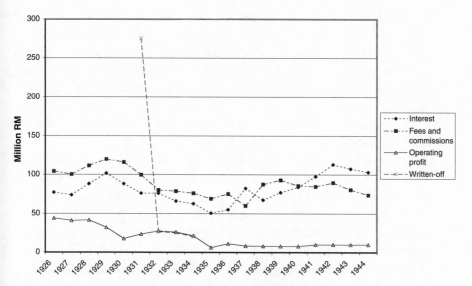

Figure 1. Deutsche Bank: income and operating profit 1926–1944.

lished accounts), it is not unreasonable to conclude that it might have
been intended to demonstrate to the Reich Economics Ministry, the
Göring plan authorities, and the tax authorities that the bank was not
making "excessive" or "unusual" profits from "aryanization." This was
particularly important at a time when Hermann Göring especially was
preoccupied with collecting as much revenue as possible (from Jews,
of course, but also from German companies) in the financial preparation for a war of conquest. The context for these accounts is then the
increasing severity of the tax authorities, and in particular the introduction of a supplemental income tax (*Mehreinkommensteuer*) on the
profits of 1938 that were over 1937 levels.[2] It was of course in 1938
that the bulk of the German "aryanizations" were carried out.

Such an interpretation would be borne out by the figures, which
seem to give rather low figures (especially for the Sudetenland, where
the bank's profits appear extraordinarily low when treated in the context of the great efforts the bank made to find purchasers for
Sudetenland property). The figures given here thus represent a very
minimal estimate. Dresdner Bank prepared estimates of "aryanization" profits, presumably for the same fiscal purpose, which used a
slightly more extended definition of "aryanization" profits and

included material on the gains derived from administering Jewish blocked accounts prior to emigration. In general, the published profits in the accounts were substantially less than the profits declared in the tax balance sheets. For instance, in 1938, the balance sheet showed a profit of RM 7,950,800, whereas the tax balance sheet showed RM 36,573,900.[3]

The unpublished supplemental material for the 1938 balance sheet (Annex 3) includes a "breakdown of profits from transactions not regularly recurring," with a sum of RM 936,812.87 as "special profits and brokerage fees in connection with aryanizations, sales of securities and real estate, fees for listing on the stock exchange, trustees, mortgage brokerage, etc." In addition, a sum of RM 553.43 was added in ink and described as "Bezirk Reichenberg" in the Sudetenland: This represented the commissions arising out of Sudeten "aryanizations." In 1939, the equivalent amount was RM 709,425.66; in 1940, RM 415,497.68; in 1941, the brokerage fees amounted to RM 153,963.51; in 1942, RM 89,736.41; and in 1943, RM 188,296.49 from mortgages and property and RM 99,088.10 from shares. In addition, further items are likely to represent direct or indirect profits from "aryanization:" It appears that particularly important or unusual cases were shown separately. In 1938, there was a special item of RM 213,310.16 representing special profits from shares of Simon Hirschland & Co. In 1939, the Krefeld branch showed a special profit of RM 264,424.20 from the acquisition of Joh. Girmes & Co. shares. In 1941, the special profit of RM 116,728.23 for H. Albert de Bary & Co. Amsterdam "due to various French loans" probably reflects the acquisition of Jewish-owned shares in the occupied Netherlands.[4]

Dresdner Bank's internal accounts show, by comparison, lower figures for a more narrowly defined entry called "brokerage fees in connection with dejudifications," RM 362,000 in 1938 and RM 285,000 in 1939. But Dresdner Bank also recorded larger figures for special receipts arising out of the administration of Jewish accounts (RM 115,000 in 1938 and RM 479,000 in 1939) and commissions on share transactions involving Jews (RM 68,000 in 1938 and a very large figure, RM 960,000, in 1939). Adding these figures suggests that Dresdner Bank made larger profits out of "aryanization" than did Deutsche Bank, an outcome that reflected its substantially closer contacts with the regime.[5]

Can these figures be supplemented by other known profits of the bank to give a more realistic estimate of the gains derived from "aryanization?" There was a second element of gain involved in participation in some "aryanizations" that is unrecorded in the balance-sheet material: the appreciation of stock when it was sold to the public. The most dramatic, and most large-scale, example of such an operation is the floating of the Norddeutsche Leder shares in 1941. The difference in the share price between the sum paid to almost entirely Jewish owners by Deutsche Bank (RM 106) and the issue price of RM 140 brought a gain of around RM 6.12 million – obviously substantially more than the modest RM 120,000 commission.

Moreover, the greatest gains appeared not on the books of Deutsche Bank itself but in the accounts of affiliated institutions, notably BUB. The dramatic turnaround of that institution from large losses, which Deutsche Bank tried to transfer to the German state, to high profitability was largely a consequence of the economic reordering that followed in great part from the persecution and expropriation of Jews in occupied Europe. To the extent that Deutsche Bank derived dividends from such banks, it participated in the fruits of their transactions.

Even adding these supplemental sources of "aryanization" gain does not show that "aryanization" produced dramatic profits for Deutsche Bank. In addition, it should be noted that we know little about the overall profits from "aryanization" before 1938, which were not listed separately. But this was a much smaller scale of activity than the massive push of state-driven "aryanization" in 1938. In this sense, the account sometimes told in which postwar prosperity and the "Wirtschaftswunder" were founded on Nazi expropriation is wholly mythological. The moral balance sheet is much harder to assess. In some cases, bank transactions directly helped individuals to transfer assets abroad; in many cases, the bank helped others achieve gains that would not have been possible without Nazi anti-Semitic policies. In addition, the bank provided assistance to a public policy that was deeply immoral and that, at least in a number of instances relating to foreign-held assets, could not have been realized by the regime alone.

Routine "aryanizations" could be, and frequently were, handled by other banks. There may be several explanations: For party ideologues, an institution such as Deutsche Bank looked too cosmopolitan, too much a relic of the internationalism of the 1920s and Weimar, to be really trusted in carrying out the national revolution. At least in some cases, Deutsche Bank's managers seem to have disliked the nature of the business. But where Deutsche Bank's internationalism was a positive attraction, as in the case of bigger enterprises interlinked with foreign corporations and entangled in foreign law (this is true of Mendelssohn, or Hirschland, or Adler & Oppenheimer), the bank provided a service that other banks, whether regional banks or state-owned companies such as the Reichs-Kredit-Gesellschaft, could not offer.

Of the foreign affiliates of Deutsche Bank during the War, BUB was most centrally involved in large-scale "aryanizations." By the time Deutsche Bank had a controlling interest in the Vienna Creditanstalt, the sudden flood of Austrian "aryanization" was over. There were simply no businesses left to "aryanize." On the other hand, BUB, together with the Dresdner Bank–owned Escompte Gesellschaft, played a central part in the "dejudification" first of the Sudetenland and then of the remainder of Czechoslovakia. BUB was built up, however, by its ambitious young management as a bank that acted on a much wider stage than that of the Protectorate. In procuring and exchanging shares and bonds in occupied western Europe, men like Walter Pohle wanted to make the Czech bank a central player in the economic reordering of Europe. A critical judgment might be that the Prague bank did the work that the Berlin bank felt was too problematic to touch. Deutsche Bank's share of BUB's profits comprised RM 687,500 for 1942 and RM 531,667 for 1943. No accounts for 1944 or 1945 were prepared, and no payments were made. However, during these years, BUB was systematically transferring assets (such as the Hohenems credit) and securities to Deutsche Bank.

With one exception – the sale of the A&O shares – Deutsche Bank did not make a large profit on "aryanization." However, Deutsche Bank was a vital element in a chain of exploitation and theft. That it was relatively poorly rewarded for these services does not lessen the extent of a moral liability.

Such calculations neglect the core element of the whole process of "aryanization." Jews were pressed or forced to sell businesses that they would not otherwise, in the absence of a viciously persecuting regime, have sold. They did not want money that could be transferred out of Germany only with great difficulties, and further losses (by

1938–39 an emigrant owning financial assets would be required to leave ninety-eight to ninety-nine percent of these behind in Germany).[6] The victims of persecution certainly would not have envisaged turning their money into the contents of a statistician's estimate of what a standard German basket of consumption would look like. If they held onto the money that resulted from "aryanization" sales, they would have found that because the money represents a claim on the German state, it lost value radically as a result of the methods used to finance Hitler's war. There was an explosion of cash, and to restore monetary stability in 1948, the Allies and the German authorities imposed a currency reform that reduced the value of Reichsmark holdings by a factor of 100:6.5 to produce new Deutschemark assets.

This is why, even in the cases in which a "fair" price in terms of stock-market valuation was paid in the 1930s, in the 1950s West German courts correctly and justly ordered the payment of additional sums or the transfer of some shares. (The Hubertus and Salamander cases are treated in detail in previous chapters.) The sums that were judged and accepted as appropriate in the 1950s are clearly less than their equivalent sums would be today, if restitution arrangements had never been made, or if they were to be looked at again – because the German economy and society are now so much more prosperous. But restitution arrangements cannot simply be reexamined at regular intervals of a decade or so. There is fundamentally no financial way of correcting an injustice perpetrated over fifty years ago. The most equitable settlements, for instance in the Hirschland case, which was based on the precedent of the Warburg settlement, involved the restitution of a capital participation, not the payment of a fixed amount.

There are thus three, almost equally unsatisfactory, ways of trying to put a figure on bank involvement. One is to take the path of Michael Hepp and make an assessment of the overall volume of Jewish assets in Germany, and then in the occupied countries, and to deduce from a bank's share of overall business what its participation in "aryanization" might have comprised.[7] But this method runs into the objection that most businesses were liquidated (especially in the case of the smaller enterprises), not transferred, and that there is no reason to assume that banks' involvements correlated with their overall business. We have seen that often the party preferred to exclude big banks and that in smaller businesses, this attempt was often successful; equally, in larger businesses, with complex transactions, owners had strong incentives to work through a large institution with international connections. The total amount of Jewish-owned wealth in Germany is estimated by Raoul Hilberg at RM 10 billion to 12 billion in 1933. German records show gross assets of RM 8,531 million in 1938 for an area that includes Austria. In her recent ground-breaking investigation of the wealth position of the Jewish population, Helen Junz estimates that 52.5 percent of this amount represents financial assets. This figure is much higher than it would have been in 1933, because of the winding-up of businesses: The proceeds were often placed in deposit accounts or in state paper. Fourteen percent (or RM 1,195 million) still represented active business capital.[8] But there is no way of getting from this estimate to a guess of what Deutsche Bank's share might have been.

The second way is to look at the internal data provided by Deutsche Bank and other banks in estimating the earnings from such one-off transactions. These were not documents prepared for public release, or even for tax purposes, and there is no reason to suppose any deliberate understatement of the earnings. But the definition of business resulting from "aryanization" is narrow (much more so in the case of the material from Deutsche Bank than in the case of Dresdner Bank). For Deutsche Bank, for instance, there is no way of seeing what earnings were received from the administration of blocked-mark accounts.

The third way is to look at published profits and to see the rise (though a very small one) in profits in 1938 at the high point of the "aryanization" process. Such figures, however, may have been manipulated to understate extraordinary profits at a moment when the party and state authorities were increasingly concerned with the position of finance capital and its profitability.

All of these approaches have obvious limitations. Such limitations do not, however, preclude reaching an overall assessment of responsibility and obligation.

9

Some Concluding Reflections

The preceding analysis of several hundred "aryanizations" of major companies conducted by Deutsche Bank in Germany, and the role of Deutsche Bank in the expropriation of Jewish businesses in occupied territories, suggests the following conclusions:

1. There is no single typical process of "aryanization," but rather a multiplicity of measures aimed at the extinction of Jewish business life.
2. Many of these measures, especially in the early years of the Nazi regime, were not directed from the central office of the bank but corresponded to local circumstances. Sometimes it was a matter of responses to pressures from local party offices and bureaucrats, sometimes of initiatives by branch managers keen to ingratiate themselves with the new regime.
3. In large cases, even at the outset of the dictatorship, political calculations were involved, and Deutsche Bank's central decision makers accommodated these pressures. An example is the case of Ullstein, where control of the media and of opinion was of paramount concern to the Nazi authorities, and where there was very rapid "aryanization."
4. The transfer of commercial property from Jews to non-Jews had an impact on a number of aspects of bank business: The bank
   - Lost loan customers
   - Earned commissions on the sale of property
   - Experienced a temporary rise in the deposits of Jewish customers as a result of the liquidation and sale of property

- Issued shares in "aryanized" companies on the stock exchange
- Transferred money out of Germany in the context of a complex exchange-control system
- Refinanced mortgages
- Lent money to purchasers of Jewish property
  Some of these measures led to losses for the bank, whereas others produced profits. In areas where there were many Jewish businesspeople, such as Frankfurt or Mannheim, the bank's managers were more worried about the loss of business than enthralled with the prospect of new sources of profit.

5. The complexity of the business transactions involved in foreign transfers of assets, across multiple frontiers, increased with the German conquests and military occupations after 1938.

6. The overall story of "aryanization" can thus be divided into several phases. In the first, from 1933 to 1937, there were no *central* state initiatives systematically to expropriate or eliminate Jewish-owned business. In the second, from 1937 to 1939, in Germany, the state aimed at the elimination of Jewish business life, and the bank's leadership accommodated this policy. In the third, from 1938 onward, the expropriation of Jewish property outside the former German territories took place in the context of a radical mobilization of anti-Semitic resentment, and then of a racial war. The seizure of property in Austria and the Czech lands, and the immediate and brutal persecution of Jews, provided a precedent for later occupation strategy.

7. The bank's motives included compliance with state policy, help to individual Jewish businesspeople, help to non-Jewish businesspeople in acquiring property, and expansion of market share – especially in previously foreign territories.

8. After 1945, the bank and its successor organizations had multiple motives, which included:
   - Compliance with the restitution legislation of the occupation authorities (and subsequently of federal law)
   - Protection of existing customers, as well as of previous and future customers who had been the victims of persecution
   - The limitation of the bank's own responsibility in restitution cases

How does the story presented here change the way in which we think historically of the terrible phenomenon of National Socialism, and how do we interpret the actions of individuals and institutions entangled in its grasp? To what extent did the realization of its destructive ideology depend on the acquiescence, the complicity, and the cupidity of existing economic and political institutions?

Explanations that rely on the profit motive as the primary explanation of business cooperation with the regime are inadequate, probably in general and certainly in this case. Later, Hermann Abs liked to say: "Profit is good, but it's not everything. As man does not live in order to breathe, he does not go about his business with the exclusive aim of making profit."[1] Deutsche Bank helped in the implementation of the regime's policies, including those which aimed at what Georg Solmssen, the bank's managing board spokesman in 1933, had presciently termed "the indiscriminate economic and moral destruction of all members of the Jewish race living in Germany."[2] It made some profit on the business transactions involved, but they were not extravagant or excessive profits, on a scale that would allow the institution to sustain a subsequent half-century of expansion. If nothing else, the regime's commitment to an anticapitalist and especially an antifinance capital ideology saw to the limitation of profits emanating from the regime and the party's measures.

The fact that the bank was not primarily driven by profit does not, of course, make its actions any more justifiable. Indeed, it might be argued that transactions that fundamentally undermined trust in contracts, and that extended the arbitrary and capricious exercise of power, are discreditable enough by themselves – but even more discreditable when they cannot be legitimated in terms of the traditional logic of business decisions. Talk of simply going on with "business as usual" in the extraordinary circumstances of Nazi Germany is thus inherently implausible, for there was nothing very usual about German business at that time.

A better way of understanding the behavior of business in that era is to think of the consequences of the regime's actions in destroying essential mechanisms of the market economy: prices (controlled by price restraints), interest rates or the price of money (which were capped), and dividends (which were limited). Profits in themselves made no sense, but capturing the political process that then increasingly shaped economic outcomes rather certainly did. Instead of competing in a market for market share, businesses competed for influence in a political market that functioned on its own terms and logic. Thus, Deutsche Bank and its chief rival, Dresdner Bank, tried not for higher profits but to extend the grasp of their influence. This was especially true when the political market was shaken up by the German conquests and when new opportunities became apparent. The dynamics of the political market are especially apparent in the story of Deutsche Bank in relation to the competing interests and pressures it encountered when it entered the politics of occupied Austria and Czechoslovakia. But the truly extraordinary fortunes were made by those who commanded the political logic more fully than banks and bankers ever could.

The most plausible rationalization of business strategies in these circumstances sees them as responding not to the existing circumstances but to future possibilities in a world in which the rules might be changed back again. This is the essence of the explanation given by Neil Gregor for the apparently illogical and certainly criminal energies of large corporations in acquiring capacity, developed with slave labor, even at a stage of the war when it was abundantly apparent that Germany had lost the war.[3] The capacity, in this interpretation, was intended to be used in the subsequent peace, as a basis for expansion in a differently ordered economy.

Although this interpretation may make sense for some business corporations, it does not really account for the behavior of Deutsche Bank as described in the previous pages. The most aggressive and brutal parts of its strategy concerned areas that could not possibly be part of a postwar reconstruction of the German economy: the occupied territories, and – for Deutsche Bank especially – the Czech lands.

We will understand this side of the company's history only if we cease being naïve about the way in which a company functions – especially in such circumstances as the 1930s, which eroded and corroded corporate life. What drove decisions increasingly was not an overall strategy but rather the ambitions of individual functionaries in the corporate hierarchy. There was a radicalization from below, reminiscent of that described by Hans Mommsen for the administration, the army, and the party.[4] Within Germany, there was some room for maneuver for individual bank managers. We have seen how much the character and aggressiveness of "aryanization" varied from branch to branch and region to region. Particularly where there were many Jewish businesspeople – in pre-1938 Germany – the bankers of Deutsche Bank tended to be hesitant. Individual managers had much greater scope outside Germany, and the extraordinary energy of a Walter Pohle found greater release here. The scope for implementing a political philosophy based on a racist nationalism became much greater.

Such a case study as this has a valuable function, in reminding us that even large corporations, complex social organisms as they might be, are made up of individuals who make choices about their actions. They cannot always be certain of what the eventual outcomes of those choices will be. At least some of the initiatives concerning "aryanization" were undertaken for legitimate and even decent motives, protecting legitimate property holders, and helping them at least to rescue parts of their assets or preserve some of their interest. This appears to be the case in the transactions concerned with the liquidation of Mendelssohn, or the transfer of the German publishing interests of S. Fischer Verlag to a man of unimpeachable decency (who nevertheless made his own compromises). Even decent motives are not enough to ensure decent outcomes, and the long, drawn-out seizure of the assets of the Adler and Oppenheimer families indicates how the initial help provided by a bank with international contacts drew that bank into a compromise with the criminal extortions of the German occupation regime in the Netherlands.

The reader will ask – if the question of judgment on individuals and their actions is raised – what of the most visible and controversial figure in Deutsche Bank's twentieth century history, Hermann Abs? He appears as a striking contrast to Erich Bechtolf, who rather courageously did not simply fail to act to take over the Bank Handlowy but even explained his course of inaction to his incredulous Polish counterpart. Bechtolf, too, had a highly influential and successful postwar career, and he was spokesman of the managing board of the successor to Deutsche Bank, Norddeutsche Bank AG, from 1952 to 1957.

Abs fully used an unusually wide range of contacts – from foreign multinationals (such as Unilever), the Vatican, through German business leaders, to the thugs who ran the takeovers and expropriations in

Austria and in Czechoslovakia, the SS and the Gestapo. While being helpful to some of the great German-Jewish dynasties, the Mendelssohns, the Hirschlands, the Oppenheimers, the Adlers, or the German-Czech Petscheks, he made money for his bank and extended his contacts and interests (and in some cases, as with the Petscheks, his personal interests). Deutsche Bank's particular "asset" in dealing with "aryanization," even before 1938, and its competitive edge over other German banks (especially the state-owned sector) had been the range of its foreign contacts. Abs was brought to the bank to continue this tradition of external orientation and its advantages for the bank. He was responsible for the bank's "foreign policy," and this ensured that he bore a direct responsibility for the brutalities of the Czech case. He surveyed carefully the extent of the Creditanstalt's industrial holdings, and then those of BUB. He was the patron who urged the appointment of the energetically inventive and destructive Walter Pohle. Under his ultimate authority, BUB worked closely with the Gestapo and the SS. He was bound in this way, by chains with multiple links, to persecution and destruction. Jonathan Steinberg commented in the previous report on the effects that such indirect links have on the issue of responsibility. Bankers are normally at a safe distance from killing, removed by a long chain of business and social interactions.[5] The most self-reflective and self-critical financier of the end of the twentieth century has addressed this anonymous and apparently responsibility-diminishing characteristic of financial markets, which is also true outside the extreme circumstances of genocidal conflict. George Soros commented on his involvement in financial markets: "If I had to deal with people instead of markets, I could not have avoided moral choices and I could not have been so successful in making money. I blessed the luck that led me to the financial markets and allowed me not to dirty my hands."[6] But relationship banking in the German tradition does of course involve "dealing with people."

Is it possible to determine whether anyone died directly as a result of any of Abs's actions? The complexity of human interactions means that the answer to this question cannot be determined with complete certainty. Where the chain of links was shortest – again, in immediately the Czech case – some of the directors of BUB lost their lives as a consequence of their dismissal and Pohle's intrigue. This constitutes responsibility.

The mixed involvements of Deutsche Bank's leading banker did not become substantially less tangled when it came to managing restitution after 1945, where again Abs took part in negotiations in many different guises, as the representative of quite diverse interests (sometimes those of new owners, sometimes those of the victims of Nazism, as well as the interests of Deutsche Bank at a time when that institution had ceased to exist). The original engagements took place as a consequence of the actions of a regime that elevated inhumanity to a daily practice. Abs justified his actions to himself by thinking of them as preserving a particular institution, a German *Grossbank*. In retrospect, it does not seem a very good justification.

Notes

CHAPTER 1 BUSINESS AND POLITICS: BANKS AND COMPANIES IN NAZI GERMANY

1 Robert A. Brady, *The Spirit and Structure of German Fascism* (London: Victor Gollancz, 1937), 321.
2 Peter Hayes, *Industry and Ideology: IG Farben in the Nazi Era* (Cambridge, UK: Cambridge University Press, 1987), 381.
3 C. W. Guillebaud, *The Economic Recovery of Germany from 1933 to the Incorporation of Austria in March 1938* (London: Macmillan, 1939) 185.
4 Ulrich Herbert, *Hitler's Foreign Workers: Enforced Labor in Germany under the Third Reich* (Cambridge, UK: Cambridge University Press, 1997).
5 Hans Pohl, *Die Daimler-Benz AG in den Jahren 1933–1945* (Wiesbaden: Steiner, 1986); Horst Mönnich, *BMW. Eine deutsche Geschichte* (Vienna and Darmstadt: Paul Zsolnay Verlag, 1989).
6 Peter Hayes, *Industry and Ideology,* 342–60.
7 Hans Mommsen, *Das Volkswagenwerk und seine Arbeiter im Dritten Reich* (Düsseldorf: Econ, 1996); Wilfried Feldenkirchen, *Siemens 1918–1945* (Columbus: Ohio State University Press, 1999), 128–38; Manfred Pohl, *Philipp Holzmann: Geschichte eines Bauunternehmens* (Munich: Beck, 1999), 262–76.
8 Wolfgang Benz, *Sklavenarbeit im KZ* (Munich: Deutscher Taschenbuch-Verlag, 1993); Beate Brüninghaus, Barbara Hopmann, Mark Spoerer, Birgit Weitz, *Zwangsarbeit bei Daimler-Benz* (Stuttgart: Franz Steiner Verlag, 1994); Dietrich Eichholtz (ed.), *Krieg und Wirtschaft. Studien zur deutschen Wirtschaftsgeschichte 1939–1945* (Berlin: Metropol, 1999); Neil Gregor, *Star and Swastika. Daimler-Benz in the Third Reich* (New Haven CT: Yale University Press, 1998); Wolf Gruner, *Der geschlossene Arbeitseinsatz deutscher Juden. Zur Zwangsarbeit als Element der Verfolgung 1938–1943* (Berlin: Metropol, 1997); Katharina Hoffmann (ed.), *Nationalsozialismus und Zwangsarbeit in der Region Oldenburg* (Oldenburg: Bibliotheks- und Informationssystem der Universität Oldenburg, 1999); Andreas Heusler, *Ausländereinsatz. Zwangsarbeit für die Münchener Kriegswirtschaft 1939–1945* (Munich: Hugendubel, 1996); Hermann Kaienburg (ed.), *Konzentrationslager und deutsche Wirtschaft 1939–1945* (Opladen: Leske & Budrich, 1996); Ernst Kaiser, Michael Knorn, *"Wir lebten und schliefen zwischen den Toten": Rüstungsproduktion, Zwangsarbeit und Vernichtung in den Frankfurter Adlerwerken* (Frankfurt: Campus, 1994); Bertrand Perz, *Projekt Quarz.*

Steyr-Daimler-Puch und das Konzentrationslager Melk (Vienna: Verlag für Gesellschaftskritik, 1991); Gudrun Pischke, *Europa arbeitet bei den Reichswerken: das nationalsozialistische Lagersystem in Salzgitter* (Salzgitter: Archiv der Stadt Salzgitter, 1995); Otto Reinhard, *"Vernichten oder ausnutzen?" "Aussonderungen" und Arbeitseinsatz sowjetischer Kriegsgefangener im Reichsgebiet in den Jahren 1941/42* (Paderborn: Universitätsdissertation, 1995); Franz W. Seidler, *Die Organisation Todt: Bauen für Staat und Wehrmacht 1938–1945* (Bonn: Bernard & Graefe, 1998); Klaus-Jörg Siegfried, *Rüstungsproduktion und Zwangsarbeit im Volkswagenwerk 1939–1945* (Frankfurt: Campus, 1999).

9 Helmut Genschel, *Die Verdrängung der Juden aus der Wirtschaft im Dritten Reich* (Göttingen: Musterschmidt, 1966); Avraham Barkai, *From Boycott to Annihilation* (Hanover: University Press of New England, 1989); Frank Bajohr, "Arisierung," in *Hamburg: Die Verdrängung der jüdischen Unternehmer (Hamburger Beiträge zur Sozial- und Zeitgeschichte)* (Hamburg: Christians, 1997).

10 Hans Safrian, *Die Eichmann-Männer* (Vienna and Zurich: Europa Verlag, 1993), 36.

11 Jonathan Steinberg, *The Deutsche Bank and its Gold Transactions during the Second World War* (Munich: Beck, 1999); Johannes Bähr, *Der Goldhandel der Dresdner Bank im Zweiten Weltkrieg* (Leipzig: Kiepenheuer und Witsch, 1999). More recently, there appeared an essentially derivative essay by Peter Hayes: "The Deutsche Bank and the Holocaust," in Peter Hayes, (ed.), *Lessons and Legacies III: Memory, Memorialization and Denial* (Evanston, IL: Northwestern University Press, 1999), 71–98.

12 Harold James, "The Deutsche Bank and the Dictatorship," in Lothar Gall, Gerald D. Feldman, Harold James, Carl-Ludwig Holtfrerich, Hans E. Büschgen (eds.), *The Deutsche Bank 1870–1995* (London: Weidenfeld & Nicolson, 1995), 227–356.

13 These files are now catalogued in the Historisches Archiv der Deutschen Bank (hereafter HADB) as "B" files and are freely available for consultation.

CHAPTER 2   THE STRUCTURE, ORGANIZATION, AND ECONOMIC ENVIRONMENT OF DEUTSCHE BANK

1 From October 1929 to October 1937, the official name of the corporation was "Deutsche Bank and Disconto-Gesellschaft." It will be referred to below simply as Deutsche Bank.

2 See Lothar Gall, "The Deutsche Bank from Its Founding to the Great War," in Lothar Gall, Gerald D. Feldman, Harold James, Carl-Ludwig Holtfrerich/Hans E. Büschgen (eds.), *The Deutsche Bank 1870–1995* (London: Weidenfeld & Nicolson, 1995), 1–127.

3 See Boris Barth, *Die deutsche Hochfinanz und die Imperialismen: Banken und Aussenpolitik vor 1914* (Stuttgart: Steiner, 1995), 20–21.

4 See Harold James, *Monetary and Fiscal Unification in Nineteenth-Century Germany: What Can Kohl Learn from Bismarck?* (Princeton, NJ: Essays in International Finance, No. 202, 1997).

5 See Manfred Pohl, Angelika Raab-Rebentisch, *Von Stambul nach Bagdad: Die Geschichte einer berühmten Eisenbahn* (München: Piper, 1999); Gall, "The Deutsche Bank from Its Founding," 67–77.

6 Manfred Pohl, *Entstehung und Entwicklung des Universalbankensystems: Konzentration und Krise als wichtige Faktoren* (Frankfurt: Fritz Knapp, 1986), 67.

7 See Enquête-Ausschuss, *(Ausschuss zur Untersuchung der Erzeugungs- und Absatzbedingungen der deutschen Volkswirtschaft) Der Bankkredit* (Berlin: E. S. Mittler & Sohn, 1930).

[8] See Caroline Fohlin, "The Rise of Interlocking Directorates in Imperial Germany." *Economic History Review* 52 (2): 307–33 (1999).

[9] On the issue of the geographic distribution of Jewish-owned businesses, see Werner E. Mosse, *Jews in the German Economy: The German-Jewish Business Elite* (Oxford: Oxford University Press, 1987).

[10] Peter Hüttenberger, "Nationalsozialistische Polykratie," in *Geschichte und Gesellschaft 2* (Göttingen: Vandenhoeck & Rupprecht, 1976), 417–42; Dieter Rebentisch, *Führerstaat und Verwaltung im Zweiten Weltkrieg: Verfassungsentwicklung und Verwaltungspolitik* (Wiesbaden: Steiner, 1989); Ian Kershaw, *The Nazi Dictatorship: Problems and Perspectives of Interpretation* (London: Edward Arnold, 1989), 42–81.

[11] Heinrich Brüning, *Memoiren 1918–1934* (Stuttgart: Deutsche Verlags-Anstalt, 1970). On the origins of the memoirs, see Rudolf Morsey, *Zur Entstehung, Authentizität und Kritik von Brünings Memoiren 1918–1934* (Opladen: Westdeutscher Verlag 1975) (only partially accurate); Gerald D. Feldman, "Jakob Goldschmidt, the History of the Banking Crisis of 1931, and the Problem of Freedom of Manouevre in the Weimar Economy," in Christoph Buchheim, Michael Hutter, Harold James (eds.), *Zerrissene Zwischenkriegszeit: Wirtschaftshistorische Beiträge: Knut Borchardt zum 65 Geburtstag* (Baden-Baden: Nomos, 1994), 307–28; William L. Patch Jr., *Heinrich Brüning and the Dissolution of the Weimar Republic* (Cambridge, UK; Cambridge University Press, 1998).

[12] See Gerald D. Feldman, "The Deutsche Bank 1914–1933," in Gall et al., *Deutsche Bank,* 264–67.

[13] See Harold James, *The German Slump: Politics and Economics 1924–1936* (Oxford: Oxford University Press, 1986), 303–7.

[14] *Lord d' Abernon's Diary, Vol. 2: The Years of Crisis June 1922–December 1923* (London: Hodder and Stoughton, 1929), 51: "He was finally released after six months and bound over for the rest of his sentence, thereafter fading into oblivion."

[15] Historisches Archiv der Deutschen Bank, Frankfurt (hereafter HADB), Rheinisch-Westfälische Bank (RWB) 27, December 15, 1953, note for Rösler.

[16] Mosse, *Jews,* 225, 227.

[17] Thomas Balogh, *Studies in Financial Organization* (Cambridge, UK: University Press, 1947), 78, noted "a secular tendency for the demand for bank loans to decline." See also *Frankfurter Zeitung,* June 3, 1934: The state had financed new credit through work-creation programs, but "the credit created in this way did not stay in the economy, because important sectors still preferred to liquidate inventories in order to repay credit."

[18] Bundesarchiv Berlin (hereafter BAB) R 8119 P24000, Deutsche Bank circular to Branch Managers, August 22, 1933.

[19] HADB, Directors' Meetings file, Directors' Meetings of October 6, 1936, and August 30, 1938.

[20] HADB, F63/1053, Deutsche Bank Special Circulars, S62/33, August 16, 1933.

CHAPTER 3   NATIONAL SOCIALISM AND BANKS

[1] Karl Marx, *Early Writings* (Harmondsworth: Penguin, 1975), 236.

[2] Martin Gregor-Dellin (ed.), *Richard Wagner: Mein Denken* (Munich: Piper, 1982), 174.

[3] See Gerald D. Feldman, *The Great Disorder: Politics, Economics and Society in the German Inflation 1914–1924* (New York: Oxford University Press, 1993), 200–02; Angelika Müller, "Der 'jüdische Kapitalist' als Drahtzieher und Hintermann. Zur anti-

semitischen Bildpolitik in den nationalsozialistischen Wahlplakaten der Weimarer Republik 1924–1933," in *Jahrbuch für Antisemitismusforschung 7* (Frankfurt: Campus, 1998), 175–207.

4 See Ralf-Georg Reuth, *Goebbels* (New York: Harcourt Brace, 1993), 52.

5 There is no reason to believe that Georg Solmssen joined the pressure to force out Wassermann, as has been suggested by Peter Hayes, "The Deutsche Bank and the Holocaust," in Peter Hayes (ed.), *Lessons and Legacies III: Memory Memorialization and Denial* (Evanston, IL: Northwestern University Press, 1999), 75.

6 Bundesarchiv Berlin (hereafter BAB), R8119 F, P55, July 1933 Report of Urbig. See also Christopher Kopper, *Zwischen Marktwirtschaft und Dirigismus: Staat, Banken und Bankenpolitik im "Dritten Reich" von 1933 bis 1939* (Bonn: Bouvier, 1995), 132–34.

7 BAB, R8119 F, P55, July 1933 Urbig report.

8 Historisches Archiv der Deutschen Bank, Frankfurt (hereafter HADB), P1/14, January 18, 1934 Urbig to Ernst Enno Russell.

9 HADB, B200, May 1, 1934 Oppenheim note; June 20, 1934 Mosler letter to Oppenheim.

10 Dieter Ziegler, "Die Verdrängung der Juden aus der Dresdner Bank," in *Vierteljahrshefte für Zeitgeschichte 47* (Munich: Oldenbourg, 1999), 187–216.

11 HADB, F38/145, November 12, 1938, Deutsche Bank branch Munich to Deutsche Bank branch Augsburg.

12 HADB, F56/6, April 19, 1937, Deutsche Bank Zentrale to Deutsche Bank branch Aachen, which noted: "It was your wish to be in agreement with Dresdner Bank, which is in the same position as yourselves. Today I should like to inform you that Dr. von Halt has agreed with Dresdner Bank that our two Aachen branches will dismiss their non-aryans on 31 December 1937 [...]." See also February 9, 1938, Deutsche Bank branch Aachen to Finanzamt Aachen-Stadt.

13 HADB, Rheinisch-Westfälische Bank, 54, December 6, 1935 Sippell memorandum; see also March 1, 1951, Rösler to Maximilian Müller-Jabusch.

14 von Halt had joined the NSDAP in May 1933: party membership number 3204950 (Berlin Document Center [BDC]).

15 Hermann Hess, *Ritter von Halt. Der Sportler und Soldat* (Berlin: Batschan, 1936), 126–29.

16 BDC, von Halt file.

17 National Archives and Records Administration (NA), Record Group (RG) 260/2/148/16, OMGUS, February 1, 1945, Tregaskes to Dougherty.

18 HADB, RWB, 31, March 20, 1950 Rösler declaration under oath.

19 Instituut voor Oorlogsdokumentatie, Amsterdam, 77–85 (RSSPF), 65 Aa.

20 NSDAP membership number 6927011 (BDC).

21 HADB, P1/4 (Personnel file Frowein), February 15, 1945, Deutsche Bank to Gau Economic Chamber Berlin.

22 BAB, R43II/245 b, fol. 1, February 18, 1943, Berlin: Meeting with Reich Minister Walther Funk.

23 NSDAP membership number 91273 (BDC).

24 Heinrich Hunke, "Verstaatlichung der Grossbanken," in *Die Deutsche Volkswirtschaft* 3 (1): 3–6 (1934).

25 NA, OMGUS, Deutsche Bank, 61.

26 See Carl-Ludwig Holtfrerich, "The Deutsche Bank 1945–1957: War, Military Rule and Reconstruction," in Lothar Gall, Gerald D. Feldman, Harold James, Carl-Ludwig Holtfrerich, Hans E. Büschgen (eds.), *The Deutsche Bank 1870–1994 (London: Weidenfeld & Nicholson, 1995)*, 357–521, 362.

27 BAB, R 8119 F, P31, fol. 27–32, September 16, 1943, Working Committee.

28 This list is contained in HADB, NL1/5; it is undated but must be from 1944 or later. It might even have been prepared as part of a denazification exercise, although I have not seen a copy of this document in the extensive material collected by OMGUS.

29 HADB, P1/14, April 9, 1933, Solmssen to Urbig.

30 Czech Republic State Archives, Finance Ministry, 9442/1939 box 1956, December 15, 1938, Duvernický sbor zrízencu Anglo-Ceskoslovenské a Prazské Úverní Banky to Ministry of Finance.

CHAPTER 4 THE PROBLEM OF "ARYANIZATION"

1 Avraham Barkai, *From Boycott to Annihilation* (Hanover: University Press of New England, 1989), 6.

2 See Harold James, "The Deutsche Bank and the Dictatorship," in Lothar Gall, Gerald D. Feldman, Harold James, Carl-Ludnig Holtfrerich, Hans E. Büschgen (eds.), *The Deutsche Bank 1870–1995* (London: Weidenfeld & Nicholson, 1995), 277–356.

3 See Heinrich Uhlig, *Die Warenhäuser im Dritten Reich* (Cologne: Westdeutscher Verlag, 1956).

4 See Frank Bajohr, *"Arisierung" in Hamburg: Die Verdrängung der jüdischen Unternehmer (Hamburg Beiträge zur Sozial- und Zeitgeschichte)* (Hamburg: Christians, 1997).

5 See Barkai, *Boycott,* 75; Peter Hayes, "Big Business and 'Aryanization' in Germany 1933–39." *Jahrbuch für Antisemitismusforschung* 3: 261 (1994).

6 As an example, the Rheydt shoe factory L. Stern & Co. was sold in November 1938 to a group of its managers, at a low price. The Düsseldorf office of Deutsche Bank noted in a letter to the Rheydt branch: "Under the new order, in view of the extremely inexpensive takeover of the real estate and machinery, the firm must expect to have to pay a substantial sum" (letter of February 17, 1939). In fact, the "aryanization levy" amounted to RM 30,000 on a transaction of RM 400,000.

7 See Mark Spoerer, *Vom Scheingewinn zum Rüstungsboom: Die Eigenrentabilität der deutschen Industriegesellschaften 1925–1941 (Vierteljahrschrift für Sozial- und Wirtschaftsgeschichte, Beiheft 123)* (Stuttgart: Steiner Verlag, 1996), 89–91.

8 Keith Ulrich, *Aufstieg und Fall der Privatbankiers: Die wirtschaftliche Bedeutung von 1918 bis 1938 (Schriftenreihe des Instituts für bankhistorische Forschung 20)* (Frankfurt: Fritz Knapp, 1998), 329.

9 June 27, 1945, Military Government Frankfurt to the director of the Reichsbank, Frankfurt: "Re. application of the Military Government's Law No. 52 concerning property of so-called 'aryanized' firms." Quoted in: HADB, F28/244, Deutsche Bank branch Mannheim to Fa. Josef Strack & Co. The original English version is kept in the Deutsche Bundesbank's archives under the signature B333/4.

10 Law No. 59 ("USREG"), in *Gazette of the Office of Military Government,* issue G, November 1947, 1. See also Bundesminister der Finanzen (ed.), *Die Wiedergutmachung nationalsozialistischen Unrechts durch die Bundesrepublik Deutschland,* Vol. 1 (Munich: Beck, 1974), 49–54.

11 Ordonnance No. 120, in *Journal Officiel du Commandement en Chef Français en Allemagne,* No. 119, 1219*ff.* See also *Die Wiedergutmachung,* 295.

12 Law No. 59 ("BrREG"), in *Verordnungsblatt für die Britische Zone,* No. 26, May 28, 1949, 152*ff.* See also *Die Wiedergutmachung,* 64.

13 Wilhelm Treue, "Bankhaus Mendelssohn als Beispiel einer Privatbank im 19. und 20. Jahrhundert," in *Mendelssohn-Studien 1* (Berlin: Duncker und Humblot, 1972), 29–80.

14 Christopher Kopper, *Zwischen Marktwirtschaft und Dirigismus: Staat, Banken und Bankenpolitik im "Dritten Reich" von 1933 bis 1939* (Bonn: Bouvier, 1995), 273.
15 See Hans Magnus Enzensberger (ed.), *OMGUS. Ermittlungen gegen die Deutsche Bank* (Nördlingen: Greno, 1985), 396 (*OMGUS. Report on the Investigation of Deutsche Bank*, November 1946, chapter 15, Table 12); Karl Heinz Roth, "Bankenkrise, Faschismus und Macht," in Kritische Aktionäre der Deutschen Bank (eds.), *Macht ohne Kontrolle: Berichte über die Geschäfte der Deutschen Bank* (Stuttgart: Schmetterling, 1990), 19; Tom Bower, *Blind Eye to Murder: Britain, America and the Purging of Nazi Germany – A Pledge Betrayed* (London: André Deutsch, 1981), 16.
16 Michael Hepp, *Deutsche Bank und Dresdner Bank: Gewinne aus Raub, Enteignung und Zwangsarbeit 1933–1944* (Bremen: Stiftung für Sozialgeschichte des 20. Jahrhunderts, 1999).
17 Eduard Rosenbaum, A. J. Sherman, *Das Bankhaus M. M. Warburg & Co. 1789–1938* (Hamburg: Christians, 1976).

CHAPTER 5 DEUTSCHE BANK AND "ARYANIZATION" IN THE PRE-1938 BOUNDARIES OF GERMANY

1 Bundesarchiv Berlin (hereafter BAB), R8119 F, P4295, fol. 106, December 1, 1933, Hutschenreuther to Franz Ulrich.
2 BAB, R8119 F, P4295, fol. 96, November 15, 1933, Eugen Schweisheimer to Urbig.
3 BAB, R8119 F, P4295, fol. 223, November 5, 1934 Rudolf Sies memorandum on negotiations in Braunes Haus, Selb.
4 Historisches Archiv der Deutschen Bank (hereafter HADB), Frankfurt, B201, October 9, 1935 Sippell note ("Confidential").
5 BAB, R8119 F, P2372, fol. 2–4, April 3, 1933, Joh. Jeserich AG to Benz (Deutsche Bank).
6 BAB, R8119 F, P2372, April 20, 1933 Benz note.
7 BAB, R8119 F, P2372, fol. 139, May 29, 1933 Benz memorandum; 177–78: July 10, 1933 Feuchtmann to Benz, 187–88; July 24, 1933 Feuchtmann to Benz.
8 Manfred Pohl, *Philipp Holzmann: Geschichte eines Bauunternehmers* (Munich: Beck, 1999).
9 BAB, R8119 F, P5218, fol. 9–10, August 30, 1933.
10 Avraham Barkai, *From Boycott to Annihilation* (Hanover: University Press of New England, 1989), 69–72.
11 Avraham Barkai, "Die deutschen Unternehmer und die Judenpolitik im Dritten Reich," in *Geschichte und Gesellschaft 15* (Göttingen: Vandenhoeck und Rupprecht, 1989), 227–47, 232.
12 Robert M. W. Kempner, "Hitler und die Zerstörung des Hauses Ullstein," in *Hundert Jahre Ullstein 1877–1977*, Vol. 3 (Berlin: Ullstein, 1977), 285.
13 Kempner, "Hitler und die Zerstörung des Hauses Ullstein," 273–75.
14 Kempner, "Hitler und die Zerstörung des Hauses Ullstein," 278.
15 HADB, B200, June 9, 1934 Mosler note.
16 Helmut Engel, Steffi Jersch-Wenzel, Wilhelm Treue (eds.), *Charlottenburg*, Vol. 1: *Die historische Stadt* (Berlin: Nicolai, 1986), 189–91.
17 BAB, R8119 F, P3481. See also Peter Hayes, "Big Business and 'Aryanization' in Germany 1933–39." *Jahrbuch für Antisemitismusforschung* 3:264 (1994).
18 BAB, R8119 F, P41, fol. 63, November 11, 1936 Rhineland-Westphalian Beirat meeting.
19 See Peter Hayes, "State Policy and Corporate Involvement in the Holocaust," in U.S. Holocaust Museum (ed.), *The Holocaust: The Known, the Unknown, the Disputed and the Reexamined* (Washington D.C., 1994).

[20] Saul Friedländer, *Nazi Germany and the Jews*, Vol. 1: *The Years of Persecution, 1933–1939* (New York: HarperCollins, 1997), 99.

[21] BAB, R 8119 F, P2947, fol. 114–15, January 7, 1938, Reichswirtschaftskammer to Reichswirtschaftsgruppen.

[22] Reichsgesetzblatt (RGBl) I 1938, 414. See also Helmut Genschel, *Die Verdrängung der Juden aus der Wirtschaft in Dritten Keich* (Göttingen: Musterschmidt, 1966), appendix II.

[23] RGB1 I 1938, 404.

[24] BAB, R 8119 F, P24002, September 25, 1935, "Niederschrift über den Besuch Dr. Schacht."

[25] RGB1 I 1938, 1902 (*Zweite Verordnung zur Durchführung der Verordnung zur Ausschaltung der Juden aus dem deutschen Wirtschaftsleben vom 14. Dezember 1938*).

[26] HADB, F38/145, Deutsche Bank branch Munich to Zentrale Rechtsabteilung.

[27] For example, Bundesverband Deutscher Banken archive (BDB), January 6, 1939, Wirtschaftsgruppe Privates Bankgewerbe to Vereinsbank in Hamburg.

[28] Special Archive (Captured German Documents), Moscow (hereafter SAM), 1458-03-0113, December 6, 1938 Göring speech. See also Friedländer, *Nazi Germany*, Vol. 1, 286–88.

[29] Staatsarchiv Leipzig (StAL), Deutsche Bank 013, October 5, 1935, October 31, 1935, and November 12, 1935 circular letters to branches marked "strictly confidential").

[30] HADB, F50/1, August 24, 1937, Deutsche Bank Zentrale to Direktionen unserer Kopffilialen.

[31] HADB, F50/1, January 7, 1938, Reichswirtschaftskammer to Reichsgruppen.

[32] BAB, R 8119 F, P24021, January 24, 1938 inquiry of the Berlin Chamber of Industry and Commerce and January 26, 1938 answer of Deutsche Bank.

[33] BAB, R 8119 F, P2947, fol. 112–13, January 14, 1938, Deutsche Bank Zentrale to Direktionen unserer Filialen.

[34] RGB1 1938 I, p. 627, *Dritte Verordnung zum Reichsbürgergesetz.*

[35] BAB, R 8119 F, P24021 August 15, 1938, Industrie- und Handelskammer zu Berlin certificate.

[36] BAB, R 8119 F, P24021, fol. 40 (n.d.), "Anmeldung des Vermögens von Juden."

[37] HADB, B214, July 4, 1938 Mosler note.

[38] Konrad Fuchs, *Ein Konzern aus Sachsen: Das Kaufhaus Schocken als Spiegelbild deutscher Wirtschaft und Politik 1901 bis 1953* (Stuttgart: Deutsche Verlags-Anstalt, 1990), 1–27.

[39] HADB, B214, Kimmich note (n.d.: July 1938).

[40] HADB, B214, September 6, 1938, Kimmich to Richard Freudenberg. See also BAB, R8119 F, P24235, Überleitung jüdischer Betriebe in arischen Besitz.

[41] HADB, B214, September 6, 1938 note.

[42] HADB, B214, September 6, 1938, Kimmich to Richard Freudenberg.

[43] Petra Bräutigam, *Mittelständische Unternehmer im Nationalsozialismus (Nationalsozialismus und Nachkriegszeit in Südwestdeutschland 6)* (Munich: Oldenbourg, 1997), 307–8.

[44] HADB, B214, September 22, 1938 Kimmich note: "Betr. Arisierungen in der Leder- und Schuhbranche."

[45] HADB, B214, September 27, 1938 Kiehl note: "Betr. Samt- und Plüschindustrie, Arisierung."

[46] Elke Fröhlich (ed.), *Die Tagebücher von Joseph Goebbels* (Munich: Saur, 1998), Part 1, Vol. 6, 182.

[47] A. J. van der Leew, "Der Griff des Reiches nach dem Judenvermögen". *Rechtsprechung zum Wiedergutmachungsrecht* 21: 383–92; 386 (1970).

[48] HADB, B214, November 24, 1938 conference in the Reich Economics Ministry "betr. Kapitalfehlleitungen und Liquidierung des Judenvermögens."

[49] SAM, 1458-2-203, November 25, 1938 conference in the Zentralverband.

[50] HADB, B214, November 26, 1938 Kimmich note: "Betr.: Sitzung bei der Wirtschaftsgruppe Bankgewerbe."

[51] HADB, F50/1, November 11, 1938 note.

[52] HADB, F50/1, NSZ Rheinpost, November 11, 1938.

[53] BAB, R8119 F, P24235, "Überleitung jüdischer Betriebe in arischen Besitz."

[54] RGB1 1938 I, 1642.

[55] HADB, B214, January 6, 1939, Wirtschaftsgruppe Privates Bankgewerbe – Centralverband des Deutschen Bank- und Bankiergewerbes to Deutsche Bank; January 13, 1939 Mosler note.

[56] HADB, B214, July 25, 1938 note (and pencil addition).

[57] BAB, R8119 F, P41, fol. 126, November 2, 1938 Rhineland-Westphalian Beirat meeting.

[58] HADB, S0441, May 16, 1938, December 20, 1938, and January 26, 1939 Elkmann notes.

[59] Sources: BAB, R8119 F, P24235, November 21, 1938 note; *Statistisches Handbuch für Deutschland 1928–1944* (Munich: Ehrenwirth, 1949), 244–45.

[60] BAB, R 8119 F, P24235, draft, n.d.

[61] BAB, R8119 F, P24330, June 21, 1938, "Niederschrift über die Sitzung der bayerischen Filialdirektoren in Nürnberg."

[62] Saxon State Archive Leipzig (StAL), Deutsche Bank files 623, December 29, 1938 letter to Berlin Filialbüro.

[63] HADB, F47/1, May 12, 1939 circular.

[64] For example, HADB, F67/16–17, on transfers for F. Raphael and M. Stern.

[65] Copy of May 30, 1938 Vermerk in Hauptstaatsarchiv Wiesbaden, 520 F 649 (Spruchkammerakten Carl Lüer: Dresdner Bank).

[66] HADB, "Sammlung deutsche Banken T–Z"; January 1, 1938, Weinmann to Martin; January 6, 1938, Martin to Schwerdtfeger; January 7, 1938, Schwerdtfeger to Martin; January 11, 1938, Martin to Weinmann.

[67] *Die Bank,* Berlin: Bank-Verlag, 1938, 1593.

[68] Information from Henning Kahmann, who is preparing a dissertation on Jacquier & Securius for the University of Regensburg.

[69] HADB, B262, Jaquier & Securius account. See also *Bank-Archiv* 37 (Berlin: Walter de Gruyter, 1938), 283.

[70] *Die Bank,* 1938, 1529.

[71] Treue, Wilhelm, "Bankhaus Mendelssohn als Beispiel einer Privatbank im 19. und 20. Jahrhundert," in *Mendelssohn-Studien 1* (Berlin: Duncker und Humbolt, 1972), 70.

[72] HADB, V1/3966, December 20, 1947 statement of Rodolfo Löb.

[73] See Julius H. Schoeps, "Wie die Deutsche Bank Mendelssohn & Co. schluckte," in *Frankfurter Rundschau,* November 27, 1998.

[74] See Johannes Houwink ten Cate, *"De Mannen van de Daad" en Duitsland 1919–1939: Het Hollandse zakenleven en der voroorlogse buitenlandse politiek.* Den Haag: Stu Uitgevers, 1995, 193–200.

[75] Abs's account of the meetings and the transaction is reproduced in Treue, "Bankhaus Mendelssohn," 76–80.

[76] BAB, R3101, 15515, June 2, 1938, Kluge to Reich Economics Ministry (with attachment).

[77] BAB, R3101, 15515, July 30, 1938, Kluge: "II. Bericht über das Bankhaus Mendelssohn & Co.," Berlin.

[78] BAB, R3101, 15515, September 3, 1938 note.

[79] BAB, R8119 F, P24130, July 26, 1938, Pohle to Abs.

[80] HADB, V1/3966, December 20, 1947 statement of Rodolfo Löb; July 31, 1970, Robert von Mendelssohn to Hermann Abs.

[81] HADB, Abs's note cards, Kempner, August 25, 1938.

[82] BAB, R3101, 15515, November 11, 1933, Walther Beyer to Ministerialdirektor Lange, Reich Economics Ministry.

[83] Die Bank, 1938, 1593.

[84] Bank-Archiv 37/38: 756, (1938).

[85] BAB, R3101, 15515, January 11, 1939 "Plan zur Arisierung des Bankhauses Mendelssohn & Co. Berlin."

[86] HADB, P1/22, October 25, 1938 Kimmich and Abs note.

[87] BDB, January 14, 1943, and February 13, 1945, Mendelssohn i.L. to Wirtschaftsgruppe Privates Bankgewerbe.

[88] April 2, 1946, Dr. Kremer memorandum: "Bericht über die Entwicklung der Firma Mendelssohn," in OMGUS/FINAD 2/169/11 and 2/181/2.

[89] Keith Ulrich, Aufstieg und Fall der Privatbankiers: Die wirtschaftliche Bedeutung von 1918 bis 1938 (Schrittenreihe des Instituts für bankhistorische Forschung 20 (Frankfurt: Fritz Knapp, 1998), 343.

[90] BAB, R3101, 15515, June 1, 1938 Fritz Fenthol to Reich Economics Ministry.

[91] Ulrich, Aufstieg und Fall, 343.

[92] BAB, R3101, 15515, July 12, 1938, Hoffmann to Reich Economics Ministry.

[93] HADB, RWB 23, July 12, 1951 note.

[94] BAB, R3101, 15515, July 19, 1938 note.

[95] BAB, R3101, 15515, July 20, 1938, "Über die heutige Verhandlung mit dem Gauwirtschaftsberater Hoffmann NSDAP Essen."

[96] BAB, R3101, 15515, July 31, 1938 Fenthol note.

[97] BAB, R3101, 15515, August 5, 1938 note.

[98] BAB, R2505, 9794, October 28, 1938 note on AfA 310504.

[99] BAB, R2505, 9794, April 21, 1939 Landwehr note, "Auswanderung der Inhaber des Bankhauses Simon Hirschland, Essen."

[100] HADB, RWB 21, March 31, 1950, "Vereinbarung über die Rückerstattung von Vermögenswerten nach Gesetz Nr. 59 der britischen Militärregierung." See also Ulrich, Aufstieg und Fall, 348.

[101] HADB, RWB 23, December 4, 1945, Burkhardt to Bechtolf.

[102] HADB, RWB 21, July 7, 1951, von Falkenhausen to Dr. Joseph Kessler.

[103] See Manfred Pohl, Konzentration im deutschen Bankwesen 1848–1980: Ein Handbuch der Bankenkonzentration in Deutschland (Frankfurt: Fritz Knapp, 1982).

[104] U.S. N.A. RG260/2 OMGUS, Interrogations, Exhibits and Annexes to Report on Reichs-Kredit-Gesellschaft, Exhibit 13: "Ergänzungen zu dem Bericht vom 6.1.1946 über die Geschäftätigkeit der Reichs-Kredit-Gesellschaft A.G. Berlin in den Jahren 1933–1945."

[105] HADB, F38/127, March 14, 1952, Landgericht Ravensburg.

[106] Hanspeter Sturm, "Salamander." Tradition 12: 309–333, 327 (1967).

[107] BAB, R 8119 F, P4150, Deutsche Bank branch Stuttgart to Zentrale, September 19, 1929.

[108] Bräutigam, Mittelständische Unternehmer, 257ff.

[109] Frank Bajohr, *"Arisierung"* in *Hamburg: Die Verdrängung der jüdischen Unternehmer (Hamburger Beiträge zur Sozial- und Zeitgeschichte)* (Hamburg: Christians, 1997), 47, citing *Hamburger Abendblatt*, March 30, 1933.

[110] Bräutigam, *Mittelständische Unternehmer*, 257*ff*, 334.

[111] BAB, R 8119 F, P4151, November 16, 1933, Deutsche Bank branch Stuttgart to Zentrale.

[112] BAB, R 8119 F, P4151, November 20, 1933, Deutsche Bank Berlin to Deutsche Bank branch Stuttgart.

[113] BAB, R 8119 F, P4151, November 27, 1933 note.

[114] BAB, R 8119 F, P4151, December 6, 1933 note.

[115] BAB, R 8119 F, P4151, July 6, 1935, Köhler to Rummel; July 3, 1935 Köhler note.

[116] BAB, R 8119 F, P4151, January 29, 1936, Deutsche Bank branch Stuttgart to Zentrale.

[117] BAB, R 8119 F, P4151, April 15, 1937, Deutsche Bank branch Stuttgart to Zentrale.

[118] Bräutigam, *Mittelständische Unternehmer*, 257, citing DAF-Abteilung "Information" to DAF-Kreisverwaltung of September 4, 1935.

[119] HADB, F9/40, December 7, 1948, Südwestbank FSAG to FIDES Vermögensbetreuungs- und Verwaltungs-GmbH, Munich; HADB, V1/1623, August 10, 1953 note of Delbrück Schickler & Co. Shares with a nominal value of RM 15,000 had been sold on August 11, 1937, and shares with a nominal value of RM 50,000, on September 11, 1937. HADB, V1/1623, "Auszug der Konten von Frau Paula Levi bei Delbrück Schickler & Co."; December 17, 1948, Hermann J. Abs to FIDES Vermögensbetreuungs- und Verwaltungs-GmbH, Munich.

[120] A brother of Salamander AG's principal shareholder Levy owned shares with a nominal value of RM 600,000 of the Schuhfabrik Luwald AG, Luckenwalde. The Deutsche Bank Hanover branch established contacts with prospective buyers of Luwald shares to "aryanize" the firm. See HADB, F88/640, October 4, 1938 Deutsche Bank Hanover note.

[121] From 1949 onward, Waldemar Strenger renewed his contacts with Hermann Abs after a longer break to be instructed about the foundation of a tobacco company under the name Deutsche Tabak Kompanie GmbH in Cologne. HADB, V1/4733, correspondence between Abs and Strenger between February 17, 1949, and February 5, 1952.

[122] BAB, R 8119 F, P4151, June 2, 1938 Sekretariat note.

[123] HADB, V1/1623, November 8, 1948, letter of Fides to Abs. See also HADB, F9/19 list without date. The persons listed are apparently the holders of a depository with Süddeutsche Bank in Stuttgart. Apart from Carl Kaess, Lederwerke Backnang, and the Stuttgart shoe producer Spieß, the names of Arthur Levi, Mathilde Weil, and Marga Engländer (neé Rothschild), who belonged to the Jewish group, are again listed as holders of shares with a nominal value of RM 461,000, 57,200, and 28,600, respectively.

[124] For instance, *Die Prognose: Finanz-, Börsen- und Wirtschaftsberichte*, 23, June 11, 1953, 135.

[125] HADB, V1/1623, June 12, 1951, Ferdinand Kremer to Alfred Kurzmeyer.

[126] HADB, V1/1623, August 21, 1957 note for Hermann Abs, signed by Abs on September 1, 1957.

[127] In the summer of 1970, Czichon published his book *Der Bankier und die Macht – Hermann Josef Abs in der deutschen Politik,* in which he made many accusations against Abs, including Abs's willing cooperation with the Nazi regime in the "aryanization" process (Eberhard Czichon, *Der Bankier und die Macht. Hermann*

Josef Abs in der deutschen Politik [Cologne: Pahl-Rugenstein, 1970]). Deutsche Bank and Abs protested against the publication of the book in its existing form and sued Czichon for the statements made in it. They won their case in the summer of 1972 (judgment of the Landgericht Stuttgart of June 27, 1972) and it was explicitly stated in the judgment that the accusations made by Czichon concerning Abs's role in the "aryanization" process were false. (The case of Adler & Oppenheimer that had been used by Czichon in his book as an example for Abs's cooperation with the Nazis consequently became part of the bank's statement of claim.)

128 HADB, V1/4919, August 26, 1971 Georg Krupp note.

129 HADB, Abs note cards, Steinbeck, June 16, 1938.

130 The former banking house Sal. Oppenheim jr. & Cie. The firm was registered under the name Pferdmenges on May 20, 1938. The name was changed again into Sal. Oppenheim jr. & Cie. in July 1947. See Michael Stürmer, Gabriele Teichmann, Wilhelm Treue, *Wägen und Wagen: Sal. Oppenheim jr. & Cie. Geschichte einer Bank und einer Familie* (Munich and Zurich: Piper, 1989), 379, 422*ff.*

131 For example, HADB, B32, December 29, 1939, Sekretariat to Paul Oppenheimer, London.

132 HADB, B31, November 30, 1938 Abs note.

133 The Wilhelm Werhahn OHG in Neuss was founded in 1871. The fast-growing and soon prosperous enterprise produced a variety of goods: grain, vegetable oil and various other foodstuffs, soap, wood, coal, and electricity. The dominating figure in the late 1930s was Wilhelm Werhahn, grandson of the founder of the Wilhelm Werhahn OHG.

134 HADB, B31, June 27, 1939, Schuller to Abs.

135 HADB, B31, November 30, 1938 Abs note.

136 HADB, Abs note cards, Steinbeck, September 23, 1938.

137 HADB, B31, February 27, 1939 Pollems note.

138 HADB, B31, "Niederschrift über die am 12. Juli 1939 zwischen Herrn Abs und den Herren Hendriks und Rykens getroffenen Absprachen betreffend Adler & Oppenheimer-Aktien."

139 HADB, B31, "Aktenvermerk über die am 12. Juli 1939 geführte Unterredung im Reichswirtschaftsministerium."

140 SAM, 1458-1-454, July 12, 1939 note.

141 HADB, B31, April 8, 1940 note.

142 HADB, B31, June 18, 1940, Hermann Köhler (Stuttgart) to Hermann Abs.

143 HADB, B31, May 30, 1940, Abs to Friedrich Herbst.

144 HADB, B33, May 3, 1940 Elkmann note.

145 HADB, Abs note cards, Steinbeck, October 2, 1940 (acquisition of 3 million shares).

146 HADB, B32, October 14, 1940 Elkmann note.

147 HADB, B32, November 11, 1940 note.

148 HADB, B32, March 24, 1941 note.

149 HADB, Abs note cards, Steinbeck, February 3, 1941.

150 HADB, B32, June 3, 1941 note.

151 HADB, Abs note cards, Huppertz, June 3, 1941.

152 HADB, B33, March 6, 1940, Deutsche Bank telegram to H. Albert de Bary & Co.

153 HADB, B32, November 3, 1940, Deutsche Bank to Amsterdamsche Leder Maatschappij.

154 HADB, Abs 1365, October 25, 1948 "Gutachten Baerns."

155 HADB, B31, November 23, 1940, Abs to August Neuerburg.

156 HADB, B32, n.d. (pencil 3/7 [July 3]) "Mitwirkung der Deutschen Bank bei den Übernahmen."

[157] HADB, B31, August 19, 1940 Elkmann note. Michele d'Alessandro, Guido Montanari, "BCI and International Capital Transfers to Poland between the Wars," paper delivered at the May 2000 conference of the European Association for Banking History, Warsaw.

[158] HADB, Abs note cards, Schaefer (Reichs-Kredit-Gesellschaft), August 9, 1938, July 16, 1941.

[159] HADB, B31, March 6, 1941 note.

[160] HADB, B30, January 6, 1941 Abs note.

[161] HADB, B31, August 4, 1941, "Placierung Norddeutsche Lederwerke A. G. Aktien."

[162] HADB, B32, March 1, 1943, Deutsche Bank to Reich Economics Ministry.

[163] HADB, V1/4919, Anlage 3, "Teilbericht der Deutschen Revisions- und Treuhandgesellschaft."

[164] HADB, V1/1365, September 30, 1948, Ulrich to Baerns, December 6, 1948 statement.

[165] Friedrich Wilhelm Erich Bechtolf was born in Elberfeld on April 8, 1891. Having finished his studies (law), he joined Deutsche Bank's Elberfeld branch as syndic in 1922. In 1925, he became director of the bank's Hamm branch until 1928, when he went as a departmental head to the Berlin head office. From 1932 until 1941, he worked as director of the Hamburg branch, changing back to Berlin at the end of 1941, where he soon became a member of the managing board. He stayed in that position until the end of the war, when the Allies insisted on his retirement. Deutsche Bank ceased to exist for the time being and was split up into smaller units. Only at the end of 1947 did Bechtolf rejoin the bank in a leading position in Hamburg. From 1952 until 1957, he was a member on the board of directors of Norddeutsche Bank – one of the three major banks that in 1957 merged to become Deutsche Bank again. For almost two years, he held the position of a managing director; from April 1959 until April 1960, he was vice-chairman; until June 1967, he was chairman of the supervisory board. Bechtolf died in Hamburg on October 30, 1969. See Manfred Pohl, Wilhelm Treue (eds.), *Deutsche Bank: Ein Teil deutscher Wirtschaftsgeschichte, Berichte und Biographien* (manuscript).

[166] HADB, V1/1365, November 3, 1948 Bechtolf to Ulrich.

[167] Settlement (*Vergleich*) between N.V. Amsterdamsche Leder Maatschappij in Amsterdam and the Norddeutsche Lederwerke AG in Hamburg of December 5–10, 1951 and settlement between the Relda Trading Co. Inc. and the Norddeutsche Lederwerke AG in Hamburg of 10, December 1951. The settlement was confirmed at the Wiedergutmachungsamt at the Landgericht Kiel-Neumünster on December 11, 1951.

[168] In spite of problems due to raw materials supply and prices and later on to the general job situation, Norddeutsche Leder AG prospered in the years following 1951. In 1961, it moved from Hamburg to Neumünster. When the situation on the leather market seriously deteriorated, the general meeting decided on May 6, 1966, that the firm should be liquidated after May 15, 1966. See *Handbuch der deutschen Aktiengesellschaften* (Darmstadt, Vienna, Zurich: Hoppenstedt, 1967/1968), 1949.

[169] See Stefan Mehl, *Das Reichsfinanzministerium und die Verfolgung der Deutschen Juden 1933–1943 (Berliner Arbeitshefte zur Sozialwissenschaftlichen Forschung 38)* (Berlin: Zentralinstitut für Sozialwissenschaftliche Forschung, 1990), 63. See also Lothar Gall, "A Man for All Seasons: Hermann Josef Abs im Dritten Reich", in: *Zeitschrift für Unternehmensgeschichte* 44, Munich: Beck, 1998, pp. 123–175.

[170] HADB, V1/4724 November 20, 1937 Steinbrinck note, cited as "Beleg 10124" in "Gutachten von Rechtsanwälten Reinhard und Hans Freiherren von Godin." L. M. Stahlbaumer, "Big Business and the Persecution of the Jews: The Flick Concern and

the 'Aryanization' of Jewish Property Before the War." *Holocaust and Genocide Studies* 13(1): 1–27 (1999).
171 BAB, R7, 1010 and 1011 for negotiations. The critical meeting was on June 28, 1939, in the Reich Economics Ministry: BAB, R7, 1011, fol. 323–28.
172 HADB, Abs note cards, Ernst Petschek.
173 Rheinbraun Archiv, 210/328, October 18, 1948 note. 374/328, October 19, 1938, Oberfinanzpräsident Hanover: "Sicherungsanordnung nach Art. 37a des Devisengesetzes."
174 RGBl. 1938 I, 1709.
175 Stahlbaumer, "Big Business" 13.
176 BAB, R8119 F, P964, Abs note ("In Register eingegang. February 21, 1939").
177 BAB, R8119 F, P964, fol. 101–04, March 11, 1939, Hubertus Braunkohle AG to Reich Economics Ministry. The valuation is set out in fol. 108–17, March 30, 1939, Dr. Josef Abs to H. J. Abs. HADB, V1/4976, Bericht über den Verkauf des Gewerbebetriebes der Hubertus-Braunkohlen A. G. and February 28, 1949 Vollmacht. See also Lothar Gall, "A Man for All Seasons.
178 See Gall, "A Man for All Seasons," 147.
179 HADB, V1/4976, November 30, 1946, Ernst Petschek to Kersting.
180 HADB, V1/4976, November 17, 1947, Abs to Ernst Petschek.
181 HADB, V1/4768, December 23, 1970, Salzgitter to Rechtsanwalt Barz; January 6, 1971, Abs to Charles Petschek.
182 HADB, V1/4948, William Petschek affidavit of April 24, 1972.
183 Felix Schwarz, "Literarisches Zeitgespräch im Dritten Reich" *Archiv für Geschichte des Buchwesens* 12: 1329–38 (1972).
184 Gottfried Bermann Fischer, *Bedroht bewahrt: Der Weg eines Verlegers* (Frankfurt: Fischer, 1986), 93–100.
185 BAB, R8119 F, P6088, May 2, 1944 and June 1, 1944 notes.
186 HADB, V1/4096, Suhrkamp statement of September 16, 1947.
187 Felix Lützkendorf, *Völkerwanderung 1940. Ein Bericht aus dem Osten* (Berlin: S. Fischer, 1940). Citations from pp. 42, 48, 57, 47.
188 Felix Lützkendorf, *Söhne des Krieges* (Berlin: Verlag Die Heimbücherei, 1940), 213.
189 Manfred Overesch, *Das III. Reich 1933–1945: Eine Tageschronik der Politik, Wirtschaft, Kultur* (Düsseldorf: Droste, 1983), 290.
190 Friedrich Lützkendorf, *Friedrich II* (Berlin: Suhrkamp, 1944), citations from pp. 132, 208, 215.
191 Ernst Penzoldt, *Korporal Mombour: Eine Soldatenromanze* (Berlin: S. Fischer, 1941); Ursula Lange, *Abschied von einem Soldaten, Sonette* (Berlin: Suhrkamp, 1942); Alexander Lernet-Holenia, *Ein Traum in Rot: Roman* (Berlin: S. Fischer, 1939). See Knut Beck (ed.), *100 Jahre S. Fischer Verlag 1886–1986: Eine Bibliographie* (Frankfurt: Fischer, 1986).
192 BAB, R8119 F, P6088, January 24, 1945, Kasack to Gauwirtschaftskammer Berlin.
193 BAB, R8119 F, P6088, October 11, 1944, "Bericht zum Jahresabschluss."
194 HADB, F28/224, November 18, 1945 note concerning "aryanizations."
195 HADB, F2/619, lists.
196 BAB, R8119 F, P24001, July 13, 1933, Pfeiffer (Kassel) to Zentrale.
197 HADB, F88/526, January 18, 1938, Deutsche Bank Hanover to Holthusen & Co.
198 HADB, F88/335.
199 HADB, F56/6, April 20, 1937, Deutsche Bank branch Aachen to Deutsche Bank Zentrale. May 7, 1937, Deutsche Bank Zentrale to Deutsche Bank branch Aachen.
200 HADB, F3/24.
201 HADB, F33/377, February 22, 1938, Deutsche Bank branch Freiburg to Filialbüro Berlin.

202 HADB, F33/377, March 5, 1938 note.

203 HADB, F33/377, March 30, 1938, Deutsche Bank Zentrale to Deutsche Bank branch Freiburg.

204 HADB, F33/377, April 4, 1938, Deutsche Bank branch Freiburg to Deutsche Bank Zentrale.

205 HADB, F33/377, April 4, 1938, Deutsche Bank Zentrale to Deutsche Bank branch Freiburg.

206 HADB, M-Blätter II–IV 1938, 97/38, No. 1129.

207 HADB, F33/377, April 30, 1938, Deutsche Bank branch Munich to Deutsche Bank branch Freiburg.

208 HADB, F33/377, May 6, 1938, Deutsche Bank branch Munich to Deutsche Bank branch Freiburg.

209 HADB, F33/377, June 17, 1938 note.

210 HADB, F33/377, August 9, 1938, Central-Kaufhaus to Deutsche Bank branch Freiburg.

211 Hayes, "Big Business," 267.

212 HADB, F33/377, July 6, 1943 "Kreditanmeldung"; HADB, F33/142, June 23, 1943 note.

213 HADB, F100/266, November 24, 1936 note.

214 HADB, F100/509, September 21, 1938 note; F100/297.

215 HADB, F88/390, January 31, 1938, Deutsche Bank Hanover to Zentrale; also September 13, 1938.

216 HADB, F88/643, June 29, 1938, Deutsche Bank Hanover to Graf von der Schulenburg-Wolfsburg.

217 HADB, F33/370, March 21, 1939, Deutsche Bank branch Freiburg to Friedrich Kreuzer.

218 HADB, F33/218, February 3, 1938 note.

219 HADB, F33/215, March 30, 1950, Walter Schindler, attorney, to Landgericht Restitutionskammer, Freiburg. See also copies of the letters of 1937 and 1938 documenting the political pressure on Hupag in Landgericht Freiburg, Or 98/49.

220 Landgericht Freiburg, dossier Or 98/49.

221 HADB, F33/216, November 9, 1951, Dr. K. Butsch, Oberrheinische Bank branch Freiburg to Eckert.

222 See *Badische Zeitung* 204:December 8 (1953) *Basler Nachrichten* 524:December 11 (1953).

223 *Badische Zeitung* 204:December 8 (1953).

224 HADB, F23/17, file.

225 Generallandesarchiv (GLA) Karlsruhe, 505/1683, July 21, 1938, Wirtschaftskammer Bade – Unterabteilung Einzelhandel to Badisches Finanz- und Wirtschaftsministerium.

226 HADB, F13/112, February 2, 1938, Filialbüro to Deutsche Bank branch Lahr.

227 HADB, F13/112, February 9, 1938 note.

228 HADB, F13/112, February 14, 1938 note.

229 HADB, F13/112, April 8, 1938, Deutsche Bank branch Freiburg to Deutsche Bank branch Lahr.

230 HADB, F13/112, October 2, 1942 note.

231 HADB, F132/0104, December 14, 1938 Deutsche Bank branch Tübingen to Deutsche Bank Zentrale.

232 HADB, F2/235, November 26, 1937 note.

233 HADB, F50/1001, May 19, 1938, "Streng vertraulich: An die Direktionen unserer Zweigniederlassungen: Aktien unserer Bank."

234 BAB, R8119 F, P10563, fol. 385, Deutsche Bank branch Bamberg to Zentrale Rechtsabteilung, BAB, R8119 F, P10562, fol. 408–09, Deutsche Bank branch Frankfurt/Main to Deutsche Bank Zentrale Rechtsabteilung.
235 HADB F88/650, November 18, 1938, Deutsche Bank branch Hanover to Deutsche Bank branch Celle.
236 BAB, R8119 F, P24151, November 10, 1938, Deutsche Bank branch Frankfurt/Main to Personalabteilung.
237 Deutsche Bank FSAG, "Bilanz auf 31. Dez. 1937. Sonderbericht zur Bilanz."
238 StA, Deutsche Bank 164, February 1, 1939, Deutsche Bank branch Leipzig to Zentrale "betr. Jahresabschluss 1938."
239 HADB B310, December 7, 1938, "Betr.: Nichtarier-Engagements per November 1938."
240 HADB, B214, July 25, 1938 note.
241 StAL, Deutsche Bank 623, January 27, 1938, Deutsche Bank branch Leipzig to Deutsche Bank Zentrale Berlin.
242 StAL, Deutsche Bank 207, July 10, 1935 note.
243 StAL, Deutsche Bank 205–12, 257–62, 300–07, 379–80. Wilhelm Harmelin, "Juden in der Leipziger Rauchwarenwirtschaft." Tradition 11: 249–82 (1966).
244 StAL, Deutsche Bank 547, February 14, 1935, Deutsche Bank branch Leipzig credit report.
245 StAL, Deutsche Bank 596, November 23, 1938 note.
246 StAL, Deutsche Bank 423, November 26, 1940 request (Deutsche Rauchwaren-Gesellschaft), October 3, 1940 memorandum.
247 HADB, F88/580, March 30, 1938, Deutsche Bank branch Hildesheim to Deutsche Bank branch Hanover.
248 HADB, F167/95.

CHAPTER 6 DEUTSCHE BANK ABROAD: "ARYANIZATION," TERRITORIAL EXPANSION, AND ECONOMIC REOREDERING

1 See for instance Hans Witek, "'Arisierungen' in Wien: Aspekte nationalsozialialistischer Enteignungspolitik 1938–1940," in Emmerich Talos, Ernst Hanisch, Wolfgang Neugebauer (eds.), NS-Herrschaft in Österreich (Vienna: Verlag für Gesellschaftskritik, 1988), 199–216; Hans Safrian, Die Eichmann-Männer (Vienna and Zurich: Europa Verlag, 1993).
2 Alan S. Milward, "The Reichsmark Bloc and the International Economy," in Gerhard Hirschfeld, Lothar Kettenacker (eds.), The "Führer State": Myth and Reality: Studies on the Structure and Politics of the Third Reich (Stuttgart: Klett-Cotta, 1981), 387.
3 Special Archive (Captured German Documents), Moscow (hereafter SAM), 1458-2-77, March 24, 1938 note.
4 On the Creditanstalt, see Dieter Stiefel, Finanzdiplomatie und Weltwirtschaftskrise: Die Krise der Credit-Anstalt für Handel und Gewerbe 1931 (Frankfurt: Fritz Knapp, 1989); Herbert Matis and Fritz Weber, "Economic Anschluss and German Grossmachtpolitik: The Take-Over of the Austrian Credit-Anstalt in 1938," in: P. L. Cottrell, Hakan Lindgren, and Alice Teichova (eds.), European Industry and Banking Between the Wars: A Review of Bank–Industry Relations (Leicester: Leicester University Press, 1992), 109–26.
5 SAM, 1458-2-305, fol. 9 (n.d., probably end of March or beginning of April 1938.

6   See Austrian State Archive, Vienna (hereafter ÖstA), 4/2-92/2165/2/8, September 15, 1938, "Rechnungshof: Strafverfahren und Haftungsansprüche gegen ehemalige Vorstandsmitglieder der Credit-Anstalt."

7   Bundesarchiv Berlin (hereafter BAB), Reichsbank, 6673, February 26, 1938, "Auf welche Weise liesse sich eine deutsch-österreichische Währungsunion durchführen?"

8   SAM, 1458-2-77, April 5, 1938 minutes of meeting of April 4, 1938.

9   Historisches Archiv der Deutschen Bank, Frankfurt (hereafter HADB), B203, March 14, 1938 Mosler note.

10 HADB, B51, March 31, 1938 note.

11 HADB, B51, April 13, 1938 Abs note.

12 HADB, B51, March 31, 1938 note.

13 BAB, R8119 F, P6507, Deutsche Bank branch Cologne.

14 HADB, B51, April 15, 1938 note on negotiation; May 7, 1938 Mosler note. ÖstA, 4/2-92/2165/0 vol. I, May 16, 1938 note.

15 See Manfred Pohl, Andrea Schneider, *VIAG 1923–1998: Vom Staatskonzern zum internationalen Konzern* (Munich: Piper, 1998), 134ff.

16 ÖstA, 4/2-92/2165/2/8, June 17, 1938, Creditanstalt to Fischböck; June 20, 1938, Deutsche Bank to Creditanstalt.

17 HADB, B51, April 14, 1938 Pollems note.

18 HADB, B51, May 21, 1938 minutes of meeting of May 20, 1938.

19 ÖstA, 4/2-92/2165/0 vol. I, May 31, 1938 Deutsche Bank memorandum.

20 HADB, B51, September 16, 1938, Deutsche Bank to Ernst.

21 SAM, 1458-2-61, September 13, 1938 note.

22 SAM, 1458-2-84, August 31, 1938 note (IV Kred. 4).

23 HADB, B51, note on meeting of September 30, 1938.

24 HADB, B51, November 7, 1938 Abs note.

25 HADB, B51, November 22, 1938 short message to Abs. ÖstA, 4/2-92/2165/0 vol. I, September 21, 1938, Reichskommissar Bürckel to Ernst.

26 HADB, B51, November 1, 1938 note.

27 ÖstA, 4/2-92/2165/0 vol. I, February 10, 1939, Bürckel to Reichskommissar Ernst; September 21, 1939, Bürckel to Ernst.

28 Staatsarchiv Leipzig (StAL), Deutsche Bank 623, May 4, 1938, Heinz Osterwind (Vienna) to Deutsche Bank Berlin.

29 ÖstA, 4/2-89/2160/00 vol. I, "Behutsame Arisierung" (n.d.).

30 SAM, 1458-2-83, November 23, 1938, "Betr.: Arisierung österreichischer Privatbankiers."

31 Figures from Dr. Schmidt, "Das Geld- und Kreditwesen der Ostmark und seine Eingliederung ins Gross-Deutsche Reich," at the meeting of the Wirtschaftsgruppe Österreichische Kreditinstitute, May 31–June 2, 1939, 57. ÖstA, 4/4-92/2165/0 vol. III.

32 SAM, 1458-2-61, September 13, 1938 note.

33 SAM, 1458-2-84, July 4, 1938, Reich Economics Ministry to Reichskommissar; 1458-2-305, August 30, 1938 note.

34 The Bunzl & Biach AG was founded on October 17, 1936. Its capital stock amounted to 20,000,000 shillings but was changed after the Anschluss at the end of 1939 to RM 14,000,000. At the same time, its name was changed to Kontropa Kontinentale Rohstoff- und Papierindustrie AG. The shares held by the Swiss holding company Bunzl Konzern Holding AG, Zug were transferred to the Österreichische Kontrollbank für Industrie und Handel AG, Wien, and in the course of a reprivatization of the company (carried out in 1942), they were taken over by a consortium of Austrian banks. The Creditanstalt received 3,830 of the 10,640

shares with a nominal value of RM 3,830,000. The shares were restored to the Bunzl Konzern Holding AG in 1947. See ÖstA, Akt Bunzl-Biach AG, information by Dr. Theodor Venus, Vienna. Bunzl & Biach was "aryanized" in 1939 by the Keppler-Büro; the Lenzinger Zellstoff und Papierfabrik AG was taken out of the Bunzl & Biach concern and sold to the Thüringische Zellwolle AG. See Hans Witek, "'Arisierungen' in Wien: Aspekte nationalsozialialisticher Enteigungspolitik 1938–1940," in Emmerich, Talos, Ernst Hanisch, Wolfgang Neugebauer (eds.), *NS-Herrschaft in Österreich* (Vienna; Verlag für Gesellschaftskritik, 1988), 209.

35 SAM, 1458-2-91, May 24, 1939, Creditanstalt to Reich Economics Ministry (Riehle).

36 SAM, 1458-2-153, 1938 report of the Deutsche Revisions- und Treuhandgesellschaft, Brüder Eisert.

37 ÖstA, Vermögensverkehrsstelle, 793K, 229V, 2695.

38 HADB, B52, January 11, 1939, Deutsche Bank to Creditanstalt.

39 BAB, R8119 F, P6510, October 22, 1940 minutes of the *Arbeitsausschuss.*

40 HADB, B53, March 3, 1942 note (Viag). B56, March 2, 1942 Hermann Abs note.

41 SAM, 1458-10-81, April 11, 1940, Riehle (Reich Economics Ministry) to Auswärtiges Amt: "These transfers, performed without the assistance, indeed without the knowledge of the Reich Economics Ministry, were reported to me over the telephone only when completed."

42 HADB, B55, May 4, 1942, Deutsche Bank to Viag.

43 BAB, R8119 F, P6510, August 12, 1941 minutes of the Arbeitsausschuss.

44 For example, SAM, 1458-9-158, November 9, 1940 note.

45 The name was changed in October 1938 to Czecho-Slovakia.

46 See Alice Teichova, *An Economic Background to Munich: International Business and Czechoslovakia 1918–1938* (Cambridge, MA: Cambridge University Press, 1974); Alice Teichova, "Instruments of Economic Control and Exploitation: The German Occupation of Bohemia and Moravia," in Richard J. Overy, Gerhard Otto, Johannes Houwink ten Cate (eds.), *Die "Neuordnung" Europas: NS-Wirtschaftspolitik in den besetzten Gebieten* (Berlin: Metropol, 1997), 83–108.

47 František Vencovský, Zdeněk Jindra, Jiří Novotný, Karel Půlpan, and Petr Dvořák (eds.), *Dějiny Bankovnictví v Českých Zemích* (Prague: Bankovní Institut, 1999), 242–45.

48 BAB, R8119 F, P24419, March 7, 1939, Stauss to Regierungspräsident Fritz Krebs.

49 Deutsche Bank, *Böhmen und Mähren im deutschen Wirtschaftsraum,* n.d. (1938?).

50 Christopher Kopper, "Die 'Arisierung' der deutsch-böhmischen Aktienbanken," in Boris Barth, Josef Faltus, Jan Kren, Eduard Kubu (eds.), *Konkurrenzpartnerschaft: Die deutsche und die tschechoslowakische Wirtschaft in der Zwischenkriegszeit* (Essen: Klartext Verlag, 1998), 236–45, 237.

51 Klaus Hildebrand, *Das vergangene Reich: Deutsche Aussenpolitik von Bismarck bis Hitler* (Stuttgart: Deutsche Verlags-Anstalt, 1995), 606.

52 Miroslav Karny, Jaroslava Milotova, Margita Karna (eds.), *Deutsche Politik im "Protektorat Böhmen und Mähren" unter Reinhard Heydrich 1941–1942: Eine Dokumentation* (Berlin: Metropol, 1997), 45.

53 SAM, 1458-10-64, August 25, 1941, Reichsprotektor to Reichswirtschaftsministerium.

54 OMGUS/Financial Administration 2/47/2, October 8, 1938 Abs note; also Exhibit 195, October 10, 1945 Abs statement; see also Christopher Kopper, *Zwischen Marktwirtschaft und Dirigismus; Staat, Banken und Bankenpolitik im "Dritten Reich" von 1933 bis 1939* (Bonn: Bouvier, 1995), 345–48.

55 SAM, 1548-10-228.

56 ÖstA, 4/2-92/2165/0 vol. I, November 24, 1938 note.

[57] See Harald Wixforth, *Die Neuordnung des Bankwesens im Sudetenland.* The paper was presented at the January 14, 2000 meeting of the GUG-Arbeitskreis "Unternehmen im Nationalsozialismus."

[58] HADB, B163, October 8 1938 Abs note.

[59] HADB, B163, October 8, 1939 Abs note on telephone conversation with Herr Koenigs.

[60] HADB, B163, October 13, 1938 Abs note cards.

[61] HADB, Hermann Abs note cards, Victor Ulbrich, October 15, 1938 conversation.

[62] HADB, B138, October 14, 1938 letter Dr. Ernst.

[63] HADB, B163, October 18, 1938, Deutsche Bank to Reichskommissar für das Kreditwesen.

[64] HADB, B138, September 19, 1938 note.

[65] HADB, B138, September 21, 1938 Rösler report.

[66] HADB, B141, January 10, 1939 Walter Pohle note.

[67] Swiss Bundesarchiv, BA E7160-07 1968/54, Band 1110, April 29, 1939, Revisionsbericht Agraria Vermögensverwaltungs-Aktiengesellschaft. This reference was kindly provided by Petra Barthelmess of the Swiss Independent Experts Commission.

[68] HADB, B138.

[69] HADB, B140, "Gedächtnisprotokoll" of June 14, 1939.

[70] HADB, B138, November 28, 1938, Deutsche Bank to Reich Economics Ministry.

[71] HADB, B143, March 30, 1939, Deutsche Bank to Direktion unserer Filialen.

[72] HADB, B143, April 1, 1939 note.

[73] HADB, B168, November 6, 1938, Deutsche Bank to Reich Economics Ministry.

[74] HADB, B143, March 30, 1939, Deutsche Bank to Direktion unserer Filialen.

[75] Reichsgesetzblatt, 1938 I, 1709.

[76] HADB, B143, May 13, 1939 Schmidt note.

[77] HADB, B143, June 2, 1939 Deutsche Bank circular.

[78] HADB, B168, November 6, 1939, Deutsche Bank to Reich Economics Ministry.

[79] HADB, B143, August 5, 1940 note.

[80] SAM, 1458-10-228, December 1, 1938 note on meeting of November 23, 1938.

[81] HADB, B173, Annex to Deutsche Bank letter to Reich Economics Ministry (Riehle), November 12, 1938.

[82] Elizabeth Wiskemann, *Czechs and Germans: A Study of the Struggle in the Historic Provinces of Bohemia and Moravia* (London: Oxford University Press and Royal Institute of International Affairs, 1938), 166–67.

[83] HADB, B163, October 27, 1938 Mosler note.

[84] Czech National Archives, Ministry of Finance 944/1939, box. 1956, December 14, 1938 memorandum of "Důvěrnický sbor 'Sdružení.'"

[85] HADB, B161, January 4, 1939 Übernahmevertrag; HADB, B165, March 7, 1939, Oberfinanzpräsident Berlin.

[86] Decree of December 2, 1939, Sudetendeutsches Verordnungsblatt, 263; see HADB, B173, September 26, 1939, Deutsche Bank branch Reichenberg to Deutsche Bank Zentrale.

[87] HADB, B173, October 17, 1939, Deutsche Bank to Reich Finance Ministry.

[88] HADB, B173, minutes of the negotiation between Deutsche Bank Karlsbad and Oberfinanzpräsident Karlsbad of December 5, 1939.

[89] HADB, B173, March 14, 1940 note.

[90] Hans-Erich Volkmann, "Die NS-Wirtschaft in Vorbereitung des Krieges," in Militärgeschichtliches Forschungsamt Freiburg (ed.), *Das Deutsche Reich und der Zweite Weltkrieg,* Vol. 1 (Stuttgart: Deutsche Verlags-Anstalt, 1979), 177–368, 331.

[91] SAM, 1458-10-228, November 28, 1938 note on November 22, 1938 meeting.

[92] HADB, B153, March 14, 1939, Deutsche Bank and Dresdner Bank to Reich Economics Ministry.

[93] HADB, B153, March 16, 1939, Deutsche Bank to Reich Economics Ministry.

[94] HADB, B153, March 23, 1939 Mosler note.

[95] Bundesarchiv Koblenz (hereafter BAK), NID-10-996.

[96] Finance Ministry of the Czech Republic, Prague (hereafter CFM), 67/1830, March 16, 1939, April 12, 1939 minutes of the Aufsichtsrat.

[97] CFM, 67/1830, June 27, 1939, September 29, 1939, minutes of the Aufsichtsrat; January 26, 1940 minutes of the Engerer Ausschuss.

[98] HADB, B167, May 19, 1939, Deutsche Bank to BUB (Pohle).

[99] HADB, B167, April 27, 1939, Deutsche Bank Zentrale to BUB (Pohle).

[100] HADB, B167, May 15, 1939, Deutsche Bank to Reich Economics Ministry.

[101] SAM, 1458-10-84, March 23, 1939, Pohle to Reich Economics Ministry and attachment.

[102] CFM, 67/1831, July 13, 1939 minutes of the Arbeitsausschuss.

[103] HADB, B167, "Stand der BUB Aktien per 28.3.39."

[104] HADB, B163, October 13, 1938 Abs note; HADB, B162, August 12, 1939 BUB to Reich Economics Ministry.

[105] HADB, B167, annex to Pohle letter to Deutsche Bank, May 22, 1939.

[106] HADB, B167, correspondence with British Overseas Bank and Société Générale, August and September 1939.

[107] HADB, B169, December 13, 1939, BUB to Deutsche Bank; HADB, B176, February 13, 1940 Abs note.

[108] HADB, B161, "Gedächtnisprotokoll" of December 12, 1939.

[109] HADB, B169, December 12, 1939 Pohle speech.

[110] HADB, B169, December 12, 1939 Pohle speech.

[111] SAM, 1458-10-234, February 10, 1939 Reich Economics Ministry note.

[112] CFM, Finance Ministry, CUB (reference files), November 28, 1950, Dr. F. Kavan, affidavit.

[113] BAB, R2, 13533, fol. 136, November 14, 1939, Deutsche Bank to Reich Economics Ministry.

[114] HADB, B162, August 7, 1939, Deutsche Bank to Emil Kreibich.

[115] CFM, 67/1831, July 13, 1939 minutes of the Arbeitsausschuss.

[116] CFM, 67/1831, April 30, 1942, October 21, 1942 minutes of the Exekutiv Komitee.

[117] CFM, 67/1831, November 27, 1940 minutes of the Engerer Ausschuss.

[118] HADB, B165.

[119] *OMGUS Ermittlungen*, 415 (OMGUS Annex to the Report on the Investigation of Deutsche Bank, March 1947, 29), Exhibit 372; HADB, B162, May 10, 1940 note.

[120] OMGUS Exhibit 194; Exhibit 195, October 10, 1945 statement of Hermann J. Abs.

[121] HADB, B162, April 18, 1940, Reich Economics Ministry to Deutsche Bank.

[122] CFM, 54/751, January 22, 1940, Deutsche Bank (Rösler/Halt) to Pohle.

[123] HADB, B189.

[124] Josef Krebs, Walter Pohle, Dr. Max Ludwig Rohde, Dr. Max Selige (until 1939), Viktor Ulbrich.

[125] HADB, B143, June 2, 1939, Deutsche Bank to Reich Economics Ministry, requesting the use of the £80,000 transaction not required for the DAIB transaction to be transferred for the purpose of acquiring BUB.

[126] BAB, R2, 13532, March 30, 1939 memorandum, 20.

[127] BAB, R2, 13533, fol. 119–20, November 13, 1939, Deutsche Bank to Reich Economics Ministry.

[128] BAB, R8119 F, P5351, fol. 147–48, June 28, 1939 Kimmich memorandum.

[129] HADB, B175, January 24, 1941 note on conversation.

[130] HADB, B175, January 24, 1941 note on conversation.

[131] HADB, B175, February 5, 1942 letter of Reich Finance Ministry.

[132] HADB, B166, April 19, 1941 Devisenprüfungsbericht.

[133] BAB, R2, 14087; BAB, R2, 13533, fol. 141, November 14, 1939, Deutsche Bank to Reich Economics Ministry; BAB, R2, 13535 fol. 300-03, January 1942 Reich Finance Ministry memorandum; BAB, R2, 13536, fol. 124–25, May 3, 1940, Deutsche Bank to Reich Finance Ministry.

[134] *Die Wirtschaft*, April 21, 1945.

[135] CFM, 67/1830, February 11, 1943 minutes of the Aufsichtsrat.

[136] BAB, R2, 13536, fol. 136–37, May 15, 1940, Reich Economics Ministry (Generalreferat Kehrl) to Reich Finance Ministry. BAB, R2, 13532, fol. 43–44, April 28, 1939 Reich Finance Ministry memorandum.

[137] In 1940 Dr. Ing. Emil Hammerschmid, living in Düsseldorf, was chairman of the supervisory board of "Gerhardt & Rahm, Schraubenfabrik und Blankeisenzieherei AG" in Rosenthal/Sudetenland. Two relatives of Emil Hammerschmid – Fritz and Gustel Hammerschmid – were members of the managing board and the supervisory board.

[138] Hans Kreibich was a German industrialist in the Sudetenland, born March 24, 1900, in Walkowitz, Kreis Saaz. He was probably a brother (or other relative?) of Emil Kreibich, who was born in the same place on March 22, 1899.

[139] Details in SAM, 1458-10-390.

[140] SAM, 1458-10-396, May 9, 1941, Reichsstatthalter im Sudetengau to Reich Economics Ministry.

[141] BAB, R8119 F, P6694, October 15, 1941, Krebs to Otten.

[142] BAB, R8119 F, P6694, October 2, 1941 note.

[143] BAB, R8119 F, P6643, December 19, 1942 note.

[144] BAB, R8119 F, P6694, December 1, 1941 note.

[145] BAB, R8119 F, P6643, November 26, 1942, BUB to Creditanstalt.

[146] Wilfried Konzett, Rechtsanwalt Bludenz, August 25, 1938, Krebs to Lauterbach (files from an attorney that Mr. Otten [his client] sent to the author).

[147] BAB, R8119 F, P6644, December 13, 1938, M. B. Neumann to Krebs (BUB).

[148] Wirtschaftskammer Vorarlberg (WKV), Otten I, August 30, 1941, Betriebsbericht, Wirtschaftskammer Alpenland.

[149] BAB, R 8119 F, P6644, October 30, 1941, Lauterbach to Deutsche Bank (Christian).

[150] WKV, Otten I, April 21, 1947, Bundesminister für Vermögenssicherung und Wirtschaftsplanung to Bundesminister für Justiz.

[151] CFM, 67/1830, March 5, 1940 minutes of the Engerer Ausschuss.

[152] CFM, 67/1830, March 5, 1940 minutes of the Engerer Ausschuss.

[153] CFM, 67/1830 March 11, 1941 minutes of the Engerer Ausschuss.

[154] HADB, B181.

[155] HADB, F50/999, Sonderrundschreiben of July 11, 1939 and October 14, 1939.

[156] HADB, B168, August 8, 1939 note.

[157] See HADB, F50/999.

[158] HADB, F33/395, June 6, 1939, BUB to Deutsche Bank Mannheim.

[159] BAB, R8119 F, P6854, fol. 58–59; fol. 131.

[160] HADB, B185, January 10, 1940, Mannesmannröhren-Werke to Deutsche Bank.

[161] SAM, 1458-10-396, January 20, 1940, Deutsche Bank to Reich Economics Ministry. Peter Hayes claimed that this was a "lucrative" transaction (Peter Hayes, "The Deutsche Bank and the Holocaust," in (ed.) Hayes, *Lessons and Legacies III. Memory, Memorialization, and Denial* (Evanston, IL.: Northwestern University Press, p. 88), in

that the Deutsche Bank sold claims of over RM 600,000 against the Bohemia Ceramics Works for RM 750,000. In fact, the Deutsche Bank and the Prague bank Petschek in liquidation each owned over RM 600,000 in claims, and each was paid RM 325,000 by the SS, with the result that each took a loss. See also Gabriele Huber, *Die Porzellan-Manufaktur Allach-München GmbH* (Marburg: Jonas, 1992), 35–36.

162 SAM, 1458-10-396, March 28, 1940, Reich Economics Ministry note.

163 Walter Naasner, *SS-Wirtschaft und SS-Verwaltung: "Das SS-Wirtschafts-Verwaltungshauptamt und die unter seiner Dienstaufsicht stehenden wirtschaftlichen Vertretungen,"* Schriften des Bundesarchivs 45 a (Düsseldorf: Droste, 1998), 143–46.

164 BAB, R2, 13536 fol. 96–7, April 18, 1940, Reich Economics Ministry to Devisenstelle Berlin; BAB, R2, 14894, fol. 6, August 25, 1939, Pohle to Benz; fol. 8–9, August 31, 1939 Benz memorandum. See also Gabriele Huber, *Die Porzellan-Manufaktur Allach-München GmbH* (Marburg: Jonas, 1992), 35–48.

165 HADB, B167, July 4, 1939, Pohle to Deutsche Bank.

166 CFM, 69/1948, May 14, 1943, BUB to BUB Budweis.

167 CFM, 69/1948: for example, Auswanderungsfonds für Böhmen und Mähren to BUB, September 23, 1942.

168 CFM, 69/1948, March 22, 1943, BUB Budweis to Zentralamt für die Regelung der Judenfrage, case of M. Neubauer Budweis.

169 Vencovský, *Dějiný Bankovnictví v Českých Zemích,* 328–29.

170 CFM, Finance Ministry, CUB (reference files), January 15, 1943, BUB to Gestapo (Dr. Arthur Czeczowiczka). Dr. Arthur C. was the owner of the three bills for CKr 5,000, which the Gestapo ordered to be transferred to Lebensborn e. V.

171 BAB, R8119 F, P11013, fol. 4, November 30, 1942 accounts. See also Hans Günther Adler, *Theresienstadt 1941–1945: Das Antlitz einer Zwangsgemeinschaft* (Tübingen: Mohr, 1960).

172 CFM, 67/1831, November 24, 1944 minutes of the Exekutiv Komitee.

173 BAB, R8119 F, P11013, fol. 136, February 28, 1945 accounts.

174 See in general Gerhard Mollin, *Montankonzerne und "Drittes Reich": Der Gegensatz zwischen Monopolwirtschaft und Befehlswirtschaft in der deutschen Rüstung und Expansion 1936–1944,* (Kritische Studien zur Geschichtswissenschaft Bd. 78) (Göttingen: Vandenhoeck & Ruprecht 1988), 187–88.

175 BAB, R8119 F, P1418, fol. 36–7, October 18, 1937 Kiehl note on conversation with Rasche and Rinn (Dresdner Bank).

176 BAB, R8119 F, P1416, fol. 11–13, July 28, 1937 Kimmich note.

177 BAB, R8119 F, P1416, fol 91–2, June 28, 1939 Kimmich note; BA R7, 2268, fol. 7–9, Reich Economics Ministry Generalreferat Kehrl.

178 CFM, 67/1831, May 30, 1940 minutes of the Engerer Ausschuss.

179 CFM, 67/1831, January 26, 1940 minutes of the Engerer Ausschuss.

180 BAB, R2, 17830, June 12, 1943 Dr. Müller memorandum.

181 Jonathan Steinberg, *All or Nothing: The Axis and the Holocaust* (London: Routledge 1990); 171.

182 BAB, R8119 F, P1416, fol. 116, June 26, 1940, Kimmich to Pohle.

183 BAB, R8119 F, P1417, fol. 84, June 23, 1939, Kiehl to BUB.

184 Willy A. Boelcke, *Die Deutsche Wirtschaft 1930–1945: Interna des Reichs-wirtschaftsministeriums* (Düsseldorf: Droste, 1983), 265. Hans Umbreit, "Auf dem Weg zur Kontinentalherrschaft," in Militärgeschichtliches Forschungsamt Freiburg (ed.), *Das Deutsche Reich und der Zweite Weltkrieg,* Vol. V/1 (Stuttgart: Deutsche Verlags-Anstalt, 1988), 3–345, 213–15.

[185] BAB, R7, 3158, fol. 4–5. 1941 Veltjens (Oberst der Luftwaffe): "Zusammengefasster Bericht über die Kapitalverflechtung mit Holland und Belgien seit der Besatzung." Also *OMGUS Ermittlungen*, 202*ff*, 221*ff*. (OMGUS Report on the Investigation of Deutsche Bank, November 1946, 184*ff*, 202*ff*.)

[186] HADB, B129, April 1, 1941 note.

[187] BAB, R8119 F, P6875 in general; see also BAB, R8119 F, P6854, fol. 349.

[188] BAB, R8119 F, P6854, October 16, 1940, Pohle to Rösler.

[189] BAB, R8119 F, P6942, November 18, 1940, Pohle to Kimmich; February 10, 1941, Pohle to Kehrl. Hayes in his essay incorrectly calculates the commission on the purchase of the Jewish sales as almost six times the actual level and, on this basis, concludes that this was "perhaps the most profitable of the BUB's services." Hayes, "Deutsche Bank," 88.

[190] CFM, 67/1831, November 27, 1940, December 16, 1941 minutes of the Engerer Ausschuss.

[191] CFM, 67/1831, February 23, 1942 minutes of the Engerer Ausschuss.

[192] CFM, 67/1831, June 11, 1941 minutes of the Engerer Ausschuss.

[193] BAB, R8119 F, P6876, fol. 321, April 20, 1944, Lippmann Rosenthal to Deutsche Bank; fol. 528, August 9, 1944, Deutsche Bank to BUB.

[194] BAB, R8119 F, P6875, July 27, 1943 note.

[195] CFM, 67/1831, March 1, 1944 minutes of the Exekutiv Komitee.

[196] BAB, R8119 F, P6931, fol. 28–30, June 11, 1942, Pohle to Bechtolf.

[197] HADB, B191, July 19, 1940, BUB to Sicherheitsdienst RF SS SD Leitabschnitt Prag.

[198] HADB, B191, May 22, 1941, "Geschäftsverteilung für den Vorstand."

[199] HADB, B191, April 25, 1941 and May 23, 1941, Rösler to Rohde.

[200] BAB, R8119 F, P6876, fol. 571–72, June 9, 1942, Pohle to Rösler.

[201] BAB, R8119 F, P6931, fol. 1–15, June 6, 1942 note.

[202] HADB, B192, June 10, 1942 note.

[203] Beate Ruhm von Oppen, *Helmuth James von Moltke: Briefe an Freya 1939–45* (Munich: Beck, 1988), 369.

[204] BAB, R8119 F, P6932, April 26, 1943 Bechtolf letter; Rolf-Dieter Müller, "Von der Wirtschaftsallianz zum kolonialen Ausbeutungskrieg," in Militärgeschichtliches Forschungsamt Freiburg (ed.), *Das Deutsche Reich und der Zweite Weltkrieg*, Vol. 4 (Stuttgart, 1983), 98–189, 140. Franz Neumann saw the supervisory board of Kontinentale Öl as "the model of a new ruling class, composed of the party, the army, the bureaucracy, and industry" and resting on "the oppression and exploitation of foreign countries and of the German people alike." Franz Neumann, *Behemoth: The Structure and Practice of National Socialism*, 2nd ed. (New York: Oxford University Press, 1944), 396.

[205] BAB, R8119 F, P7236, fol. 33, October 30, 1940, Pott to Kiehl; fol. 43–48, January 29, 1941 Kiehl note.

[206] BAB, R8119 F, P6932, May 5, 1943, Bechtolf to Pohle; BAB, R8119 F, P6931, fol. 315–16, March 3, 1942, Rohde and Pohle to Bechtolf.

[207] BAB, R8119 F, P1416, fol. 141, October 19, 1944, Deutsche Bank managing board to Dresdner Bank.

[208] BAB, R8119 F, P6854, fol. 123, fol. 204; BAB, R8119 F, P6855, fol. 188–93.

[209] BAB, R8119 F, P6855, fol. 179, July 20, 1943 Rösler note.

[210] SAM, 1458-10-234, February 13, 1939 memorandum. ÖstA, Ministerium für Wirtschaft und Arbeit (1939), No. 32577, March 21, 1939 Exekutiv-Ausschuss of the Creditanstalt.

[211] SAM, 1458-10-66, September 6, 1941 note; SAM, 1458-10-233, April 26, 1940 report of Finance Ministry Bratislava.

212 HADB, B174, August 22, 1940 letter of BUB.

213 SAM, 1458-10-66, October 29, 1940 Dr. Fritschler speech.

214 See SAM, 1458-10-66, July 4, 1941, Deutsche Gesandtschaft to Reich Economics Ministry.

215 Archive of the National Bank of Slovakia, Bratislava (hereafter NBS), UB353/1, August 20, 1941, November 3, 1941, September 28, 1943 minutes of the Verwaltungsrat and credit files NBS, U283 and U317.

216 NBS, UB353/1, August 20, 1941 minutes of the Verwaltungsrat.

217 NBS, UB353/1, November 3, 1941 minutes of the Verwaltungsrat. See in general Livia Rothkirchen, "The Situation of Jews in Slovakia between 1939 and 1945." *Jahrbuch für Antisemitismusforschung* 7: 46–70 (1998).

218 HADB, ZA40/1, January 19, 1956, Minister für Wirtschaft und Verkehr des Landes Nordrhein-Westfalen to Rheinisch-Westfälische Bank.

219 HADB, ZA40/3, November 25, 1958, Deutsche Bank Berlin to Deutsche Bank Rechtsabteilung.

220 NBS, UB1 1945 memorandum Česká Banká Union v likv.

221 The Geneva agreement of May 15, 1922, which dealt with the future constitutional and legal conditions of Upper Silesia, was signed by the German and Polish representatives on June 11, 1922. Concerning the German banks' branches in East Upper Silesia (which had become Polish territory after the referendum of 1921) – the Bank für Handel und Industrie, Deutsche Bank, and Dresdner Bank, the Geneva agreement stated that these banks were entitled for the following fifteen years to go about their business as before. The same applied to the Polish banks in the German part of Upper Silesia – the Bank Przemyslowców and the Polski Bank Handlowy. See RGBl 1922 II, 375.

222 SAM, 1458-15-167, May 3, 1937 note; April 8, 1938 note.

223 SAM, 1458-15-124, December 12, 1939, Deutsche Bank to Reichsaufsichtsamt für das Kreditwesen.

224 New archive, Warsaw (hereafter ANN), GG 1291, 17, September 8, 1939, Devisenfahndungsamt Teschen; September 23, 1939 Beauftragter des Devisenfahndungsamts, Krakau.

225 HADB, P 24222, September 19, 1939, Kiehl to Theusner; September 22, 1939, Theusner to Kiehl.

226 SAM, 1585-15-124, April 30, 1940 Report of Reichsbankstelle Litzmannstadt.

227 SAM, 1458-15-61, January 17, 1940 note of Forschungsstelle für Wehrwirtschaft.

228 SAM, 1458-15-128, June 3, 1940, Paersch to Riehle (Reich Economics Ministry).

229 SAM, 1458-15-129, May 29, 1941, "Betr. Bankeinflüsse und Behörden."

230 Harold James,"The Deutsche Bank and the Dictatorship," in Lothax Gall, Gerald D. Feldman, Harold James, Carl-Ludwig Holtfrerich, Hans E. Büschgen (eds.), *The Deutsche Bank 1870–1995* (London: Weidenfeld & Nicholson, 1995), 277–356. 301. HADB, P1/35; *Süddeutsche Zeitung*, November 2, 1964.

231 HADB, F119/119.

232 HADB, F119/207.

233 HADB, F119/279.

234 HADB, F119/917.

235 HADB, F119/167, May 7, 1941, Deutsche Bank Zentrale to Deutsche Bank branch Kattowitz. Joachim von Stülpnagel was possibly a close relative of Carl-Heinrich Stülpnagel, who took part in the conspiracy against Hitler on July 20, 1944. He was born in Glogau, Silesia, on March 5, 1880, and began his military career in 1898. After the First World War, he rose to the rank of general, working for some time at the Reich War Ministry. Apart from his military career, he worked as a publisher – he was man-

aging director of the publishing firm Die Wehrmacht – and was a member of several supervisory boards. See *Reichshandbuch der Deutschen Gesellschaft*, Vol. 2 (Berlin: Deutscher Wirtschaftsverlag, 1931), 1876–77. See also *Wer leitet?* (Berlin: Hoppenstedt, 1940), 884.

236 SAM, 1458-15-81, September 24, 1940, Deutsche Bank to Reich Economics Ministry.

237 SAM, 1458-15-125, April 26, 1940 note of Reichsaufsichtsamt für das Kreditwesen.

238 HADB, B54, August 27, 1943, Ulrich to Abs referring to the minutes of the Arbeitsausschuss of Creditanstalt-Bankverein of October 12, 1939.

239 SAM, 1458-15-125, October 21, 1940, note of Reichsaufsichtsamt für das Kreditwesen.

240 HADB, B52, November 2, 1940, Deutsche Bank to Reich Economics Ministry.

241 BAB, R8119 F, P6510, September 3, 1940, minutes of the Arbeitsausschuss of Creditanstalt-Bankverein.

242 HADB, B52, January 24, 1941, Deutsche Bank to Creditanstalt.

243 ANN, Kom. Rzadu Mienie Nieprzyjec, 20/318, June 27, 1942 to Kommissar für die Behandlung feindlichen Vermögens.

244 ANN, Kom. Rzadu Mienie Nieprzyjec, 10, fol. 27.

245 HADB, B53, April 10, 1942, Kiehl to Generalkonsul Winkelmann (Danzig).

246 ANN, Bank Handlowy 331, August 7, 1945 account of Dr. Wachowiak.

247 ANN, GG 1342, November 2, 1942 note (visit of Wachowiak, October 27, 1942).

248 ANN, GG, 1265, 141-142, *Krakauer Zeitung: Wirtschafts-Kurier* 1942, No. 240.

249 ANN, GG 1388, August 24, 1943 note of Aufsichtsstelle on visit of Glathe August 21, 1943.

250 HADB, B54, October 22, 1942 Hermann Abs note.

251 ANN, GG 1265, 141–42, *Krakauer Zeitung* 1942, No. 240.

252 ANN, GG 1401, Bankaufsichtstelle July 27, 1942.

253 I owe this information to Bertrand Perz. See *"Profil"* September 14, 1998: "Das grauenvolle Geheimnis der CA" and interview with Perz.

254 ANN, GG 1401, June 10, 1943, Bankaufsichtsstelle.

255 ANN, GG 1403, fol. 27, 1944 report of the Treueverkehr: Gründungsprüfung der Creditanstalt Aktiengesellschaft Krakau.

256 BAB, R8119 F, P6511, July 28, 1943 Arbeitsausschuss.

257 ANN, GG 1401, October 20, 1942 Bankaufsichtsstelle (visit of Tron, October 12/13, 1942.)

258 ANN, GG 1401, August 30, 1943 Bankaufsichtsstelle (visit of Tron, August 25, 1943.)

259 BAB, R8119 F, P6511, April 26 and 27, 1944 Arbeitsausschuss.

260 BAB, R8119 F, P6511, June 13, 1944 Arbeitsausschuss.

261 See Walter Naasner, *Neue Machtzentren in der deutschen Kriegswirtschaft 1942–1945* (Boppard: Boldt, 1994), 412–13.

262 ANN, GG 1388, July 31, 1944, Bankdirigent der Emissionsbank to Staatssekretär Generalgouvernement.

CHAPTER 7   JEWISH-OWNED BANK ACCOUNTS

1 Bundesarchiv/Zentrale [Zwischenlager Hoppegarten] (Box 39283, Regal 2197), November 22, 1935 Depositenkasse A to Kreditbüro Dresden; November 28, 1935, Deutsche Bank branch Dresden to Zentrale-Filialbüro. The original Rundschreiben was 72/35, November 12, 1935.

2 Commerz- und Privatbank, Enstehung und Verwendungsmöglichkeiten der verschiedenen Arten von Reichsmarkguthaben für Ausländer.

3 *Reichsgesetzblatt* 1938 I, 414.
4 Herbert Wolf, "Zur Kontrolle und Enteignung jüdischen Vermögens in der NS-Zeit." *Bankhistorisches Archiv* 16(1):56 (1990).
5 Avraham Barkai, *From Boycott to Annihilation* (Hanover: University Press of New England, 1989), 171.
6 BA/ZE [Zwischenlager Hoppegarten] (Box 39283, Regal 2197), November 14, 1938: Verfügungen nichtarischer Kunden.
7 BA/ZE [Zwischenlager Hoppegarten] (Box 39283, Regal 2197), November 15, 1938 note.
8 Historisches Archiv der Deutschen Bank, Frankfurt (hereafter HADB), B214, January 6, 1939 Wirtschaftsgrupe Privates Bankgewerbe – Centralverband des Deutschen Bank- und Bankiergewerbes to Deutsche Bank. January 13, 1939 Eduard Mosler note.
9 HADB, F28/204, February 21, 1939 Oberfinanzpräsident Karlsruhe: Genehmigungsbescheid 57903. The rest of the information in this paragraph comes from the account file in F28/204.
10 Barkai, *Boycott,* 179–80.
11 Special Archive (Captured German Documents), Moscow (hereafter SAM), 1458-1-1044, April 4, 1941, Bekanntmachung (Baden Interior Ministry).
12 *Reichsgesetzblatt* 1941 I, 303.
13 There is, however, no evidence that any bank refused to make the transfer to the Reich on the grounds that the account holder had been deported to Auschwitz.
14 Cited in Wolf, "Kontrolle," 60.
15 Bundesverband deutscher Banken, Rundschreiben 180/1941.
16 Bundesarchiv Berlin (BAB), R13 VIII/6, March 19, 1942, Deutsche Bank to Wirtschaftsgruppe Privates Bankgewerbe.
17 BAB, R13 VIII/7, April 13, 1942 note (Roer).
18 BAB, R13 VIII/6, March 11, 1942, Wirtschaftsgruppe Privates Bankgewerbe note (Roer).
19 BAB, R13 VIII/6, May 8, 1942, Deutsche Bank to Wirtschaftsgruppe Privates Bankgewerbe.
20 For example, Staatsarchiv Marburg 314–15 Oberfinanzpräsident Nr. 36, UA 2, May 6, 1942, Deutsche Bank to Oberfinanzpräsident Hamburg. This document, in which the Hamburg branch points out that one person named on the list had not been "evacuated" but had been seen in the bank, was published and erroneously been interpreted by Karl Heinz Roth as a *"Denunzieren"* and *"Beihilfe zum Judenmord"* ("denouncing" and "acting as an accessory to the murder of the Jews"). The bank was clearly stating that this particular account could not be subject to asset confiscation (*"Vermögensbeschlagnahme"*). See Karl Heinz Roth, "Hehler des Holocaust: Degussa und Deutsche Bank." *1999 Zeitschrift für Sozialgeschichte des 20. und 21. Jahrhunderts* 13(2): 137–44 (1998). In fact, the accountholder concerned emigrated to Cuba in 1942.
21 Wirtschaftsgruppe Privates Bankgewerbe, Rundschreiben 141, October 9, 1942.
22 HADB, F28/7.

CHAPTER 8   THE PROFITS OF THE DEUTSCHE BANK

1 For example, HADB, F33/218, the Hupag case (1.5%); HADB, F88/514, Firma Lindgens Söhne (3%); HADB, F38/139, Lederwerke Cromwell AG (1.5%); HADB, F88/390, Gebr. Thalheimer, Hanover (2% proposed; the transaction was not realized); HADB,

F88/529, December 8, 1941, Terraingesellschaft Gross-Berlin to Deutsche Bank Hanover refers to 3% as *"die übliche Provision"* for the sale of real estate.

2 The issue of tax law changes and corporate profitability has been excellently treated in the illuminating work of Mark Spoerer, *Von Scheingewinn zum Rüstungsboom: Die Eigenrentabilität der deutschen Industriegesellschaften 1925–1941 (Vierteljahrschrift für Sozial- und Wirtschaftsgeschichte Beiheft 123)* (Stuttgart: Steiner Verlag, 1996). The older literature includes Erich Kosiol, *Bilanzreform und Einheitsbilanz: Grundlegende Studien zu den Möglichkeiten einer Rationalisierung der periodischen Erfolgsvermittlung, Schriften des Betriebswirtschaftlichen Ausschusses Sudetenland 5* (Reichenberg, Leipzig, Vienna, 1944); Samuel Lurie, *Private Investment in a Controlled Economy: Germany 1933–1939* (New York, Columbia University Press, 1947).

3 BAB, R2/56808, Attachment to March 13, 1940 Poensgen letter, fol. 160.

4 From HADB, B308–B314 (balance sheets).

5 BAB, R8119 F, P11752 (a file of Dresdner Bank, erroneously classed by the former Zentrales Staatsarchiv Potsdam as part of Deutsche Bank's archives), Rentabilität 1937–1939.

6 Helmut Genschel, *Die Verdrängung der Juden aus der Wirtschaft im Dritten Reich* (Göttingen: Musterschmidt, 1966), 204*ff*, 256*ff*.

7 Michael Hepp, *Deutsche Bank und Dresdner Bank: Gewinne aus Raub, Enteignung und Zwangsarbeit 1933–1944* (Bremen: Stiftung für Sozialgeschichte des 20. Jahrhunderts, 1999).

8 Raoul Hilberg, *The Destruction of the European Jews* (New York: Holmes and Meier, 1985). Helen Junz, "Report on the Wealth Position of the Jewish Population in Nazi-Occupied Countries, Germany and Austria," in *Independent Committee of Eminent Persons, Report on Dormant Accounts of Victims of Nazi Persecution in Swiss Banks* (Bern: Staempfli, 1999), Appendix S, A127–A206.

CHAPTER 9   SOME CONCLUDING REFLECTIONS

1 Cited in *Der Spiegel* 51(December 20): 52 (1999).

2 Harold James, "The Deutsche Bank and the Dictatorship," in Lothar Gall, Gerald D. Feldman, Harold James Carl-Ludwig Holtfrerich, Hans E. Büschgen (eds.), *The Deutsche Bank 1870–1995* (London: Weidenfeld & Nicholson, 1995), 337.

3 Neil Gregor, *Daimler-Benz in the Third Reich* (New Haven, CT: Yale University Press, 1998).

4 See Hans Mommsen, "Hitler's Position in the Nazi System," in Hans Mommsen, *From Weimar to Auschwitz* (Princeton, NJ: Princeton University Press, 1991, 163–88.

5 Jonathan Steinberg, *The Deutsche Bank and Its Gold Transactions during the Second World War* (Munich: Beck, 1999), 72: "The further the gold gets from the victims the more the moral responsibility seems to dissipate and the transactions to normalise themselves."

6 George Soros, *The Crisis of Global Capitalism: Open Society Endangered* (New York: Public Affairs, 1998), 197.

Bibliography

Adler, Hans Günther, *Theresienstadt 1941–1945: Das Antlitz einer Zwangsgemeinschaft*. Tübingen: Mohr, 1960.

Bähr, Johannes, *Der Goldhandel der Dresdner Bank im Zweiten Weltkrieg*. Leipzig: Kiepenheuer und Witsch, 1999.

Bajohr, Frank, *"Arisierung"* in *Hamburg: Die Verdrängung der jüdischen Unternehmer (Hamburger Beiträge zur Sozial- und Zeitgeschichte)*. Hamburg: Christians, 1997,

Balogh, Thomas, *Studies in Financial Organization*. Cambridge, UK: University Press, 1947.

Barkai, Avraham, *From Boycott to Annihilation*. Hanover: University Press of New England, 1989.

Barkai, Avraham, "Die deutschen Unternehmer und die Judenpolitik im Dritten Reich," in *Geschichte und Gesellschaft 15*. Göttingen: Vandenhoeck und Rupprecht, 1989, 227–47.

Barth, Boris, *Die deutsche Hochfinanz und die Imperialismen: Banken und Aussenpolitik vor 1914*. Stuttgart: Steiner, 1995.

Beck, Knut (ed.), *100 Jahre S. Fischer Verlag 1886–1986: Eine Bibliographie*. Frankfurt: Fischer, 1986.

Benz, Wolfgang, *Sklavenarbeit im KZ*. Munich: Deutscher Taschenbuch-Verlag, 1993.

Boelcke, Willy A., *Die Deutsche Wirtschaft 1930–1945: Interna des Reichswirtschaftsministeriums*. Düsseldorf: Droste, 1983.

Bower, Tom, *Blind Eye to Murder: Britain, America and the Purging of Nazi Germany – A Pledge Betrayed*. London: Andre Deutsch, 1981.

Brady, Robert A., *The Spirit and Structure of German Fascism*. London: Victor Gollancz, 1937.

Bräutigam, Petra, *Mittelständische Unternehmer im Nationalsozialismus (Nationalsozialismus und Nachkriegszeit in Südwestdeutschland 6)*. Munich: Oldenbourg, 1997.

Brüning, Heinrich, *Memoiren 1918–1934*. Stuttgart: Deutsche Verlags-Anstalt, 1970.

Brüninghaus, Beate, Hopmann, Barbara, Spoerer, Mark, Weitz, Birgit, *Zwangsarbeit bei Daimler-Benz*. Stuttgart: Franz Steiner Verlag, 1994.

Bundesminister der Finanzen (ed.), *Die Wiedergutmachung nationalsozialistischen Unrechts durch die Bundesrepublik Deutschland*. Munich: Beck, 1974.

Czichon, Eberhard, *Der Bankier und die Macht. Hermann Josef Abs in der deutschen Politik*. Cologne: Pahl-Rugenstein, 1970.

Deutsche Bank, *Böhmen und Mähren im deutschen Wirtschaftsraum*. n.d. (1938?)

Eichholtz, Dietrich (ed.), *Krieg und Wirtschaft. Studien zur deutschen Wirtschaftsgeschichte 1939–1945*. Berlin: Metropol, 1999.

Engel, Helmut, Jersch-Wenzel, Steffi, Treue, Wilhelm (eds.), *Charlottenburg*, Vol. 1: *Die historische Stadt*. Berlin: Nicolai, 1986.

Enquête-Ausschuss, *(Ausschuss zur Untersuchung der Erzeugungs- und Absatzbedingungen der deutschen Volkswirtschaft) Der Bankkredit*. Berlin: E. S. Mittler & Sohn, 1930.

Enzensberger, Hans Magnus (ed), OMGUS. *Ermittlungen gegen die Deutsche Bank*. Nördlingen: Greno, 1985.

Feldenkirchen, Wilfried, *Siemens 1918–1945*. Columbus: Ohio State University Press, 1999.

Feldman, Gerald D., *The Great Disorder: Politics, Economics and Society in the German Inflation 1914–1924*. New York: Oxford University Press, 1993.

Feldman, Gerald D., "Jakob Goldschmidt, the History of the Banking Crisis of 1931, and the Problem of Freedom of Manouevre in the Weimar Economy," in Christoph Buchheim, Michael Hutter, Harold James (eds.), *Zerrissene Zwischenkriegszeit: Wirtschaftshistorische Beiträge: Knut Borchardt zum 65. Geburtstag*. Baden-Baden: Nomos, 1994, 307–28.

Feldman, Gerald D., "The Deutsche Bank 1914–1933," in Lothar Gall, Holtfrerich, Gerald D. Feldman, Harold James, Carl-Ludwig Holtfrerich, Hans E. Büschgen (eds.), *The Deutsche Bank 1870–1995*. London: Weidenfeld & Nicolson, 1995, 130–276.

Fischer, Gottfried Bermann, *Bedroht bewahrt: Der Weg eines Verlegers.* Frankfurt: Fischer, 1986.

Fohlin, Caroline, "The Rise of Interlocking Directorates in Imperial Germany." *Economic History Review* 52 (2): 307–33 1999.

Friedländer, Saul, *Nazi Germany and the Jews,* Vol. 1: *The Years of Persecution, 1933–1939.* New York: HarperCollins, 1997.

Fröhlich, Elke, (ed.), *Die Tagebücher von Joseph Goebbels.* Munich: Saur, 1998.

Fuchs, Konrad, *Ein Konzern aus Sachsen: Das Kaufhaus Schocken als Spiegelbild deutscher Wirtschaft und Politik 1901 bis 1953.* Stuttgart: Deutsche Verlags-Anstalt, 1990.

Gall, Lothar, "The Deutsche Bank from Its Founding to the Great War," in Lothar Gall, Gerald D. Feldman, Harold James, Carl-Ludwig Holtfrerich, Hans E. Büschgen (eds.), *The Deutsche Bank 1870–1995.* London: Weidenfeld & Nicolson, 1995, 1–127.

Gall, Lothar, "A Man for All Seasons: Hermann Josef Abs im Dritten Reich." *Zeitschrift für Unternehmensgeschichte* 44: 123–175 1998.

Genschel, Helmut, *Die Verdrängung der Juden aus der Wirtschaft im Dritten Reich.* Göttingen: Musterschmidt, 1966.

Gregor-Dellin, Martin (ed.), *Richard Wagner: Mein Denken.* Munich: Piper, 1982.

Gregor, Neil, *Star and Swastika. Daimler-Benz in the Third Reich.* New Haven, CT: Yale University Press, 1998.

Gruner, Wolf, *Der geschlossene Arbeitseinsatz deutscher Juden. Zur Zwangsarbeit als Element der Verfolgung 1938–1943.* Berlin: Metropol, 1997.

Guillebaud, C. W., *The Economic Recovery of Germany from 1933 to the Incorporation of Austria in March 1938.* London: Macmillan, 1939.

Harmelin, Wilhelm, "Juden in der Leipziger Rauchwarenwirtschaft." *Tradition* 11: 249–82 (1966).

Hayes, Peter, *Industry and Ideology: IG Farben in the Nazi Era.* Cambridge, UK: Cambridge University Press, 1987.

Hayes, Peter, "State Policy and Corporate Involvement in the Holocaust," in U.S. Holocaust Museum (ed.), *The Holocaust: The Known, the Unknown, the Disputed and the Reexamined.* Washington D.C., 1994.

Hayes, Peter, "Big Business and 'Aryanization' in Germany 1933–39." *Jahrbuch für Antisemitismusforschung* 3: 254–281 (1994).

Hayes, Peter, "The Deutsche Bank and the Holocaust," in Peter Hayes (ed.), *Lessons and Legacies III: Memory, Memorialization and Denial*. Evanston, IL: Northwestern University Press, 1999, 71–98.

Hepp, Michael, *Deutsche Bank und Dresdner Bank: Gewinne aus Raub, Enteignung und Zwangsarbeit 1933–1944*. Bremen: Stiftung für Sozialgeschichte des 20. Jahrhunderts, 1999.

Herbert, Ulrich, *Hitler's Foreign Workers: Enforced Labor in Germany under the Third Reich*. Cambridge, UK: Cambridge University Press, 1997.

Hess, Hermann, *Ritter von Halt. Der Sportler und Soldat*. Berlin: Batschan, 1936.

Heusler, Andreas, *Ausländereinsatz. Zwangsarbeit für die Münchener Kriegswirtschaft 1939–1945*. Munich: Hugendubel, 1996.

Hilberg, Raoul, *The Destruction of the European Jews*. New York: Holmes and Meier, 1985.

Hildebrand, Klaus, *Das vergangene Reich: Deutsche Aussenpolitik von Bismarck bis Hitler*. Stuttgart: Deutsche Verlags-Anstalt, 1995.

Hoffmann, Katharina (ed.), *Nationalsozialismus und Zwangsarbeit in der Region Oldenburg*. Oldenburg: Bibliotheks- und Informationssystem der Universität Oldenburg, 1999.

Holtfrerich, Carl-Ludwig, "The Deutsche Bank 1945–1957: War, Military Rule and Reconstruction," in Lothar Gall, Gerald D. Feldman, Harold James, Carl-Ludwig Holtfrerich, Hans E. Büschgen (eds.), *The Deutsche Bank 1870–1995*. London: Weidenfeld & Nicholson, 1995, 357–521, 362.

Houwink ten Cate, Johannes, *"De Mannen van de Daad" en Duitsland 1919–1939: Het Hollandse zakenleven en der vooroorlogse buitenlandse politiek*. Den Haag: Stu Uitgevers, 1995.

Huber, Gabriele, *Die Porzellan-Manufaktur Allach-München GmbH*, Marburg: Jonas, 1992.

Hüttenberger, Peter, "Nationalsozialistische Polykratie," in *Geschichte und Gesellschaft 2*. Göttingen: Vandenhoeck Rupprecht, 1976, 417–42.

James, Harold, *The German Slump: Politics and Economics 1924–1936*. Oxford: Oxford University Press, 1986.

James, Harold, "The Deutsche Bank and the Dictatorship," in Lothar Gall, Gerald D. Feldman, Harold James, Carl-Ludwig Holtfrerich, Hans E. Büschgen (eds.), *The Deutsche Bank 1870–1995*. London: Weidenfeld & Nicolson, 1995, 277–356.

James, Harold, *Monetary and Fiscal Unification in Nineteenth-Century Germany: What Can Kohl Learn from Bismarck?* Princeton, NJ: Essays in International Finance, No. 202, 1997.

Junz, Helen, "Report on the Wealth Position of the Jewish Population in Nazi-Occupied Countries, Germany and Austria," in *Independent Committee of Eminent Persons, Report on Dormant Accounts of Victims of Nazi Persecution in Swiss Banks.* Bern: Staempfli, 1999, Appendix S, A127–A206.

Kaienburg, Hermann (ed.), *Konzentrationslager und deutsche Wirtschaft 1939–1945.* Opladen: Leske & Budrich, 1996.

Kaiser, Ernst, Knorn, Michael, *"Wir lebten und schliefen zwischen den Toten": Rüstungsproduktion, Zwangsarbeit und Vernichtung in den Frankfurter Adlerwerken.* Frankfurt: Campus, 1996.

Karny, Miroslav, Milotova, Jaroslava, Karna, Margita (eds.), *Deutsche Politik im "Protektorat Böhmen und Mähren" unter Reinhard Heydrich 1941–1942: Eine Dokumentation.* Berlin: Metropol, 1997.

Kempner, Robert M. W., "Hitler und die Zerstörung des Hauses Ullstein," in *Hundert Jahre Ullstein 1877–1977,* Vol. 3. Berlin: Ullstein, 1977.

Kershaw, Ian, *The Nazi Dictatorship: Problems and Perspectives of Interpretation.* London: Edward Arnold, 1989.

Kopper, Christopher, *Zwischen Marktwirtschaft und Dirigismus: Staat, Banken und Bankenpolitik im "Dritten Reich" von 1933 bis 1939.* Bonn: Bouvier, 1995.

Kopper, Christopher, "Die 'Arisierung' der deutsch-böhmischen Aktienbanken," in Barth, Boris, Faltus, Josef, Kren, Jan, Kubu, Eduard (eds.), *Konkurrenzpartnerschaft: Die deutsche und die tschechoslowakische Wirtschaft in der Zwischenkriegszeit.* Essen: Klartext Verlag, 1998, 236–45.

Kosiol, Erich, *Bilanzreform und Einheitsbilanz: Grundlegende Studien zu den Möglichkeiten einer Rationalisierung der periodischen Erfolgsvermittlung, Schriften des Betriebswirtschaftlichen Ausschusses Sudetenland 5.* Reichenberg, Leipzig, and Vienna, 1944.

Lange, Ursula, *Abschied von einem Soldaten, Sonette.* Berlin: Suhrkamp, 1942.

Van der Leew, A. J. "Der Griff des Reiches nach dem Judenvermögen." *Rechtsprechung zum Wiedergutmachungsrecht* 21: 383–92 (1970).

Lernet-Holenia, Alexander, *Ein Traum in Rot: Roman.* Berlin: Fischer, 1939.

Lord d'Abernon's Diary, Vol. 2: The Years of Crisis June 1922–December 1923. London: Hodder and Stoughton, 1929.

Lurie, Samuel, Private Investment in a Controlled Economy: Germany 1933–1939. New York: Columbia University Press, 1947.

Lützkendorf, Felix, Friedrich II. Berlin: Suhrkamp, 1944.

Lützkendorf, Felix, Söhne des Krieges. Berlin: Verlag Die Heimbücherei, 1940.

Lützkendorf, Felix, Völkerwanderung 1940. Ein Bericht aus dem Osten. Berlin: Fischer, 1940.

Matis, Herbert, Weber, Fritz, "Economic Anschluss and German Glossmachtpolitik: The Take-Over of the Austrian Credit-Anstalt in 1938," in Cottrell, P. L., Lindgren, Hakan, Teichova, Alice (eds.), European Industry and Banking Between the Wars: A Review of Bank–Industry Relations. Leicester: Leicester University Press, 1992, 109–26.

Marx, Karl, Early Writings. Harmondsworth: Penguin, 1975.

Mehl, Stefan, Das Reichsfinanzministerium und die Verfolgung der Deutschen Juden 1933–1943 (Berliner Arbeitshefte zur Sozialwissenschaftlichen Forschung 38). Berlin: Zentralinstitut für Sozialwissenschaftliche Forschung, 1990.

Milward, Alan S., "The Reichsmark Bloc and the International Economy," in Hirschfeld, Gerhard, Kettenacker, Lothar (eds.), The "Führer State": Myth and Reality: Studies on the Structure and Politics of the Third Reich. Stuttgart: Klett-Cotta, 1981), 377–413.

Mollin, Gerhard, Montankonzerne und "Drittes Reich": Der Gegensatz zwischen Monopolwirtschaft und Befehlswirtschaft in der deutschen Rüstung und Expansion 1936–1944 (Kritische Studien zur Geschichtswissenschaft Bd. 78), Göttingen: Vandenhoeck & Ruprecht, 1988.

Mommsen, Hans, "Hitler's Position in the Nazi System," in Hans Mommsen, From Weimar to Auschwitz. Princeton, NJ: Princeton University Press, 1991, 163–88.

Mommsen, Hans, Das Volkswagenwerk und seine Arbeiter im Dritten Reich. Düsseldorf: Econ, 1996.

Mönnich, Horst, BMW. Eine deutsche Geschichte. Vienna and Darmstadt: Paul Zsolnay Verlag, 1989.

Mosse, Werner E., Jews in the German Economy: The German-Jewish Elite. Oxford: Oxford University Press, 1987.

Morsey, Rudolf, Zur Entstehung, Authentizität unnd Kritik von Brünings Memoiren 1918–1934. Opladen: Westdeutscher Verlag 1975.

Müller, Angelika, "Der 'jüdische Kapitalist' als Drahtzieher und Hintermann. Zur antisemitischen Bildpolitik in den nationalsozialistischen Wahlplakaten der Weimarer Republik 1924–1933," in *Jahrbuch für Antisemitismusforschung* 7. Frankfurt: Campus, 1998, 175–207.

Müller, Rolf-Dieter, "Von der Wirtschaftsallianz zum kolonialen Ausbeutungskrieg," in Militärgeschichtliches Forschungsamt Freiburg (ed.), *Das Deutsche Reich und der Zweite Weltkrieg*, Vol. 4. Stuttgart: Deutsche Verlags-Anstalt, 1983, 98–189.

Naasner, Walter, *Neue Machtzentren in der deutschen Kriegswirtschaft 1942–1945*. Boppard: Boldt, 1994.

Naasner, Walter, *SS-Wirtschaft und SS-Verwaltung: "Das SS-Wirtschafts-Verwaltungshauptamt und die unter seiner Dienstaufsicht stehenden wirtschaftlichen Vertretungen"* (Schriften des Bundesarchivs 45 a), Düsseldorf: Droste, 1998.

Neumann, Franz, *Behemoth: The Structure and Practice of National Socialism*, 2nd ed. New York: Oxford University Press, 1944.

Overesch, Manfred, *Das III. Reich 1933–1945: Eine Tageschronik der Politik, Wirtschaft, Kultur*. Düsseldorf: Droste, 1983.

Patch, William L. Jr., *Heinrich Brüning and the Dissolution of the Weimar Republic*. Cambridge, UK: Cambridge University Press, 1998.

Penzoldt, Ernst, *Korporal Mombour: Eine Soldatenromanze*. Berlin: Fischer, 1941.

Perz, Bertrand, *Projekt Quarz. Steyr-Daimler-Puch und das Konzentrationslager Melk*. Vienna: Verlag für Gesellschaftskritik, 1991.

Pischke, Gudrun, *Europa arbeitet bei den Reichswerken: das nationalsozialistische Lagersystem in Salzgitter*. Salzgitter: Archiv der Stadt Salzgitter, 1995.

Pohl, Hans, *Die Daimler-Benz AG in den Jahren 1933–1945*. Wiesbaden: Steiner, 1986.

Pohl, Manfred, *Konzentration im deutschen Bankwesen 1848–1980. Ein Handbuch der Bankenkonzentration in Deutschland*. Frankfurt: Fritz Knapp, 1982.

Pohl, Manfred, *Entstehung und Entwicklung des Universalbankensystems: Konzentration und Krise als wichtige Faktoren*. Frankfurt: Fritz Knapp, 1986.

Pohl, Manfred, *Philipp Holzmann: Geschichte eines Bauunternehmens*. Munich: Beck, 1999.

Pohl, Manfred, Raab-Rebentisch, Angelika, *Von Stambul nach Bagdad: Die Geschichte einer berühmten Eisenbahn*. München: Piper, 1999.

Pohl, Manfred, Schneider, Andrea, *VIAG 1923–1998: Vom Staatskonzern zum internationalen Konzern*. Munich: Piper, 1998.

Pohl, Manfred/Treue, Wilhelm, (eds.), *Deutsche Bank: Ein Teil deutscher Wirtschaftsgeschichte, Berichte und Biographien* (manuscript).

Rebentisch, Dieter, *Führerstaat und Verwaltung im Zweiten Weltkrieg: Verfassungsentwicklung und Verwaltungspolitik*. Wiesbaden: Steiner, 1989.

Reinhard, Otto, *"Vernichten oder ausnutzen?" "Aussonderungen" und Arbeitseinsatz sowjetischer Kriegsgefangener im Reichsgebiet in den Jahren 1941/42*. Paderborn: Universitätsdissertation, 1995.

Reuth, Ralf Georg, *Goebbels*. New York: Harcourt Brace, 1993.

Roth, Karl Heinz, "Bankenkrise, Faschismus und Macht," in Kritische Aktionäre der Deutschen Bank (eds.), *Macht ohne Kontrolle: Berichte über die Geschäfte der Deutschen Bank*. Stuttgart: Schmetterling, 1990, 13–23.

Roth, Karl Heinz, "Hehler des Holocaust: Degussa und Deutsche Bank." *1999. Zeitschrift für Sozialgeschichte des 20. und 21. Jahrhunderts* 13(2):137–44 (1998).

Rothkirchen, Livia: "The Situation of Jews in Slovakia between 1939 and 1945." *Jahrbuch für Antisemitismusforschung* 7:46–70 (1998).

Ruhm von Oppen, Beate, *Helmuth James von Moltke: Briefe an Freya 1939-45*. Munich: Beck, 1988.

Safrian, Hans, *Die Eichmann-Männer*. Vienna and Zurich: Europa Verlag, 1993.

Schoeps, Julius H., "Wie die Deutsche Bank Mendelssohn & Co. schluckte," in *Frankfurter Rndschau*, November 27, 1998.

Schwarz, Felix, "Literarisches Zeitgespräch im Dritten Reich." *Archiv für Geschichte des Buchwesens* 12:1329–38 (1972).

Seidler, Franz W., *Die Organisation Todt: Bauen für Staat und Wehrmacht 1938–1945*. Bonn: Bernard & Graefe, 1998.

Siegfried, Klaus-Jörg, *Rüstungsproduktion und Zwangsarbeit im Volkswagenwerk 1939–1945*. Frankfurt: Campus, 1999.

Soros, George, *The Crisis of Global Capitalism: Open Society Endangered*. New York: Public Affairs, 1998.

Spoerer, Mark, *Vom Scheingewinn zum Rüstungsboom: Die Eigenrentabilität der deutschen Industriegesellschaften 1925–1941 (Vierteljahrschrift für Sozial- und Wirtschaftsgeschichte Beiheft 123)*. Stuttgart: Steiner Verlag, 1996.

Stahlbaumer, L. M., "Big Business and the Persecution of the Jews: The Flick Concern and the 'Aryanization' of Jewish Property Before the War." *Holocaust and Genocide Studies* 13(1): 1–27 (1999).

Statistisches Handbuch für Deutschland 1928–1944. Munich: Ehrenwirth, 1949.

Steinberg, Jonathan, *All or Nothing: The Axis and the Holocaust*. London: Routledge, 1990.

Steinberg, Jonathan, *The Deutsche Bank and its Gold Transactions during the Second World War*. Munich: Beck, 1999.

Stiefel, Dieter, *Finanzdiplomatie und Weltwirtschaftskrise: Die Krise der Credit-Anstalt für Handel und Gewerbe 1931*. Frankfurt: Fritz Knapp, 1989.

Stürmer, Michael, Teichmann, Gabriele, Treue, Wilhelm, *Wägen und Wagen: Sal. Oppenheim jr. & Cie. Geschichte einer Bank und einer Familie*. Munich and Zurich: Piper, 1989.

Sturm, Hanspeter, "Salamander," *Tradition* 12: 309–333 (1967).

Teichova, Alice, *An Economic Background to Munich: International Business and Czechoslovakia 1918–1938*. Cambridge, MA: Cambridge University Press, 1974.

Teichova, Alice, "Instruments of Economic Control and Exploitation: The German Occupation of Bohemia and Moravia," in Overy, Richard J., Otto, Gerhard, Houwink ten Cate, Johannes (eds.), *Die "Neuordnung" Europas: NS-Wirtschaftspolitik in den besetzten Gebieten*. Berlin: Metropol, 1997, 83–108.

Treue, Wilhelm, "Bankhaus Mendelssohn als Beispiel einer Privatbank im 19. und 20. Jahrhundert," in *Mendelssohn-Studien 1*. Berlin: Duncker und Humbolt, 1972, 29–80.

Uhlig, Heinrich, *Die Warenhäuser im Dritten Reich*. Cologne: Westdeutscher Verlag, 1956.

Ulrich, Keith, *Aufstieg und Fall der Privatbankiers: Die wirtschaftliche Bedeutung von 1918 bis 1938 (Schriftenreihe des Instituts für bankhistorische Forschung 20)*. Frankfurt: Fritz Knapp, 1998.

Umbreit, Hans, "Auf dem Weg zur Kontinentalherrschaft," in Militärgeschichtliches Forschungsamt Freiburg (ed.), *Das Deutsche Reich und der Zweite Weltkrieg*, Vol. V/1. Stuttgart: Deutsche Verlags-Anstalt, 1988, 3–345.

Vencovský, František, Zdeněk Jindra, Jiří Novotný, Karel Půlpán, and Petr Dvořák. (eds.), *Dějiny Bankovnictví v Českých Zemích*. Prague: Bankovní Institut, 1999.

Volkmann, Hans-Erich, "Die NS-Wirtschaft in Vorbereitung des Krieges," in Militärgeschichtliches Forschungsamt Freiburg (ed.), *Das Deutsche Reich und der Zweite Weltkrieg*, Vol. 1. Stuttgart: Deutsche Verlags-Anstalt, 1979, 177–368.

Wiskemann, Elizabeth, *Czechs and Germans: A Study of the Struggle in the Historic Provinces of Bohemia and Moravia*. London: Oxford University Press and Royal Institute of International Affairs, 1938.

Witek, Hans, "'Arisierungen' in Wien: Aspekte nationalsozialialistischer Enteigungspolitik 1938–1940," in Emmerich Talos, Ernst Hanisch, Wolfgang Neugebauer (eds.), *NS-Herrschaft in Österreich*. Vienna: Verlag für Gesellschaftskritik, 1988, 199–216.

Wixforth, Harald, *Die Neuordnung des Bankwesens im Sudetenland*. Paper presented at the January 14, 2000 meeting of the GUG-Arbeitskreis "Unternehmen im Nationalsozialismus."

Wolf, Herbert, "Zur Kontrolle und Enteignung jüdischen Vermögens in der NS-Zeit." *Bankhistorisches Archive* 16(1): 55–62 (1990).

Ziegler, Dieter, "Die Verdrängung der Juden aus der Dresdner Bank," in *Vierteljahrshefte für Zeitgeschichte 47*. Munich: Oldenbourg, 1999, 187–216.

Index

Abs, Clemens, 100, 103, 105
Abs, Hermann Josef, 7, 8, 17–18, 30,
  66, 71, 74–77, 91, 99, 189, 217
  and Adler & Oppenheimer, 92–98,
  160
  and Böhmische Union Bank, 140,
  144, 157, 160, 216
  and Creditanstalt-Bankverein,
  Wien, 131–35, 140
  as partner of Delbrück Schickler &
  Co., 86, 87, 105
  becomes Director of Deutsche
  Bank, 29
  moral responsibility of, 215
  and Petschek, 100–104
  and postwar restitution
  negotiations, 89–90, 102–104
  and views on profits, 213
  and Salamander, 86–90
  and Suhrkamp, 105, 106, 110
Abs, Josef, 100, 101
Abshagen, Otto, 78
ACM, 77, 80, 81
ADCA, 144
Adefa (Arbeitsgemeinschaft deutsch-
  arischer
  Konfektionsfabrikanten, or
  Working Group of German-
  Aryan Clothing Manufacturers),
  59, 60
Adler, Alfred, 98
Adler, Anna Luise, 98
Adler, family, 90, 95, 99, 120,
  215–216
Adler, Hans, 90
Adler & Oppenheimer, 38, 82,
  87–88, 90–94, 98–99, 160, 208
AEG, 12
Agraria Vermögensverwaltungs AG,
  146
Ahlmann, Wilhelm, 105–106
Air Ministry, 52
Almy, 91, 94–95, 98
Amann, Max, 48–49
Allalemjian, Mirham, 124
Allgemeine Deutsche Creditanstalt
  (see ADCA)
Allgemeine Elektrizitätsgesellschaft
  (see AEG)
Allgemeine Handels- und
  Creditbank, 180
Allgemeiner Jugoslawischer
  Bankverein, 135
Allgemeiner Polnischer Bankverein,
  187
Amsterdamsche Bank, 94,

Amsterdamsche Crediet
Maatschappij (see ACM)
N.V. Amsterdamsche Leder
Maatschappij (see Almy)
André, Erich, 111–112
Apitzsch, Walter, 164
Antimon Berg und Hüttenwerke AG,
181
Argentina, 6, 198
Ariowitsch, Max, 124
Ariowitsch (Ariowitsch & Jacob Fur
Co. Ltd.), 124
Ariowitsch (J. Ariowitsch), 124
Ariowitsch (J. Ariowitsch &
Company, Anglo-American Fur
Merchants Corporation), 124
Army Ministry, 30
Gebr. Arnhold, 68
Aronwerke Elektrizitäts AG, 49
Arpol, 188
Assuschkewitz (Gebr.
Assuschkewitz), 124
Aufhäuser (H. Aufhäuser), 29, 46,
69, 76
Auschwitz, 4, 200
Austria, 10, 61, 127–129, 131,
134–139, 156, 167, 210, 212,
214, 216
Awag AG, 83

Badische Bank, 114–116–118
Bähr, Johannes, 6
Bally, 95
Bagehot, Walter, 17
Bajohr, Frank, 4, 37
Bamberger, Ludwig, 12
Banca Commerciale Italiana, 97, 189
Banca Commerciala Romana, 140
Banca Alemán Transatlántico (see
Deutsche Ueberseeische Bank)

Bandeisen + Blechwalzwerke AG
Karlshütte, 176
Bank der Deutschen Luftfahrt, 21
Bank für Industrie-Obligationen
Bank Handlowy, 189–191, 215
Bank of England, 17, 147
Bank Polski, 191
Bankverein AG Belgrad, 179
Bankverein für Kroatien, 179
Banque de Bruxelles, 189
Banque des Pays de l'Europe
Centrale (see Länderbank)
Barkai, Avraham, 4,6,36–37
Bary (H. Albert de Bary & Co. N.V.),
206
Bass & Herz, 69
Bata, 84
Bausback, Ferdinand, 48
Bayerischer Lloyd, 173
Bebca, 142–145, 149, 153–154, 163,
170, 181
Bechtolf, Erich, 29, 99, 190–191,
194, 215
Belgium, 76, 139, 174, 183
Benz, Ottomar, 46
Bergen-Belsen, 117
Berghütte Dombrowa, 179
Berghütte-Komplex, 175–178, 181
Bergisch-Märkische Bank, 12–13
Berg- und Hüttenwerksgesellschaft
Karwin Trzynietz, 176
Berg- und Hüttenwerksgesellschaft
Teschen, 176, 179
Berg- und Hüttenwerksgesellschaft
Wegierska Gorka, 176
Berkovits, Josef, 166
Bernstein, Kurt, 83
Betzen (ehemals Israel Schmidt),
148
Beyer, Walther, 74
Biedermann, D., 124

Bituma Bergbau und Chemische
    Industrie AG, 144, 158
Blaut (Marcus Blaut), 60
Blessing, Karl, 92, 178
Blinzig, Alfred, 27, 46
Blumenstein, Alfred, 118
Blumenstein, family, 117, 126
Blumenstein, Joseph, 116–118
Bodenkreditanstalt, 17, 132
Boehm & Reitzenstein, 69
Böhmisch-Mährische
    Stickstoffwerke, 176
Böhmische Escompte Bank &
    Creditanstalt (see Bebca)
Böhmische Escompte-Gesellschaft,
    208
Böhmische Kupferwerke, 144, 163
Böhmische Metallwerke, 144
Böhmische Union-Bank (see BUB)
Boernicke, Hellmut, 29, 30
Bösing, Wilhelm, 62–63
Bohemia-Moravia (Protectorate),
    129, 141, 143, 148, 151–154,
    157–159, 167, 170, 172,
    176–177, 195
Bohemia Keramikwerke, 144, 158,
    168–169, 183
Bormann, Martin, 29
Bower, Tom, 41
Brady, Robert, 2
Bratislava Handels- und Kreditbank
    AG, 152
Braunkohlen- und Brikettindustrie
    AG (see Bubiag)
Breker, Arno, 105–106
Brinckmann Wirtz & Co., 81
Brinkmann, Rudolf, 133, 137
British Chartered Bank, 121
British Overseas Bank, 156, 160,
    189
Bruckmann, Hugo, 105

Brüning, Heinrich, 16–18
Brünn-Königsfelder Maschinen- und
    Waggonsfabriks AG, 172
Brünner Waffenwerke, 172–173
BUB, 8, 31, 140–145, 151, 155–156,
    158–168, 172–175, 179,
    207–208, 216
    and "aryanization", 169–171
    and Bratislava branch, 180–181
    and Creditanstalt, 153, 160, 180
    and Gestapo, 154, 157, 170–171,
        176
    Jewish directors and personnel,
        149, 154
    Jewish-owned accounts, 149,
        169–171
    postwar liquidation of, 182–184
    profits of, 162
    Sudeten branches of, 150
Bubiag, 100
Bulgaria, 134
Bunzl & Biach AG, 138
Bürckel, Josef, 4, 134–135
Bunnell, Sterling, 154
Burkhardt, Otto, 78, 81
Burkhardt & Co., 80–81

Canada, 183
Cautio, 48
Central-Kaufhaus GmbH, 113–114
Česká Banka Union (see BUB)
Chaim Eitingon AG, 124
Christian, Johannes, 165
Ciba, 95–96
Coburg-Werke, 176
Commerzbank AG, 28, 49–50, 57,
    84–86, 143–144, 186, 200–201
Compagnie Belge de l'Etranger, 139
Compagnie voor Belegging en
    Administratie (Coba), 77, 80

Creditanstalt AG Krakau, 194
Creditanstalt-Bankverein, Wien, 38,
    128, 130–136, 139–140,
    152–153, 160, 178, 180–, 182,
    191, 193–194, 208, 216
    and "aryanizations", 137–138
    and operations in Poland, 129,
    189, 192
Croatia, 163
Czech National Bank, 147
Czechoslovakia(after, 1938 Czecho-
    Slovakia), 10, 116, 128, 141,
    146, 148, 150–151, 153, 157,
    169, 180, 208, 212, 214, 216
Czech Republic, 7–8, 183
Czichon, Eberhard, 7, 90, 104

Dachau, 169
Daelen (H. Daelen & Co.), 102
DAF, 41, 78, 91–92, 111, 114, 117
DAIB, 128, 144–147, 149, 153, 155,
    160, 162, 169
Daimler-Benz, 3
Danatbank (see Darmstädter und
    Nationalbank)
Darmstädter und Nationalbank, 13,
    24
    and, 1931 crisis, 16–18
Degele, Wilhelm, 119
Delbrück Schickler & Co., 29,
    86–88, 91, 97, 105, 160, 179
Delbrück von der Heydt, 102
Deutsche Arbeitsfront (see DAF)
Deutsch-Bulgarische Kreditbank
    Sofia, 136, 140
Deutsche Agrar- und Industriebank
    (see DAIB)
Deutsche Bundesbank, 92
Deutsche Erdöl-AG, 100
Deutsche Genossenschaftsbank, 186

Deutsche Golddiskontbank, 16, 66,
    79–80, 134, 147, 168, 199
Deutsche Industrie AG, 100
Deutsche Kohlenhandelsgesellschaft
    mbH, 100
Deutsche Mühlenvereinigung AG,
    45
Deutsche Rauchwaren Gesellschaft,
    125
Deutsche Reichsbank, 6, 12, 16–17,
    25, 39, 48, 58, 70–71, 73–75,
    77, 79, 90, 92, 116, 130,
    132–133, 135, 147, 178, 182,
    184–185, 187, 190–191, 200
Deutsche Revisions- und
    Treuhandgesellschaft, 138, 162
Deutsche Ueberseeische Bank
    (Banco Alemán Transatlántico),
    11
Deutscher Verlag KG, 48
Diamant, 60
Disconto-Gesellschaft, 13, 56
Döblin, Alfred, 105
Dönitz, Karl
Dresdner Bank AG, 6, 13, 64, 66, 78,
    129, 141, 161, 180, 194, 201
    and, 1931 crisis, 16–18
    and Bebca, 142–143, 153–154
    and conflicts and rivalry with
    Deutsche Bank, 44, 60, 76,
    85–86, 113, 115, 128, 134, 136,
    138, 154, 161, 172, 186, 191,
    214
    and collaboration with Deutsche
    Bank, 57–59, 63, 131, 152
    and Darmstädter und
    Nationalbank, 16–18
    and employment of Joseph
    Goebbels, 22
    and Mercurbank, 128, 131, 134
    and personnel policy, 28, 111–112

activities in Poland, 29, 184,
186–187
profits from "aryanization", 41,
205–206, 210,
and Sudetenland, 141–143, 208
Dreyse, Fritz, 71, 74
Droop, Ewald, 104

Eher (Franz Eher Verlag), 48–49
Eichtersheimer (M. Eichtersheimer),
198
Eisenwerke AG Kriebich, 158
Eisenwarenfabriken Lapp-Finze AG,
139
Eisenwerke Rohau-Neudek, 144
Eisert (Brüder Eisert AG), 138
Eisner, Ernst, 69
Elektrische Licht- und Kraftanlagen
AG, 49
Elektrische Walzenmühle Dalezman
& Co., 188
Eleventh Decree on the Citizenship
Law [Elfte Verordnung zum
Reichsbürgergesetz] of
November, 25, 1941, 200–202
Elimeyer (Philipp Elimeyer), 39
Elkmann, Gerhard, 64, 93
Elsässische Tabakmanufaktur, 121
Engels, Emil, 50
Erft-Bergbau AG, 50, 101–103
Ermeler, 120
Ermen & Engels AG, 50
Ernst, Friedrich, 71, 74, 131,
143–144, 149
Erste Böhmische Glasindustrie AG,
158
Erste Brünner Maschinenfabriks-
Gesellschaft, 172
Erste Donau-
Dampfschiffahrtsgesellschaft,
136

Escompte und Volkswirtschaftliche
Bank, 152, 180
Esders & Dyckerhoff, 165

Fahr (Gebr. Fahr), 60
Falkenhausen, Gotthard von, 78–81
Federal Reserve Bank of New York,
17
Feichtmann, Emil, 138
Feinstahlwerke Traisen AG vorm.
Fischer, 136
Feit, Hans, 114
Feldenkirchen, Wilfried, 3
Feldman, Gerald D., 6
Fenthol, Fritz, 78–79
Feuchtmann, Eugen, 46
Freund, Otto, 154
Fischböck, Hans, 127, 132–133,
135–137, 139, 189
Fischer, Gottfried Bermann, 105,
110
Fischer, Samuel, 105
Fischer (S. Fischer-Verlag), 105,
107, 110, 215
Fontane, Theodor, 106
France, 22, 76, 94, 98, 173–175, 183
Friedländer, Saul, 51
Friedrich Flick AG, 100
Flick, Friedrich, 78, 172
Four-Year-Plan, 5, 38, 51, 116, 131,
163, 178, 205
Frank, Theodor, 25, 26
Französisch-Italienische AG der
Dombrowaer Kohlengruben, 175
Fränkel (S. Fränkel), 69
Freudenberg, Richard, 60
Friedenshütte, 179
Frisch, Joseph, 86
Fritscher, Ludwig, 181–182
Fröhlich (G.A. Fröhlich's Sohn), 158
Frowein, Robert, 29

Fürstenberg, Familie, 118
Fürstenberg, Max Egon Fürst zu, 116
Fuld, Lothar, 46
Fuld, Ludwig, 27, 45–46
Funk, Walther, 78, 174, 190

Gall, Lothar, 6
Galopin, Alexandre, 157
Geisler, Fritz, 48
Generalgouvernement, 186, 189,
    190–192, 194
Genschel, Helmut, 4
Gerber, Alois, 114
Gerber & Oefelein, 114
Gestapo, 77, 106, 109, 154, 157,
    170–171, 176, 197, 199, 202,
    215
Gewerkschaft Beiselgrube, 102
Ginzkey (J. Ginzkey), 162
Girmes (Joh. Girmes & Co. AG), 60,
    206
Glathe, Arthur, 191
Goebbels, Joseph, 22, 30, 48–49, 51,
    60, 105
Göring, Hermann, 43, 51, 61, 63,
    100, 130–131, 173–174, 179,
    205
Goetz, Carl, 57–58, 78
Goldschmidt, Jakob, 16, 24
Graber (M. Graber & Sohn), 168, 181
Gräff, 120
Gräflich Schaffgott'sche Werke, 100
Graf, Julius, 60
Graf von Ballestrem'sche
    Güterdirektion Gleiwitz, 179
Great Britain, 94, 98, 183
Greece, 136
Grodetsky & Pollak, 167
Grödel, Josef Baron, 163
Gruber, Heinrich, 109

Guillebaud, Claude, 2–3
Gumpel, 69
Gutmann, 137
Gutmann (A. Gutmann & Co.), 115
Gutmann, Sigmund, 115

Hácha, Emil, 142, 170
Hadega, 171
Haffner, Alex, 87
Hagen & Co., 69
Hänggi, Paul, 102
Halt, Karl Ritter von, 29, 46, 177
Hambros, 189
Hamburger Hypothekenbank, 79
Hammerschmid, Emil, 163
Handels-Aktiengesellschaft
    Grunewald, 116, 118
Hanneken, Hermann von, 177
Hardy, 69
Hasslacher, Franz, 130, 132, 138
Hauptmann, Gerhard, 105–106
Haupttreuhandstelle Ost (Central
    Trustee Office for the East, see
    HTO)
Hayes, Peter, 3–4, 114
Hefft'sche Kunstmühle AG, 45
Helimont AG Glarus, 100
Heliowatt-Elektrizitäts AG, 49
Henckel von Donnersmarck-
    Beuthen, 100
Henkel-Konzern, 85, 89, 97
Hepp, Michael, 209
Herbert, Ulrich, 3
Hermannsthaler Papierfabrik, 144
Hertel, Franz, 187
Hertie-Kaufhaus-Beteiligungs GmbH,
    47
Hesse, Hermann, 106
Hessische und Herkules
    Bierbrauerei, 111

Heydrich, Reinhard, 143, 170
Heyl (Cornelius Heyl AG), 92, 168
Heyl zu Herrnsheim, Cornelius
  Freiherr, 92
Hilberg, Raoul, 210
Hirschland, family, 77–81, 216
Hirschland, Georg, 77, 79, 81, 110
Hirschland (Simon Hirschland),
  67–69, 71, 77, 80–82, 90,
  208–209
Hitler, Adolf, 1, 18, 24, 29, 30, 33,
  36–37, 48, 50–51, 60, 84, 92,
  108, 128, 132, 142, 153, 186,
  199, 209
Hoffmann, Paul, 78–81
Hofmannsthal, Hugo von, 105
Hohenemser Weberei und Druckerei
  AG, 165
Hohenemser Weberei und Druckerei
  Josef Otten, 166
Holy See, 6, 215
Holzmann (Philipp Holzmann AG),
  3, 46
Holzzellstoff- und Papierfabrik
  Neustadt (see Hupag)
HTO, 175, 187–188, 191
Huber, Robert, 192
Hubertus Braunkohlen AG,
  100–104, 110, 209
Hütter & Schranz AG, 139
Hungary, 134–135, 163, 179
Hunke, Heinrich, 30
Hupag, 116–117, 126
Huta Bankowa, 174–175
Hutschenreuther (Lorenz
  Hutschenreuther AG), 44–45,
  47
Idealspaten und Schaufelwalzwerke
  vormals Eckhardt & Co. KG,
  163

I.G. Farbenindustrie AG, 2–4, 100,
  198–199
I.G. Farben Auschwitz, 188
I.G. Kattowitz, 177
International Business Machines
  Corp., 190
Israel (N. Israel), 64

Jacobsson, Per, 8
Jacquier & Securius, 69
Janina, 174
Jedicke, 120
Jeserich (Johannes Jeserich AG),
  46–47
Jewish Restitution Successor
  Organization, 203
Jörissen (L. Jörissen & Co.), 165
Joham, Josef, 130

Kärntnerische Eisen- und
  Stahlwerksgesellschaft, 136
Kahla Porzellan AG, 79
Kaiser, Hermann, 182
Karlsbader Kristallglasfabriken AG,
  144, 158
Karstadt AG, 29, 87
Kasack, Hermann, 109
Kassen- Aufzugs- und Maschinenbau
  AG F. Wertheim & Co., 139
Kassner (Josef & Moritz Kassner),
  124
Kavan, F., 153–154, 156–159
Kehl, Werner, 25
Kehrl, Hans, 8, 178
Kempner, Paul, 70, 72–75
Keppler, Wilhelm, 132
Kersting, Hans, 102–103
Kiehl, Johannes, 186, 189–190
Kienböck, Viktor, 132

Klöckner, Peter, 172
Kimmich, Karl, 19, 26, 58–59, 62,
  64, 76, 78, 110, 172–173
  and circulars concerning
  "aryanization", 55, 66, 123
Kluge, Erich, 72–73
Kobe, Ernst, 119
Koch (Erich-Koch-Stiftung), 63
Köhler, Hermann, 85–86, 115
Kohn (A. Kohn), 69
Kommerzialbank (subsidiary of
  Dresdner Bank in Cracow), 194
Kontinentale Öl AG, 178
Kopper, Christopher, 40
Kossack & Böhme, 123
Krebs, Joseph, 154, 165, 169,
  176–177
Kreditanstalt der Deutschen, 146
Kreibich, Hans, 163
Kremer, Ferdinand, 76–77
Kroatischer Bankverein (see
  Bankverein für Kroatien)
Krupp (Fried. Krupp AG), 81
Kubinsky, Friedrich Freiherr von,
  167
Kurz, Hermann, 46
Kurzmeyer, Alfred, 75–76, 89, 97
Kuxe Renaud, 174

Länderbank, 131, 152
Lange, Kurt, 61, 78
Lange, Ursula, 108
Langermann, 60
Laupheimer Werkzeugfabrik, 83
Lauterbach, Alexander, 165
Lebensborn e.V., 171
Lederer & Wolf, 158
Legiobank, 139, 181
Leibig & Co., 162

Leising, Karl, 101
Lenz, Richard, 69
Lenz (Richard Lenz & Co.), 69
Lernet-Holenia, Alexander, 109
Levi, family, 84–86, 88
Levi, Max, 84, 86
Levi, Paula, 86–88
Levi, Rolf, 88
Levi, Wolf Josef, 164
Levy (A. Levy & Co.), 68
Ley, Robert, 114
Lindgens, Ursula, 83
Lippmann, Rosenthal & Co., 175
Löb, Rudolf, 70, 72–75
Lüdinghausen, Reinhard Freiherr
  von, 141, 154
Lützkendorf, Felix, 105–108
Luther, Hans, 17

Mährische Bank, 153
Mafrasa Textilwerke AG, 82
Mann, Thomas, 105
Mannesmann AG, 144, 168, 175,
  181
Mannheimer, Franz, 70–72, 75
Margarinefabrik Paul Hofmann &
  Co., 188
Margarine-Union, 92
Martin, Eduard, 67–68
Marx, 69
Marx, Karl, 22
Maschinen- und Waggonfabrikations
  AG vorm. H.D. Schmid, 136
Mautner & Ahlswede, 124
Mayer (L. Mayer), 119
Mendelssohn, family, 216
Mendelssohn, Franz von, 70
Mendelssohn, Giulietta von, 72, 76
Mendelssohn, Joseph, 70

Mendelssohn, Marie von (neé
Westphal), 71–72, 75
Mendelssohn, Moses, 70
Mendelssohn, Robert von, 70,
72–73, 75–76, 110
Mendelssohn-Bartholdy, Elsa von,
71–72, 74, 76
Mendelssohn-Bartholdy, Paul von,
71, 76
Mendelssohn & Co., 38, 40, 67–71,
74–77, 82, 86, 89, 90, 208, 215
Mendelssohn & Co. (branch
Amsterdam), 72
Merck, Finck & Co., 78, 137
Mercurbank, 128, 131, 134
Merkur (Kaufhaus Merkur), 114
Metall- und Farbwerke AG, 126
Metallwalzwerke AG, 168
Milward, Alan, 127
Mitteldeutsche Stahlwerke AG, 100
Moos, Rudolf, 84
Mosler, Eduard, 19, 26, 28, 49, 55,
57, 131, 184
Moltke, Hans Adolf von, 178
Moltke, Helmut James Graf von, 8
Mommsen, Hans, 3, 214
Moser (Ludwig Moser & Söhne), 158
Mühlig-Union Glasindustrie, 144,
158
Müller-Klemm, Wolfgang, 79

National City Bank of New York, 154
National-Bank AG, 78–79
Naundorff (Ernst Naundorff Nachf.
Holzstoff- und Pappenfabrik),
163
Netherlands, 80, 93–94, 98–99, 116,
118, 127, 136, 174–175, 183,
206, 215

Neudeker Wollkämmerei, 144
Neuerburg, August, 96
Neuerburg GmbH, 87, 97
Neugebauer, Georg, 187
Neumann (M.B. Neumann's Söhne
ostmärkische Weberei und
Druckerei AG), 164, 166
Neumann (M.B. Neumann's Söhne
Union-Textilindustrie- und
Druckfabriks AG), 39, 164, 166
Neurath, Konstantin von, 170
Neusch, Johann, 121
New York Hanseatic Corporation, 80
Norddeutsche Bank AG, 215
Norddeutsche Lederwerke AG
(Nordleder), 93, 95–99, 207
Norddeutsche Überseegesellschaft in
Hamburg mbH, 121
Nordwolle, 16
Norway, 183
Novalis, 106
Nussbaum (J & S Nussbaum),
112–113

Oberhütte, 179
Österreichische Industriekredit AG,
133
Österreichische Kontrollbank für
Industrie und Handel AG, 137
Österreichische Nationalbank,
132–133
Ölfabrik Sigmund Arzt, 188
Offenburger Rosshaarspinnerei, 123
Olscher, Alfred, 135
Oppenheim, Hermann, 27–28
Oppenheimer, Clemens, 94–95
Oppenheimer, family, 95, 99, 120,
215–216
Oppenheimer, Ferdinand, 98

Oppenheimer, Fritz, 105
Oppenheimer, Julius, 87
Ordinance on the Registration of
Jewish Assets [*Verordnung über die Anmeldung jüdischen Vermögens*] of April, 26, 1938, 51, 197
Ordinance on the Exclusion of Jews from German Economic Life [*Verordnung über die Ausschaltung der Juden aus dem deutschen Wirtschaftsleben*] of November, 12, 1938, 51, 197–198
Ordinance on Investment of Jewish Property [*Verordnung über den Einsatz des jüdischen Vermögens*] of December, 3, 1938, 63, 101, 122
Osterwind, Heinz, 136
Osthafenmühlen-AG, Berlin, 45
Ostmark-Keramik AG, 139
Otten, Joseph, 165–166

Paersch, Fritz, 190, 192
Participia AG, 163
Penzoldt, Ernst, 108
Petschek, Ernst, 100–103
Petschek, family, 100, 102–104, 110
Petschek, Frank, 100
Petschek, Ignaz, 100
Petschek, Karl, 100, 103–104
Petschek, Wilhelm, 100, 101, 103–104
Petschek-Konzern, 4, 100–101, 168, 172
Petschek-Zuckerwerke, 156, 167
Petzold-Kaolin, 144
Petzold-Döll-Werke, 158
Pfälzische Hypothekenbank, 63

Pferdmenges & Co., 91, 97
Pischner, Wilhelm, 188
Plassmann, Clemens, 29
Pleiger, Paul, 172
Plüsch-Loewi, 144
Pohl, Hans, 3
Pohl, Manfred, 3
Pohle, Walter, 8, 74, 153, 155, 156, 158–159, 169, 175–177, 183, 195, 208
and Adler & Oppenheimer, 160
and Creditanstalt-Bankverein, Wien, 131, 140
and Gestapo, 154, 157, 216
personality of, 178, 215–216
Poland, 7, 10, 10–108, 129, 146, 184, 189, 192
Pollack (Hermann Pollack's Söhne), 163
Pollack, Oscar, 130
Pollems, Helmut, 131, 133–134
Polnische Emissionsbank, 190–191
Polysamplex GmbH, 163
Portland Zementwerke, 119
Portugal, 6, 94
Porzellan-Manufaktur Allach-München, 169
Poznanski (I.K. Poznanski), 96
Preussische Bergwerks- und Hütten-AG, 101
Preussische Staatsbank (Seehandlung), 137, 200
Private Banking Business Group, 52, 56, 61, 75, 200–201

Quandt, Günther, 168

Radomsko Metallurgia, 174, 179
Rafelsberger, Walther, 136

Rasche, Karl, 154, 172
Ratjen, Christoph, 105
Rech, Heinrich, 188
Reemtsma, Philipp, 14
Reemtsma-Konzern, 105, 120, 181
Rehberg, Hans, 105, 108
Reich Chancellery, 86
Reichenberg-Maffersdorfer und
     Gablonzer Brauereien AG, 144,
     158
Reich Economics Ministry, 5, 38, 52,
     57, 59–63, 66–67, 70, 72–75,
     78, 81–83, 85–87, 91–97,
     100–101, 111, 121, 128, 130,
     132–, 135, 137, 143, 147–148,
     151–153, 155–157, 160–162,
     165, 174–175, 177–178,
     186–187, 190, 205
Reich Finance Ministry, 48, 132,
     137, 151, 160, 170, 191
Reich Group Banks, 63, 69, 198, 202
Reich Ministry of Food, 162
Reich Propaganda Ministry, 30,
     48–49, 60, 105–106
Reichs-Kredit-Gesellschaft, 21, 82,
     128, 208
     and "aryanization", 71, 75, 83,
     90–91, 97
     and Creditanstalt-Bankverein,
     Wien, 133–135
"Reichskristallnacht", 51
Reichsvereinigung der Juden in
     Deutschland, 197, 199
Reichswerke "Hermann Göring", 41,
     52, 100, 104, 136, 172–177,
     179, 181, 199
Reiniger & Co., 164
Relda Trading Co. Inc., 99
Rentenbank-Kreditanstalt, 45
Reuter, Fritz, 111

Revisions- und Organisations-
     Gesellschaft mbH, 162
Revisni Jednota Bank, 156
Rheinbraun, 102
Rheinische Aktiengesellschaft für
     Braunkohlenbergbau und
     Brikettfabrikation (see
     Rheinbraun)
Richter, Wolfgang, 143
Riedel, Walter, 142
Riehle, Joachim, 8, 153
Ripper (M. Rippers Söhne), 182
Roddergrube, 102
Rodrian, Wilhelm, 188
Rösler, Oswald, 26, 29–30, 144–145,
     152–153, 158, 176–178, 180
Rohde, Max Ludwig, 62, 140, 160,
     162, 176, 182
Rohdewald, August, 182
Romania, 134
Rosenfeld & Co., 169
Rosenthal, Charles, 46
Rosenthal, Josef, 164
Rosenthal, Philipp, 164
Roth, Karl-Heinz, 40
Roth-Händle, 120–121
Rothschild (bank), 137
Rothschild, Bertha, 86
Rothschild, family, 129, 172
Rothschild, Isidor, 86
Rottenberg, Franz, 130
Rudaer Steinkohlegewerkschaft,
     179
Rummel, Hans, 26, 50, 55, 66, 152
Russia, 6, 189

Saar-Pfälzische Vermögens-
     Verwertungs-GmbH, 62
Sächsische Staatsbank, 83
Safrian, Hans, 4

Salamander AG, 42, 84, 86–90, 93, 209
Salomonsohn, Adolph, 56
Salzdetfurth AG, 100
Salzgitter, 104
Samulon, Adolf, 111
Schaaffhausen (A. Schaaff-hausen'scher Bankverein), 26
Schacht, Hjalmar, 8, 25, 48, 52, 58, 86–87, 133, 184
Schäffer, Hans, 48
Schellin, Erich, 194
Schering, 92, 95
Schilling, Joseph, 50
Schlegel, August Wilhelm von, 106
Schlieper, Gustaf, 26
Schmidt, E.W., 148
Schmitt, Carl, 15
Schmoller, 119
Schneider-Creusot, 175
Schocken, 59
Schubert, Karl, 188
Schulenburg-Wolfsburg, Günther Graf von der, 116
Schuller, Erwin, 92
Schultheiss-Patzenhofer Brauerei, 16, 25
Schwabe & Co., 69
Schweizerische Creditanstalt, 102
Schweizerischer Bankverein, 95
Schwerdtfeger, Arnold, 68
Seckbach (W & C Seckbach), 123
Semperit Gummiwerke, 139
Seyss-Inquart, Arthur, 127, 132
Siemens AG, 3, 12, 49–50
Siemens, Georg, 11
Siemens, Werner von, 11
Siemens und Halske, 11
Siemens-Schuckert-Werke, 49
Sigle, family, 84–86

Sigle, Jakob, 84, 86
Jakob Sigle & Co., 84
"Sigma" Buchdruck M. Lesay (vorm. S. Hauser), 181
Simm & Söhne, 167
Sippell, Karl Ernst, 26
Skoda, 172
Slovakia, 7, 156, 181
Société Générale de Belgique, 139, 156–157, 160
Solmssen, Georg, 25–26, 34, 56, 213
Sosnowitzer Bergwerks- und Hütten-AG, 174
Sosnowitzer Röhren- und Eisenwerke, 174
Soviet Union, 1, 129
Spain, 6
Stadler, Eduard, 48
Stauss, Emil Georg von, 25
Stein, Leopold, 144–154
Steinbeck, Ernst, 91
Steinberg, Jonathan, 6, 9, 173, 204,216
Steinbrinck, Otto, 100
Stern, Ernst, 46
Stern (Jacob Stern), 69
Stern (L. Stern & Co.), 126
Steyr-Daimler-Puch AG, 136
Steyrische Gussstahlwerke AG, 136
Strenger, Waldemar, 87
Streicher, Julius, 27
Stülpnagel, Joachim von, 188
Süddeutsche Bank AG (SDB), 88–89
Südwestbank, 115, 118, 203
Suhrkamp, Peter, 105–106, 109–110
Suhrkamp Verlag, 105–106, 108–110
Sweden, 6, 183
Switzerland, 6, 76, 94–96, 98, 102, 105, 116, 118–119, 128, 161, 167, 183

Tack, 60
Tatra Bank, 152
Teplitzer Eisenwerke Schaufel- und
    Zeugwaren AG, 163, 167
Terboven, Josef, 78
Tiso, Josef, 153, 182
Thalheimer, family, 115
Thalheimer (Gebr. Thalheimer), 115
Theresienstadt, 170–171, 202–203
Theusner, Felix, 186
Theodor Thorer, 124
Thyssen, Fritz, 78
Thyssen-Konzern, 97
Tietz (Hermann Tietz & Co.), 37, 47
Toussenel, Alphonse, 22
Traub, Edmund, 168
Treue, Wilhelm, 40, 70
Tricotindustrie C.M. Koblenzer, 121
Tron, Walter, 140, 193–194
Troppauer Zuckerfabrik, 144, 158,
    162
Tuka, Vojtech, 180
Turkey, 136

UBB, 153, 180–181
Ukraine, 156
Ullmann, Ernst, 87–88
Ullstein-Verlag, 38, 48–49, 211
Ulbrich, Victor, 144–145, 167, 171
Ulrich, Franz Heinrich, 98
Unilever N.V., 92, 215
Union-Bank Bratislava (see UBB)
Union Rheinische Braunkohlen
    Kraftstoff AG, 101
Universale Hoch- und Tiefbau AG,
    139
Urbig, Franz, 25, 33, 44–45
United States of America, 1, 3, 5–6,
    9, 75, 94, 98, 124, 159, 183

Vereinigungsgesellschaft Rheinische
    Braunkohlenbergwerke mbH
    (see Verges)
Vereinigte Holz und Industrie AG,
    181
Vereinigte Industrieunternehmen
    AG (see VIAG)
Vereinigte Sauerstoffwerke GmbH,
    198
Verges, 103
VIAG, 103, 133–135, 138–140
Volkswagen AG, 3

Wachowiak, Stanislaw, 190–191
Wagner, Adolf, 114
Wagner, Richard, 22
Walz, Karl, 115
Warburg, Erich, 81
Warburg, Max, 24
Warburg (M.M. Warburg), 69, 71, 76,
    81, 209
Wassermann (A.E. Wassermann),
    67–68
Wassermann, Oscar, 16–17, 24–26
Wassermann, Sigmund, 67
Wassermühle Skotschau, 188
Watson Business Machines, 190
Weberei, Samt- und Druckfabriks
    AG Warnsdorf, 158
Wehrli Bank, 146
Weikersdorfer Textilwerke Samt-
    und Druckgewerbe, 144
Weil, Mathilde, 86
Weingartner, Fritz, 111
Weinmann, Erich, 67–68
Werhahn, family, 92
Wertheim, family, 83
Wiener Bankverein, 129, 134

Wiener Brückenbau- und
Eisenkonstruktions-AG, 139
Wiener Creditanstalt, 16–17
Wieringer, 60
Winkelmann, Hugo, 190
Winkler, Max, 48
Wintershall AG, 100
Wintermantel, Fritz, 26
Witkowitzer Bergbau- und
Eisenhüttengesellschaft,
172–174

Wohlthat, Helmuth, 100

Yugoslavia, 134–135, 179, 183

Zarnack, Wolfgang, 101
Zentral-Textil-Gesellschaft, 187
Zettlitzer Kaolinwerke AG, 144
Ziegler, Dieter, 28
Živnostenska Bank, 67, 143